Saul Bellow

RUTH MILLER

SAUL BELLOW

A Biography of the Imagination

St. Martin's Press New York

(Permissions continue on page 387)

SAUL BELLOW: A BIOGRAPHY OF THE IMAGINATION. Copyright © 1991 by Ruth Miller. All rights reserved. Printed in the United States of America. No part of this book may be used or reproduced in any manner whatsoever without written permission except in the case of brief quotations embodied in critical articles or reviews. For information, address St. Martin's Press, 175 Fifth Avenue, New York, N.Y. 10010.

Design by Judith Stagnitto

Library of Congress Cataloging-in-Publication Data

Miller, Ruth.
    Saul Bellow : a biography of the imagination / Ruth Miller.
        p.   cm.
    ISBN 0-312-03827-1
    1. Bellow, Saul.   2. Novelists, American— 20th century—Biography.
    I. Title.
PS3503.E4488Z7945   1991
    813'.52—dc20
                                        89-28983
    [B]

First Edition: March 1991

10 9 8 7 6 5 4 3 2 1

For my sister Adele

Contents

CONTENTS

viii

Acknowledgments

I would like to thank my gentle men on whom I called: Stuart Nelson and Meir Berger, Benilde Montgomery, and my dear friend Sidney Gelber. I would like to thank my not so gentle women Joan Dickie and June Jordan, who listened but did not read, and Adrienne Munich and Louise Vasvari, who read and would not listen. Their good sense steadied me, as often it threw me. My special thanks to Jesse and Ethel Holland for their hospitality when I came to New York and for their friendship over more than forty years.

I greet Thomas Broadbent, who encouraged me and had confidence. And a warm handshake to my editor, Michael Denneny, a man of grace, whose skills in the trade turned a private manuscript into a published book.

Ruth Miller

"But to look back from the stony plain along the road which led one to that place is not at all the same thing as walking on the road; the perspective, to say the least, changes only with the journey; only when the road has, all abruptly and treacherously, and with an absoluteness that permits no argument, turned or dropped or risen is one able to see all that one could not have seen from any other place."

—James Baldwin, *Go Tell It on the Mountain*

Introduction:

"This is where

you should be"

Whenever I meet Saul Bellow, I am surprised once again at the quiet of the man, the stillness of his face, the resting eyes, his hands soft, open, waiting, or if clasping, then each palm pressing the other, diffident hands that never have held a heavier burden than a pen. Has he forgotten who I am or why I have come? What am I after? Always there are those few moments of uncertainty, as if he must first place himself in a scene that includes me, gives me a significance to which he can then respond. Perhaps it is I who am timid. He chooses a better place for me to sit, offers tea, an apple, an Andes mint, and when all that is over, lapses into a patient silence, staring at the pattern of the carpet or the view out the window, as if to give me time to collect myself. I look at his bookshelves and his desk—orderly but a work place, books open, magazines open, a pile of letters—and nearby on an old typing table is his Smith-Corona, with the ream of white paper waiting on the one side, and the pages of typescript on the other side, done, and on a fragile music stand, the manuscript book. I'm thinking that knowing the man has never helped me figure out how this can be the Bellow on whom nothing is lost.

I always have to remind myself that his hooded sleepy eyes see everything, that he hears far beyond anything I can think to say, and no matter how gentle and kind and reassuring I sense he means to be, his self-effacement always puzzles me. But then, Bellow's heroes also appear to be small men, third-raters, second-stringers, with souls capable of striving to become equal to the power of the world.

In 1938, I graduated from Von Steuben High School in Albany Park in Chicago. A child of the Depression, a plumber's daughter raised in a ghetto, I did not know the difference between teachers' training college and a college of liberal arts, let alone a university; I could not tell the difference between a job and a profession, fiction and literary criticism. I knew only that I did not want to be a secretary until such time as I found a good husband. When I was offered a work-scholarship to Pestalozzi-Froebel Teachers College, I gladly accepted. The word *College* was on the letterhead; the names of Pestalozzi and Froebel were in *Compton's Picture Encyclopedia*, which my mother had bought on time payments from a book salesman who came to our door.

English Composition is a course required of first-year college students no matter where they may be. At Pestalozzi, it was in the hands of pickup help, that year an odd fellow who had no idea what he was supposed to do twice a week with a class of Illinois girls, many just off the farm, and the rest, city girls from the scattered neighborhoods beyond the Loop. At the first meeting, he simply distributed a list of novels and told us to hand in a book review each week. Our class consisted of his reading one or two papers aloud and then going on to tell us what he thought, not of our essays but of the book and its author. I have the list still: *Crime and Punishment, Madame Bovary, Portrait of the Artist as a Young Man, Sons and Lovers, Chrome Yellow, Winesburg, Ohio, Sister Carrie, Manhattan Transfer,* and *A Farewell to Arms.* The teacher was Saul Bellow.

He kept office hours, and whenever I went to discuss my weekly theme, he read to me from the manuscript of a novel he carried about with him, the lined legal-sized yellow pages that eventually became *Dangling Man.*

Bellow invited me to visit him at his home, a one-bedroom apartment in a large old building on Fifty-seventh Street and Harper, and gave me exact instructions on how to get there, for I had never been to the South Side of Chicago. Afraid to risk such a journey alone, I asked my only friend at Pestalozzi, Alice Jennison, to go with me, and all during the train ride we tried to guess what his wife would be like. Bellow found us standing within the protective iron gates of the Illinois Central Railroad, but before taking us to his apartment, he offered to show us around the neighborhood. We walked along the Midway Plaisance on Fifty-ninth Street, past International

House, past Ida Noyes Hall, and Rockefeller Chapel, and turned right, through the passageway between two long gray stone buildings, Harper Memorial Library and the Social Sciences Research Building, and there, in front of us, I saw what I now know to be the beginning of the Quadrangles, a miniature park cut through with paths leading to a wilderness of buildings: stone benches, trees, and squirrels. "What is it?" I asked. He opened his arms wide, as if to encompass the whole, and said, "The University of Chicago. This is where you should be." I was sixteen years old; he was twenty-two.

He was proud of his apartment, with its so-called Pullman kitchen, the small bedroom down a short hall, past the small bathroom, and the large room neatly spaced off with four pieces of furniture, a card table set between two windows looking out on the courtyard, the couch, the desk, and a huge bookcase.* There was his wife, Anita, wearing a dirndl skirt and a peasant blouse, unwrapping the strudel her mother, Sophie, had sent over. What should I say to her? I told her my Aunt Goldie made strudel the same way but without the nuts. "No, no, that's not possible. There have to be nuts." Poor Aunt Goldie. I'm sure she, too, chopped the walnuts. Why did I deny her? Alice Jennison said nothing.

Anita served tea. We each had a cup of hot water and a tea bag, which we dipped up and down. Alice and I were very polite, careful, uneasy in the presence of the new bride. Anita Bellow said, "I always wanted to do this," and she raised her arm high over her head and whirled her tea bag in the air, and Saul Bellow took his up, and the two of them, laughing and shouting "Hey! Hey!", swung those wet sops around and around, splattering walls, windows, curtains, rug, couch, easy chair, the desk, and the books. Alice and I were made to join. I aimed my tea bag out of the way of the books. The following week, I was admitted as a freshman to the University of Chicago. I wish I knew what became of Alice Jennison. Bellow and I have remained friends from that time on.

I found an entry in an old journal of mine,† dated April 15, 1939: "Saul was talking to me today and we decided that I needed taking in hand. He said he would like to introduce me to a friend of his, Isaac Rosenfeld." Isaac was studying philosophy at the University of Chicago, and although we met and talked a few times, I never understood a word he said to me—too

---

*Asa Leventhal lives in such an apartment, transposed to Irving Place in Manhattan. See *The Victim.*

†One year, I took a course with Professor E. K. Brown—it was on E. M. Forster and Virginia Woolf. He solemnly advised all who would be writers to keep a journal, and from then on, I faithfully kept a record of my significant thoughts and conversations. Thus, after a talk with Bellow, I would hurry to put down—as well as I could remember—what Bellow had said to me.

much mind. I wanted to be a writer—golden goal! But how? That night, I wrote in my journal:

> Saul said the first thing that I needed was to look at myself and understand myself, and then understand society. Realize that I owe something to society, and that we are all based on one another. I must first be honest, lay aside all my prejudices, and see, really see, the life about me. "Someday you'll meet a fact in a dark alley and the fact will come out the better for it, and you'll be weeping beside a rubbish can filled with empty beer tins."*

I did not understand that, either, but it was more poetic and worth a try.

Now, as I reflect on his odd formula for learning to write, I see in it the germ of his belief in the inevitable clash between the literal world and the internal world of feeling, akin to old Sammler's vision—his one eye observing the world and his shaded eye gazing into himself, his memories, his passions, and his sympathies—but then I thought it meant I had to study society. I declared myself a major in the Division of Social Sciences and floundered my way through economics and logic and philosophy and Russian, but all this defeated me. I withdrew and edged my way into the English department. Bellow threw up his hands and laughed, challenging me, but I thought I could study literature even if the professors were "dried-up old birds" or, as Bellow said so often, "only purveyors of literature."* I was determined to become a willing and happy victim of Cobb Hall, sitting in the classrooms of Frederick J. Hoffman and David Daiches, Norman Mac-Lean and Elder Olson, Walter Blair and Napier Wilt, and above all R. S. Crane. All this was a long way from learning to be a kindergarten teacher.

By the time I graduated, Bellow and Rosenfeld had gone off to New York. The action was there. We caught up with each other in the 1950s. I was teaching at Brooklyn College, and, of course, I was writing a novel. Every few weeks, I took a chapter to him. Now, I know he was always kind to young writers, but then, I thought he was taking special pains with me.

*Bellow has never changed his mind about the uselessness of English departments. Large audiences at his public lectures heard his diatribes against academia; a wide number of readers could find the same thing in his essays (for example, "Cloister Culture," "Skepticism and the Depth of Life," and "Culture Now"). Usually he accepted a short lecture series or a transient position in an English department for a single semester or a year or two. When he signed a contract for a permanent position at the University of Chicago in 1963, it was as a member of the highly diversified faculty that made up The Committee on Social Thought. I asked him why he had finally agreed and it seemed to me he was saying he needed the steady income. But it was more than that. In 1963—it was after *Herzog*—he believed he had earned the right. Years later Bellow was invited to join the Department of English at the University of Chicago, and he accepted.

Our sessions were much the same as our first meetings during his office hours at Pestalozzi-Froebel. I would take my new pages or a section revised according to our last discussion and watch him glance through them quickly, always knowing he would stop halfway along in his reading and say he would show me, and putting my pages aside, take up his own manuscript and begin to read. He was then writing a memoir of his early life in Lachine, as a sort of tribute to his father. I paid attention to every word, for I was trying to write a passage of reminiscence into my own novel. So it was that years later I recognized those very pages when they appeared in *Herzog* as the long recollection of Moses's childhood in Montreal. Like Sammler's daughter Shula, rummaging about in her dustbins, Bellow searches through his old memories and experiences and finds good things to save, someday to fit a better use and larger purpose.

On one of those afternoons, in 1955, I took him a chapter that worked, finally worked, and Bellow, elated, kissed me. After about ten seconds, I moved my head and opened my mouth to breathe and ask a question. "Listen," I said, "do you remember what you told me when I asked why you married Anita?" "Yes. But I was wrong. Let me explain it." And then we both began to laugh. "I know, Saul, I talk too much. I ask too many questions." He said that with me he needed to talk. I thought he meant to keep me for an intellectual companion, to prove he could relate to a woman for this purpose. I was going to be the example of a relationship that was not erotic.

That was all right with me. By then, I was married and had two children. I had reality instructors. I wanted a literary instructor, an encourager, not a lover. So indeed we have kept on talking intermittently for more than forty-five years: about his wives and children, his family and friends, his enemies, ostensible and real, about his books and the critics, his ideas, his memories.

I was proud of Bellow's wish to single me out, to form me into a sympathetic companion, to tell me how it was with him, but I have long since understood I was certainly not the only one. I remember Harold Rosenberg saying to me, when my husband, a painter, and I came to visit Rosenberg, "Oh, you're one of Bellow's girls!" Further, I need not have been at Pestalozzi-Froebel Teachers College to learn about this man. I have shared him with a million readers. Bellow talks with the same honesty to whoever will listen; he would make of us all his sympathetic companions, explaining his thoughts, exploring his feelings, revealing his conflicts and jeopardies, his spasms of courage and fits of trembling.

In the opening paragraph of Bellow's first novel, *Dangling Man,* Joseph says:

> There was a time when people were in the habit of addressing themselves
> frequently and felt no shame at making a record of their inward transactions.
> But to keep a journal nowadays is considered a kind of self-indulgence, a weak-
> ness, and in poor taste. For this is an era of hardboileddom.

Refusing the code of the tough boy, Bellow begins his lifelong narrative of
his inward transactions, and for thousands of pages over a passage of five
decades, we all may hear his voice explaining, crying out, keeping us posted,
reminding us of what else there is to know, exhorting us to look, to understand, and to pity.

Keeping in touch, losing touch, restoring. If I never had seen Bellow
again after 1938, I would still know what had happened to my first teacher.
He need not have been a friend to be my friend. I have observed the writer
grow older, more respectable, successful, but so may any reader notice that
Augie's torn undershirt eventually gives way to Charlie Citrine's custom-
made pima cotton shirt and a Countess Mara necktie; so may any reader
discover that steam hissing from a radiator in a seedy boardinghouse gives way
to cocktail music at the Plaza, or that the Western Avenue streetcar turns
into a Boeing 747. From Osaka, from Jerusalem, from London, from Detroit,
any reader can keep in touch with Bellow.

"Cousins," a story published in 1984, begins with an agitated middle-
aged Ijah Brodsky:

> To catch up with European time, I stayed up late playing solitaire with a pack
> of outsized cards that made eyeglasses unnecessary and this put me in a frame
> of mind to get into bed without a fit of exuberance. Given calm and poise, I
> *can* understand my situation. Musing back and forth over the cards, I under-
> stand. . . .*

I have seen Bellow at his solitaire. I visited him at his rented farm-
house in Vermont a few summers ago and there I met his, then, fourth wife,
Alexandra. In the evening, we moved into the living room "for some conversation." He laid out his well-worn cards on the coffee table. He never missed
a word. He never missed a card. A field mouse ran across the room and
burrowed behind the drapes. Alexandra ran for the broom and gave it to Saul,
lengthwise. He told us to go into the kitchen for a while. He would tell us
when we could come back. Alexandra held a mop to protect the hallway, and
I, from halfway up the stairs, listened to the rattling and running. He said
he chased the mouse out the door. I never believed him about this. He

*From "Cousins," *Him with His Foot in His Mouth and Other Stories*, 1984.

returned to the couch and evened out the rows of cards on the table and went on with the game and the talk. It was as if part of him had withdrawn, as if, in the presence of trusted friends, he could recover his calm and poise, he could play out the game, see how the puzzle of his life would this time, this one time, reveal its meaning.

We are all the trusted friends of Saul Bellow. Withdrawing from the experiences that are taking place between the fictions, the writer retreats to his room, takes up his pad of paper or his manuscript book, and sits down to tell us his story anew, hoping thereby to divine some pattern to his progress and decline, his winnings and defeats, his life of prize and loss and prize again. Telling the story—or some fragment of the story—again, he may bring to light a finer perception of his character, discover a new significance in the course of events, arrive at a truer understanding of his world.

The next morning, we went to see the house he was building for himself and Alexandra. Set far back from the road, out of the sight of neighbors, beyond the noise of traffic, the concrete foundation had been poured. He explained his simple floor plan and then we walked around a scrub where a pond was to be excavated so that he could swim and listen to the croaking of the frogs at twilight. He said he had never built a house before. He led me along a footpath that went deeper into the forest. I could not see the sky—ferns in Vermont grow as do my rhododendrons on Long Island— and after about a hundred yards, we came to a clearing. This was where he was going to build his studio. He too would have a cabin in the woods. Unlike Thoreau, he would have hired help.

"You plan to walk here and back each day? Three, four times a day?" He nodded.

I said no more and am glad now I did not. I have before me the final sentences of "Cousins":

And when the girl, noticing that I seemed unable to walk, offered me her arm, I wanted to say, "What d'you mean? I need no help. I still play a full set of tennis every day." Instead I passed my arm through hers and she led us both down the corridor.

Bellow does not understand why I have come to talk about his books. I have them. What more do I need? He would rather read to me from the manuscript he is working on, and he does. The voice is crystal clear and carries across the lawn. I listen, thinking, He is right. His job is to get the words onto the page. It is all he can do. It is the best he can do. My job is to say what my intuition and my imagination conceive to be the way to understand his writings.

That has been my project since 1977, when I visited Bellow in his office in that same Social Sciences Research Building where he has taught for many years as a member of the faculty of The Committee on Social Thought, and more recently also as a professor in the English Department. We stood in that same passageway and Professor Edward Shils passed by, then turned back to congratulate Bellow on receiving the Nobel Prize, apologizing that he could not go to Washington, D.C., to hear the Jefferson lecture,* and, Shils said, he would have to miss the Chicago talk as well, adding with a small smile, it was because he had no tuxedo. Well, I supposed, Bellow did have a tuxedo.

Knowing Bellow over a long period of time helps; walking onto the Quadrangles and entering Cobb Hall to graduate—as we said then—out of the stable of R. S. Crane helps; best of all, reading everything he has published from his first stories to his most recent novel is surely the best way to know the man who wrote the books, for I believe the books reflect that man, and it was always the books that intrigued me. Bellow the man, I know intermittently, but I have endless access to the writer and can read his words as often as I like. When I read them together, as it were, I find patterns in his form, consistencies in his queries, unfoldings in his ideas, and a casting and recasting of characters, as if they were, despite all their modulations, Bellow's personal archetypes.

I have read many fine monographs and perceptive essays about Bellow, studies that throw much light on his ideas and comic style, on his influences, his sources, his symbolism, his attitudes, his significance as a major American writer. Worthwhile as they are, they lead me away from my goal: to interpret the progress of the writer from the time he first appeared in print to his most recent publication, taking into account especially the critical reception that greeted each work as it came from Bellow's hand.

No doubt I would have profited from talking with many of Bellow's friends and associates, his former wives, his present wife, and members of his family, but I chose to let Bellow's written work speak about his life, his personal relationships, his goals and quandaries, his literary aspirations and disappointments, his social and political distractions; all of this is present in his essays, lectures and speeches, his reviews and interviews, and overwhelmingly present in his novels and short stories and plays. In a career that spans some sixty years, there are enough facts and details on record, and it was always the transformation of his facts into his fiction that interested me. In his imaginative writings, there are truths enough.

---

*Prestigious annual lecture in the humanities sponsored by the National Endowment for the Humanities; Bellow gave his first lecture in Washington, D.C., March 30, the second in Chicago, April 1, 1977.

To thank Saul Bellow for the many hours of conversation we have shared over a long span of years may suggest he is in part responsible for what I have written. He is not. Indeed, I understand that Bellow disagrees with much of what I say in this book and, I am told, now denies having said many of the things I quite clearly recall him saying, things I often recorded in my journal at the time. Of course, I must stand by my memory and my notes. I express my gratitude to him for allowing me to read his letters and papers deposited in the archives of the Regenstein Library at the University of Chicago, although he ultimately decided not to let me quote from them.

Ruth Miller
State University of New York at Stony Brook
1990

Saul Bellow

1

"Where are you going?"

"Chicago. In America"

The opening lines of *The Adventures of Augie March* are spoken by an aggressively self-aware man, poised for experience:

> I am an American, Chicago born—Chicago, that somber city—and go at things as I have taught myself, free-style, and will make the record in my own way: first to knock, first admitted; sometimes an innocent knock, sometimes a not so innocent. But a man's character is his fate, says Heraclitus, and in the end there isn't any way to disguise the nature of the knocks by acoustical work on the door or gloving the knuckles.

Few Americans, Chicago-born, were likely to share the bravado of Augie March. His declarations of free-style independence and self-assertion, his sense that were he first to knock he would indeed be first admitted, would cause some 1 million immigrant Chicagoans to shake their heads.

Near the end of the film *Fiddler on the Roof,* the dispossessed Jews are finishing the romantic life of their shtetl, wrapping the few mementos of their Sabbath peace and tossing the shards of their workday staggerings onto a rubbish heap, closing their doors on poverty and cold, peddling and po-groms, service in the army of the czar. While loading their belongings onto their wheelbarrows and their backs, they call out to one another: "Where are you going?" One city after another of the Diaspora is named, and to this day wherever the film is shown, someone in the audience shouts "Hurrah!" or whistles for his city.

"Where are you going?" Tevye asks Lazar Wolf.

"Chicago. In America."

"I am going to New York, America. We'll be neighbors. Goodbye Lazar Wolf."

"To my brother-in-law in Chicago. In America. I hate him, but a relative is a relative."

Between 1881 and 1924, 2 million Jews came to America. In 1920, 125,000 Jews were settled in Chicago. How did they choose their neighborhood, their Maxwell Street and Douglas Park and Humboldt Park and Ravenswood? If the streetcar went there, you went there; if you could get kosher meat and walk to the synagogue, you rented a flat, and when you found a job, you saved your money and sent for your relatives.

Immigrants could always sew and sell until they learned enough to buy and hire. Crowding two, three, and four in a room in railroad flats, they soon came to know the police, the landlords and aldermen, the man who came to read the gas or electric meter, the telephone company man at the door to collect the nickels from the coin box, filling a little leather bag, then emptying it on the dining-room table to separate lead slugs from buffalos. Someone's relative delivered the milk or bread rolls or firewood; someone's cousin was the peddler who hawked fruits and vegetables from his rented wagon; someone's mother sold aprons and pot holders, pins and shoehorns, climbing the stairs of the two-stories, three-stories, and six-flats on her route. Everyone knew the man at the newsstand, the druggist, the tailor, the butter and egg man, the streetcar conductors, the schoolteachers and assistant principal, the supervisors and managers, cashiers and ushers, the movie stars, the vaudeville stars, and each voice on the radio. All knew Sam Insull and Big Bill Thompson and Al Capone.

No one knew Heraclitus.

Aunt Zelda asks Moses Herzog whether he ever finished his project, "that study of whatchamagig. You never did wind it up, did you?"

Writing in a shaky hand, from Hot Springs, Arkansas, where he waited for the climate to help him recover his health, Saul Bellow's father congratulated his son on the success of *Augie March*. Saying that it was a nationwide success, he reminded his now-famous son that he was still the head of the family and expected letters once in a while.

Abraham Bellow had no legal right to live outside the pale without a resident permit, but for a long time he went about his business unmolested in St. Petersburg, importing figs from Turkey, onions from Egypt, until in 1913 he got into difficulties with the authorities and had to leave everything behind to begin his life again in Canada. He fled to his two sisters and a brother, who lived in Lachine, a suburb of Montreal. Early in November, his family followed him to that tough industrial town where Poles, Italians, Ukrainians, and Jews lived alongside French Canadians and Indians. Bellow still keeps in his desk his mother's original passport:*

>   Lescha Belo avec ses enfants
>   Zelda, 7 ans
>   Movscha, 5 ans
>   Samuel, 2 ans
>   Se rendent à l'étranger de St. Petersburg
>   Signé,
>   Conte Adlersberg

I recall Bellow saying in 1985 that he was not yet part of that family. I did not know whether he meant then or to the present day, but he seemed disheartened yet at the same time proud. Holding the old permit to emigrate in his hand, it was as if they were all still in his keeping. It seemed to me he felt that he had always kept himself separate, aloof, but never from the family, although he always knew he did not fit and was not approved of. He had to go it alone from his earliest days.

Abraham hustled to feed his family, rising in the middle of the night to work in a bakery, then driving the wagon through the rutted back streets to make deliveries.

Saul Bellow was born in Lachine on June 10, 1915. It was a Sicilian who owned the cottage where he was born. The doctor had to be fetched from the saloon to deliver him.

His mother had always wanted her youngest son to be a talmudic scholar. At four years of age, he recalls, he had already memorized whole passages from the Old Testament, not because it was his duty, or for the sake of shining at his Hebrew lessons, taught by Mr. Stein who lived across the street, but because to him the stories were real. He had his own version of Genesis. To him, it was literally so. Looking out the window into a deluge of rain, he listened for God's voice. Watching a boat making its way through

---

*In *Herzog*, Moses searches through his father's desk while Tante Taube is in the kitchen. "Now he began to search for those rubles. Those he found in a small compartment with old passports, ribbons sealed in wax, like gobs of dried blood. *La Bourgeoise Sarah Herzog avec ses enfants, Alexandre huit ans, Helene neuf ans et Guillaume trois ans,* signed by Count Adlersberg, *Gouverneur de St. Petersburg.*"

the locks of the canal was like watching the passage through the Red Sea. Monkey Park was Sodom and Gomorrah. He made little distinction between the patriarchs and his relatives, quarreling as did his aunts and uncles and cousins and brothers, fiercely quarreling and always making peace to begin again. One aunt was a Jezebel, so his father said; another was Bathsheba, so his uncle said; the neighbor lady was an ancient imperious Sarah, so Bellow knew when he created Grandma Lausch. His family was a tribe cautiously wandering among Philistines. How different had their fate been, brought by stormy seas and cast up on this alien shore of Canada, clinging to one another, engaged in exotic and incomprehensible activities, yet living side by side with anyone at all?

Moses Herzog reflects on his mysterious continuity:

> Napoleon Street, rotten, toylike, crazy and filthy, riddled, flogged with harsh weather—the bootlegger's boys reciting ancient prayers. To this Moses' heart was attached with great power. Here was a wider range of human feelings than he had ever again been able to find. The children of the race, by a never-failing miracle, opened their eyes on one strange world after another, age after age, and uttered the same prayer in each, eagerly loving what they found.

His mother was a Rachel, a Rebekah, the center of all human connectedness. To her, the children were central and you knew you were cherished.

Herzog remembers how his mother petted and babied him, protected him:

> Once, at nightfall, she was pulling me on the sled, over crusty ice, the tiny glitter of snow, perhaps four o'clock of a short day in January. Near the grocery we met an old baba in a shawl who said, "Why are you pulling him, daughter?" Mama, dark under the eyes. Her slender cold face. She was breathing hard. . . . "Daughter, don't sacrifice your strength to children," said the shawled crone in the freezing dusk of the street. I wouldn't get off the sled. I pretended not to understand. One of life's hardest jobs, to make a quick understanding slow.

He was a Joseph, dreaming his brothers loved him although they left him behind again and again to wait, alone, until they returned, laughing and teasing. And he was an Ishmael, cast out, alone in the wilderness. At eight, suffering from tuberculosis, he was placed in a hospital ward, separated from his family. Where were they? He was frightened of the empty beds he often had to face on a morning after a child had hemorrhaged and died in the night. He was afraid of the Christian lady who visited the wards and gave him a different Bible. She always sat down beside him to listen to the Jewish boy read aloud the passages she chose for him from the New Testament. He complied, eager to please, anxious for some way to find good luck. He never showed her the funny papers his mother had given him, his Boob McNutt and Barney Google.

In *Humboldt's Gift,* Charlie Citrine remembers the lonely boy when he describes his childhood to his own daughter, Mary:

> Oh, I loved them all terribly, abnormally. I was all torn up with love. Deep in the heart. I used to cry in the sanatorium because I might never make it home to see them. I'm sure they never knew how much I loved them, Mary. I had a TB fever, and also a love fever. A passionate morbid little boy. . . . At home if I was first to get up in the morning I suffered because they were still asleep. I wanted them to wake up so that the whole marvelous thing could continue.

To make the marvelous thing continue, the boy in the ward promised himself the light. Citrine remembers:

> I became very thoughtful here and I think the disease of the lungs passed over into an emotional disorder so that I sometimes felt, and still feel, poisoned by eagerness, a congestion of tender impulses together with fever and enthusiastic dizziness. Owing to the TB I connected breathing with joy, and owing to the gloom of the ward I connected joy with light, and owing to my irrationality I related light on the walls to light inside me.

When I asked Bellow to explain to me what he wished to do as an artist, he answered with an anecdote about his childhood. As a boy, he said, he loved to sit alone on the curb, staring into the gutter. He would watch the iridescent colors shifting on the oil and water and he figured out that the slop of the St. Dominique Street gutter was reflecting the sunlight overhead. A small boy, just sitting there, he had emotional feelings, very powerful, of gladness and mystery, and he wanted to say something, to tell someone, about *that.* But there was no one to whom he could speak. He knew his brothers would laugh; he feared his father would scoff; and his mother, well, maybe his mother, but she would probably dampen his hair and comb it, and send him to the store. Or, if he felt that odd constriction in his chest and told her, she would drop everything and take him to the dispensary. To the present day, Bellow says, when he writes about what he calls the light within, the sense he always has had of the mystery of joy in life, he gets this same tightness in his chest and with it, the old sense of trepidation. He was sometimes afraid to go on. He always knew he had the talent. He wanted to write but he was afraid of the gift. Probably no one in his family ever understood what he was doing. He knew he would cut himself off from his parents, his brothers and sister, his aunts and uncles, his cousins; and yet, how could he hide it? Lose the joy? He was always afraid that if he allowed the fire to burn, he would die. If he allowed the fire to go out, he would die. So the gift was dangerous. If he used it, he would kill himself. If he let it lie hidden, he would kill himself. To confront it head-on would be too much to bear; but how could he throw it away?

In *More Die of Heartbreak,* published in 1987, there is an early description of his beloved Uncle Benn by nephew Ken; he talks first of his uncle's eyes, with their extraordinary faculty of seeing, "of seeing *itself;* what eyes are actually for. The light pries these organs out of us creatures for purposes of its own. You certainly don't expect a power like the power of light to let you alone."* Ken goes on to tell the readers of the novel something of the singular childhood of Benn:

> Now let's return to Uncle: A while back I spoke of an influential irregularity, and I'll explain this now. Let's start with childhood. You're a kid in a poor neighborhood, your parents are immigrants, you have to play with milk bottles on the back porch, you study the esthetics of dust motes, you sit on the curb. And by and by you make your decision to become this or that when you grow up. I don't speak now of doctoring or electrical engineering, or even Streets and Sewers, but of singular choices. You decide upon something singular and then you *become* it. Just like that? How do you know that there's a future in it? You don't. But this is what Professor Popper calls an Open Society, and in an Open Society what's to stop you? Nothing except ideas of regularity, which gain ascendancy over you as you grow older and more cagey. How can you trust a small child of a singular bent? Not even little Samuel in the Temple recognized that God was calling to him; he thought it was the High Priest, needing a drink in the night. Well, prophets are secured to God. Our times are riskier. The venturesome child is like a space walker whose lines may tear loose from the mother ship. If they do, he'll be sucked away into outer space.

Bellow was that small child of singular bent, that venturesome space walker, cut off, compelled to take the risk, at first cautiously, eventually, as he saw it, tearing himself to shreds and gluing the fragments back together, time after time.

*Ithiel Regler, in *A Theft,* published in 1989, is described as a man who looks at the century with his "singular inborn eye."

* * *

In 1924, the Bellow family left Abraham's sister in Quebec and moved on, to live near his cousin in Chicago. Now the tenement stood in Humboldt Park; the boy no longer sat on the curb staring at the colors of the oily water but ran after his brothers on the streets of Chicago, to see it all. Everybody was an immigrant. Everyone belonged to a special neighborhood. He wanted to become a tough guy, shrewd, street-wise. That meant to know pool halls, movie houses, vaudeville shows, prizefights, to hang around exotic Division Street, that clamorous melting pot where he could listen to musicians screeping on their violins, listen to Socialists and Zionists and Health Faddists and watch the street dancers, and roam in the Christian cemeteries, where he and his buddies stole ribbons and flowers and gold letters off the wreaths they found abandoned on some new grave. They sneaked everywhere, mooched into everything. Bellow learned to be a wiseacre, a smartass.

Bellow remembers exactly the schools he attended and he delights in rattling off their names—the Lafayette School, Columbus Elementary School, Sabin Junior High, Tuley High. He can recall the name of his first black friend, Milton Littlejohn. It was in the schools, Bellow says, he first met Americans. His teacher, Miss Jenkins, had an uncle who fought at Andersonville.* She literally knew the American past. Soon he began to realize all of the kids in the class were being treated not as Jews but as Americans. He embraced it. Not immigrants, not aliens, but Americans all! They were part of a new mixture, not tribes, more than families. He read James Fenimore Cooper and became Natty Bumppo lost in the woods, making his way in an Indian canoe on freshwater. An American.

By ten, he knew he wanted to be a writer. In grammar school, he was writing. He wrote imitations of things that stirred him. He read Jack London and wrote a Jack London story. He read and imitated O. Henry. He sat long hours on a chair in the public library on North Avenue and Rockwell Street reading, collecting his models. Bellow has left a record of the progress of his reading in *Augie March*. Grandma Lausch sends the boy, Augie, to the library:

> Once a year she read *Anna Karenina* and *Eugene Onegin*. Occasionally I got into hot water by bringing a book she didn't want. "How many times do I have to tell you if it doesn't say *roman* I don't want it? You didn't look inside. Are your fingers too weak to open the book? Then they should be too weak to play

*Andersonville was a Civil War prison camp in the South, a notoriously cruel place where prisoners were horrendously abused, punished excessively, even starved to death.

ball or pick your nose. For that you've got strength! *Bozhe moy!* God in Heaven! You haven't got the brains of a cat, to walk two miles and bring me a book about religion because it says Tolstoi on the cover."

Grandma bought a set of the *Encyclopedia Americana* and required Augie and his brother, Simon, to read it. So Augie begins to look inside, his fingers avidly turning the pages. When Einhorn makes Augie a present of the Harvard Classics, Augie keeps the volumes in a crate under his bed and starts on Plutarch, goes on to Luther's letters to the German nobility, and then Darwin's *The Voyage of the Beagle*, in which he gets as far as the crabs who stole the eggs of stupid shorebirds. As his adventures continue, Augie carries with him the five-foot shelf of books, reading from them when he can. When Augie begins thieving for Padilla, who has "a racket swiping books," he is "struck by the reading fever."

> I lay in my room and read, feeding on print and pages like a famished man. Sometimes I couldn't give a book up to a customer who had ordered it, and for a long time this was all that I could care about.

Padilla turns over to Augie all orders for books on theology, literature, history, and philosophy, and so Augie reads von Ranke's *History of the Popes* and Sarpi's *Council of Trent* or Burckhardt's *The Civilization of the Renaissance in Italy*. Then there is Robey, the millionaire, who needs an assistant to do research for a book that will be a spiritual guide for the rich; Robey hires Augie to read and report on the books he assigns. "It suited me fine to sit in the library amid a heap of books." Now, Augie reads Weber and Tawney and Marx and Aristotle, whoever proposed a theory of happiness.

In high school, Augie hangs around with a few boys "who read whopping books in German or French and knew their physics and botany manuals backward, readers of Nietzsche and Spengler." That is young Bellow at Tuley High; among his friends were Oscar Tarkov, Sam Freifeld, Sidney Harris, Studs Terkel, Dave Peltz, and Isaac Rosenfeld, any one of whom could have read those whopping books. In a memoir written for *Partisan Review* on Isaac's death in 1956,[2] Bellow recalled:

> It is late afternoon, a spring day, and the Tuley Debating Club is meeting on the second floor of the old building, since destroyed by fire. The black street doors are open, the skate wheels are buzzing on the hollow concrete and the handballs strike the walls with a taut puncturing sound. Upstairs, I hold the gavel. Isaac rises and asks for the floor. He has a round face, somewhat pale,

glasses, and his light hair is combed back with earnestness and maturity. He is wearing short pants. His subject is *The World as Will and Idea*, and he speaks with perfect authority. He is very serious. He has read Schopenhauer.

After high school, Bellow and Rosenfeld together entered the University of Chicago. Two years were enough for Bellow. He knew he wanted to be a writer, but the study of literature, especially as it was taught there, seemed to him not the best way to learn. In 1935, he transferred to Northwestern University, where he worked under Melville J. Herskovitz in anthropology, graduating with honors. It was always literature, however, that drew him and he decided for graduate study he would switch to the Department of English at Northwestern. It was not so easy. He was told by William Frank Bryan, chairman of the department (1936–1938), that as a Jew and the son of Russian Jews, he would probably never have the right "feeling" for Anglo-Saxon traditions, for English words. Bellow has never forgotten Bryan's refusal to admit him. In 1985, when I asked him about the anti-Semitism he had experienced when he began to make his way into the literary world, his voice was cold with indignation, as if to say, Now get this straight. At least you get this straight. His parents spoke Russian to each other, Yiddish to the children, but he and his brothers spoke English to one another. He learned English on the streets when he was two years old. He always spoke English. French was an accompaniment, like the Hebrew he learned in *heder*, the Jewish elementary school. To be viewed as an interloper in the great democracy! Who in America was not the offspring of immigrants? Bellow turned again to anthropology.

Herskovitz arranged for a fellowship to the University of Wisconsin at Madison. Rosenfeld, still pursuing his studies in philosophy, followed Bellow to Madison, remained there to graduate, then went with his wife, Vasiliki, to New York to continue at New York University. Bellow was unable to tolerate academic life. It was Alexander Goldenweiser who told him what Bellow knew well: He was not cut out for science. Every time he worked on his thesis, it turned out to be a story. Goldenweiser was right. During the Christmas holidays, in 1937, Bellow went home to Chicago and never returned to the university. He married Anita Goshkin, moved into his mother-in-law's flat in Ravenswood, and sat down at the bridge table in the back bedroom to write.

Bellow remembered that money was a great problem for them when they were starting. They never had any money. His brother occasionally gave him hand-me-downs, always too big. He seldom had enough money on which to live. When they gave him money, he did not like to take it. It was as if they were all waiting for him to come to his senses, to come into the real world and do something practical.

He could earn money. That was not the problem. He accepted odd jobs as they came along, working for the federally funded Writers' Project, compiling information on American subjects, writers—I was not to ask who—rivers, cities—I was not to ask which—and went twice a week to Pestalozzi-Froebel to teach by the hour. He didn't mind that; the school was on Michigan Boulevard and he could walk to the library on Randolph Street or to the Crerar Library or the Art Institute. He did research work on the "Syntopicon," the index scheme for the new edition of the *Encyclopaedia Britannica*. As Robey hired Augie March, so Mortimer Adler hired Bellow to read some fiction and some history. From the "Great Books," he indexed passages on happiness, reading Plutarch and Tacitus, *War and Peace,* some Plato, some Aristotle—the *Nichomachean Ethics* and the *Metaphysics*—and Hobbes's *Leviathan,* and Herodotus and Thucydides.

The larger problem was what to do about the goal: He sat there learning a discipline. As Bellow recalled, he believed he was here to interpret the world as brilliantly as possible, but how? When Isaac and he decided to be artists, it was a little like taking an oath without having read the bylaws of the organization they had joined. What were they supposed to do? How were they to go about it? What were they going to write about? What did they have to say? Joining was one thing; what to do next was something else again.

Bellow has frequently described how and why and when he appointed himself to be an artist; sometimes, he speaks in his own voice, in interviews, essays, or in formal lectures, but the best account of his awakening to the power and purpose of art is embedded in a story, published in 1974, called "Zetland: By a Character Witness."[3] Zetland is Isaac Rosenfeld, Saul the character witness.

In the story, Bellow portrayed two boys growing up together, clever kids, listening to the Wobblies on Division Street, developing their physical strength playing tennis and swimming, rowing on the public lagoon while one reads Keats to the other. Zetland is a junior Kant, a witty Voltaire, a sentimental Rousseau; he is an ingénu with a Dickensian heart. This Zetland needs shabby disorder to stimulate thought, to liberate feeling, to generate inventiveness. "Living in a kennel he embraced the universe." All this may be said as well of the character witness, for there is as much of Bellow as there is of Rosenfeld in the character of Zetland.

Zetland leaves provincial Chicago, "the most boring place in the world," for New York, sophisticated New York, where no excuses are needed for the life of the intellect, for dedication to art, for pursuit of the transcendent, where there is "deeper meaning in the air." The "Wittgenstein of the West Side" plunges ecstatically into the ferment of Manhattan but falls sick and lies alone in his bed. Restless, disconnected, he finds himself reflecting on different kinds of issues, no longer asking who is right, John Dewey or Lenin, but what has he, Zetland, to say, what does he, Zetland, think, for what is he here, what human messages has he to give and to receive?

> So Zet laid aside his logic books. They had lost their usefulness. They joined the funny papers he had put away when he was eight years old. He had no more use for Rudolf Carnap than for Boob McNutt. He said to Lottie, "What other books are there?" She went to the shelf and read off the titles. He stopped her at *Moby Dick*, and she handed him the large volume. After reading a few pages he knew that he would never be a Ph.D. in philosophy. The sea came into his inland, Lake Michigan soul, he told me. Oceanic cold was just the thing for his fever. He felt polluted, but he could read about purity. He had reached a bad stage of limited selfhood, disaffection, unwillingness to be; he was sick; he wanted *out*. Then he read this dazzling book. It rushed over him. He thought he would drown. But he didn't drown; he floated.

On the surface, this is certainly Rosenfeld, who resigned from New York University; at the same time it is Bellow, that boy who stared at the slime in the gutter and saw in it the reflections of sunlight. Zetland discovers the truth of the imagination, finds the way to heal the sickness of his soul; the character witness records Zetland's excited words:

> "Oh Lottie, it's a miracle, that book. It takes you out of this human world."
> "What do you mean, Zet?"
> "I mean it takes you out of the universe of mental projections or insulating fictions of ordinary social practice or psychological habit. It gives you elemental liberty. What really frees you from these insulating social and psychological fictions is the other fiction of art. There really is no human life without this poetry."

Perhaps Rosenfeld did say something of the sort to his wife. Rosenfeld did, in fact, go East to live; he did, in fact, leave his studies in philosophy to enter the dangerous career of the writer. But when, in 1974, Bellow described Zetland's conversion from schoolman to artist, it is the character witness who testifies to his own beginnings, to his own beliefs. Bellow declared publicly, many times, that art has the power to pull one out of the muck of traditional expectations and the habits of limited selfhood; said often enough it was the independence, the freedom, the autonomy that attracted him to the life of the artist. Bellow engaged in a lifelong quarrel with the writers of social and psychological fictions, the philosophers and historians, the academicians and theorists, with their projects and their programs, who purport to teach the truth but know nothing of the poetry of human life. They are still his target in *More Die of Heartbreak*.

In the same year he wrote "Zetland," Bellow published a personal sketch called "Starting Out in Chicago,"[4] and there he described again how and why he became an artist, how the son of immigrants, a child of the Depression, decided he would make of himself a major American writer. In Bellow's memoir, it is again books that play a part, and once again freedom is the prize. "I did not go to the public library to read the Talmud, but the novels and poems of Sherwood Anderson, Theodore Dreiser, Edgar Lee Masters and Vachel Lindsay." He recounted how he searched in books to find a way to live that would teach him how to confront the ordinary, how to withstand convention, how to sidestep the commonplace, how to escape the dragging net of society, to hold himself aloof from an environment that offered him pigeonholes.

"I felt that I was born to be a performing and interpretive creature, that I was meant to take part in a peculiar exalted game," a game that was a celebration and an act of praise. The allusion is to the medieval parable of the juggler, humbly content to display his art before the statue of the Virgin Mother. Bellow adapted the parable to himself and gave himself an even more exalted audience: "At its noblest, this game is played, under discipline, before God himself." He had no humility about his project: The purpose of the exuberant performer is to become "the representative of beauty, the interpreter of the human heart, the hero of ingenuity, playfulness, personal freedom, generosity, and love." The metaphor recurs in *More Die of Heart- break*, reaching beyond the activity of the artist to signify the goal of every man, any man: "We human creatures should be at play before the Lord—the higher the play, the more pleasing to God. . . . 'Before the earth was made,' says the Book of Proverbs, I was with the Lord 'forming all things, and was delighted every day, playing before Him at all times, playing with the world. And my delights were to be with the children of men.'"

Bellow knew, when he began his play before the Lord, he would have to pay a price. He was willing to live poor, to be lonely, to arouse suspicion. Very well. So long as he remained free to explain the world as *he* perceived it, so long as in fantasy he could live a life of significance, find a fate good enough, create of his secular life a spiritual reality, it was worth it. He had the primary instrument for pursuing his project of art: the imagination. He needed one thing only: freedom.

In 1978, four years after writing "Zetland" and "Starting Out in

Chicago," Bellow once again explained to the large audience invited to listen to his Jefferson lectures how he began as a writer in Chicago. He had already received his Nobel Prize; he had already been called the "heir to Faulkner and Hemingway"; through his hands a million dollars and more had passed; he had fathered three sons born of three wives and was now the husband of his fourth wife, who sat encouragingly before him. He recollected his story again. He told his listeners—cautioned to wear evening dress, warned not to take photographs or tape his words—how he sat in his three-dollar room, which he had civilized with his books and his prints of Velázquez and Daumier, and taught himself not to mind the musty sour smell, the desiccated wallpaper, the soiled carpets, the greasy upholstery of armchairs used by countless others before him, the cockroaches and the mice.

He explored his earliest striving as a longing for real life, for contact, not so much with the external world as with the self. Kinship, roots, community counted for less than the private self. With this lack of connection came a wonderful freedom for those who could endure it.

Then, however, he admitted, freedom itself, that cherished freedom, placed him in jeopardy; for how could he interpret the world if he lived enwrapped in a cocoon of isolation, dissociated from the business of the world? He remembered himself, when starting out, as did his first hero, Joseph, the dangling man, as a young man who chose solitary purity for the sake of his art, discomfited by his solitariness and not so sure of his purity. His friends had all gone their way—to New York, to California, to North Africa—and where was he? Bellow ironically observed he was on the far outside, in Ravenswood, merely an observer of the world around him. He needed to become a participant. Yet the least step in that direction unnerved him. The need to belong drew him and the need to resist membership drew him. Ruefully, Bellow admitted to his audience that the artist as a type was unstable, stubborn, and nervous. To cure that unstable, stubborn, nervous self would be a lifework.

On the platform, Bellow, speaking of the imbalance of his early days, asserted that there was no reasonable solution to the condition of the artist, it simply had to be accepted as the condition of creativity. When he began, Bellow went on to say, he believed he could cure his ignorance, overcome his sense of inadequacy, his limitations, with books, and once again he described his passion; he recalled he was reading Russian, French, English, German books and he thought he could write about Chicago as had H. G. Wells of his London, as had Arnold Bennett of his Five Towns, as had Joyce of his Dublin. Yes, he was very much at home in Chicago. Then he confessed he began to have doubts about Chicago.

What was the use of this Chicago, this prairie city, this restless, scheming, nose-thumbing Chicago? It was no City of Light. Reading Balzac and Dostoevski, Conrad and Rilke, hearing incredible news from the great world of culture, Bellow admitted he gazed down at his so-called white-knuckle city and worried. Was a man at home on the streets of Chicago likely to understand the truth of America? Was he still out of line, too solitary, still a strange case, not because he was poor, or going to be a writer, but because he was ignorant of the significant world—how could the place where he had grown up be significant? It wasn't enough to be a bright talented fellow, not enough to be educated, ambitious. What of Nietzsche? Freud? Marx? D. H. Lawrence? Joyce? Tolstoi? Gide? Dickens? How could one match them riding the streetcar on Kedzie Avenue?

He searched the great authors for hints. He disciplined himself for his great purpose; but what was the purpose? Dostoevski knew. Pound knew. Walt Whitman knew. Joyce and Proust, Mann and Kafka knew. Bellow read thousands of pages in every discipline, the familiar and the esoteric, and by the time he came to deliver his Jefferson lectures, he had been identified by reviewers and critics and scholars alike as the most widely read, the most intellectual writer in America. However, he always quarreled with what writers had to tell him, or found nothing in them to his purpose, as those in the audience who had read *Herzog* were aware. Perhaps they had missed Bellow's irony when he described Herzog trying to straighten out his life by citing Locke and Mill, or failed to notice Sammler choosing only one book for his guidance, *Meister Eckhart.* It took years for Bellow to release himself from his attachment to books.

In 1982, in the novella *Him with His Foot in His Mouth,* Shawmut recalls his visit to his old college library:

> The heavy library doors were open, and within there were green reading lamps and polished heavy tables, and books massed up to the gallery and above. A few of these books were exalted, some were usefully informative, the majority of them would only congest the mind. My Swedenborgian old lady says that angels do not read books. Why should they? Nor, I imagine, can librarians be great readers. They have too many books, most of them burdensome. The crowded shelves give off an inviting, consoling, seductive odor that is also tinctured faintly with something pernicious, with poison and doom.

In 1987, in *More Die of Heartbreak,* Kenneth Trachtenberg, a young man in his thirties, returns to his shabby dormitory room:

> . . . coming into my comfortless sanctuary, I wanted to throw out all the books and papers—the same books on which I depended for clarification, for keeping

up with the twentieth century. After so much mental fussing, nothing was clear anyway.

Well, all that was to come. When starting out in Chicago, Bellow decided he could not leap toward the marvelous while sitting on a bench in Jackson Park in blacktop Chicago reading *Partisan Review*. Bellow went to New York.

He had been called into the army but then given a deferment. Eventually, the Merchant Marines took him and sent him off to the Maritime Camp in Sheepshead Bay for sea training and then gave him a shore job with the Maritime Commission in New York. When the war ended, Bellow took his wife and year-old son, Gregory, to a flat on Pineapple Street in Brooklyn Heights and supported himself writing notices of fiction and nonfiction books. Victor Weybright was founding Penguin Books and preparing his first list and asked Bellow to read for him. *The New York Times* and *New Republic* gave him review copies, which he sold to secondhand book dealers. He went to *Time* magazine and lasted there one day. Bellow described the fiasco to Melvyn Bragg in a 1975 interview for *The Listener:*

> I was fired at the end of the day by Whittaker Chambers. I came into Chambers' office, and he took one look at me. He was obviously determined to get rid of me and he said: "Do you know who Wordsworth was?" I said: "Yes." He said: "Who was he?" I said: "A poet." "Don't tell me that, young man," he said, "I want to know what sort of poet he was." I said: "Well, he was a romantic poet. But I don't see what that has to do with reviewing moving pictures." He said: "Never mind that, there's no room for you in this organisation, you're fired." My friends told me: "Chambers hates the romantic Wordsworth—he cares only for *The Excursion,* he adores *The Excursion,* which is not a romantic poem." So I lost my job.[5]

In *New York Jew,* Alfred Kazin recalled his first impressions of Bellow:

> Through the Chicago writer Isaac Rosenfeld—whose wife, Vasiliki, was my secretary—I met Saul Bellow, who was also just in from Chicago, and who carried around with him a sense of his destiny as a novelist that excited everyone around him. Bellow was the first writer of my generation . . . who talked of Lawrence and Joyce, Hemingway and Fitzgerald, not as books in the library but as fellow operators in the same business. . . . He had the gift . . . of making you see the most microscopic event in the street because *he* happened to be seeing it. . . . Bellow had not yet published a novel; he was known for his stories and evident brilliance only to intellectuals around *Partisan Review* and the University of Chicago. Yet walking the unfamiliar Brooklyn streets, he seemed to be measuring the hidden strength of all things in the universe, from the industrial

grime surrounding Brooklyn Bridge to the prima donnas of the American novel, from the lasting effects of Hitler to the mass tensions of New York. He was measuring the world's power to resist *him,* he was putting himself up as a contender. Although he was friendly, unpretentious, and funny, he was ambitious and dedicated in a style I had never seen in an urban Jewish intellectual; he expected the world to come to him. He had pledged himself to a great destiny. He was going to take on more than the rest of us were. . . . Life was dramatically as well as emotionally a contest to him. In some way I could not define, he seemed to be always training for it. And he was wary—eager, sardonic, and wary.[6]

It was true. Bellow's public image was one of indisputable confidence. He typed a letter to James Laughlin, editor of *New Directions,* on April 2, 1942, in which he suggested that *New Directions* publish a novella as well as a poet of the month. He, himself, could offer several stories of sixteen to twenty thousand words, and, he asserted, a story is either good or bad and new directions have nothing to do with it. He asked for a prompt reply. Bellow had published a single story.

2
The Jason
from Chicago

Partisan Review celebrated its fiftieth birthday in 1984. Bellow refused to participate in the festivities. When I asked him why, his answer had nothing to do with my question. He told me nobody got him on *Partisan Review,* not Delmore, not Isaac. He just submitted his manuscript to Dwight Macdonald and Philip Rahv and they took it.

In the May–June 1941 issue, there appeared "Two Morning Monologues," one subtitled "9 A.M. Without Work," the other "11:30 A.M. The Gambler." A year later, there appeared "The Mexican General," and the year after that, *Partisan Review* printed a long excerpt from *Dangling Man.* [1]

In his first story, little more than a sketch of four pages, Bellow presented a narrator whose adventures we will follow through all the novels and short stories to come. Like the adolescent described years later in the Jefferson lectures, he is young, poor, impractical, disapproved of by his father, adrift on a stage on which he does not belong, an interloper in a world that may have no part for him to play.

It's my father's fault that I'm driven from the house all morning and most of the afternoon. I'm supposed to be looking for a job. I don't exaggerate when I say driven. That's what it is. He's created an atmosphere in which if he found me at home, say at eleven in the morning, I'd feel intensely wrong and guilty.

... "A good boy, a smart boy, American, as good as anybody else—but he hasn't got a job."

Ill at ease, dissociated from family, ostensibly an ordinary man, he is fully aware of his far-from-ordinary distinctive self. He interprets the very sandwich he carries in his pocket as a sign: ". . . in the afternoon a faint spicy smell would spring out. One of the closely curled leaves of my identity." And, of course, he is a reader: "I brought my books home and read them on the kitchen table."

To fill up his days, he wanders about Chicago, riding a streetcar into the Loop, giving a passing glance out the window, and we recognize on the first printed pages the device of the writer who will pause, always pause, to tell what may be seen and then reflect on the reality as it affects a man of feeling.

The point of view is in place—the direct address to the reader. He confides to us his state of mind, as will every Bellow hero from first to last. "I needn't tell you how much I'd like to get away. . . . I know a great deal about myself in as well as out, privately, that is, as well as statistically. I'm very nearly sunk."

Before the sketch ends, Bellow has made a start on his dangling man—touchy, hopeful, unhappily stuck at home, here with an anxious mother and a nagging father, soon to become anxious mistresses and wives, nagging brothers, uncles, cousins, manipulating friends, disapproving mentors, and here, too, at the outset, planning an escape:

> I often find myself wishing that mine had been one of the first draft numbers so that I'd be parted from both of them, especially from him, on official grounds. Perhaps I should become a volunteer.

In the second monologue, "The Gambler," we can recognize Bellow's beloved crook, the first in his long line of mobsters, con men, shysters, drifters, who were as much a part of his growing up in Chicago as were the elevated tracks or the Loop or the Lake or the six-flats. The gambler is the sad loser, the shabby sport. So enters the prototype of all Bellow's reality instructors who will try to show every narrator from Augie March to Tommy Wilhelm to Herzog to Dean Corde and Shawmut and Brodsky how to live. Win by fighting, by sharking, says the progenitor of Einhorn and Tamkin, Zaehner and Vilivitz, all on the lookout for the main chance. Like Bellow himself, the gambler has to make it, to find his way through the cracks, to manage right and never die.

The second story, "The Mexican General," begins deceptively, seeming to lay the ground for an erotic sketch:

> "This is your room, the center one, Señor el General," said the clerk. . . . "That on the left is for the ladies and this on the right for the two gentlemen. Everything is just as you asked for it in your telegram."

General Felipe is fussy, observant, and cautious; the women are silky and lascivious; the two gentlemen are the General's lieutenants, Paco, a fat dumb ox of an aide, and Citrón, a thoughtful man of good education. Any reader familiar with Bellow's fiction will recognize in Citrón the prototype of Bellow's sensitive observer.

The party has just arrived in Patzcuaro; the General needs to rest, to relieve his tension and strain, for he has just concluded an investigation of the murder of an old man in Coyoacan. Citrón describes to Paco what happened, and the reader discovers that the *viejo*, whose skull was split by an ice pick, is Trotsky, Citrón is the compassionate soldier who guarded the assassin, and the old standing bull of a General is the man "who took charge of history in Coyoacan." Like ordinary tourists, the General and his entourage eat and drink and go off to see the sights of the town, with its *zócalo*, its church and colorful marketplace. Interwoven with the details of place are flashbacks to the violent death of the founder of world socialism, the panic of the killer, the grief of the widow, and the corrupt manipulations of the Mexican General.

Bellow was for a time a Trotskyite. He had been led to the Party when the show trials in the U.S.S.R. were in full swing, and signatures were affixed to pledges of neutrality that gave substance to the shadows of Hitler and Stalin, Mussolini and Franco. While pogroms raged and countries went under—Bohemia, Moravia, Slovakia, Lithuania, Latvia, Estonia, Finland, Poland, Hungary, Rumania, Bulgaria, Denmark, Norway, Holland, Belgium, Luxembourg, France, Spain—Bellow and Rosenfeld attended socialist meetings in Chicago and stood solemnly, singing, as did the few dozen people with them in some second-floor loft. Bellow withdrew from the Party after a year of listening to speeches that failed to explain to his satisfaction the way things were in the real world, and he took upon himself the role of mentor through the medium of words, his words, his interpretation of significant history and meaningful action. His horror at the assassination of the man he respected was crystallized in imagery:

> The old man, his face alone appearing between the cone of bandages and the sheet, seemed already dead. There were two stripes of blood running from his temple to his beard.

The corpse of Trotsky is treated like a side of beef, turned this way and that so that it could be photographed from every angle; the General, dressed in full military regalia, presides at the burial. Citrón reflects, first on Trotsky, and a few pages later, on the event.

> I felt sorry for the *viejo*. He deserved a more manly antagonist. Everything about him was of much consequence and all based on principle, principle. I remember him expounding the principle when they chopped up his room with bullets and how he complained in statements that rang in with the French Revolution and ended with predictions of victory. . . . And people like me who are carried along and not being in major positions have an opportunity to look into the works, we are struck by a lack of fitness that throws suspicion on everything and makes us sure there must have been precisely such vanities and blunders in the greatest Passions. Although it would be cheap to discredit them for that.

"What did happen at Coyoacan besides what I already know?" Paco asks Citrón. Citrón answers in Bellow's second published story in a way that is already recognizable Bellow—his rendering of the dilemma of the small man who would be part of great events yet knows he can never make any real difference, who is a member but in no way effective, a flunky who is aware and understands but can do little more than watch the progress of the world from the sidelines. Citrón is Bellow's proxy for the ordinary reader who sits with book or newspaper in hand, trembling or nodding at the shattering news in print. Citrón is the survivor.

Few people bother to read *Fanshawe* by Hawthorne or *Watch and Ward* by Henry James, both first novels, both difficult to find outside of university libraries, but *Dangling Man* has remained in print and is still the subject of study. Yet Bellow always disparages his early work, often scoffing, saying he has not read that stuff since he saw the galleys. He wondered why I bothered with it, as if he did not really know what he was doing or even wanted to do in *Dangling Man*. At the Friday-night banquet for the winners of the Nobel Prize, Bellow said, "I feel that I have scarcely begun to master my trade." On such an occasion, he can indulge in a semblance of humility. At a public reading in New York in 1985, when Bellow was asked by a member of the audience what he thought of his early novels, he replied, "I should have spent my youth more productively." However, that was a clever retort and the audience laughed, delighted at the display of careless fame.

Yet there are startling connections between *Dangling Man* and later works. Four decades intervened between *Dangling Man* and *The Dean's December*. Joseph dangles at the end of a rope, choosing, as well as doomed, to be cut down by reality, to fall into the abyss of the real world:

> I had not done well alone. I doubted whether anyone could. To be pushed upon oneself entirely put the very facts of simple existence in doubt. Perhaps the war could teach me, by violence, what I had been unable to learn during those months in the room. Perhaps I could sound creation through other means. Perhaps. But things were now out of my hands. The next move was the world's.

Dean Corde dangles from a gantry that rides along the rib of the dome of the Mount Palomar observatory: "You live alone, you die alone," he thinks while staring at the absolute sky, at the "something more," the "something beyond," but he knows his sightings must be taken on earth. If one is to learn how to live a good life, he must learn in the company of his fellows.

> Rocks, trees, animals, men and women, these also drew you to penetrate further, under the distortions (comparable to the atmospheric ones, shadows within shadows), to find their real being with your own.

Bellow rendered Joseph's ethical question, and his gradual discovery of the only feasible way to resolve it, as a series of dated entries in a journal in which Joseph records the events or nonevents of his days, beginning on December 15, 1942, when he has left his job and waits for the draft board to induct him, and concludes on April 9, 1943, when, demoralized at his failure to find any meaning in his life, inward or outward, he forces the draft board to act. Winter to spring is a favorite time span for Bellow, who often catches his man in a state of discomfiture in dormant December and releases him outdoors, bearing a plan for recovery, in the spring.

Despite the promise in the opening lines of the book—"If I had as many mouths as Siva had arms and kept them going all the time, I still could not do myself justice"—there is not much to record. By day, he asks himself serious questions: What is the relationship between the interior life and outer reality? Is there a common humanity that survives in the midst of ugliness? In the middle of the night, he wakes in a panic: "How will I die? How will it be? How?"

The quest for identity does not do much to help him live a good life. As a son, a brother, an uncle, a husband, he argues; as a friend, he is unstable, envious, intolerant; as a roomer, he is suspicious and quarrelsome; as a walker on the streets, he is insulted and wounded. He is an apprentice to suffering and humiliation, a weakling who fancies himself strong, willful and passive, arrogant and peaceful. Joseph believes he is a man of reason, but he is ready to take a punch at Captain Briggs, takes offense when the maid lights a cigarette without asking his permission to smoke, and shouts at Mr. Vanaker, who urinates without closing the toilet door. Joseph believes in his special destiny but is enraged when a former Communist acquaintance refuses to say hello, when his tailor charges fifteen cents to sew on a button, when his wife leaves him a list of tasks to perform for the day.

Inside his room, he does little: He listens to the radio, watches the maid dust and wash the windows, polishes shoes. Against the chaos of the world, which intrudes day by day in the newspapers that he buys, he creates balance and structure for himself by reading the newspaper in the same orderly fashion each day: first the comic strips, then the news and the columnists, then gossip and the family page with its recipes, then the obituaries and society notes and the ads, and finally the puzzles.

Outside his room, he does little: He looks in on a dime store, goes to a shooting gallery, a tailor shop, a bank, a Christian Science Reading Room; he takes a haircut, eats in a restaurant, visits his relatives, goes to a party. He dangles. His friend Abt is in Washington, Adler in San Francisco, Pearl in New York, Tad in Algiers, Stillman in Brazil, and Joseph roams about the neighborhood, bored and irritable, or rocks back and forth in his chair. The more he tries to identify his unique character, the more blank his mind becomes. If he is not like everyone else, if he has a special destiny, why is his will immobilized?

On February 3, the "Spirit of Alternatives" arrives. Also called "*Tu As Raison Aussi*" or "On the Other Hand," the Spirit has come to assess the pass to which Joseph has come—impasse rather—and asks why he is so quarrelsome, why he refuses to recognize that he belongs to the world. "Why don't you join?" Joseph asks, "With whom?" The world "shunts you back and forth, abridges your rights, cuts off your future, is clumsy or crafty, oppressive, treacherous, murderous, black, whorish, venal, inadvertently naive or funny," and he tells his Spirit he will not enter such a world unless he has prepared himself with a good plan or program. The "Spirit of Alternatives" is willing to aid Joseph in his search for a serviceable ideal construction: Try politics; try philosophy; try history; try religion. None of the alternatives satisfy Joseph. He laments to his Spirit, "What of the gap between the ideal construction and the real world, the truth?" What, Joseph demands, have fine theories to do with coarse reality? The Spirit has no answer.

To avoid the damnation of a meaningless life, Joseph has given himself time and freedom. By February 14, he falters: "If I were a little less obstinate I would confess failure and say I do not know what to do with my freedom"; and a week after that, he takes another hesitant step, admitting it has not been the lack of an idea or a program that has immobilized him but his vain requirement that a meaningful life be lived in isolation. On what basis has he demanded such exclusivity? Because he is in pursuit of higher truths or because of his own vanity and egotism?

On March 16, the "Spirit of Alternatives" comes a second time: "Aren't you tired of this room? Wouldn't you rather be in motion, outside, somewhere?"

Joseph concedes. The only truth he is likely to discover is the truth that unlocks the imprisoning self. He has put himself in his room. He can take himself out. "Prepare to live and not to die." Freedom is not a state of being but the exercise of choice. There are no ideal constructions, no prescriptions for living that precede living. Ideas are abstractions and abstractions are irrelevant in the real world. Activate the will to open the door. Afterward, a man can indulge himself in mental exercises and play with reasons.

Joseph asks his Spirit a final question: "Do I have a separate destiny?" There is no reply; and so Joseph takes his letter to the draft board:

> I hereby request to be taken at the earliest possible moment into the armed
> services. I am available at any time.

His father presents Joseph with a watch. His brother gives him a suitcase. His sister-in-law and niece give him a leather sewing kit, complete with a scissors and buttons.

The dangling man is the prototype of the Bellow hero who pursues the chimera of instruction and rejects the instruction, seeks the guide who will teach him how to contend with reality and dismisses the guide, searches for the way to maintain his freedom and gives to the world the right to interfere with his independence. By the time we have read through the canon of Bellow's fiction and reach *More Die of Heartbreak*, written in 1987, Bellow will have looked at the programs of all significant writers, until, after forty years, he has brought before his court every major ideal construction that has found its way into the record of Western civilization, from Aristotle to Freud to Heidegger. None can help. In one guise or another, Bellow will have tested every extrusion of significant history, every institution, every mode of escape, and he will have satisfied himself with no program, no answer. He will have chosen many testing grounds, from Sixty-third Street on the South Side of Chicago to upper Broadway in New York, to Acatla, to Baventai, to Paris,

Madrid, Bucharest, Kyoto, and always his narrator will ask Joseph's question—How shall a good man live?—and always his adversaries will present answers to which he will listen with half an ear, for he is attending to his "Spirit of Alternatives," the Spirit that whispers the only advice Bellow will ever sanction: "Prepare to live and not to die." That is, as Citrine tells himself, "Dance, dance, dance, dance!" Mastery of the game, paddle ball or life, depends upon dancing.

Poor old Sammler hasn't much pep left in him and the spirit of Charlie Citrine needs metaphysical help to confront the intellectual dandyism, the erotic fantasies, the money swindles, the insanities and shabby defeats that bar the way to harmony and balance and order. Albert Corde is torn apart by the urban predators of Bucharest and Chicago, by the mayhem and murder in a world where corpses are lined up awaiting their turn in crematoria or living bodies are thrown from third-story windows. Still he asks, How shall a good man live? Still the answer is choose to dance. *Tu as raison aussi.*

Thoreau and Whitman and Emerson put to themselves in their time the same question. Their good man was an individual sanctified by his divine origin, with his traits of character tucked into his genes, his goodness and wisdom and moral integrity inherent in the life spark generated by a Cosmic Soul. However, the nineteenth-century man is a wistful memory. It is 1942. Joseph is not so sure about innate goodness, though he desires to believe he is on the side of the winning smile. Joseph recalls:

> In high school I became friendly with a boy named Will Harscha, a German. I used to visit him at home and I knew his sister and his younger brother, as well as his mother. But I had never met his father, who kept a store in a distant neighborhood. However, when I came to call one Sunday morning, the father happened to be at home, and Will took me in to meet him. He was a fat man, blackhaired and short, but kindly-looking.
>
> "So this is Joseph," he said as he shook hands with me. "Well. *Er ist schön,*" he said to his wife.
>
> "*Mephisto war auch schön,*" Mrs. Harscha answered.

This throws Joseph. He spends sleepless hours thinking of what Mrs. Harscha had said. She had seen through him by some instinct, and where others saw nothing wrong, she had discovered evil.

> There might be some justice in the view that man was born the slayer of his father and of his brother, full of instinctive bloody rages, licentious and unruly from his earliest days, an animal who had to be tamed. But, he protested, he

Tough Enough

3

to Hold

William Targ, in a memoir called *Indecent Pleasures,* wrote of his early days in Chicago.

> During my years as a bookseller, one of my steady customers was a shy, quiet, but intensely cultivated young man named Saul Bellow. He bought many used books from me, and one day he took along with him a twelve-volume set, *The Works of Tolstoy.*
>
> A number of my steady customers bought on the installment plan: so much down, so much a week. Bellow paid for the Tolstoy set on that basis. . . . Years passed. One night I ran into Bellow in New York; I think it was at the opening of his play, *The Last Analysis.* As he saw me approaching, he took out his wallet, extracted a bill, and handed it to me.
>
> "What's that for?" I asked.
>
> "I remembered that I owed you for one final payment on the Tolstoy set—five dollars. Sorry it took me so long; here it is."
>
> I was speechless.
>
> "I can't take it, Saul," I said. "Statute of limitations. Besides, please don't . embarrass me."
>
> "Embarrass, hell! I owe it to you. It's about twenty-five years overdue, and you could really add a hell of a lot of interest to the debt."
>
> I refused to take it. "I'd rather be able to tell my friends you owe me five dollars," I said.
>
> A few more years passed. Then one evening, in New York, I met Saul's new

could find in himself no such history of hate overcome. He could not. He believed in his own mildness, believed it piously.

By the time Joseph has confronted himself, scrutinized himself wholly, he will have understood the real world is Sodom and only Sodom; Gomorrah is the inside of the heart. And he will find in himself a history of hate overcome.

Joseph is the first of Bellow's heroes, the progenitor of all who follow, down to the young nephew Ken, torn between Eros and Thanatos, unstable, "a bit on the weird side," "notorious for the kinkiness of his theories," but devoted to his special project, to make of his life a turning point, in search of revelation that will enable him to live a significant life, to become by force of will a citizen of eternity. And, like Joseph, he fails but does not give up the trying. The Bellow hero begins and will end as an ordinary man, not so good, not so evil, confused, intolerant and quarrelsome, irritable and contemptuous, envious and vain, *and* well-intentioned, loving, kind, tender, compassionate and brave, split between emotion and reason, indulging his erotic desires, devising tests for the wisdom writers and failing them. This first dangling man is a Jason from Chicago, sent by himself to find a golden fleece that may or may not exist, equipped with attributes that may or may not enable him to retrieve it. Such a man will strive through ten novels and many short stories and a few plays to connect with cosmic unity and learn he cannot and refuse to believe it.

In 1989, Bellow published two novellas, *A Theft* and *The Bellarosa Connection*. In *A Theft*, Clara Velde is the female counterpart of the dangling man: She has the old "anti-rest character," is still a prey to her demons, still beset by confusion and disorder, still "unstable," split between emotion and logic. Her golden fleece is Ithiel Regler, an elderly "Spirit of Alternatives," who may enable her to live a significant life, who can center her, unify her, give her balance, concentration, and heart. In *The Bellarosa Connection*, it is the aged man of memory, a senior citizen Jason, identified only as the founder of the Mnemosyne Institute, who is dangling in a mansion in Philadelphia, and longs to connect, to reconnect, with Sorella Fonstein, a woman of a deeper nature, an oddball beautiful person, a superior person of intelligence and taste, in whose presence he can find stability, final calm, final connection. Old Sorella is a dead "Spirit of Alternatives."

wife. On being introduced she said, "Oh, Bill Targ! We owe you five dollars." Whereupon she opened her purse and pulled out a five-dollar bill. The ensuing conversation was a repetition of my previous one with Saul. I refused to take the money.

Let it be known to the world that Saul Bellow owes me five dollars. His children will be involved in this matter in years to come—probably with my grandchildren. I will continue to hold out. An inscribed copy of his Nobel award speech will settle the debt.[1]

Targ came to New York and worked many years as editor in chief for Putnam's; he left to form his own publishing house, bringing out limited signed editions of distinguished authors. In 1979, Targ Editions announced in a flyer:

> Saul Bellow—*Nobel Lecture* (with Banquet Speech). Designed and printed by Ronald Gordon. Hard-bound. Limited to 350 copies, signed by Mr. Bellow. (Edition about 85% subscribed.) Winter, 1979. $50.

The twenty pages were bound in white, stamped in gold.[2]

Few people who hear Bellow speak call him a spellbinder. On Sunday, December 12, 1976, when he delivered his Nobel Prize speech, the large crowd gathered in the royal hall to hear him applauded with polite enthusiasm. For the occasion, Bellow explained a view of art he had discovered as an undergraduate forty years before when, laying aside the heavy books on money and banking required for a course in which he was enrolled, he studied the novels of Joseph Conrad. To Conrad, the artist had no unique talent or access to heavenly inspiration but a capacity to share in a universal fellowship of human hearts. The artist may trust that his most secret thoughts, most private experiences, will have meaning for each person who opens his book because there is in each person the same gift of sensibility.

Bellow believed Conrad. On a podium where the light focused the world's attention on him, Bellow spoke of the dark and silent cave where the artist lives in total isolation, and declared it was Conrad who taught him that the lonely quest was the means for connection with his fellowman.

> To begin with, the artist had only himself; he descended within himself and in the lonely regions to which he descended he found "the terms of his appeal." He appealed, said Conrad, "to that part of our being which is a gift, not an acquisition, to the capacity for delight and wonder . . . our sense of pity and pain, to the latent feeling of fellowship with all creation—and to the subtle but

> invincible conviction of solidarity that knits together the loneliness of innumera-
> ble hearts . . . which binds together all humanity—the dead to the living and
> the living to the unborn."

Near the end of his address, Bellow arrived at his own view of art, recognizably the truth of Conrad, but carried to a startling, if to Bellow logical,
extreme, for without hesitation or embarrassment Bellow gave a concrete
name to the source of universal connection and declared it to be the soul.

The gift of fellowship, vested in each human heart because of the
presence in each human heart of the spirit, was at once individualizing and
transcendent. For Conrad, the loneliness of innumerable hearts arose out of
a longing for connection; Bellow acknowledged this to be true but added that
the human spirit longs even more for understanding. Diverse as every man's
experience may be, each person yearns to have answers to abiding questions:
What are we? Who are we? What is this life for? The artist must hunt down
the answers, track, on behalf of every man, the essence of the human condition, in all its complexity and confusion and pain. The tough part is that
insights appear and disappear as do flashes of light, that intuitions, however
true, are fragile and transient; it is the task of the artist to represent that
which is evanescent in a way that appears to be concrete, to render fragmentary intuitions of the spirit as if they were palpable and reasonable.

> This essence reveals, and then conceals itself. When it goes away it leaves us
> again in doubt. But our connection remains with the depths from which these
> glimpses come. The sense of our real powers, powers we seem to derive from
> the universe itself, also comes and goes. We are reluctant to talk about this
> because there is nothing we can prove, because our language is inadequate, and
> because few people are willing to risk the embarrassment. They would have to
> say, "There is a spirit" and that is taboo. So almost everyone keeps quiet about
> it, although almost everyone is aware of it.
>
> The value of literature lies in these intermittent "true impressions." A novel
> moves back and forth between the world of objects, of actions, of appearances,
> and that other world from which these "true impressions" come and which
> moves us to believe that the good we hang onto so tenaciously—in the face of
> evil, so obstinately—is no illusion.

Sitting alone at his desk in Chicago, Bellow wrote his thoughts honestly and
polished his words carefully. Then, reading them aloud from a world forum
in Stockholm, they seemed still to say exactly what he believed, precisely what
his books intended to express. Bellow looked up and saw his brother and sister,
for whom, so long ago—fifty-five years ago—he had waited each morning to

get up and dress and come to the kitchen table: "I wanted them to wake up so that the whole marvelous thing could continue." There sat Samuel and his wife, Sam's daughter Lisa, named for Bellow's mother, and her husband and three daughters. There sat his three sons, Gregory, Adam, and Daniel, each of a different mother, and there, radiant and shy, not having dreamed of so public a marriage gift, sat his new wife, Alexandra Ionescu Tulcea, her mother and her aunt beside her, two elderly women who had secured permission to travel from watchful but yielding government officials in Rumania. If he wished, he could have caught a glimpse of his German publisher, Nevin Dumont, his English publisher, Tom Rosenthal, his American publisher, Tom Ginsburg, his British agent, Hester Greene, and his American agent, Harriet Wasserman. They had all come, and sat among the knights, the writers, the critics, the academics, the professional and businessmen, and anyone else who could secure the gilt-edged invitation. Who there, in all this audience, expected Bellow to bear witness to the progress of the soul, to explain in the presence of a king that there are two realities, two worlds, the world of objects, actions, and appearances, and the world beyond, from which true impressions come?

When news of the prize was made public, his oldest son called to congratulate him. Richard Stern, a Chicago writer and friend, told the readers of *The New York Times Magazine* that he had heard Bellow say, "Thank you, Greg. Now you know why I was after you to be quiet thirty years ago."[3] More than thirty years before, in 1945, Bellow and Anita and Gregory had been in New York and he was writing *The Victim.*

Dangling Man had been well received, for a first novel;[4] *The New York Times* led the way printing two reviews of it, on Saturday, March 25 (John Chamberlain) and again the following day in its Sunday book review section (Kenneth Fearing). In the first week of publication, two major weeklies reviewed it, *The New Yorker,* coming on April 1 (Edmund Wilson) and the *New Republic* on April 3 (George Mayberry). The *New York Herald Tribune* book review section (Herbert Kupferberg) and the *Chicago Sun Book Week* (Peter De Vries) caught up on April 9, and the following week there were reviews in *The Nation* (Diana Trilling) and *Saturday Review* (Nathan Rothman). All this excitement led *Time* magazine to take a longish look in its May 8 issue at the "carefully written book" by an "introspective stinker." The monthlies had to wait for their summer issues and *Partisan Review* (Delmore Schwartz) and *Kenyon Review* (Mark Schorer) and *Politics* (Irving Kristol) all gave space to *Dangling Man.*

As would be true throughout Bellow's career, notice was taken of the book but there was little agreement among the reviewers on its quality or meaning. On the one hand, the book was "perfectly realized," "grave and vibrant," "a successful piece of work everywhere you examine it," "superb in its restraint, dignity and insight," and on the other hand, the book was "too raw, too lumpish and unrefined," "talented and clever" but "offensive." Diana Trilling summed up for one side: "I find myself deeply opposed to novels of sterility—or, rather, to small novels of sterility." Edmund Wilson summed up for the other:

> [The] book is an excellent document on the experience of the non-combatant in time of war. It is well-written and never dull. . . . It is also one of the most honest pieces of testimony on the psychology of a whole generation who have grown up during the depression and the war.

Bellow observed, ruefully, in 1984, that this was the first and last notice Edmund Wilson ever took of him. Wilson never wrote a word about Bellow again.[5]

Good reviews or bad, Bellow had been brought to the attention of the intellectual community.

William Barrett, in *The Truants* (1982), remembered Bellow as a past master at protecting himself in his relations with the group, Barrett's coterie of New York intellectuals. Whenever he was in New York, Barrett recalled, Bellow made contact with the *Partisan Review* circle but did not allow himself to become entangled in it. "He needed to observe the New York intellectuals, to be stimulated by them, and learn from them what he wanted—that was his job as a writer." Barrett was impressed by Bellow's single-minded devotion to his art. He seemed always to hover on the edge of the circle, cautious, as if to guard his talent was the best way to succeed in his vocation.

> He was the kid from Chicago, carrying a chip on his shoulder, and ready to show these Eastern slickers that he was just as street-smart (intellectually) as they were. He made me think at times of the great Chicago welterweight Barney Ross, who had come to New York a few years earlier and beaten all the Eastern contenders. Not that there was anything raucous or overtly aggressive in his behavior; on the contrary, his manner was civilized and gentle; but the chip of self-confidence was there on the shoulder just the same. And Bellow never faltered in this single-minded dedication to his muse; the solid body of work he went on to create is to be admired as, among other things, a triumph of character.[6]

I asked Bellow about his desire to join the New York scene and he said ironically that he had come to seek sanctuary in what corners of culture one could find in this country, there to enjoy his high thought and to perfect himself in the symbolic discipline of an art, and then he dismissed it all with a shrug, as if to say, What did they know about art? There wasn't an artist in the lot.

Still, Bellow wanted a community, a quiet zone where he could practice his art in accord with his unique sensibility, to be free to chase around town and meet a Barrett, an Irving Howe, a Philip Rahv, a Lionel Abel, a Dwight Macdonald, a Dan Bell, a James Laughlin—whoever—or retreat to his room to listen to his spirit and his imagination quarrel with his reason, free to record the dialogue between his heart and his elusive, or illusory, heart's companions.

On December 16, 1942, Joseph confides in his diary, "I have begun to notice the more active the rest of the world becomes, the more slowly I move, and that my solitude increases in the same proportion as its racket and frenzy." On what racket and what frenzy does Joseph turn his back? Between that December and the coming spring, a mile or so away from Joseph's rooming house, beneath the closed football stadium of the University of Chicago, an elite community of scientists (Szilard, Fermi, Oppenheimer) were working in secret on the Argonne Project and here they achieved their first dependable nuclear reaction. When they emerged they went to Oak Ridge and Los Alamos. On December 16, 1942, the Russians began their counteroffensive on the Don and by the middle of January were fighting the Germans in Leningrad; in February, they repossessed Stalingrad, then Rostov, then Kharkov. By spring, they took back Rzhev. Between December and spring, Joseph sits in his rented room meditating on responsibility. U.S. soldiers sat in their prison cells in Bataan and Corregidor. Luckier soldiers were dropping bombs on the Gilbert and Marshall islands, on Midway and Guadalcanal, New Guinea and the Solomon Islands. General MacArthur was shooting his way around the South Pacific; General Eisenhower was in North Africa; and in the spring, General Patton would be on his way to Tunisia, and then Palermo. The FBI had arrested eight saboteurs off Long Island and Florida; Gandhi had been taken off to prison; Roosevelt and Churchill had met in Casablanca; Lidice had been wiped out; and in 1942, the serious liquidation of the Jews had begun—the gas chambers were ready to go into full operation. Pictures would not become available until the camps were liberated in 1945, but meanwhile, the newspapers and magazines and newsreels had good prints of other rackets and frenzies as they occurred daily.

At the end of *Dangling Man*, Joseph decides to enter the war; he cuts himself down to fall into the fellowship of men in action. However, at the beginning of *The Victim*, Asa Leventhal is only modestly active in the real world; in the main, he is withdrawn, confused, anxious, living a solitary life.

In 1947, when *The Victim* was published, U.S. and U.S.S.R. troops had met at Torgau and embraced. Mussolini and his mistress, Clara, had been hanged. Hitler and his mistress had committed suicide. F.D.R. had died of a stroke. Hiroshima and Nagasaki were finished. The concentration camps had been razed. The Allies had reorganized themselves into the United Nations. The Arab Nations had formed their league. Churchill lost the election and went to Missouri to warn the world of Red expansion. China was at civil war. India was partitioned to avoid a civil war. U.S. troops sat down in South Korea; U.S.S.R. troops sat down in North Korea. We had digital calculators, synthetic vitamin A, rockets and missiles, ranch houses, bebop. A goat boy found the Dead Sea Scrolls. The Nuremberg trials were ended.

With all this going on during the writing of *The Victim*, Bellow sat at his desk, his back to the door, and imagined what it felt like to be Asa Leventhal, a small man, living on Irving Place in Manhattan, working for a minor trade journal, helping his brother's wife, whose youngest son was ailing, and quarreling with a shabby annoying person by the name of Kirby Allbee. Over a span of eight weeks, in settings that are commonplace—a dreary flat in Staten Island, a squalid couple of rooms in Manhattan, a fancier apartment uptown, a print shop, some cheap restaurants, a ferryboat, a park, a hospital room, a funeral parlor—Bellow placed his adversaries on chairs with a table between them and they talk. What about? Moral responsibility.

Bellow may have thought that was one major issue of the war, and let the war be ended, and the international tribunal convene at Nuremberg to hear the evidence against twenty-two Nazi leaders accused of war crimes; to Bellow, who day by day read the arguments raised in defense of the Nazis responsible for the horrors of the concentration camps, who heard their testimony that they were just following orders, such trials and enactments of international justice did not eliminate hate and fear, could not fix blame and guilt, had nothing to do with evil. To Bellow, it was psychological anomie, the fear of isolation, the dread of mortality that throbbed with each beat of each human heart that was the source of suspicion and lawlessness and violence. One hangs a few Nazis: That does not eliminate evil, deters nothing, placates no one. The moral responsibility of predators and victims transcends time and place and is as much an issue for clerks as generals, is present outside the war and thrives in the marketplace. "Who ran things?" the Nazis on trial in Nuremberg were asked; "Who runs things?" Leventhal asks Allbee.

Bellow took all the complexities and confusions of the trial and compressed them into the pursuit of the Jew, Leventhal, by the anti-Semite, Kirby Allbee. Leventhal is not a hapless Jew cut down by fascist bullets or gases in a van or shower stall; he is the son of immigrant Jews in America, born in Hartford, Connecticut. Allbee is not a black-booted, black-shirted, ironfisted Nazi; he is a descendant of Governor Winthrop. At the center of *The Victim* is the question of anti-Semitism in America.[7]

Bellow has always denied that the issue was anti-Semitism. In 1979, I asked him about this and he said it was the immigrant about whom he was talking, the immigrant in America, the man who does not belong. He wants in; he is always kept out. He tries to come in, to belong, but he cannot. He was talking about the outsider in all of us. That may be true. As Bellow sees it, the Jew is dissociated in the alien world of WASPs because a man is dissociated in the world of his fellows. An Allbee does track down a Leventhal on the streets of Manhattan, but a Leventhal allows himself to be pursued and caught. A glance at the events in *The Victim* shows how prevalent, it seems to me, is the issue of anti-Semitism. Not only is Allbee guilty; finally, so is Leventhal.

Leventhal feels ill at ease in his place of employment. He has over-heard the slurs of Mr. Beard, his employer: "Takes unfair advantage. . . . Like the rest of his brethren. I've never known one who wouldn't. Always please themselves first." Asa's brother Max has married Elena, an Italian girl, and when their son fights to breathe in his darkened room, Asa fears the censure of Elena's mother: "A Jew, a man of wrong blood, of bad blood, had given her daughter two children, and that was why this was happening." In a movie theater, when Asa's wife, Mary, asks a woman to remove her hat because it blocked her vision, the woman turns and mutters something about "the gall of Jews." At a party at Asa's friend's house, a girl is singing old ballads and some Negro spirituals. Allbee, who is present, interrupts her: "Why do you sing such songs? . . . It isn't right for you to sing them, you have to be born to them. If you're not born to them, it's no use trying to sing them. . . . Sing a psalm . . . any Jewish song. Something you've really got feeling for. Sing us the one about the mother."

Leventhal is offended by the attitude of Jews themselves toward anti-Semitism. He believes his friends are insensitive to slurs, too eager for Gentile approval. When he observes his friends laughing at themselves, telling jokes that deride their own traditions, he refuses to smile at their self-deprecating humor.

In Kirby Allbee Bellow renders his notion of the prototype of the anti-Semite; he pursues Leventhal everywhere and always he taunts the Jew: When Leventhal refuses to drink with him, Allbee says:

"You're a true Jew, Leventhal. You have the true horror of drink. We're the sons of Belial to you, we smell of whiskey worse than of sulphur. When Noah lies drunk—you remember that story?—his gentile-minded sons have a laugh at the old man, but his Jewish son is horrified."

The usual stereotypes are present:

> "You people don't do business on Saturday."

> "You people take care of yourselves before everything. You keep your spirit under lock and key. That's the way you're brought up. You make it your business assistant. . . . Nothing ever tempts you to dissolve yourself."

When Leventhal finds Allbee in Asa's bed with a whore, Allbee smirks at Asa's outrage:

> "But what's there to be so upset about? Where else, if not in bed? . . . What do you do? Maybe you have some other way, more refined, different? Don't you people claim that you're the same as everybody else? That's your way of saying that you're above everybody else."

When he sees that Asa's wife is pregnant, Allbee says, "Congratulations. I see you're following orders, 'Increase and multiply.' " Bellow's own memory of his experience trying to get into the English Department at Northwestern still rankles. Allbee says:

> "It's really as if the children of Caliban were running everything. . . . I go into the library once in a while, to look around, and last week I saw a book about Thoreau and Emerson by a man named Lipchitz. . . . A name like that? After all, it seems to me that people of such a background simply couldn't understand."

Allbee pursues Leventhal, on the street, into a cafeteria, into his home, reading his mail, drinking his whiskey, stealing his keys, finally settling down in Asa's flat, demanding money, badgering Asa to get him a job because he believes it was Leventhal who caused him to be fired from his job in retaliation for his anti-Semitic slurs.

Leventhal resents the charge but wavers about the truth of the accusation, and in his turn, he pursues all his friends who might have an opinion about his culpability. He asks his Gentile friend Williston and is appalled to discover Williston agrees with Allbee.

Did he or did he not intend Allbee to lose his job? How had it happened? Allbee had recommended him for a job open at his place of employment. At the interview, Leventhal lost his head completely, filled with disgust at his needing so measly a job, contemptuous of that pompous employer, an ass who had the right to say yes or no. Was that why he was reduced to such vulgar brutal behavior, disparaging Rudiger's newspaper, calling him a two-bit big shot, an empty wagon, or was it his secret belief that Rudiger was right to treat him like dirt? "He made me believe what I was afraid of." He, too, was ashamed of his own Jewish friend Harkavy, a burlesque Jew, who "when he spoke his hands flew and his brows slanted up, sharpening the line of his nose," and his Jewish traits became accentuated. And worse, he recognized he was all too much an Allbee. Enemies they may be, but his reaction went beyond any evening party or job interview; his hatred rose out of his sense that there was an affinity between them: He, too, had drifted, had been jobless and lonely, accepted mediocre jobs, lived in dirty hall bedrooms. Yes, he had been there, a transient, a scrounger, an effaced man. He despised in Allbee what he had once been; worse—what potentially he is, even now, for he can be fired at any time, his friends can close their doors to him, and they were probably talking of him behind his back. In Allbee, Leventhal recognizes he is observing a man as unstable as himself: Both appeal and cower, both plead and taunt, both lose control and shout, both are irrational and violent.

Near the end of the novel, Leventhal's fears are confirmed. He goes to a birthday party, and drinking too much wine, cannot make his way back home and sleeps the night on Harkavy's couch, awaking disheveled, defeated, lost, trembling, vacillating, without a plan, his reasoning faculties at an end. He has become an Allbee.

Why does Allbee pursue Leventhal and why does Leventhal allow himself to be caught? The anti-Semite and the Jew are equal partners in alienation. Leventhal is at war with Allbee because he is at war with himself. Allbee is at war with Leventhal for the same reason. Behind the appearance of the issue of anti-Semitism is the reality of self-disgust, self-contempt. Leventhal is isolated and dreary, ignoble on the job, incompetent among friends and family, desolate in his apartment, disgruntled in the neighborhood restaurant. Worse than exclusion is the belief that he deserves to be kept out. Why, he asks himself, is he so shamed and angry, so bitter and suspicious, so nervous and irritable? Why is he always on the verge of losing control? Why is he so withdrawn from the community of men?

Reflecting on the issue of human vulnerability, Leventhal realizes a man's psyche is precarious because he has the birthright of mortality. His sense of alienation arises out of his fear of death, and it is his fear that generates hate, fear that generates discomfiture and irrational antagonism.

Thus it is that in every man there is the same propensity to hate. Love is unnatural; love needs to be cultivated; we hate one another instinctively, as we breathe. The myth of the hairy glove of Esau on the hand of Jacob has been transformed to mean the dual nature of man, the simultaneity of good and evil in every man.

Awakened in the middle of the night by sounds of a commotion in the street, Leventhal thinks how little he knows of evil in the real world. He sleeps with the bathroom light burning. Evil is present and it has nothing to do with Kirby Allbee. Hatred is an innate attribute of man. He is no victim of Allbee; Allbee is no victim of Leventhal. In this world where evil is inherent and lies there rotting the heart of every man, every man is a victim.

Leventhal stares sadly at Mickey in his coffin and is struck by the softness of the boy's face, by the absence of signs of recoil or fright. That is the one sure way to be quiescent, to be passive, to avoid entanglement, to be sure the surface is not penetrated. While one lives, there is hatred and outbursts of irrational rage.

Why should a child, who is as far from malevolence as is a seed from its flower, sicken and die, however? Is God no respector of persons? Do the same rules apply to Jew or Gentile, man or child? Who runs things? The common man drifts in a world he has no part in making. The Jew suffers the same complex and confused private feelings, the same fear, hatred, anguish, insecurity, and shame as does the Gentile. We are all in the same boat when it comes to our destiny. So what do we owe? And if we owe, how can we pay? And if we can pay, to whom? What is to be done?

It is the old Jew, Schlossberg, a tired man, still holding fast to his standards, who tells what is to be done. Schlossberg has a unique program of how a man shall act and it is as near as Bellow came, in this novel, to an answer:

> "I'll tell you. It's bad to be less than human and it's bad to be more than human. What's more than human? . . . If I can talk myself into it that I never sweat and make everybody else act as if it was true, maybe I can fix it up about dying, too. We only know what it is to die because some people die and, if we make ourselves different from them, maybe we don't have to? Less than human is the other side of it. . . . So here is the whole thing. Good acting is what is exactly human. . . . This is my whole idea. More than human, can you have any use for life? Less than human, you don't either."

In his quiet zone, Leventhal reflects on what Schlossberg has said:

> Leventhal disagreed about "less than human." Since it was done by so many, what was it but human? "More than human" was for a much smaller number.

But most people had fear in them—fear of life, fear of death, of life more than of death, perhaps. But it was a fact that they were afraid, and when the fear was uppermost they didn't want any more burdens. . . . They said, "Just let me alone, that's all I ask." But either they found the strength to meet the costs or they refused and gave way to dizziness—dizziness altogether, the dizziness of pleasures before catastrophes. . . . he liked to think "human" meant accountable in spite of many weaknesses—at the last moment, tough enough to hold.

Is he tough enough to hold? He had better be. There is no other way.

Allbee is not tough enough to hold. He puts his head in the oven and turns on the gas. Leventhal leaps to the kitchen stove and turns off the gas. He smashes down his door and violently throws Allbee down the stairs. He saves himself; and he saves Allbee. Whatever life means or does not mean, this life they are all leading, there will be no choosing to die, no further helpless participation in disintegration. Asa's next act is to arrange with Mrs. Nunez, the superintendent's wife, to come with her broom and mop to clean the flat for Mary's return.

It is a mark of the restoration to order of Leventhal, just as there will be in *Herzog* the steady scratching of Mrs. Tuttle's broom, cleaning the house in Ludeyville in preparation for Ramona's visit, the same sign of the restoration to balance of Herzog. After great upheavals of spirit and heart and mind, Leventhal reclines peacefully on his couch, conceding there is no answer, only that he must hold.

Three years later, Allbee and Leventhal meet in a theater during the intermission. They have a hurried exchange before each goes back to watch the play. Allbee grins: "I've made my peace with things as they are. I've gotten off the pony—you remember, I said that to you once. I'm on the train."

"A conductor?"

"Conductor, hell! I'm just a passenger. . . . Not even first class. I'm not the type that runs things. What do I care? The world wasn't made exactly for me. What am I going to do about it? . . . Anyway I'm enjoying life."

In his second novel, Bellow crystallized the dilemma of every passenger on all trains, of every man making his way through his life span, the led, the oppressed, the saved, who share the fate of a common destiny but take no comfort in the fellowship because there is in every man the desire to have a unique destiny, to live a good life, a significant life despite the omnipresence of corruption and failure. Allbee's question "What am I going to do about it?" becomes the question of Augie March, Henderson, Herzog, Sammler, Citrine, Corde, Crader, and Ken Trachtenberg. It is Bellow's question.

In Sweden, thirty years after writing *The Victim,* Bellow said outright what the story of Asa Leventhal portrayed:

> In private life, disorder or near-panic. In families—for husbands, wives, parents, children—confusion; in civic behavior, in personal loyalties, in sexual practices . . . further confusion. It is with this private disorder and public bewilderment that we try to live. We stand open to all anxieties. The decline and fall of everything is our daily dread, we are agitated in private life and tormented by public questions.

"Jewish suffering does not drive us from human nature"

When *The Victim* was published, Elizabeth Hardwick said, "On the basis of these two novels it would be hard to think of any young writer who has a better chance than Bellow to become the redeeming novelist of his period."

However, the young writer—he was then thirty-two—was to become known as the young Jewish writer, the redeeming Jewish novelist of his period. From the time of the appearance of *The Victim,* Bellow has always been identified as a Jewish writer, despite all his protests or challenges, demurrals or denials. Richard Match, in the *Herald Tribune,* compared *The Victim* favorably to Arthur Miller's *Focus* and Laura Z. Hobson's *Gentleman's Agreement,* and identified the book as "a subtle and thoughtful contribution to the literature of twentieth-century anti-Semitism." *Time* said, "On the surface this is a competent little story about a solemn and touchy Jew accused by a fantastic Gentile of having ruined him." The qualification persisted down to the publication of *The Dean's December,* when Hugh Kenner titled his remarks in *Harper's* "From Lower Bellowvia: Leopold Bloom with a Ph.D." and informed his readers the protagonist was "not a Jewish Dean from the Bellow Repertory Company," but Bellow, that "sardonic connoisseur of Old Testament motifs," who has ostensibly given us an Irishman. Diane Johnson, in *The New York Review of Books,* reassured everyone that despite the fact that Corde is a Huguenot, "He and his family seem like nice Jewish characters."[1]

When Isaac Bashevis Singer was chosen to receive the Nobel Prize in 1978, a Swedish knight who had found his way on to the faculty at Stony Brook stopped me near Melville Library and said, "Aren't you glad about our giving the prize to another one of your people?" I mentioned this to Bellow and he said there was always a lot of that going on. He told me of a woman from an Italian news-agency network who called to ask why did he think so many Jews won the Nobel Prize? He told her it was because they were better. She asked why do you think that Jews are writing for an elite all the time, and he said, they were the only people in the world that have been made into an elite. By force of circumstance, he said, there were only a few left. They have become an elite not by choice.

To be sure, many critics sought to go beyond the victim's Jewishness and eventually spoke of Leventhal as a metaphor for urban man, or all minorities, or isolation in general, but it made very little difference. For example, Martin Greenberg, writing for *Commentary,* recognized that although *The Victim* was a "Jewish novel," the Jewishness was not to be viewed as a special world of experience, but as a quality that informs all of modern life. "The Jew expresses the experience of modernity itself." Leslie Fiedler, writing for *Kenyon Review,* gave his highest praise to the novel because it was extraordinarily like Lionel Trilling's *The Middle of the Journey;* both novels proposed sincerity as an alternative to form.[2] Fiedler was aware, but dimly, that there was another level of meaning in the book:

> Leventhal is realized with such passionate patience and skill, achieved with such scrupulous regard for detail rising from a sense that the meanings of each trivial fact are inexhaustible and mysterious that he becomes, deeply as he is a Jew, human, and infinitely, as he is particularized, universal.

Alan Downer, writing for *The New York Times Book Review,* was simpler, sharper, and unequivocal:

> The novel is at once overcontrived and undercontrived, as if Mr. Bellow had not quite determined what kind of novel he was writing. . . . It is never clear what *The Victim* is about. Leventhal is a Jew and Allbee is anti-Semitic; but the problem of prejudice is only incidental. Leventhal searches for the truth about his tormentor and himself, but we are never told how his knowledge frees him from Allbee, and we are plainly shown that it has no effect upon his character.[3]

In all his prose writings, Bellow has addressed the issue of his Jewish identity only twice on his own initiative—the first time close to the year *The Victim* was published, the second not long after *Mr. Sammler's Planet* appeared. In 1949, he wrote a piece for *Commentary* called "The Jewish Writer" and said those who use the label accept the stereotype of the Jew as a person "without birth, without upbringing." He argued here as he had in *The Victim* that Jewish pain has fundamentally the same meaning as does pain for everyone. "Jewish suffering does not drive us from human nature."

In 1974, in the imaginary interview printed in *The American Scholar,* Bellow said:

> But I started out to recall what it was like to set oneself up to be a writer in the Midwest during the thirties. For I thought of myself as a midwesterner and not a Jew. I am often described as a Jewish writer; in much the same way one might be called a Samoan astronomer or an Eskimo cellist or a Zulu Gainsborough expert. There is some oddity about it. I am a Jew, and I have written some books. I have tried to fit my soul into the Jewish-writer category, but it does not feel comfortably accommodated there. I wonder, now and then, whether Philip Roth and Bernard Malamud and I have not become the Hart, Schaffner & Marx of our trade. We have made it in the field of culture as Bernard Baruch made it on a park bench, as Polly Adler made it in prostitution, as Two Gun Cohen, the personal bodyguard of Sun Yat-sen, made it in China. My joke is not broad enough to cover the contempt I feel for the opportunists, wise guys, and career types who impose such labels and trade upon them. In a century so disastrous to Jews, one hesitates to criticize those who believe that they are making the world safer by publicizing Jewish achievements. I myself doubt that this publicity is effective. . . . People who make labels should be in the gumming business.[4]

That Bellow, when he wrote his imaginary interview, should have chosen to comment on himself as a Jewish writer was itself an ironic gesture, for his interviewers always put the question to him. Over and over again, they asked him to affirm or deny that he was a Jewish writer. Always he said, "No." In 1964, he told Nina Steers: "I have no fight about being a Jew. I simply must deal with the facts of my life—as a basic set of primitive facts. They're my given."[5] In 1965, he explained very carefully to Gordon Lloyd Harper how he began as a writer, emphasizing it was the craft of writing that had excited him, that it had been a matter of finding the proper form.[6]

> My first two books are well-made. I wrote the first quickly but took great pains with it. I labored with the second and tried to make it letter-perfect. In writing *The Victim* I accepted a Flaubertian standard. Not a bad standard, to be sure,

but one which in the end, I found repressive—repressive because of the circumstances of my life and because of my upbringing in Chicago as the son of
immigrants.

Whatever else he said to Gordon Lloyd Harper made very little difference.
From then on anyone—Jews and non-Jews alike—who wished to comment
on Bellow's fiction had Bellow's own words to affirm his ethnic identity; he
himself had pointed out he was the son of immigrants, and that was that.
Nobody seemed to notice he had gone on to describe the harm he had
experienced in being identified as a Jew instead of an American.

> I had good reason to fear that I would be put down as a foreigner, an interloper.
> It was made clear to me when I studied literature in the university that as a Jew
> I would probably never have the right *feeling* for Anglo-Saxon traditions, for
> English words. I realized even in college that the people who told me this were
> not necessarily disinterested friends. But they had an effect on me, nevertheless.
> This was something from which I had to free myself. I fought free because I
> had to.

Bellow may have fought free of the need to prove he did have the right feel
for English words; he never fought free of the label.

In 1969, he told Jim Douglas Henry: "I don't have any sense of
ethnic responsibility. That is not my primary obligation. My primary obligation is to my trade and not to any particular ethnic group."[7] In 1970, a Hindu
professor of American literature, Chirantan Kulshrestha, went to Chicago to
do research for his monograph on Bellow. They met and Kulshrestha published the interview.[8] "I was trying to pin him down to a firm and concrete
statement on the Jewish quality of his work, and he was vehemently repulsing
the overture calling the Jewish tag 'false and wrong.' " To be a Hindu, to be
a Jew, he told Kulshrestha, is simply a fact of your life.

> That's how I view my own Jewishness. That's where the great power of it comes
> from. It doesn't come from the fact that I studied the *Talmud*, or anything of
> that sort. I never belonged to an orthodox congregation. It comes simply from
> the fact that at a most susceptible time of my life I was wholly Jewish. That's
> a gift, a piece of good fortune, with which one doesn't quarrel.

Kulshrestha was not satisfied: "I am told that in recent years there has been
a great change in the attitude of the Jewish community towards your work.
To what do you attribute this change? Would you describe yourself specifi-
cally as a Jewish writer?"

I don't really know the answer to that. I don't think that any literature should be so special that it can't be understood by non-communicants. . . . I have never consciously written as a Jew. I have just written as Saul Bellow. I have never attempted to make myself Jewish. I've never tried to appeal to a community. I never thought of writing for Jews exclusively. . . . I think of myself as a person of Jewish origin—American and Jewish—who has had a certain experience of life, which is part Jewish.

Bellow made the same point, more strongly, before a large audience in Tel Aviv, where he was asked the same question, now put to him by a panel of Israeli writers.

I will say one further thing about the Jewish writer in America, and that is that the Jewish community in America was delighted when the Jewish writers appeared on the scene because they felt it would be good for the Jews in America. This put us in a rather awkward position of doing public relations, unwillingly, for the American Jews, and we were also expected to refrain from any sharp criticism of persons who were Jews. And this was extremely disagreeable because it seemed to me to be an imposition on truth to have to make things come out nicely as Israel Zangwill did, and give the people a pleasing impression. Other Jewish writers bent over backwards just because there was this pressure put on them and they decided that they would be, on the contrary, or out of contrariness, quite nasty in their realistic portrayal of Jews. This is an accusation that has been brought against Philip Roth, who has gone much farther in this direction than I ever dreamed of going. But he went farther in that direction because he felt the provocation. Or the challenge, I think, whereas I always refuse to be provoked or challenged and simply went my stubborn, mulish narrow way without accepting either the task of making good public relations for the Jews or reacting strongly against this demand.[9]

In May 1971, Bellow replied to a question from Joseph Epstein:

There is an implied put down in the label American Jewish writer. . . . I must say I find the label intellectually vulgar, unnecessarily parochializing and utterly without value—especially since, from a personal point of view it avoids me both as a writer and as a Jew.[10]

In 1973, he still had to answer the question for students at Franklin and Marshall College: "This whole Jewish writer business is sheer invention—by the media, by critics and by 'scholars.' I'm well aware of being Jewish and also of being an American and of being a writer. But I'm also a hockey fan, a fact which nobody ever mentions."[11]

Humor, indignation, careful explanation, patience, irritation—nothing made much difference. That Eugene Henderson was a Connecticut Yankee off to the wilds of Africa to learn the truth of his identity from Queen Willatale and King Dahfu was an amusing fiction; that Charlie Citrine took instruction in the art of meditation according to Rudolf Steiner was discounted as a lapse in common sense; that Albert Corde was an Irishman was a mere disguise.

In April 1979, I met Bellow in New York. "Why do you think," I asked as we were walking toward the garage where my car was parked, "that the critics always mention the Jewish aspect, always point to you as the Jewish American writer?" His answer was abrasive, but then Bellow has never been tolerant of literary critics. He said it was probably because critics don't bother to read what he is saying, just follow one on the other, with someone getting a general notion of what's there, and then the rest going on to describe that, book by book. Bellow always has accused the critics of being part of an establishment, a business, writing to make it in the establishment, saying only what the establishment said. He feels they don't relate to literature; they don't respond or react as human beings; they write what they think will get them ahead in their business. Bellow always has claimed he does not read the critics, that after only a few paragraphs, he puts the pages down in sadness. They just did not get it, he lamented. He was particularly outraged that no one, nobody at all, bothered to read Steiner, although they all reviewed *Humboldt's Gift,* one leaning on the other, not reading the book or Steiner, but one another.

I was going to drive him to the airport and he carried his two suitcases and a shopping bag full of books he had picked up at the bookstore of the Anthroposophical Society on Madison Avenue. He also was carrying along a banana, runny ripe, and an orange, the last of the bowl of fruit the Hotel Carlyle had given him on his arrival. He did not want to leave the fruit behind; they would think he did not appreciate the gesture. On the street, I asked him why Rudolf Steiner had so much appeal for him: "What are you, a Jewish theosophist?" He said that he did not believe in clairvoyance or the Ouija board or spirits, but the world of the spirit, yes, the cosmic reality, the soul, yes.

Then, since we still had two hours, we stopped in for a drink at Berkeley's, a bar across the street from the Algonquin Hotel. He did not want to go to the Algonquin, for there would be too many people there. He did not like that scene. Too many coming over to his table to talk to him. He doesn't need that. Bellow, as usual, was dressed to the nines, now in a wonderfully smooth velvety gray flannel suit, a black and white bold-striped shirt, and his soft silky tie, very full and flowing, this time a strong floral print, the blacks, grays, and raspberry tones challenging. Always the face struck me, the worn-out face, heavier now, jowly, lined, but the body still thin, still lithe, no sags, no paunch. I thought, remembering him long, long days ago in the wrinkled seersucker suits worn in hot Chicago when I visited him in the basement space in the Social Sciences building, people working there on the Hutchins-Adler Syntopicon project, the place off-limits to any student of R. S. Crane in those days. We stare a long time to catch glimpses of what we were, but then, finally, we take it on faith that we are still those same people, with the same voices, the same thoughts. The visible signs are gone. But we have our names.

In the bar, at a table in a dark corner, he held his Jack Daniels on ice, cooling his hands, he said, and began to talk about the meaning of Steiner. It was a question of the difference between romanticism and realism, a distinction that began with the Greeks and ran through the Middle Ages to the nineteenth century and modern times. He said that any sense of the yonder side of life had always been lost; every culture, whatever the time, wherever the place, always strove toward materialism. It was the here and now that concerned men, and anything else was interpreted as foolish romanticism. He never agreed with that. Maybe it was the same with Steiner.

Bellow said that people don't like to think about such things as the soul, the spirit, or the afterlife. He does. And, he said, Whitman was close to it; Whitman was, in fact, a serious religious poet. He also said that Tolstoi understood it but he drew back, he got scared, he refused to name it although he knew it existed. In the story "The Death of Ivan Ilyich," the closest Tolstoi let himself come was "The light! The light!" Tolstoi never had the courage to say what the light was.

We walked to the garage, just a few doors away, and waited for the car to be brought down. Bellow tipped the parking attendant and we took off.

As we drove to La Guardia, he said that maybe in his next book he ought to have a woman as his main character. He had never really written about a good woman as a main character. I reminded him of Willatale in *Henderson the Rain King* and he smiled and said yes, that was right.

Musing aloud, he said he ought to take someone like John L. Lewis's daughter, a remarkable woman whom Lewis adored, and who adored him, always together but never able to get along. He could handle that, he said ruefully, and then, quiet for a long time, he went on as if no time at all had passed, to say he could work in something about unions and labor, the hither side of reality, and let the woman live more on the yonder side. As he spoke, I had the feeling he was more interested in John L. Lewis than in the daughter, that he was not sure fiction could handle Steiner's interpretation of reality. Maybe poetry could, but fiction worked better on facts, on concrete reality.

Bellow was not to write about any so-called John L. Lewis or his daughter. Ten years later, when he published *A Theft* in 1989, Clara Velde, his heroine, was a remarkable-enough woman but on no yonder side of reality. Clara adores her mentor, Ithiel Regler, and in her mind at least, they are inseparable, but it is Regler who is the singular person, committed to high civility, with a genius for understanding politics and history, possessing an amazing range of information, with an indisputable grasp on reality, preoccupied with significant thoughts, powerful, secretive, sensual, whose one subject was love and happiness, resigned to his having neither love nor happiness. On a scale of one to ten, Regler was a clear ten. Bellow could handle that.

We got into a traffic tieup on the Brooklyn–Queens Expressway. "Real New York traffic," I said. "And I'm not so sure we're on the right road to La Guardia."

Bellow began to get out of the car to ask someone. I grabbed his arm and shouted, "No way! Are you crazy? You are certainly not getting out of this car. You'll be killed." He shrugged as if he did not care, one way or the other.

When I left him at the airport, he stood on the curb, watching me pull out. He seemed reluctant to be alone. I saw him in my rearview mirror, standing there with his suitcases and his shopping bag of Steiner.

Women have a part to play in Bellow's fiction, but they are only instruments in a man's quest for identity of his solitary self.[12] Joseph's unease and Leventhal's irritability have nothing to do with their wives but, rather, of their awareness of human frailty and helplessness in the face of the reality of death. When Joseph slips into bed with Kitty, he knows the affair is only part of his wanting to miss nothing.

> A compact with one woman puts beyond reach what others might give us to enjoy, the soft blondes and the dark aphrodisiacal women of our imagination are set aside. Shall we leave life not knowing them? Must we?

As soon as Joseph recognizes he is only using Kitty to satisfy his avidity for experience, he brings the affair to a close. Joseph is dissatisfied with his wife because of her reluctance to be guided and formed by him. She did not fit his dreams "inspired by Burckhardt's great ladies of the Renaissance and the no less profound Augustan women" who were in his head, not hers. She preferred such things as "clothes, appearances, furniture, light entertainment, mystery stories, the attractions of fashion magazines, the radio, the enjoyable evening." What could he say to her? "Women—thus I reasoned—were not equipped by training to resist such things. . . . she is as far as ever from what I once desired to make her. I am afraid she has no capacity for that."

Joseph knows it is arrogant to think of women as blighted because they lack worthwhile ideas, even though he himself thinks that worthwhile ideas count for very little in the actual world, but he cannot understand why, once shown the way, women remain reluctant to learn.

> . . . no one came simply and of his own accord, effortlessly, to prize the most truly human traditions, the heavenly cities. You had to be taught to struggle your way toward them. Inclination was not enough. Before you set your screws revolving, you had to be towed out of the shallows. But it was now evident that Iva did not want to be towed.

There is no Iva in *The Victim.* Leventhal's wife is out of town; Allbee's wife is dead. It's the men who argue about right conduct; women watch over their children, serve tea and cakes, carry a mop and a bucket, or take off their clothes for a couple of dollars. Alas, only women indifferent to the heavenly cities will attract the heroes in Bellow's stories.

From *Augie March* to *More Die of Heartbreak,* the Kitty Daimlers take over. Only in *The Dean's December* has Bellow portrayed women who can act together as a sisterhood of caring and efficiency and strength, arousing respect and awe in Albert Corde. The little nieces of the Mexican general, the erotic, the gay and faithless, the little beauties, aesthetes of sensuality charm and trap the narrator with their youth and exuberance, their aggressive sensuality. Once he wins her, he will change her. Not one of Bellow's narrators succeeds; each is helpless to resist or reform a Thea, a Lily, a Ramona, a Renata. Even old Sammler fails to improve Angela. Not one minor character succeeds, be he brother, father, uncle, cousin, friend, acquaintance, son-in-law, or taxi driver. One may well ask how can a man expect to dominate a woman whom he requires to be the aggressor? How can he form the mind of a woman whom he requires to be sensuous?

The narrator asks no such question. He weeps. Another man is in Kitty's bed; Thea runs off with Talavera; Madeleine shuts Herzog out of his own house—her lover Gersbach is waiting inside; Renata runs off with Flonzaley, leaving Citrine holding her black velvet cloak in a rooming house in Madrid. From Augie March to Uncle Benn and Nephew Ken, who pursues a Treckie and settles for a Dita who endured a face peeling to attract him, women afflict the narrator. He tries to fathom why women are frumps, predators, trollops, cheats, mousies, doxies, harridans, emasculators, manipulators, betrayers, or rigid unyielding martinets, paranoids, dollies, or chumps.

Until 1989, when *A Theft* was published, only two stories portray women from the woman's point of view: "Dora" (1949) about a seamstress who does not even know there is such a thing as a significant life, and "Leaving the Yellow House" (1957), which gives us Hattie, an independent woman, drunken, fat, ailing, living out her last joyless days on Sego Desert Lake.

Bellow wrote "Dora" just after completing *The Victim*. Dora, brought up in an orphanage, lives in a rented room in a boardinghouse, worrying about her poor teeth and poor digestion. She sews beautiful dresses for her few private customers and pretty costumes for the Metropolitan Opera Company, and because she has nothing else to do, she baby-sits when some family needs her. At night, she lies in her bed waiting to fall asleep, listening to sounds of crying or shouting or screaming. She reflects on their meaning, not as so commonplace a Dora might do, but as Bellow's Dora must—detached, forlorn, fearful, alone.

> But worse than the father and daughter and wife is to hear *one*, not two people answering each other, but one person who shouts and screams by himself, screams so thick you can't even tell who is screaming, whether it's a man or a woman or even an animal, because you're so accustomed a human voice should mean something. . . . But anyway, when this screaming starts, nobody can do anything about it. And it isn't like animals' sound after all, but a language everybody knows but never uses. And I suppose every grownup knows that it is about painful mistakes. It's the pain that causes you to make the mistakes, from which comes pain and then more mistakes again—on and on. It must stop somewhere. You hope it will. The person knows it will. But the person *within* the person doesn't really believe it until the moment it finally has to. No more mistakes nor anything else either. The last mistake has been made. And that is what you hear. An animal couldn't make a cry like that.[13]

She hears a terrible cry, a howl of anguish from the bedroom down the hall and then a heavy thud, as if a tree had fallen in the forest. This is no matter for abstract reflection; it is the sound of her neighbor; it is real business. She enters the room and finds the man lying on the floor, naked, comatose. "I put my ear to his chest and heard beating." She places a pillow under his head and phones Bellevue.

Doctors tell her it was a stroke and there is nothing to be done for him; he may get better or he may never speak or move again. There is nobody to notify. Dora refuses to leave him to die unknown to anyone, and so each day she visits him.

> When I get into the street with my shantung dress and feel the fit over my hips while I wait for the bus and see in my imagination the brilliantine shining on my hair and the poppy color of the lipstick—it is something. It is more as if I was going to a parade for a general back from Africa or Burma instead of Bellevue. I haven't missed a day this week. I take the bus to Second Avenue and transfer. I make better time on it than on the subway, though the street is rough. Most of the way there is that old brick paving from years and years back.

Dressed in her best clothes, with orange-red lipstick on her lips and her hair set in curls, she sits beside his bed on her mission of mercy to a man she does not know and who can never see her in her new good looks, never hear what she says, never speak a word. So Bellow explores connection from the woman's point of view.

Both "Dora" and Chapter 1 of *Augie March* were published in November 1949. That Bellow should have been thinking of so drab a woman at the same time he was reveling in the glossy memories of Augie March is no more mysterious than the fact that *Harper's Bazaar* chose to publish "Dora." The cheerful fashion magazine designed for well-heeled, self-indulgent women printed "Dora" among advertisements for mock pearl chokers and dangle earrings, sporty watches from Geneva and handwoven tweeds from the Hebrides. The eye may wander from the final lines of the story of two aimless lives and contemplate an ad for Toujours Moi, the perfume of lasting fragrance imported from France for America's smartest women. What can one do about the Doras of the world? Buy a new two-toned compact with a satin silver finish.

A few months earlier, Bellow had sent a different kind of story to *Partisan Review*, "A Sermon by Doctor Pep,"[14] and it is also a wonder they should have chosen to print it. Dr. Pep is a con man, like a circus shill, addressing a street crowd on Bughouse Square, where anyone can put up an American flag, climb on a soapbox, and say what's on his mind. Dr. Pep is flashy and ebullient in spirit, learned to the point of stupefaction. His discourse on nutrition and the human spirit is proved by examples of the ground-up children of Thyestes and the chicken croquettes of Thompson's restaurant; allusions join together the Lincoln Park zoo and star-browed

Apollo, the Guiana spider and Acheron, the Heavenly City and Auschwitz, Henry George with his Single Tax and Abraham and Isaac.

"A Sermon by Doctor Pep" was to *Partisan* what "Dora" was to *Harper's Bazaar. Partisan Review* was doctrinaire in its politics, and committed to the promotion of modern writers from abroad—Joyce, Flaubert, Lawrence, Pound—and here was Dr. Pep deriding all programs as spurious, talking fast in a stream of consciousness that was a zigzag of thoughts, not the tracks of the unconscious of the mythic man but the exuberant public speech of a shyster on the sidewalk in front of the Newberry Library, on Walton Street and North Clark. Listen to Dr. Pep. Hold on to his thread of logical illogic and follow him out of the Minotaur's cave of ignorance and emerge into the light, where your idea of culture and his idea of culture can be distinguished. Dr. Pep will tell you why your pseudogentility and foolish self-immolation for the sake of causes and ideas must be put by, for it leads only to the embracing of death. Dr. Pep says the heart of a good man, admittedly an insignificant man, is also filled with love and compassion. It's as if Bellow was saying to the intellectual travelers who read *Partisan* seriously, page by earnest page, Come now, come off it, stop parading all this so-called civilization and culture and profundity of thought. "I sit in the Newberry," says Dr. Pep, "and compassionate with the tender girls who have never felt anything warmer than a washcloth upon them." You dream of building the City of Man? You believe that art and civilization go together? Dr. Pep tells you that beautiful Versailles and the shaped trees of Fontainebleau fed the dream of Robespierre, who was prepared to murder millions of his countrymen to see it real. "Were the fierce moppers of Auschwitz inspired by their squared and polished home towns and the pleasant embroidery of the regulated Rhine?"

Perhaps the editors of *Partisan Review* were preoccupied with more ticklish problems raised for them by their beloved modern writers, especially D. H. Lawrence and Ezra Pound, to pay much attention to the choice of Bellow's story for their May–June issue. Lawrence, who had so impressed the *Partisan Review* crowd a decade earlier with his advocacy of sensual ecstasy as the means for merging with the cosmos, was not so easy to defend in the forties, with his celebrations of blood brotherhood. Ezra Pound, with his sparse diction and cold sensibility, had exhilarated readers and editors a decade earlier, but now his broadcasts for the fascists dismayed them all. Pound sat convicted of treason, confined in St. Elizabeth's Hospital for the Insane. In 1949, he was chosen to receive the Bollingen Award for his *Pisan Cantos.* On the committee, acting for the Library of Congress, which sponsored the prize, sat Robert Lowell, and Allen Tate, Conrad Aiken, Louise Bogan, W. H. Auden, T. S. Eliot, Robert Penn Warren, and Karl Shapiro, all respected members of *Partisan*'s respected establishment.[15] Only Karl Shapiro voted no. He refused to be shaken from his point of view that anti-Semitism does indeed vitiate art. All through that spring, summer, and fall of 1949, the argument was kept alive. The magazine published an attack on the prize by William Barrett in April, and it also published a defense of the prize by Auden and Tate in the issue in which "Dr. Pep" appeared. To balance their position, the editors published another attack by Karl Shapiro in their November number, the same issue in which Chapter One of *Augie March* was printed.

Bellow was far out of the way of the controversy, on his first trip abroad, with a Guggenheim award to support two years of travel. He had left behind him, in New York, his newly acquired literary agent, Henry Volkening; he had negotiated a fine contract with a well-established press, leaving Vanguard for Viking; and he had found a subject matter he was sure would carry him as far as possible from Flaubert, and beyond the reach of the conventional well-made novel, well past what the New York scene expected him to write, out of the range of labels, and maybe, with luck, maybe, he could leave, as well, his old self behind. He had thought of an old playmate, and his project was to write an imaginary life of that early friend growing up in Chicago: What would he be like? What might have become of him? The first chapter was already in the offices of *Partisan Review* before Bellow took off for Europe.

Three prose pieces written by Bellow enable us to piece together how he felt about his experiences traveling on the Continent. The first was titled "The French as Dostoevsky Saw Them."[16] In it, Bellow remembered finding a copy of Dostoevsky's *Winter Notes on Summer Impressions* (in French, *Le Bourgeois de Paris*) at a bookstall. "It may be appropriate," he began, "to recall the circumstances under which I first read *Winter Notes* and to tell how I was feeling when the gods placed it in my hands."

Nineteen forty-eight was a cold winter in Paris. Always depressed in bad weather, Bellow was "sunk in spirit" in the city that lay under fog, with the grime and medicinal smells of the Seine enveloping him. "Gay Paris? Gay, my foot!"

> Only the coldest of foreigners can arrive in Paris without experiencing a wild excitement. . . . Renting an apartment in Paris was not a simple matter in 1947, but a good friend of mine, Nicolaus, had found one for us on the right bank, in a fussy building. I had bought a new Remington portable typewriter, which the landlady had absolutely demanded, as a gift. . . . It was a steep rental. Nicolaus, however, said the apartment was worth the money. He knew Paris,

and I took his word for it. . . . As soon as Madame left, I turned a somersault over the Chippendale chair and landed thunderously on the floor. This lightened my heart for a time, but in subsequent dealings with Madame and others in France I could not always recover my lightness of heart by such means.

Like Dostoevsky, who had complained a hundred years earlier that he was treated like an interloper by the French, Bellow was dismayed to be accused of materialism by a people whose worship of economic power and whose pompous defense of their superiority appalled him. He tried to argue himself out of his dislike of the French.

Because you have paid the price of admission and have come with your awkward affections in your breast and dollars in your pocket, do you expect these people to press you to their hearts, and to take you into their homes? You must try to appreciate the fact that they have other and more important concerns. Only three years ago Hitler was deporting thousands, shooting hostages. A war has been fought here. . . . And now the communists are trying to drag France into Russia. America presses from the other side. Armies of tourists are pouring in. And must you inject your irrelevant self?

Reasoning so did not help him much. He could not detach himself from his indignation at a people whose prejudices seemed to him more apparent than their nobility, whose tradition of culture seemed more hypocrisy than idealism.

It is not easy to be a good tourist. A good tourist is selfless. He is unarmored. His nervous receptors are open. . . . The good tourist is he who, going from Mont St. Michel to the Louvre and from the Louvre to Chartres, Chartres to Vézelay, Vézelay to Avignon, Avignon to Nice, to Venice, to Florence, to Rome, can still, though weary, lift up his heart like a father immersed in a crowd who hoists his small boy on his shoulders to watch the parade he himself cannot see.

Bellow was not such a tourist. "It demands strength, humility, forbearance, and a great many more qualities I do not possess."

Spain was worse. Bellow visited Spain to get the feel of the people, not to see the monuments, and there, too, he felt out of place, was again the suspect American, envied, scoffed at, gypped. He wrote about his experience in Spain in a travel sketch called "Spanish Letter," printed in *Partisan Review* in 1949.

No Prado, no Escorial, no Alhambra, Seville, or Cadiz; at a railroad junction, he entered the station restaurant and described the man behind the

counter; he entered the dining room of his pension and described the board-
ers he met at the table. No colorful bullfights, no flamenco dancers; he
observed the police. He watched the peddlers of stolen goods—pens, jewelry,
cigarettes—and the beggars. He attended a political trial in Alcala de
Henares, the birthplace of Cervantes; three pages are devoted to the proceedings, and all the ugliness of Spain, the hypocrisy, injustice, dishonor, and
despair are compressed into the description of the court action, and of the
two petty criminals—an old man and a boy—who are under arrest. He might
well have been a "barbarian from a vast and backward land" but what was
so advanced, so refined in the muck of Franco's Spain?

Bellow was not a good visitor abroad. He much preferred to sit
quietly alone at a table and write about Augie March growing up in Chicago;
he would arrange his notebooks on some corner table of a restaurant, or
balance his papers on his knees, sitting on a bench off to the side in a public
garden, and allow his words to pour out. In a feature article, "How I Wrote
Augie March's Story," printed in *The New York Times Book Review* on
January 31, 1954, Bellow looked back on this time and recalled the ease with
which the novel seemed to be writing itself.

> I was at that time writing in a tiny hotel room on Rue des Saints Pères. . . . It
> was Chicago before the Depression that moved my imagination as I went to my
> room in the morning, not misty Paris with its cold statues and its streams of
> water running along the curbstones. . . . The book was writing itself very rapidly.
> I was coming to be strangely independent of place. Chicago itself had grown
> exotic to me. . . . In the spring of 1950 I began to travel southward with my
> family. One chapter of "Augie" . . . was written at Schloss Leopoldskron,
> Salzburg, the late Max Reinhardt's baroque castle, while I was teaching in the
> American Seminar. Another was written in Florence in May at various café
> tables. . . . In Rome I wrote every morning for six weeks at the Casino Valadier
> in the Borghese Gardens. In this marvellous place, overlooking the city from the
> Pincian Rock, I happily filled several student notebooks and smoked cigars and
> drank coffee, unaware of the close Roman heat as long as I did not move about.
> . . . My old Mexican briefcase was growing fat with manuscript as we traveled.
> I wrote in all kinds of conditions, in hotels and eating places, on a rooftop
> in the town of Positano, south at Sorrento, at the Crystal Palace Hotel,
> London. . . .

All he had to do was hold the notebook to catch the spill of words from
well-meaning Augie in search of a fate good enough for him. When Bellow
returned to New York in 1950, he simply went right on writing:

> . . . in the apartment of my friend Ladov on West Ninety-fifth Street in Forest
> Hills, in a cold-water flat on Hudson Street, in the Hotel Meany in Seattle, in

a motel in Portland, Oregon, at Yaddo in Saratoga Springs, in the Pennsylvania Station, in a Broadway hotel, in an office at the Princeton Library. . . .

Wherever he went, he carried his notebooks and his old briefcase, embossed leather bought years ago in Mexico, with him.

On his return to America, Bellow sublet Ladov's flat in Forest Hills for his family and he rented a cold-water flat in the Village for himself so that he could work without disturbance or distress. As a writer, he recognized he had broken through conventional form and style and plot and character and tradition and passive modes of thought. The American tourist had left the oppressive old world behind him. Now, with *Augie March* safely on its way, and singing, he was about to leave his old self behind. He had a sense of excitement, feelings of vigor, of renewal that gladdened his heart. Before *Augie March* was set in type, he had already published three short stories and six book reviews, tried his hand at playwriting (*The Wrecker*), and translated from the Yiddish I. B. Singer's short story "Gimpel the Fool," the first work by Singer to appear in English.17

I visited the apartment in Forest Hills. I don't know what I expected. Exuberance? Joy? Light? To look at photographs? Mementos of the years abroad? The room was dark, the curtains drawn, a single lamp burning in the early afternoon, Saul talking in a low voice. Soon he said he did not think I should stay much longer. His wife probably did not like strangers in the house. He walked with me to the subway. I thought, then, no one could keep up with the kind of man Bellow was turning out to be, a man wholly devoted to the fire that burned at his heart's center, a man eager to meet people, to talk, and joke, and laugh.

After their divorce, Anita Goshkin went to California to live, taking Gregory with her; eventually, she remarried, enjoying a quieter life with her son and eventually his wife and in time her grandchildren. She always wished Saul well, as he did Anita. There is a letter from her in the archives written to congratulate Bellow on his third marriage, to Susan Glassman, hoping it would work this time. When she died suddenly of a stroke in 1985, Bellow recalled their breaking apart with deep sadness.

Bellow closed down the New York operation and went off to Princeton as an assistant to Delmore Schwartz. He was paid to be a Creative Writing Fellow, and he had a good sum of money from the National Institute of Arts and Letters. It pleased him to give lavish parties for a whole new set of friends with whom he could drink and gossip, to whom he could talk about writing and politics and strategies, or even quarrel, not about his character and personality but about his ideas. At his Christmas party, there were Delmore Schwartz and Elizabeth Pollet, John Berryman and Eileen Simpson, Ralph Ellison, triumphant that year with the publication of *Invisible Man,* and Helen Blackmur (left behind by Richard). At Berryman's house, he met Arthur Koestler, Irving Howe, Edmund Wilson, Walter Clemons, and Carlos Baker. It was in Princeton that he gave the finished manuscript of *Augie March* to Berryman to read. Berryman was ecstatic. He told his wife, Eileen Simpson, "I'm going to have lunch with him and tell him he's a bloody genius." Bellow enjoyed Berryman's praise but he was already so sure of *Augie March,* he had allowed parts of it to be printed well before it was finished.[18]

At Viking Press, Bellow had met an attractive young woman, Alexandra Tschacbasov—Sasha, Sandra, Sondra—and it was with her that he celebrated the National Book Award given to him in 1953 for *The Adventures of Augie March;* and it was with her that he drank champagne when the book was chosen to be an alternate choice of the Book of the Month Club. She went to live with him that same year when he accepted an appointment at Bard College as a professor of American literature. It was for her he bought his house in Tivoli. They married in 1956.

"By-blow of a travelling man"

When his family moved to Humboldt Park in Chicago in 1924, Bellow was nine years old. An imperious old lady lived in the house next door. Her neighbors were her business. Augie March is about the same age when Grandma Lausch instructs him on what to say to the social worker at the eye dispensary. Augie grows up in Bellow's old neighborhood, living among the immigrant families Bellow knew and transformed into Einhorns and Coblins and Renlings, Dingbat, Clem Tambow, Five Properties, Sylvester, Padilla, Guzynski, Kayo Obermark, Iggy Moulton, Hyman Basteshaw, Mintouchian—all those wonderful names that disguise the real people circulating through Bellow's world as he grew up in Chicago between 1915 and 1948.

Like Bellow, Augie goes to grammar school, high school, and college, does odd jobs, travels to Mexico, joins the Merchant Marines, musters out, and goes off with his wife to Europe. Like Bellow, Augie wants to help mankind. There perhaps the likeness ends, for Bellow always knew he would become a writer despite his family's view that it was childish folly, then adolescent folly, and, as he said to an interviewer years later, "they still think it is folly." Augie March does not know exactly how best to live and he agrees to fit himself into every plan proposed to him but never does so wholeheartedly, for Augie is as much an escape artist as he is a joiner. By the end of the novel, he has tested a dozen experiments with reality and rejected them all as illusory, and not only because they are not true but not good enough for him who seeks a transcendent fate. All he has learned by the end of his adventures is that he must not become a disappointed man.

At the end of the book, Augie is married to a would-be actress who has a small part in a second-rate movie being filmed in Paris. She lies to him; she cheats; she is busy. To pass the time, he has been writing a memoir—this book—in order to tell his friends—and they are those who read his book—all that has happened to him, from his childhood to the present time, how he began as a bright ambitious boy and ended up still dreamy, disconsolate, and lonely, yet in an odd way still tolerant and peaceful, still confident that his drifting existence will yet become meaningful. To the world he appears idle, yet he knows he has been hard at work, not at business but with the work of mind and heart and spirit:

> I felt settled and easy, my chest free and my fingers comfortable and open. And now here's the thing. It takes a time like this for you to find out how sore your heart has been, and, moreover, all the while you thought you were going around idle terribly hard work was taking place. Hard, hard work, excavation and digging, mining, moling through tunnels, heaving, pushing, moving rock, working, working, working, working, working, panting, hauling, hoisting.

What is this secret work he has been performing? Learning. Learning he is "powerless and unable to get anywhere, to obtain justice or have requital," learning he must labor, wage combat, "settle scores, remember insults, fight, reply, deny, blab, denounce, triumph, outwit, overcome, vindicate, cry, persist, absolve, die and rise again."

All this internal action is the work of Bellow's memory. Like a kaleidoscope, then, that fragile tube with its fragments of colored glass, Augie March rolls about Bellow's modules of family, friends, mentors, public events, private actions, between the two flat plates of experience and memory. The source of light is Bellow's imagination and as he peers down on each stage of Augie's search for meaning, and invents the sentences to describe what he sees, the truths of Augie's discoveries about illusion and reality, appearance and the hiding self, are not mere invention but come from another source of light, the inner light of Bellow's intuition. In this sense, in the narrative of Augie's adventures it is Bellow who is reflecting on how he was formed, how he emerged free, an amalgam of all the influences lined up waiting to create him, and at the same time how he became an individual with his own way to go. Tied *and* loose. Bound *and* liberated. The breakthrough Bellow sought came not by turning his back on himself but by sitting down face-to-face with that meek Joseph and whining Asa Leventhal and telling himself he must represent a more vigorous "Spirit of Alternatives," and fight the Allbees to a standstill and laugh at a world that sought to thwart him. His third novel would go over the ground again and do it bigger and better and truer. And that is *The Adventures of Augie March.*

The novel is spacious, moving slowly from the time Augie was starting out in life to his emergence as an adult preparing to start out in life "kissed by the rocky face of clasping experience." In his thirty-three years, Augie has worked at twenty-two jobs, but the only work he ever really loved was his brief volunteer job as a teacher:

> It moved me while I did it; it was no problem to be my natural self with the kids—as why, God help us, should it be with anyone? But let us not ask questions whose answers are among the world's well-kept secrets. In the classroom, or outside in the playground holleration, smelling pee in the hall, hearing the piano trimbles from the music room, among the busts, maps, and chalk-dust sunbeams, I was happy. I felt at home. I wanted to give the kids my best and tell them all I knew.

His wish at the end of his adventures is to create a kind of academy–foster home, to gather a group of children, take his mother out of the Home for the Blind, and his brother Georgie out of the state asylum, and bring them to his home, one of those "Walden or Innisfree wattle jobs under the kind sun, and there live content, keep bees and teach the children."

What does this would-be teacher know? Each job Augie holds represents a tier of his learning, each a practical test of some higher truth by which a man ought to live in the wilderness of a shifting reality. Taken all together, they represent stages in his search for wisdom and for a "good enough fate." Augie asks Joseph's old question: "Do I have a separate destiny?" Augie asks Leventhal's question: "Who runs things?" The tough little street kid, without a dime to back him, and no special skills, a Castor whose Leda was a woman who sewed buttonholes in a coat factory, whose Zeus was the driver of a laundry truck, this Augie, the "by-blow of a travelling man," with a hotshot older brother and a retarded younger brother, feels himself to be set apart for a great purpose, reserved to achieve a life of truth, love, bounty, usefulness, and harmony. That's all. He allows himself to be adopted, counseled, directed, guided, helped by reality instructors, and abandons each, one after the other, reneges, escapes, refuses their lessons because no reality instructor understands Augie's fate must be good enough. He believes in his special destiny from the time he goes out with Stashu Kopecs to steal "coal off the cars, clothes from the lines, rubber balls from the dime store and pennies off the newsstands" to the time he wanders about Paris supervising illicit business deals for his friend the Armenian lawyer, Mintouchian.

Within the family circle, Grandma Lausch is his first teacher. Her subject is strategies. "Nobody asks you to love the whole world, only to be honest." But Augie soon perceives Grandma is a manipulater, organizing and controlling the household, that she is only monitoring Augie's progress in telling believable lies. Augie's brother Simon takes the boy, only a fragment trained, into the real world. He teaches Augie to cheat, to wheel and deal, to take the main chance, to hustle. His brother Georgie, too, teaches Augie, but the example of Georgie's docility, sweetness of temper, and patience must wait to take effect when Augie arrives at the end of his apprenticeship; for now, Georgie is dismissed as subnormal, a student in the "dummy school," and will be sent to a "Home for Boys," where all he will learn is broom making and basket weaving, and then he will be admitted to Manteno, where he will become skillful in cobbling shoes. Between the polarities of Simon and Georgie, Augie will find his way.

Augie takes a job in Willie Einhorn's house, where he receives lessons in power on a larger scale. Einhorn owns a forty-flat building, six stores, a poolroom, and manipulates insurance companies. Here is scope for learning. What can be done in the city of Chicago? Swindle. Abandon illusions and become street-smart. Prepare for the big grab. Of what? Whatever. When the stock-market crash wipes out Einhorn and he descends from dollars to nickels, from plans to connivance, Augie moves on. Under the guidance of Joe Gorman, he learns how to rob a leather-goods store. Now Augie is ready to enter society.

Mrs. Renling teaches him "what a rich young man enjoys," to dress well, eat and drink with social ease, say witty things, dance, and cultivate a handsome-devil smile. He is acquiring the demeanor for love, like his brother Simon, who has become a sport and is out to catch a rich girl. Augie watches his brother turn himself into a sycophant of the Magnus family, and worse, become a brutal, uncaring, greedy, overfed, overdressed, dishonest hypocrite. Willie Einhorn, too, alters; his fortunes mend, by swindle, and he comes out of his poolroom, moves into a modern flat, is gussied up, but Augie thinks he looks drearier. Einhorn is still shabby, desiccated, but he is crowingly lascivious, preening himself because a foot cripple called Mildred has fallen in love with him. Augie laughs, but he is still an old-fashioned loyal youth (of the dummy school) and he admires Einhorn's chanticleer spirit—his "male piercingness, sharpness, knotted hard muscle and blood in the comb, jerky, flaunty, haughty and bright, with luxurious slither of feathers." Observing a Simon and an Einhorn, the fatuous Mrs. Renling and her vague husband, Augie realizes that individuals need to survive the ups and downs of life, must pit themselves against the shifts, the unsteadiness and alterations of fate. They cannot do so if they refuse to understand that life is not "a single line that a stick draws on the ground but a vast harrow of countless disks." Humankind does not have simplicity; no single truth operates in all real circumstances. Augie learns to accept complexity (no single program!) and he remembers Einhorn had once told him force and strength are as important as humility and kindness.

> One should choose or seize with force; one should make strength from disadvantages and make progress by having enemies, being wrathful or terrible; should hammer on the state of being a brother, not be oppressed by it; should have the strength of voice to make other voices fall silent—the same principle for persons as for peoples, parties, states. This, and not a man-chick, plucked and pinched, with scraggle behind and anxious face full of sorrow-wrinkles, human fowl chased by brooms.

Is Einhorn right? The old matchmaker, Kreindl, has also told Augie the élan vital had nothing to do with idealism and spirit but good jig-jig: *"Take, take if they give you! Never refuse. To come together with a peppy little woman who sings in your ear. It's the life of the soul!"*

Augie is midway through his memoir. He is still nothing, a nonentity whose one skill is adaptability and one asset is adoptability. He is learning to accept facts but chooses to believe in nonfacts, in ideas that go beyond reality. Meanwhile, he reads like a shark roving the waters for living food.

> I sat and read. I had no eye, ear, or interest for anything else—that is, for usual, second-order, oatmeal, mere-phenomenal, snarled-shoelace-carfare-laundry-ticket plainness; unspecified dismalness, unknown captivities; the life of despair-harness, or the life of organization-habits which is meant to supplant accidents with calm abiding. Well, now, who can really expect the daily facts to go, toil or prisons to go, oatmeal and laundry tickets and all the rest, and insist that all moments be raised to the greatest importance, demand that everyone breathe the pointy, star-furnished air at its highest difficulty, abolish all brick, vaultlike rooms, all dreariness, and live like prophets or gods? Why, everybody knows this triumphant life can only be periodic. So there's a schism about it, some saying only this triumphant life is real, and others that only the daily facts are.

Simon scoffs at Augie's books and his pretensions; he wants Augie to come down to earth, to emulate him. Simon is going to marry fat, rich Charlotte Magnus and he wants Augie to take her cousin Lucy. Augie prefers to wait for love, true love, but Simon is practical.

> I'll never go for all the nonsense about marriage. Everybody you lay eyes on, except perhaps a few like you and me, is born of marriage. Do you see anything so exceptional or wonderful about it that makes it such a big deal? Why be fooling around to make this perfect great marriage? What's it going to save you from? Has it saved anybody—the jerks, the fools, the morons, the *schleppers,* the jagoffs, the monkeys, rats, rabbits, or the decent unhappy people or what you call nice people? They're all married or are born of marriages, so how can you pretend to me that it makes a difference that Bob loves Mary who marries Jerry? That's for the movies.

Augie agrees to try Simon's way. He dresses to please the Magnus family, drives Simon's car, wears his clothes, spends his money, even sits in Simon's chair in the barbershop at the Palmer House, rising with glossy nails and well-cut hair. He escorts Lucy to nightclubs, sorority dances, night football games, and strokes her thighs above her garters. He cannot sustain the charade for long, however. Opposition is a stronger force than adaptability.

Despite Simon's contempt, Augie continues to live in a rooming house on the South Side and his neighbors are Mimi Villars and Kayo Obermark. From them, he learns truths that appall him, that he considers and rejects although he believes it is his duty to remain loyal to them, for they are his chosen friends. Mimi believes in a shared fate, but her way of sharing is physical, "Her actual body was her recruiting place," and when she loves, it is passionately, yes, but promiscuously. She "issued her own warrant, license, diploma, asserting what she was." She "banked all on her clinching will, her hard reason, and her obstinate voice." That was right, this about liberty and individuality, but Augie observes that all her talk of love hides a deep underlying bitterness, a contempt for, not a celebration of, life. When Mimi becomes pregnant, Augie is shocked to discover she will have an abortion, that she will choose to destroy the "little scallop." Her justification? To the fetus, she says, "You don't know how lucky you are, what makes you think you would have liked it?"

Kayo Obermark is even more cynical: Human fellowship simply does not exist.

> He thought the greatest purity was outside human relations, that those only begot lies and cabbage-familiarity, and he told me, "I prefer stones any time. I could be a geologist. I'm not even disappointed in humankind. I just don't care about it, and if there's one thing that's sure, it's that this world is certainly not enough, and if there isn't any more they can have it all back."

Augie is no recruit for the unearned bitterness and gloom of Mimi Villars or Kayo Obermark; their pessimism arises out of their single-track program for getting through life. "You don't," he thinks, "take so wide a stand that it makes a human life impossible, nor try to bring together irreconcilables that destroy you, but try out what of human you can live with first." Still he remains devoted. When he is supposed to appear at the Magnuses' door, he chooses to wait in a hospital ward while doctors cleanse Mimi's womb. He cannot understand why the Magnus family should turn him out. So he adds to his understanding of people the principle of inconstancy. Admittedly, he, too, can be inconstant; he, too, can practice duplicity; he, too, is a manipulator. Still he believes he serves a higher good, which he fondly calls "love." He is ready for Thea Fenchel.

Thea lives outside Augie's familiar world. On her way to Mexico to hunt iguanas with an eagle as her predator, she takes Augie along for a different kind of training. He does not oppose what she wishes him to become, an Abercrombie & Fitch lover, and he happily packs his new leather jacket, his new high boots and Stetson hat, his checks, plaids, and suedes, all that she has bought for him, and he is ready to experiment in the world of nature. He visits the Lincoln Park zoo to observe an eagle. *Bozhe moy!* as Grandma Lausch once said. Was this the way to set himself apart, to test his worthiness? God in heaven! Yes, he has lived under the glittering eyes of Einhorn and Grandma Lausch, under the glowering eyes of Simon and Mrs. Magnus, but now he recognizes they were peanuts to Caligula, a ferocious eagle whose gaze is one of "awful despotism." Can he sustain himself under the eyes of a Caligula? Will that be easier than maintaining his balance under the measuring lustful eyes of Thea?

Mexico is a country of death. The people he meets in Acatla live on the periphery of life—wastrels, scoundrels, drunks, gamblers. The beautiful world of nature where he will hunt with Thea is dangerous, cruel, unreliable, unpredictable. As it turns out, the dreaded predator Caligula, the fierce, is afraid of a lizard; as it turns out, the docile good old horse Bizcocho kicks Augie in the head. Now Augie knows his quest for the significant life must take into account the incontrovertible facts of betrayal and death. Caligula is a washout; Bizcocho, a betrayer. Augie, another washout, lies in bed recovering from a cracked skull; Thea, another betrayer, is off hunting snakes and copulating with Señor Talavera. The Garden of Eden is a fantasy "set up by hopes and art," by the writers of utopias, who have overlooked the truth of the world of nature. The signal truth about the natural world is mortality; the salient fact is death. "It takes some of us a long time to find out what the price is of being in nature, and what the facts are about your tenure."

Convalescing from a badly mauled skull in Iggy Moulton's villa, Augie reflects on Iggy's words: "You don't know the score yet. . . . You always had it too good. You got to get knocked over and crushed like this." What was the score? Lying in a darkened room, he asks himself, "If I didn't have money or profession or duties, wasn't it so that I could be free, and a sincere follower of love?" Was he really love's servant? And his brain jars: Am I, too, a pretender?

> Suddenly my heart felt ugly. I was sick of myself. I thought that my aim of being simple was just a fraud, that I wasn't a bit goodhearted or affectionate, and I began to wish that Mexico from beyond the walls would come in and kill me and that I would be thrown in the bone dust and twisted, spiky crosses of the cemetery, for the insects and lizards.

The truths about a man's fate are all at once too much for him to bear. Was it not better to be dead than wise? Must he be so honest with himself? Must he continue? Yes. "This terrible investigation had to go on." Augie must understand himself, devastating as the knowledge may be. He pushes himself into further questioning and asks himself whether all his search was a long deception. What was he doing, after all, learning or sucking up, pleasing or showing everyone that just when they thought they had him, he could leave, check out, as if to say he was better than they knew? Was he better? How was he so different? Did anybody care about the other fellow? Did he? Why did he pretend? If humankind is indeed not simple but, as he has already discovered, a vast harrow of countless disks, then why should human complexity lead to dissemblance? If there was no such thing as simplicity, why should we fear complexity? Yes, a man is weak and timid, yes, dishonest; but was that not because ultimately he is afraid to admit he is powerless? Is it not better to maintain the appearance of power than to face the reality of helplessness? Appearances for whom? No one really cared to know anything about the other: "Do you think every newcomer is concerned and is watching? No. And do you care that anyone should care in return? Not by a long shot." Does he care? Not really. He is like everyone else.

So then, if that is true, what of his special fate? His unique destiny? And what is he supposed to do, with or without his sense of himself reserved for a fate good enough? "With everyone going around so capable and purposeful in his strong handsome case," why should he still go on pretending to be limp, feeble, poor, a silly, harmless, laughing creature? Was he not pretending? Was there an alternative Augie March? If not, dared he to create one? He must, Augie realizes, invent the man who can stand before the terrible appearances. True or not does not matter; a man must invent the self.

> No, you have to plot in your heart to come out differently. External life being so mighty, the instruments so huge and terrible, the performances so great, the

> thoughts so great and threatening, you produce a someone who can exist be-
> fore it.

Augie March perceives that artifice is the strategy of all human beings, invention the means of survival, illusion—of power and certainty and energy—necessary, and duplicity the required apparatus for human existence. A man cannot get justice and he cannot give justice; he can only live.

> And this is what mere humanity always does. It's made up of these inventors
> or artists, millions and millions of them, each in his own way trying to recruit
> other people to play a supporting role and sustain him in his make-believe.

What is true in the private world, Augie realizes now, is true in the public world.

> The great chiefs and leaders recruit the greatest number and that's what their
> power is. There's one image that gets out in front to lead the rest and can impose
> its claim to being genuine with more force than others, or one voice enlarged
> to thunder is heard above the others. Then a huge invention, which is the
> invention maybe of the world itself, and of nature, becomes the actual world—
> with cities, factories, public buildings, railroads, armies, dams, prisons, and
> movies—becomes the actuality. That's the struggle of humanity, to recruit
> others to your version of what's real. Then even the flowers and the moss on
> the stones become the moss and flowers of a version.

So Augie perceives, but at the present moment, what is real for Augie is his abandonment by Thea. Like a hermit, he retreats to lament in the wilderness, his only companion a degenerate Russian who has decamped from his tour with a cossack chorus. After listening to Augie's long and woeful tale, he says, "Wait . . . you haven't seen anything yet. Don't you know how many things there are to be disappointed in besides love?" Augie adapts the words to his own needs: "Not that life should end is so terrible in itself, but that it should end with so many disappointments in the essential."

In Mexico, Augie has fallen recruit to a variety of persuasions: how foolish to love, how wasteful to strive, how mournful to hope, how easy to cheat, and oh, how pleasant to eat and drink and go out for a walk in the sun. He is ready to return to America.

On his way back to Chicago, he stops in Pinckneyville to visit Georgie, who is equipped with nothing at all and lives happily cobbling shoes. He visits his mother, who is now blind and alone but sits content in her room in the Home for the Blind with her Gulistan carpet on the floor, touching the postcards arranged on her bureau. He visits Simon, who takes him through an ivory white door into his apartment with its walls veneered in mahogany and its candy dishes filled with chocolate-covered coconut balls and apricot marshmallows. Simon is rich, fat, brutal, autocratic, lecherous, vulgar; he drives a Cadillac and has a million dollars in his bank account. Augie visits Einhorn and Mimi and Padilla and Clem Tambow, all his former mentors, each with some sarcasm to throw his way: You're going against history! You have a nobility syndrome! How is your campaign after a worthwhile fate?

No one recognizes he has changed, that he is about to make a concession to life, to give up his search for transcendence in order to experience simple commonplace joy. He wants nothing more than a place of his own, to marry, to gather children around him and teach them how to live. Does he know? He knows he does not know. His wisdom is that there is no wisdom. It does not matter. He can live a good life and pretend, during his inconsequential tenure, that he is living a good life. It is the only way he knows to outwit death.

Luckily, the war breaks out. Like Joseph, Augie volunteers but unlike Joseph, he plans for his return. Already wearing his white uniform, he meets Stella on the street in New York City, Stella, that passionate girl smelling so sweet under the blankets on a deserted roadside in Mexico. In a frenzy of passion, in a swoon of love, he asks her to marry him. There is a new reality instructor, Mintouchian, "another of those persons who persistently arise before me with life's counsels and illumination throughout my entire earthly pilgrimage."

Mintouchian is the most sophisticated, perhaps the most cynical, of all of Augie's tutors, the kind of man Simon fancies himself to be, a big spender, a wheelsman of deals, with a mistress and a wife, a habitué of "scarlet-and-gold-door places." What does the proxy elder brother teach Augie? Life, says Mintouchian, is a dichotomy of illusion and reality, in which each part loses distinctness and merges until no one can discern one from the other. Illusion is as real as facts. Truth is a deliberate strategy of lies; we have come all the way back to Grandma Lausch. Love, the romantic ideal, is a rationalization for adultery; we have come all the way back to Simon and Einhorn and Kreindl. Augie listens to Mintouchian declare that in every consciousness, in every single human mind, there are secret thoughts and conniving duplicity.

> "I stand in awe of the genius of the race. But a large part of this genius is devoted to lying and seeming what you are not."

Every single self is a double self, a multiple self: secret over secret, lies on lies.

> "Complications, lies, lies, and lies. . . . Disguises, vaudevilles, multiple personali-
> ties, diseases, conversations. And since this is the essence of human nature, who
> knows the ultimate, and where is the hour of truth?"

That is not as evil as it first appears to be. Dissimulation is only change.
Duplicity is only transience. That, and only that, is the law of the universe.

> "On any certain day, when you're happy, you know it can't last, but the weather
> will change, the health will be sickness, the year will end, and also life will end.
> In another place, another day, there'll be a different lover. The face you're
> kissing will change to some other face. It can't be helped. . . . You make your
> peace with change. . . . You must be flexible. . . . You kiss the woman and you
> show how you love your fate, and you worship and adore the changes of life. You
> obey this law. . . . Erratic is nothing. Only system tops the laws of life."

What Mintouchian says dismays Augie but he cannot deny the possibility
that all of this is true. The wound to his ego is sharp; his heart bleeds. What
if I cannot achieve a triumphant life? What then?

> "I have always tried to become what I am. But it is a frightening thing. Because
> what if what I am by nature isn't good enough?"

Mintouchian has the answer to which the entire road to wisdom has been
heading:

> "You must take your chance on what you are. And you can't sit still. I know
> this double poser, that if you make a move you may lose but if you sit still you
> will decay. But what will you lose? You will not invent better than God or nature
> or turn yourself into the man who lacks no gift or development before you make
> the move. This is not given to us. . . . It is better to die what you are than to
> live a stranger forever."

So Augie can go to his wedding carrying flowers. He will take his chance on
what he is. Although he cannot identify himself, he is prepared to move,
never mind to where or to what.

On the *Sam MacManus,* Augie acts as the advisor to all the men on
the ship; he has, as he says, a daily clientele. What does he tell them? How

does he advise them? It makes no difference. A torpedo hits the ship and they all are blown out of life except for Augie and Basteshaw, the ship's carpenter.

The two drift in a lifeboat on an empty sea, Basteshaw talking and talking, the final theoretician of Augie's record. Uneasily listening, Augie recognizes in Basteshaw's harangue his own hard-won discoveries. Basteshaw is from Chicago; he knew Einhorn, grew up in the same neighborhood, could tolerate no formal schooling, shifted from one thing to another, was a skating champion, a stamp expert, a socialist, a musician, now a carpenter and a psychobiologist. He is addicted to medical and scientific facts, describes his bizarre relatives, tells unlikely stories, mixes personal anecdotes with explanations of Pascal, Ghiberti, Shelley, Michelangelo. Basteshaw tells Augie he had once been a skinny kid with a soul that longed for distinction. His soul told him he was meant to astonish the world. "You, Hymie Basteshaw, *Stupor Mundi!* My boy, brace up. You have been called, and you will be chosen."

Bellow enjoys such ironic twists, Augie's truths on the lips of a maniac. Bellow likes to spoof Bellow. Basteshaw explains his program for the salvation of the human race:

> "But the reality situation is what I have described. A billion souls boiling with anger at a doom of insignificance. Reality is also these private hopes the imagination invents. Hopes, the indispensable evils of Pandora's Box. Assurance of a fate worth suffering for. In other words, desiring to be cast in the mold of true manhood. But who is cast in this mold? Nobody knows. . . . After much effort to live up to a glorious standard there came fatigue, wan hope, and boredom. I experienced extreme boredom. I saw others experiencing it too, many denying, by the way, that any such thing existed. And finally I decided that I would make boredom my subject matter. That I'd study it."*

He tells Augie when the fatigue of blighted hopes sets in, the very cells of the body change, and he is certain that if the cell structure can be reversed chemically, the glorious standard of true manhood will never weaken or disappear. Reverse the disease of boredom and the soul will thrive.

Basteshaw wishes to recruit Augie to help in his research. Why? For the good of mankind.

> "March, when liberated from this boredom, every man will be a poet and every woman a saint. Love will fill the world. Injustice will go, and slavery, bloodshed, cruelty. They will belong to the past, and, seeing all these horrors of past times,

*As a professor on the faculty of The Committee on Social Thought, Bellow directed the dissertation of a doctoral student working on a history of boredom.

all mankind will sit down and weep at the memory of them, the memory of blood and the horrible life of monads, at misunderstanding and murderous rages and carnage of innocents. The breasts and bowels will melt at this vision of the past. And then a new brotherhood of man will begin. . . . Real freedom will manifest itself, not based on politics and revolutions, which never gave it anyhow, because it's not a gift but a possession of the man who is not bored."

It is the madman who believes that every man can be a poet, every woman a saint, that love can permeate the tissues of the world. Here it is Basteshaw who articulates Bellow's dream. However, Augie's dream, his program for the triumphant life, is for his own triumphant life. He tells Basteshaw:

I'm dead against doing things to the entire human race. I don't want any more done to me, and I don't want to tamper with anyone else. No one will be a poet or a saint because you fool with him. When you come right down to it, I've had trouble enough becoming what I already am, by nature. I don't want to go to the Canaries with you. I need my wife.

Basteshaw's final words to Augie are a temporary lapse in optimism: "The power of an individual to act through his intellect on the reason of mankind is smaller now than ever." Basteshaw enters a hospital, Augie March is off to Paris, and Bellow will take up that sentence and challenge it in his writings for decades to come. Henderson will be obsessed with his research on boredom; Herzog will question the relevance of the intellect; that reason is flaccid, limp, useless, will sadden Artur Sammler, Citrine, Corde, Victor Wulpy, Benn Crader, Ken Trachtenberg, Ithiel Regler, and the authority on memory, the unnamed narrator of *The Bellarosa Connection.* Bellow will contrast the erotic life and the life of reason, reflect on appearance and reality, distinguish between the aspiring soul and the querulous body, between the power of wisdom and the power of expedience, and he will dream that by representing life in all its various quests for significance, he can in some way assist mankind.

"Go! My child is missing. The world is chaos"

What pleased Bellow most about *Augie March* was his discovery of an original style. Because he felt so free while writing the book, he believed he had succeeded in throwing off all influences, traditional writers as well as contemporary models. He told an interviewer:

> A writer should be able to express himself easily, naturally, copiously in a form which frees his mind, his energies. Why should he hobble himself with formalities? With a borrowed sensibility? With the desire to be "correct"? Why should I force myself to write like an Englishman or a contributor to *The New Yorker*? I soon saw that it was simply not in me to be a mandarin.[1]

But like the art critics who searched through nineteenth-century art, and beyond, to find some historical tradition to give respectability to the new and puzzling Abstract Expressionist art of the fifties, book reviewers ranged widely in their hunt for the progenitors of *Augie March*. Robert Gorham Davis chose the narratives of post-Renaissance Europe, especially *Tom Jones* and *Wilhelm Meister;* Norman Podhoretz found Thomas Urquhart, Smollett, and Dickens; Ray B. West, Jr., said Cervantes, and Anthony West, Henry James's *The American.* T. E. Cassidy said "cheap Proust" and Harvey Webster said Joyce. Robert Penn Warren called Augie a "latter-day example of the Emersonian ideal Yankee"; Delmore Schwartz said a modern rendering of *Huckleberry Finn;* Henry Popkin named *The Great Gatsby* and Nathaniel West's *A Cool Million* and for good measure added the *schlimazl* of Jewish folklore. Maxwell Geismar said Theodore Dreiser and Thomas Wolfe.[2]

In an interview with Harvey Breit in *The New York Times,* Bellow said, "Today, the novelist thinks too much of immortality and he tries to create form. He tries to make his work durable through form. But you have to take your chances on mortality, on perishability. That's what I felt. I kicked over the traces . . . I took my chance."[3]

Nevertheless, to the present day the search goes on for the single book that ignited Bellow's imagination. In 1970, Professor Sara Chapman, of Marshall University in West Virginia, wrote to Bellow to ask for his comment on her view that nineteenth-century American romanticism in general and Melville's *Pierre* in particular influenced *Augie March.* Bellow responded with a kind letter, apologizing that he could not confirm her theory. When writing his novel, he was unacquainted with *Pierre;* he was only familiar with *Moby Dick* and Melville's short fiction; rather he had been immersed in Chicago, the world in which Augie March was growing up, in the twenties and thirties. As to her query about romanticism, he comments wryly about his own education in the Chicago public schools, recalling that pupils did read Longfellow, Whittier, Bryant, Fenimore Cooper and the Transcendentalists, and the New England moralists, which in Depression Chicago was irrelevant and funny.[4]

True, in *Moby Dick* Bellow had a great example of a mixed style that could knock an effete aestheticism right out of the ring. *Moby Dick* combined realism and romanticism in so disorderly a manner, few could—or cared to—distinguish one from the other. Bellow could observe in *Moby Dick,* with its cetology, sermons, tracts, reflections, lyrical musings, tall tales, dramatic interludes, mingling with introspective passages where quaking hearts and blustering wills were revealed, how a tapestry of chronicle and oratory and set pieces and flashbacks served as a background for the story of a young man on a quest for knowledge. He could observe that Melville thought it fit to confuse the emotions of his readers, subjecting them to his shifts from despair to humor to optimism to religious fervor and vanity and humility and pathos. Didacticism and ambiguity may drift side by side, and merge, and part again. Why not? However, none of this is proof of influence; it is only a matter of likeness of style.

Augie March brought Bellow wide attention but not universal praise. Even those who wrote him excited letters when they finished reading the novel had some reservation, some caution, some good advice to give. Consider the letters he received from Frederick Dupee, Bernard Malamud, and Leslie Fiedler.[5]

Dupee told Bellow he finally had gotten a few evenings free and read *Augie*. He felt Bellow's people were wonderful, his Chicago was wonderful, and being a Chicagoan himself, he had had constant twinges of recognition. However, he feared people would say that if Joyce's Dubliners seemed paralyzed, Bellow's Chicagoans would seem to be afflicted with elephantiasis or St. Vitus' dance.

Bernard Malamud wrote to tell Bellow how greatly he had enjoyed the book. Then, after explaining that he saw Augie as a latter-day Dante visiting the rings of Inferno, he wondered whether Augie was not too passive, too much a listener, too much a guest in the house, too reluctant an actor. Malamud would have preferred Augie to initiate actions rather than learn, absorb, evaluate, and reject. It may have been Malamud's gentle protest that led Bellow to think of a Gene Henderson, who indeed initiates some action, usually ending in disaster, but beyond *Henderson the Rain King,* Malamud's hope was never fulfilled. No Bellow hero initiates an action; each remains alone in some house or apartment or rented room, reflecting on his past, on actions done to him, on some form of victimization. All are haunted, never far from tears, shatterable indeed, and, eventually, through an act of will, emerge tattered and, by self-assertion, unshatterable. Malamud concluded with qualified praise for Bellow's style, calling it a thing of unique strength. Above all he commends Bellow's extraordinary memory, his ability to call all things by some name. Malamud did not explain further and concluded by thanking Bellow for a unique experience in zestful reading and for all Bellow had taught him about writing.

Leslie Fiedler began ecstatically, telling Bellow he had roared with delight while reading *Augie.* He was fascinated especially that Bellow had managed to write such an *American* book. However, he said, he was troubled that Bellow had made sex so bucolic, and that seemed to Fiedler to be out of touch with the American spirit. Nevertheless, he found it was good writing and he took great pleasure in its reception, and he ended his letter with the wish he could have lined up a review someplace so that his enthusiasm could join the chorus of praise.

A glance through the reviews of *Augie March* would have dampened Fiedler's thrill of discovery that good writing can also be liked; and instead of lining up a review so that he could also join the roster of universal admirers, Fiedler would have found himself entering into controversy. One writer was spellbound; another found the book tedious. For one, the book was a revelation; for another, woolly. One said the book gave us a sense that life is worth living; another said it slumped. *Augie March* was shapeless, fragmentary, and inconclusive, without order or direction; *Augie March* had unparalleled unity and was finely tuned. The book was flighty and violated good taste and we got into nothing deeply enough; *Augie March* was a genuine dramatic vision. One reviewer wondered what, after all, did Bellow mean? Another declared Bellow's meaning was clear: The theme of the book was America itself and the main character was the paradigm nonconformist, the unconventional, innately free, and self-possessed individual for whom politics and social conventions were useless. No, said another, the theme of the book had nothing to do with America; Bellow did not understand America, and his theme was the phenomenal energy of an unmolded national character almost pathological, even vicious, the embodiment of the urban jungle, where the need for change is compulsive. One said Bellow interpreted nothing; because his characters were purged of belief, the book was therefore without ultimate meaning. No, Augie was a tribute to the mystery and grandeur of the human personality, a tribute to the power of hope.

If Bellow's meaning seemed elusive, what did his reviewers have to say about his characters? Bellow's characters were memorable. Bellow's people were too willful, too self-determined. All the characters came off. None of the characters came off. They were exact. They were inauthentic. Augie was on quest to find himself. Augie already knew who he was. Augie grew. Augie did not develop. He should have been given a capacity for deeper commitments, for more joy, more sorrow. Augie was fully realized. Augie was shadowy. Augie suffered from an effortful exuberance, a strained spontaneity. Augie was sentimental. Augie was psychopathic. The book was nothing but a collection of thumbnail sketches. The book itself was schizoid, a book written deliberately to please everybody.

None of the preceding qualifying phrases sound like universal acceptance. Although Fiedler may have been unaware of so much attack and counterattack, certainly Bellow was not. He wrote to Lionel Trilling to thank him for his remarks on *Augie March* written for *The Griffin,* * the monthly publication of a recently launched book club, *The Readers' Subscription,* and then tried to explain himself.

The letter, dated October 11, 1953, assured Trilling of Bellow's

---

*Trilling was on the board of editors of the book club intended to appeal to an elite audience. The September selection was *The Adventures of Augie March.* Several years later, when the Modern Library reprinted the novel as part of its series of American Classics, Trilling allowed his *Griffin* essay to be used in its original form as the introduction to the text.

gratitude for his brilliant article, which had played a part in the success of the book—a success, with its bonus of large sales, he had never expected. Bellow was surprised at Trilling's insight that the eagle represented an antihero, but then, he said, he seldom intends deliberate symbols, and alluded, with good humor, to his bafflement at Anthony West's review (in *The New Yorker*) with its discussion of Simony. To Bellow, Augie's brother's name, Simon, was Augie's brother's name.

At length, respectfully, Bellow took up the main error in Trilling's interpretation of Augie as an instrument for propaganda of Bellow's point of view. First he quotes Emerson's ironic portrait of the dissociated highbrow transcendentalist:[6]

> "We are miserable with inaction. We perish of rest and rust: but we do not like your work."
> "Then," says the world, "show me your own."
> "We have none."
> "What will you do, then?" cries the world.
> "We will wait."
> "How long?"
> "Until the universe beckons and calls us to work."
> "But whilst you wait, you grow old and useless."
> "Be it so; I can sit in a corner and *perish* (as you call it) but I will not move until I have the highest command . . . your virtuous projects, so-called, do not cheer me. If I cannot work at least I need not lie. . . ."

Then he urged Trilling to consider Augie as a representation of this Emersonian inner-directedness, a member of the detached majority, a floater with good intentions but unable to find any function in society. To Bellow, Augie's character was the source of the comedy, and not meant to be didactic. Perhaps Trilling was out of touch with such young men, part of Bellow's generation, and had therefore not recognized the function of Augie, to represent the typical young American. Bellow had intended to suggest that the Augie Marches of our time could begin to function if they could come to understand how to love, to truly love another person.

In his letter to Trilling, Bellow began his long refusal to accept any interpretation of his fiction that suggests he is drawing upon his own experiences for his subject matter, that he ever allowed his own point of view to enter into his theme. Indeed, he may believe he has only to dismiss the idea of the autobiographical substratum in order to free himself of the charge of "propaganda," that is to say, a didactic purpose—the reliable word at the time was *rhetoric*—but there is no getting around the fact that Augie March is a singular representation of a prototype, Bellow's prototype, a very special sort of "floater," anything but a typical young American, for, typically, an American youth does not harbor the notion that society can be reformed by a dedication to love. Augie's discovery about reality and illusion, about the nature of the significant life, is the discovery of all of Bellow's narrators, and by the time Ken Trachtenberg joins with his mentor Benn in the same quest, the postwar generation of footless young men has been left far behind.

Indeed, the critical reception of *Augie March* was mysterious. There may have been disagreement on what *Augie March* meant; there was no disagreement on how Bellow wrote. Almost everyone disliked the style. Anthony West did not confine himself to taking issue with Bellow's "wrongheaded symbolism"; he called the book an American *Of Human Bondage* and wished Bellow had accepted his proper rank, on a par with Somerset Maugham and James Gould Cozzens, for his minor talent for entertainment could carry him no higher up the scale. He thought Bellow ought not to reach out so desperately to imitate James and Melville. Saying the writing was wooden and dead, West cautioned his *New Yorker* readers that they would find Bellow too much like Jean de Meung, who also read and remembered everything, and nothing he remembered could he keep out.

In his memoir, *Making It,*[7] Norman Podhoretz told the story of how his negative review of *Augie March* had endeared him to Philip Rahv and Dwight Macdonald and "clinched" for him his reputation at *Commentary* and won him an invitation to write for *The New Yorker* as well as *Partisan Review*. Podhoretz declared he "was virtually the only reviewer of the book who was able to see and understand it," and because of his courage in telling the truth of Bellow's achievement he was "adopted into the family" of New York intellectuals for good. What had Podhoretz said? That *Augie March* was strained, tortured, excessive in its language, with "an overwhelming impulse to get in as many adjectives and details as possible, regardless of considerations of rhythm, modulation, or for that matter, meaning." That Augie speaks "jargon," and his perspective is "limited." That Augie remains nothing but a mere device, that he never comes to life, and yet Augie is more "real" than any other character in the one-dimensional, nondramatic, ambiguous book. Podhoretz conceded Bellow had potential: "It is no disgrace to have failed in a pioneer attempt." Podhoretz entered the family of literary critics with his badge of the well-worn phrase worn proudly: "It doesn't quite come off."

Time called the "over-enthusiastic prose" bloated; Orville Prescott complained it "frays nerves and lacerates patience"; and Milton Crane found it shapeless and inconsistent. Arthur Mizener disliked the piling up of modifiers, the faulty use of clauses, the confusing colloquialisms; Robert

Gorham Davis lamented the lack of clarity and coherence; Maxwell Geismar thought the writing too genteel, too timid; Granville Hicks referred briefly to the "nervous, aggressive, individualized" style; and V. S. Pritchett called the style affected and arch, monotonous, singsong, garrulous, and characterized it as "goo," admitting Bellow had a gift for imagery but that in the main his poetic side was artificial and pretentious. Only Charles Rolo observed Bellow wrote in a "freshly personal style" and only Robert Penn Warren thought Bellow had "found humor and eloquence to add to his former virtues." Oddly enough, the wordsmith Delmore Schwartz had nothing whatever to say of style but wrote of theme, subject matter and character, of authenticity and freedom, as if the craft was irrelevant.[8]

Not even Bellow talks much about his style. Search as we may in his long letter to Trilling, we find a great deal on what he meant to say but nothing about how he wrote. Only in his review of *Mottel the Cantor's Son* by Sholom Aleichem (trans. 1953) written a few months before the publication of *Augie March* can we find a clue to his style.[9] Here he said the Jewish writer's comic sense arises out of the disparity between what the Jews of the ghetto, the Chosen People, thought they were—living on terms of familiarity with all times and all greatness—and what they actually were—utterly poor and powerless. Such "powerlessness," he said, "appears to force people to have recourse to words." When Bellow described how Jews of the ghetto use language, it is as good a description as we can find of Bellow's way with words.

> The most ordinary Yiddish conversation is full of the grandest historical, mythological, and religious allusions. The Creation, the fall, the flood, Egypt, Alexander, Titus, Napoleon, the Rothschilds, the Sages, and the Laws may get into the discussion of an egg, a clothes-line, or a pair of pants.

There is, of course, a deluge of words in *Augie March*—the arias and catalogues, the superabundance of details, the lavish allusions, the inexhaustible cornucopia of images, the long, long sentences packed with wandering addenda, where punctuation marks are but spaces to draw breath, short rests during which one gathers strength to qualify further. There is a disparity between what Augie is and what he aspires to be, between what he believes is true—hopes is true—and what is actually true in the real world, between how he thinks and how he acts. Out of irrationality and disorder in the system placed side by side with the clichés of harmony and progress comes the laughter. Bellow's vision of reality and his unique manner of representing disparity is the very essence of his style.

There are hundreds of examples of grandiose allusions in *Augie
March*. Augie is born in the ghetto and dreams of a fate good enough; he
is weak, poor, tearful, not sure whether he is a man of hope or foolishness,
kind or stupid. Augie is equally a Cato, a young Lincoln, an Alcibiades, a son
of Hagar, a soldier in Crassus's army. Shopping for clothes with Thea
Fenchel, he is Leicester and she is Queen Elizabeth; training their eagle in
Texarkana, they are Paris and Helen of Troy. His brother Simon carries Augie
as Napoleon carried his brothers. Crippled, conniving Einhorn is a Ma-
chiavelli, a Caesar, a Croesus. When Augie assists him in the toilet, it is as
if a courtier is helping the Sun King at Versailles. Sister-in-law Charlotte is
a Lady Macbeth; Kreindl's niece is a Briseis. Grandma Lausch is a Pharaoh
or a Caesar, always on the verge of transformation into a god; she has hatreds
like Jehovah, plays chess or klabyasch like Timur, with a partner who is like
Frederick the Great. Clem Tambow is a Stuart in exile, a young Calhoun;
Lieutenant Nuzzo is a Valentino, a Lord Nelson. Basteshaw is a Moses. I
counted four hundred such allusions before I gave up, noting references that
created such unlikely combinations as Sophie Tucker, Medea, and Athena,
Big Bill Thompson and Socrates, Jake the Barber and King Arthur. The
absurd kinships inflate the low-class characters and deflate their high-class
counterparts. When a Chicago nightclub, the Chez Paree, is likened to the
Schönbrunn Palace and the Baths of Caracalla, Chicago stumbles onto the
stage of world history.

Ridiculous, yes, but there is also a sense of pathos, a hint of despair
hidden in the allusions. In a way unique to Bellow, the bright laughter
generates anxiety, a suspicion of loss, a realization we have descended in the
scale of great aspirations and significant striving. Take, for example, a paragraph in which Augie, working for a union boss, Grammick, thinks about his
job as a labor organizer.

> He had to have my help in South Chicago that night in a gauze and bandage
> factory he had organized more or less in passing. For it was like a band of Jesuits
> landing where a heathen people thirsted for baptism in the dense thousands,
> thronging out of their brick towns. I had to fill a bag with literature and blanks
> and race over to the Illinois Central to get the electric train and meet Grammick
> at his headquarters in a tavern, a rough place but with a ladies' and family
> entrance, for many of the gauze-winders were women. I can't say how they kept
> bandages clean in that sooty, plug-ugly town built as though so many fool
> amateur projects for the Tower of Babel that had got crippled at the second story
> a few dozen times and then all hands had quit and gone in for working in them
> instead. Grammick was in the middle of this show and busy organizing. He was
> as firm as a Stonewall Jackson, but he was also as perfectly pacific as a woodshop
> instructor in a high school or some personage of the Congress party, somebody

from that white-flutter India setting out to conquer the whole place flat. By the power of meekness.

The modern John the Baptist is bringing the word in the form of union flyers to gauze-winders. The new Babel is the plug-ugly town of South Chicago— and we know how many South Chicagos there are in the United States— never built past the second story. The gigantic struggle for nationhood by Gandhi and Nehru and Patel is reduced to "white-flutter India."

From the smallest example, when Grandma tries to wheedle Augie into using his brains and says, "If Kreindl's son can be a dentist you can be governor of Illinois," to the long obituary—like an aria—Einhorn writes for his father, the Commissioner, it is the same startling juxtaposition, the same joltings of the writer who says he is "kidding his way to Jesus."

> Einhorn kept me with him that evening; he didn't want to be alone. While I sat by he wrote his father's obituary in the form of an editorial for the neighborhood paper. "The return of the hearse from the newly covered grave leaves a man to pass through the last changes of nature who found Chicago a swamp and left it a great city. He came after the Great Fire, said to be caused by Mrs. O'Leary's cow, in flight from the conscription of the Hapsburg tyrant, and in his life as a builder proved that great places do not have to be founded on the bones of slaves, like the pyramids of Pharaohs or the capital of Peter the Great on the banks of the Neva, where thousands were trampled in the Russian marshes. The lesson of an American life like my father's, in contrast to that of the murderer of the Strelitzes and of his own son, is that achievements are compatible with decency. My father was not familiar with the observation of Plato that philosophy is the study of death, but he died nevertheless like a philosopher, saying to the ancient man who watched by his bedside in the last moments . . ." This was the vein of it, and he composed it energetically in half an hour, printing on sheets of paper at his desk, the tip of his tongue forward, scrunched up in his bathrobe and wearing his stocking cap.

It is well known that Bellow is meticulous in his descriptions. Where one writer would say "glass chandelier" and let it go at that, Bellow says "the big fixtures of buffalo glass hanging on three chains." His seagulls do not fly, they "let the air currents carry them around." Dingbat doesn't wear a pinstripe suit, he is "in stripes like a locust's leg." Like the device of allusions, descriptions, too, have a more complex function and do more than paint exact pictures; Bellow's physical representations enable us to perceive unspoken feelings. When Augie is at a resort in Benton Harbor, he is infatuated with a rich, snobbish girl, Esther Fenchel, and asks her to go dancing. "With you?" she says. "I should say not. I certainly won't." Her refusal is predictable. His response is not. He faints dead away. When he comes to, another scarcely known young lady stands in the doorway staring. Instead of Esther, it is a girl who will take no further part in the action, but Bellow lavishes on her a description of what Augie sees, so that the great gulf that exists between Augie and all Esther Fenchels becomes apparent.

> Meantime Miss Zeeland was standing in the doorway, the daughter of the famous corporation lawyer, looking at me, in her evening feathers, and her body in the long drape of her dress making a single unbroken human roll. She had on golden shoes and white gloves to the elbow, and looked visionary, oriental, with her rich hair swept up in a kind of tower that was in equilibrium to her big bust. Her face was clear and cold, like a kind of weather, though the long clean groove of her upper lip was ready to go into motion, as if she were going to break her silence with something momentous and long-matured; explain love to me, perhaps. But no, her ideas remained closed to me, though she didn't leave until I got up to turn off the phonograph, and then she glided or fanned away.

Like an exotic bird, Miss Zeeland is dehumanized, inaccessible; the similes and details of the description convey how he feels.

Augie does not say outright he cannot belong to the Magnus family; he asks himself, "Indeed, who *was* I to be sharing their gold soup of supper light and putting their good spoons in my mouth?" When he is dismissed by Lucy Magnus, whose garters he stretched, he looks at her and in his mind's eye sees her in such metaphors and allusions and with such details that reveal a subliminal rage at all Lucy Magnuses who victimize all Dantes.

> The large-mouthed smile she gave me, staying at her seated distance instead of coming to kiss me, was curious—that pretty sketch of charm, in lipstick, widening, the relative of the awful cleft running the other way, of the schismatics in the sixth bulge of hell, hit open from the bottom and split through the face.

Only Bellow can so describe the effect on Augie of his seeing Trotsky in front of the cathedral in Acatlan with a metaphor so apt that it characterizes Augie's humility and Trotsky's worldliness simultaneously.

> When you are as reduced to a different kind of navigation from this high starry kind as I was and are only sculling on the shallow bay, crawling from one clam-rake to the next, it's stirring to have a glimpse of deep-water greatness.

Bellow always finds a way to present an ephemeral feeling or an abstract concept in wholly material terms. Take, for example, how he concretizes deceit: Augie, thinking wistfully about how he and his friend Sylvester will inevitably lie to each other about what they are doing in Mexico, says:

> That's how it is. One day's ordinary falsehood if you could convert it into silt would choke the Amazon back a hundred miles over the banks. However, it never appears in this form but is distributed all over like the nitrogen in potatoes.

Bellow's sentences are convoluted miracles of syntax with catalogues of details that are colorful explosions, as if he was trying to create in prose the simulacrum of those fireworks displays that went off night after night at the Chicago World's Fair. Augie is describing a group of Chicago businessmen:

> This was what you heard when the connoisseurs' club of weighty cronies met, who all showed by established marks—rings, cigars, quality of socks, newness of panamas—where they were situated; they were classified, too, in grades of luck and wisdom, darkness by birth or vexations, power over or subjection to wives, women, sons and daughters, grades of disfigurement; or by the roles they played in comedies, tragedies, sex farces; whether they screwed or were screwed, whether they themselves did the manipulating or were roughly handled, tugged, and bobbled by their fates; their frauds, their smart bankruptcies, the fires they had set; what were their prospects of life, how far death stood from them.

Bellow's catalogues interweave universal history and the narrative of his minuscule Augie, pitting the small man against the vast world, vast in length of time and breadth of place. The little guy simply turns his back on it all and votes for himself. Augie has been listening to his friend Frazer talk, and talk:

> But as you listened to this brilliant educational discussion it was somewhat scary too; like catching hold of high voltage.
> Declarations, resolutions, treaties, theories, congresses, bones of kings, Cromwells, Loyolas, Lenins and czars, hordes of India and China, famines, huddles, massacres, sacrifices, he mentioned. Great crowds of Benares and London, Rome, he made me see; Jerusalem against Titus, Hell when Ulysses visited, Paris when they butchered horses in the street. Dead Ur and Memphis. Atoms of near silence, the dead acts, that formed a collective roar. Macedonian sentinels. Subway moles. Mr. Kreindl shoving a cannon wheel with his buddies. Grandma and legendary Lausch in his armor cutaway having an argument in the Odessa railroad station the day the Japanese war broke out. My parents taking a walk by the Humboldt Park lagoon the day I was conceived. Flowery spring-time.
> And I thought there was altogether too much of this to live with. Better

forget it, in part. The Ganges is there with its demons and lords; but you have a right also, and merely, to wash your feet and do your personal laundry in it. Or even if you had a good car it would take more than a lifetime to do a tour of all the Calvaries.

"Even if you had a good car it would take more than a lifetime to do a tour of all the Calvaries." No wonder Bellow said the book simply poured out! This is the style of a writer who has found out the best way to be free: to write as he chose.

He has an ear for common speech, the vulgarisms, the slang, the foreign phrases, the curses, and it is not only the speech of the lower classes or of immigrants but recognizably that of Chicagoans. Anyone from the Chicago of Augie's youth remembers such phrases as "ladies' bloomers," "dry goods windows," "bushwah," "outfits to match," "I don't like to chew my cabbage twice," "I stayed with this deal." Our relatives, too, tortured the syntax with such constructions as:

Besides having round eyes, Mama had circular glasses that I went with her to the free dispensary on Harrison Street to get.

Coblin's uncle, a bank officer, was buried out of Kinsman's.

Death is going to take the boundaries away from us, that we should no more be persons.

It's not just the crimson Bunte candy box or the soldier caramels and the three monkeys—hear no evil–see no evil–speak no evil—and it's more than the streetcars, the Medinah Club and the Drake Hotel, the Oriental Theater with its vaudeville show, where Augie goes "to hear Sophie Tucker whack herself on the behind and sing 'Red Hot Mama.'" Every kid in Chicago did what the fourth-rate prizefighter, Nails Nagel, did on the excursion boat to Muskegon.

Nails stayed in the Salon, trying to win a prize on a machine called the Claw, a little derrick in a glass case filled with cameras, fountain pens and flashlights embedded in a hill of chickenfeed candy. For a nickel you could maneuver it by two gadgets, one that aimed and another that gripped the claw. . . . He wanted a camera for his mother.

Augie finds his mother living alone in a room off the kitchen in Kreindl's flat. "She was upright in her posture and like waiting for the grief to come to a stop; as if this stop could be called by a conductor." Augie visits his mother in the Home for the Blind. She sits on her bed, "fitting pins into Roosevelt campaign buttons" at ten cents a hundred, "earning a few dollars a week by the goodheartedness of the precinct captain." Chicagoans know those red streetcars and their conductor's calls—few riders could read the street signs and every old-timer can name the streets on the car line from memory. We all remember Roosevelt's election campaigns, or can surmise them from the tumults of Eisenhower and Stevenson, or Nixon or Carter or Reagan or Bush.

But there is more to Bellow's use of detail. He establishes authenticity for his 1930s Chicago, where one bought a Bismarck to go with a cup of coffee, or a Dixie Cup at the movies, and a box of Cracker Jacks in Lincoln Park, and rode the streetcar to Clarendon Beach. What happens to Augie happens first, indisputably, in Chicago; but by implication in America. New Yorkers can substitute a Danish pastry for the Bismarck, and Coney Island for Clarendon Beach, and Central Park for Lincoln Park, and then recognize that Chicago represents America. Perhaps only people from Illinois remember Governor Horner; Americans remember Mayor Cermak, who took the bullet for FDR; Americans remember the sermons of Father Coughlin; and Veloz and Yolanda did dance their tangos across the country. Such details are Bellow's device for establishing the authenticity of his fiction. He leaves the well-made novel behind and finds instead another way to convince his readers that all his events happened just as he tells them, not because there is precedent in some earlier event, or some trait of character hinted at or foreshadowed on earlier pages to give credence to what takes place in later pages, but because he places private experiences into the flow of public events. His way to authenticate the imagined world is to keep before his readers reference points in the real world to verify events in the fabricated world. We recognize the literal and so believe the fantasy. I recognized the refusal to be comforted when Anna Coblin, whose son has run off to fight the rebels in Nicaragua, cried, "Go! My child is missing. The world is chaos." When I telephoned my mother to talk about Kennedy's assassination, she interrupted me: "Never mind all that; your Cousin Ralphie died in his sleep last night. This morning they found him at ten o'clock like a piece of ice under the covers." Bellow keeps before his readers the Cousin Ralphies *and* the Kennedys. We know there were Kennedys. There must have been Cousin Ralphies. We know we sent soldiers to fight the rebels in Nicaragua. There must have been Anna Coblins who wept.

When Augie distributes handbills for Sylvester's Star Theater, Barney Balaban was operating his Paradise Theater on Crawford Avenue. Jacob Arvey, who eventually brought in Illinois for Harry Truman, started out as a precinct captain. Yellow Kid Weil was the most famous con man of his time. Everyone played the stock market bewitched by Samuel Insull; the crash that wiped out the Coblins and the Einhorns wiped out $30 billion in 1929. Julius Rosenwald did give out large sums of money to Negroes and not to Jews, as Grandma Lausch complained. There was a Roger Touhy, a John Dillinger, the Aiello Brothers, and there certainly were gangsters' funerals to which Augie could deliver his large wreaths of flowers. There were also noisy, rickety trucks distributing bundles of Chicago *Tribune*s and *Herald Examiners* for Augies to pick up at four o'clock in the morning to begin the paper route. The Twentieth Century Limited was indeed the fancy overnight train that left Chicago for New York from the LaSalle Street station where Simon and Augie elevated themselves to work their newsstand for the Federal News Agency. When Dingbat manages Nails Nagel, King Levinsky was beginning his fight career. Ira Berkow, in his book *Maxwell Street,* describes the famous match between King Levinsky and Joe Louis.

> Shortly before the remarkable bout on August 8, 1935, between the great heavyweight boxer Joe Louis and Maxwell Street's King Levinsky, an unusual kind of tension was building in the King's dressing room. According to Barney Nagler, author of the Louis biography, *The Brown Bomber,* the fight promoter feared that the trembling Levinsky might bolt the dressing room at Comiskey Park and run home to Maxwell Street (about three miles north), where his family had been long-time fish peddlers.
> The promoter hurried to the boxing officials and said, "We'd better start the fight now."
> An official said, "But we have a half hour to go."
> "Well, but it might start raining," replied the promoter, looking up into the balmy sky.
> The King went down and out in the first round. Some ringsiders say that the King wasn't really knocked out; what happened was he fainted. Still others, thinking back, wonder if he hadn't been weakened by pain in his feet. Legend has it that the King once complained to his trainer that his feet were killing him. The trainer duly checked and found that the King had put the right shoe on the left foot and the left shoe on the right foot.[10]

If it happened to the Kingfish, it could happen to Nails Nagel. It works both ways. If it happened to Nails Nagel, that is how it happened to the Kingfish. If it happened to Einhorn, that is how it happened to Americans caught in the Crash. If the fantasy is authentic, so is the reality.

All of Augie's irrational, illogical minglings of disparities and discontinuities and discordances, all his leaps and lapses and flounderings and recoveries are Bellow's way to render a public world with its own design of leaps and lapses. The style itself reenacts the disjunctive nature of reality, private and public, the fitful discontinuity of experience, individual and social. History itself becomes a disassembly of parts that leads to no progress.

Conventional chronology is abandoned. Begin at the beginning? End at the end? What began what? Where does any of it end? So Augie tells his story after his story concludes. By recall and flashback and discontinuous episodes, we meet Augie and all his family and friends; at the same time, all the public occurrences of his years find their place; all the public figures that may or may not have any logical relevance appear. We read of the near and the familiar and we read of the far and esoteric, yoked together only by exuberance and comic ironies, a kind of connected disconnection that would become the manner of Bellow's style for decades to come. For six hundred pages, Augie looks back on all that had happened to bring him to his present state, and he claims no wisdom. He has no idea why it started, what started, and to where it got. He is, at the end of his long self-scrutiny, unable, unwilling, to predict what he will do next. What Augie does next appears in the next novel. Bellow's Afterword.

Bellow had good cause to be pleased with his writing style, to revel in the exuberance of his comic manner. Did he eventually come to think Augie was too much an ingénu? Too larky? That may be. Bellow can disparage his early work without permission. Yet Augie, like Joseph and Leventhal, is the prototype of Bellow's skimpy hero, with his aspirations and his desires, which shipwreck him *and* which keep him afloat. "Not waving, but drowning."

Like Joseph in *Dangling Man,* Augie is ready to enter the world and search for a fate good enough for the man he believes himself to be. The search will become Henderson's quest; it will be Herzog's story, a story that will be told again in *The Last Analysis* and *Mr. Sammler's Planet* and *Humboldt's Gift, The Dean's December* and *More Die of Heartbreak.* Although the age of the narrator changes and the places he lives vary, the form of a Bellow novel remains a peripatetic journey through events that are long past and among people who are lost to him, as well as a short trip through present events and present companions. Augie is on a quest—as are all who follow him—for transcendence, or for connection, searching for some way, someone, to join, to unite himself to his fellowman or to God, or to reunite with his spirit, his core self. Bellow changes his terms, realigns his polarities, as if he were a pendulum in motion, his imagination swinging back and forth across widening spaces of memories and experiences and observations, never fixed. He is himself a living being viewing a world itself inchoate. "Go! My child is missing. The world is chaos."

Bellow's style is itself an ironic jest, a spoof of his own aspirations and desires. Consider. Bellow deplores realism, insisting there is no way to distinguish between appearance and reality, and yet there is no metaphor or simile or allusion, no description at all, that does not rest wholly on concrete details, on verifiable facts. Bellow means anytime and anyplace, yet his focus is always on the literally identifiable street on an exact day—it's a gauze and bandage factory in South Chicago at nine o'clock in the morning. Bellow believes in the primacy of art, in the power of the imagination, and he never misses an opportunity to lampoon the vanities of intellect, yet his Augie March ignores art and reads all the great books he can lay hands on in order to find the truth. Bellow believes in the innate goodness of man, yet his Augie encounters betrayal, treason, greed, rage, and outrage. Bellow believes in courage and strength of will, yet his Augie dissolves in tears again and again. He follows and follows; listens publicly, disputes and refutes privately. Bellow knows it is impossible to communicate the truths of the heart, yet his Augie talks and talks and reflects and remembers, chasing after his most fleeting emotion. Bellow believes in the power of faith, but only Georgie of the "dummy school" is faithful.

Zany? No. Bellow is dead serious. To represent the idea of simultaneity and polarity—a truer principle than the idea of cause and effect—he creates a style free of the constraints of fiction and cares not a scrap for what the new critics or old critics may say. Well, perhaps he does care. He hopes they like it. If not? So be it.

Bellow leaves the *Partisan Review* crowd behind because old aesthetics, like old politics, no longer satisfy him. Political organizations and social theories and philosophical positions go the way of new criticism and academia. He has found his writing style; fixed theories and fixed forms will go the way of his wives. He has the right way to represent his vision of reality; he remains on quest for the right vision.

When Bellow was asked in an interview given in 1973 at Skidmore College whether he retells the same story, he replied:

> I sometimes think the wisdom of life can be discovered in 10 or 15 jokes. I'll tell you one which, I think, answers this question. An American tenor was performing, making his debut at La Scala. He sings his first aria early in the first act. The applause is tremendous and people shout "Ancora, vita, vita." So he sings the aria once more. The second time the applause is even more tremendous; the Scala roof seems to go off with everybody shrieking "Ancora, vita," so he sings the aria a third time. After he's sung it a third time, they call for it a fourth time. He holds up his hands and, with tears in his eyes, he makes a little speech. He says he never hoped for anything like this, that this is the greatest hour of his life, that his mother is a poor laundress in Kansas City and that his father decamped early and left them alone and after a cheap rotten start

he'd studied at the Juilliard, and he'd studied in Paris, and in Rome, and in Milan, and this was an unforgettable night for him, it justified a belief in himself, justified himself to his mother. But, the cast is waiting, the Maestro is waiting, the orchestra is waiting, we must go on with the performance. But the crowd shouts—"No, no!" and he says "how many times must I sing this aria?" Someone shouts, "you gonna sing until you get it right!"[11]

1

"Is that perhaps the cousin from New Orleans they were expecting?"

From Sutcliffe Star Route in Reno, Nevada, I received a letter from Bellow thanking me for the gift of a canister of exotic tea, a tin of imported cookies, and a drawing, sent along by my husband, Irving Kriesberg.

Writing on November 5, 1955, Bellow talked wistfully of his isolation and loneliness, having left a dude ranch for a cabin out of reach of civilization. The experience of utter solitude had its dangers, but he probably needed it, for his recent life in New York had been frenetic and now he felt like a diver who had come up out of the depths too quick, too soon.

Bellow explained that he was in Reno to establish the required residency of six weeks, perhaps more, for his divorce, but he would break up the time by visiting old friends in San Francisco, seeing Sondra, who had been waiting in Los Angeles.

Bellow did remain a good while longer, yet not so totally alone. In March, he had a letter from Arthur Miller asking for his help:

March 15, 1956

Dear Saul:

Congratulations. Pat [Covici, their publisher] tells me you are to be married. That is quite often a good idea.

I am going out there around the end of the month to spend the fated six weeks and have no idea where to live. I have a problem, however, of slightly unusual proportions. From time to time there will be a visitor who is very dear to me, but who is unfortunately recognizable by approximately a hundred million people, give or take three or four. She has all sorts of wigs, can affect a limp, sunglasses, bulky coats, etc., but if it is possible I want to find a place, perhaps a bungalow or something like, where there are not likely to be crowds looking in through the windows. Do you know of any such place?

Bellow found a vacant cabin nearby on the edge of the Paiute Indian Reservation in the Nevada desert and there they stayed, working their way through residencies, settlements, charges, and countercharges: Bellow divorcing Anita Goshkin to marry Sondra Tschacbasov; Miller divorcing Mary Slattery to marry Marilyn Monroe.

We can perceive something of the overstimulation with which New York had left him by looking at two pieces—the first a one-act play called *The Wrecker*, written in 1953; the second a short story called "A Father-to-be," published in 1955. In the play, *The Wrecker*,[1] Bellow depicted the disintegration of a marriage; in "A Father-to-be,"[2] he described a worried man ambivalent about his mistress. Both women—wife and mistress—reappear in "Seize the Day"[3]: Margaret in Brooklyn, preying on Tommy Wilhelm; Olive waiting impatiently for him in Roxbury.*

The play depicts a middle-class man's fantasy of violence, the first direct representation we have of Bellow's droll interpretation—at once serious and a spoof—of the therapeutic methods he practiced during his short time in Reichian analysis. Years later, in 1978, during a long, cold afternoon in December, we met at the Arts Club for lunch and ended up at Bentley's in the Sheraton. At the elitist Arts Club everyone greeted Bellow with respect, many stopping at our table to say nice words. One especially well-preserved rather pretty matron gushed that she had been his student at Pestalozzi-Froebel Teachers College, that he was her one claim to fame. By one of those odd coincidences we all experience from time to time, she had interrupted our conversation precisely when Bellow was describing what had happened while he was waiting to get his car at the underground parking lot in Grant Park, before driving to the Arts Club. A woman beckoned him and

*Olive becomes Lily, waiting for Eugene Henderson to return to his home in Connecticut after he has gotten Africa out of his system. Only Henderson is impatient. It is Lily who becomes Madeleine, the killer-wife of Herzog. Madeleine is impatient only for the day she can throw Herzog out of the house.

reminded him she had known him years ago and since he had not recognized her, she told him her name. He had felt wounded to tears. When he had known her she had been an attractive, bright, and lively woman with whom he had "necked a little," a Chicago expression well known to me from the Thirties. Now there she was, her hand grasping her handbag, a fat, over-stuffed, overdressed woman, her hair treated so many times it couldn't live anymore. This was what had become of that nimble earbiting. I thought he was harsh saying she was nothing any longer and never could be. "Well," I said, "this former student does not look as if she has missed out on much," and he laughed and said yes, but he had not necked with her.

Bellow seemed to want to talk about his therapy. At the same time he hesitated, drew back, and after a pause went on to reminisce about Isaac Rosenfeld. I sensed it was Isaac Rosenfeld who was more on his mind than Wilhelm Reich. Both he and Isaac had wanted a new way to live; both wished to live a creative life. They were not even sure that it was possible to live a writer's life in those times. They did not really know what that was, and it seemed to them that it had to be something more than writing. Bellow laughed at their innocence, and I recall he wondered why writers always thought that to write takes more than writing.

In my journal I jotted down Bellow's interpretation of Reich's idea that civilization has so twisted man's sexual nature, so overtaxed him, that a sexually neurotic man can hardly become a moral man. To restore him, therapy seeks out the neurosis, manifested in the physical bearing of the patient. Undressed, the patient sits, stands, walks, runs, under the scrutiny of the doctor, whose task it is to perceive the nature of the neurosis while observing the body in motion and at rest.

He seemed reluctant to explain further, but he did mention the orgone box, another physical part of the treatment. The box was specially designed to transmit the vital energy in the natural world to the body. The patient sat in the orgone box, absorbing the flow. Bellow said he had one in his apartment in Queens, and Isaac had one in his apartment in the Village. A doctor in New York still had his orgone box from the time he had himself been a patient in his own Reichian analysis and had treated some of his patients with it. The doctor got one remission for cervical cancer and one near remission. Bellow chuckled at the idea of a near remission. Perhaps, he said, he did feel better for a time—he cured a couple of warts and improved his breathing—but he gave it up years ago. Then he thought again of Isaac, Isaac who dragged his orgone box with him to St. Albans but left it behind when he went back to Chicago. Maybe, Bellow said softly, maybe Isaac should have transported the box.

We walked over to Bentley's, not far, but it was cold. How fragile

he looked, his color almost transparent—I could make out his bone structure—and his worn-out face, the skin creased and lined. He walked slowly,
his elbows holding himself close, as if supporting his rib cage. But he was
beautifully dressed, in a smooth-finish deep green gabardine suit, a striped
shirt with white collar and cuffs, and a perfectly matched green tie—bright,
those greens—and his plaid topcoat, and then, what I came to recognize as
his trademark, his hat, always his hat, this time a neat little Homburg, years
later, in Vermont, the khaki sports cap, and all the spring, summer, fall, and
winter models in between. No one had worn hats in Chicago except when
our mothers pulled on our knitted stocking caps when the temperature
dropped down to zero.

In Bentley's we both sat quietly listening to a few musicians playing some frantic song on the far side of that cavernous room—Bentley's—
all those empty tables and no one there but us. They were practicing for
the crowd to come, I supposed. Had Bellow believed in this therapy? For a
time he had; he said the advice of the Reichian therapist had probably been
useful. Bellow talked a bit of the method of "acting out," re-enacting in
sessions at the office, or privately at home, simulations of repressed rages—
the desire to murder, to strangle, to beat, to afflict—to release aggression.
Bellow feared for a time he was losing control, becoming unstable. If someone just pushed him in the subway, he was ready to fight. To be violent
seemed therapeutic.

Aside from our conversation, we have the play, and eventually the
novel—Henderson the Rain King—to explain in fiction what we may miss
in fact.[4]

In The Wrecker, the scene is a railroad flat in an empty apartment
building. A tense and angry husband and his bewildered wife are the last to
move. Albert has decided to pack nothing, to wreck the place, to smash down
the walls of his confinement. "Today I'm a man of deeds, like a hero out of
Homer." He glares around the living room filled with "all the cherished
objects of the woman's temple" and takes up a sledgehammer: "I feel like
Samson in the Temple of Gaza! Take cover ye Philistines." The Philistines
are his tearful wife Sarah, his annoyed mother-in-law, and an indignant city
inspector, who watch while Albert pries up and strikes down, hacks and
smashes his way to health.

> See what a difference the point of view makes. I never was better. I am a
> magician. This joint is enchanted, you see. I'm getting rid of a lot of past life,
> dangerous to the soul. The past, you understand, is very dangerous if you don't
> deal with it. If I had a warehouse I could put this harmful past life into, or if
> I could take it to sea in a scow and dump it, let the seagulls have it, I'd be

satisfied. You can't drag your heavy, heavy history around with you. Suppose the humming bird had to keep remembering that in the ancient past it was a snake?

They have not been happy in any room. "Not even the bedroom?" Sarah asks wistfully.

HUSBAND   Sometimes you ought to give in to your violent feelings, Sarah. It's great to be angry. Anger is beautiful. It gives you a sense of honor. It brings back your self-respect.

Albert hands her a hatchet. Why pretend? Be honest. Pitch in.

HUSBAND   Does it say anywhere that Achilles ever built anything? Or Ulysses? They tore down Troy and killed everyone in it. Who were the heroes of the war? The fellows who dropped the bombs on cities. A hero destroys the links with the past when they bother him. He frees himself from what other men have done before him.

Sarah hesitates.

HUSBAND   You're far too rigid—far, far. You have to learn to be more flexible. It's a practical matter. For the sake of your health.

WIFE   How many ideas you have. Do you want me to believe that what you're doing you're doing for your health's sake?

HUSBAND   Of course it's for my health. Now why else do you think I'm being so truthful? It's risky. If I say too much you'll get sore. But if I don't do it I feel sick. . . . Let's wipe out some of the falsehood. Let's admit what our souls tell us is true and stop denying it for the sake of keeping the peace or preserving the marriage and the home. Yes, just because of health. . . .

Albert attacks shelves, door, mirror, floor, bric-a-brac, chandelier, and climbs a ladder to reach the ceiling. "Rip it all up! Smash it!" Sarah at last picks up the hatchet and starts chipping away, at the fireplace first, gradually, tentatively, fearfully, until she, too, climbs and begins to strike hard at the bedroom ceiling. Albert, watching her fall into an ecstasy of destruction, is no longer so sure.

The Wrecker would be an expensive play to produce. The curtain comes down on a completely destroyed set.

In the short story "A Father-to-be," Rogin is on his way to the apartment that his fiancée, Joan, shares with her cousin, a young divorcée.* His thoughts are a mixture of love and complaint. "How difficult she was, and how beautiful." Joan is a costly mistress but has so sweet and small, so daring, shapely, timid, defiant, and loving a face that Rogin can deny her nothing. He pays her bills, not cheerfully, but he pays.

> A clear idea suddenly arose in Rogin's thoughts: Money surrounds you in life as the earth does in death. Superimposition is the universal law. Who is free? Who has no burdens? Everyone is under pressure. . . . everyone has some weight to carry.†

Perversely, his realization that everyone has trouble puts him in a good mood. He stops at the deli and fills a bag with extravagant purchases for their dinner, fondly choosing frozen raspberries and heavy cream and, at the last moment, adding some ice cream.

Carrying his gifts into the subway car, he happily observes all the richly diverse passengers riding with him. The transport of joy does not last long. Beside him sits a man of forty, a dandy of respectability, a tasteless fourth-rate person, ordinary, complacent, bourgeois, dull. The worst is that the man resembles Joan, and worse than that, Joan's detestable father. Such a man, Rogin thinks, will be my son in forty years' time. "If I should marry Joan I will father this revolting man." As the train rumbles along, he sits in cold dread, staring at his presumptive son.

> What the blazes am I getting into? To be the father of a throwback to her father. The image of the white-haired, gross, peevish, old man with his ugly selfish blue eyes revolted Rogin. This was how his grandson would look. Joan, with whom Rogin was now more and more displeased, could not help that. For

*Sondra Tschacbasov shared an apartment for a time with Pearl, Alfred Kazin's sister.
†This Rogin is an experiment—a dry run—for Tommy Wilhelm.

her it was inevitable. But did it have to be inevitable for him? Well, then, Rogin,
you fool, don't be a damned instrument. Get out of the way!

Seething, in a bitter state of mind, Rogin arrives at the apartment. Joan offers
to shampoo his hair. He submits. Grousing inwardly, he promises himself he
will face her down, he will tell her off, later.

> "Do you think," he was going to tell her, "that I alone was made to carry the
> burden of the whole world on me? Do you think I was born to be taken
> advantage of and sacrificed? Do you think I'm just a natural resource, like a coal
> mine, or oil well, or fishery, or the like? Remember, that I'm a man is no reason
> why I should be loaded down. I have a soul in me no bigger or stronger than
> yours. . . ."

As Joan begins to wash his hair, Rogin is transfixed by the sensation of the
water pouring gently over his head. The water carries off his anger, its source
flowing from somewhere deep within him.

> It was the warm fluid of his own secret loving spirit overflowing into the sink
> green and foaming, and the words he had rehearsed he forgot, and his anger at
> his son-to-be disappeared altogether.

In February 1956, Bellow mailed to all his friends a tiny printed card that
said simply:

> *Married*
> *Miss Alexandra Tschacbasov*
> *and*
> *Mr. Saul Bellow*
> *the first of February*
> *Nineteen hundred and fifty-six*
> *Reno, Nevada*

It was not until spring that Bellow wrote to tell me of his plans to return to
New York. In a letter dated April 10, 1956, Bellow talked of his indifference
to money. The settlement had been costly, true, but no matter. He forgot
about money when he was writing well. These thoughts brought him to the
collection of stories to be published in the fall. Among them was a novella
that especially pleased him, a long piece of fiction with far less description

than was usual for him, a taking leave of that style of writing. I would be able to see it in the summer.[5]

"Seize the Day" is the long piece of fiction everyone would read and some praise when it appeared in *Partisan Review* in the summer of 1956. It is indeed a story written by a swimmer in trouble, a story compressed and agitated and painful. The time span is only half a day in the life of Tommy Wilhelm, but a day of reckoning.

> . . . today he was afraid. He was aware that his routine was about to break up and he sensed that a huge trouble long presaged but till now formless was due. Before evening he'd know.

He is about to take his final gamble on the commodities market with Dr. Tamkin for his guide. Either he will make it or be irretrievably wiped out.

The setting is contracted. Wilhelm moves spasmodically within the range of a very few blocks on upper Broadway; for the most part, he is confined in the spaces of his residential hotel—the Gloriana—often standing in an elevator, motionless, as he is carried between his room on the twenty-third floor, his father's room on fourteen, Tamkin's room on twelve, and the lobby. When he changes place, he does not go far: a stop at the newsstand to buy his morning paper and a few cigars; a short cross from the lobby into the dining room for breakfast with his father and Mr. Perls; and out into the lobby again, where he meets Tamkin; then back into the restaurant, to sit at a different table while Tamkin eats. Once outside, Wilhelm crosses Broadway and walks a few yards to the brokerage office, and a door or two farther on is the cafeteria where Tamkin and Wilhelm lunch. Then it is back to the broker's office, with Wilhelm stopping to help old and nearly blind Mr. Rappaport cross the street to La Magnita, where Rappaport can buy his special brand of cigars. Wilhelm pleads with his father in the massage room of the health club located in the basement. The smallest space of all is the phone booth in the lobby, where Wilhelm stands pleading with his wife. He strikes the wall of the telephone booth with a clenched fist, then races through the door of the hotel back onto Broadway, but he gets only as far as a funeral parlor in the next block. He steps into the line of mourners and walks with them, foot by foot, and stops, finally, before the coffin of a stranger. That is as far as he goes, physically.

Mentally, Wilhelm travels widely; he never stops thinking. From his mercurial thoughts and arguments and memories, we perceive a longer time and larger place, encompassing his childhood, youth, college days, marriage, separation, a new love, and his various jobs; remembering Wall Street, Times

Square, West End Avenue, Riverside Drive, Flatbush, Queens; remembering Hollywood, Santa Barbara, Roxbury, Cuba. Unlike Augie, Wilhelm is no ingénu in search of a fate good enough; he has met his fate and his life has been a passage from failure to failure. A man in his forties, with half his life over and a dreary, depressed half his life left to live through, he is a loser: The past is irretrievable; his mother is dead, his father, in the last stage of his life, is contentious and scornful; his job is lost, his money lost, his wife and children lost; he is a man of sorrows, rejected by all, despised, as Henderson will say of Christ and himself, and Wilhelm is heart-scathingly alone. All he wants is a second chance, to try again, start over, to find a way to live well, live right, despite the reality of defeat. In the face of isolation and solitude and rejection, despite his awareness of the inexorable presence of death, he wants to love and to belong.

Wilhelm has a single adversary, his father, old Dr. Adler, and a single mentor, Tamkin, an old crook. The action is a progress in the gradual divestment of masks and hypocrisies. Wilhelm starts his day with the determination to conceal his troubles, to put on a brave front, and episode by episode finds himself stripped of all his pretenses. He thinks of himself as attractive, a man of charm, and he tries to look dapper, but his clothes are shabby; he wants to appear poised and in control, but he has tics. He stammers, his gut is fat, his skin sallow, his hair scruffy, and he is unable to restrain his outbursts of anger. He wants to appear distinguished and successful, but he has no job or profession. He can't even play a decent game of gin rummy. He wants to be known as a man of truth, but he lies about his education, his screen test, his seven dreary years as a hanger-on in Hollywood, and his reason for leaving the Rojax Corporation, pretending it was a matter of moral integrity. He wants to be known as a smart operator on the commodities market but knows nothing at all of lard or rye and relies on the expertise and goodwill of a man he knows to be a four-flusher, a charlatan. He wants to appear clever but stupidly gives Tamkin power of attorney and is helpless when Tamkin absconds. He smokes cigarettes avidly and hides the butts in his jacket pocket. He takes phenophen pills and says they are vitamins.

There is no suspense in such a story. The reader is never in doubt that by afternoon Wilhelm will be flat broke and wholly unraveled, cheated by Tamkin, turned out by his father. However, it is Bellow writing the story. There is a surprise at the end. What the reader cannot predict is the effect on Wilhelm of his demoralization, that by afternoon, when he stands bare and exposed, in full view of a crowd of strangers, his hands covering his face, sobbing aloud, Wilhelm will feel his heart eased, his soul's yearning fulfilled—not cramps after all, but a compression that explodes in release. This ending derives from a second line of action, present, perhaps overlooked, as Wilhelm tried to do.

All through his climb on his own Via Dolorosa, and Golgotha lay on a height, Wilhelm feels a tug, "a great pull at the very center of his soul." He reflects:

> The spirit, the peculiar burden of his existence lay upon him like an accretion, a load, a hump. In any moment of quiet, when sheer fatigue prevented him from struggling, he was apt to feel this mysterious weight, this growth or collection of nameless things which it was the business of his life to carry about. That must be what a man was for . . . [he] was assigned to be the carrier of a load which was his own self, his characteristic self. There was no figure or estimate for the value of this load.

He comes gradually to understand what his soul requires, that the question is not what a man should do but what his soul is for. Intuitions of the truth of his existence reach him from remote elements in his thoughts; his eyes fill with tears. The closer he gets to recognizing his core soul, the greater his need to weep.

> . . . the business of life, the real business—to carry his peculiar burden, to feel shame and impotence, to taste these quelled tears—the only important business, the highest business was being done. Maybe the making of mistakes expressed the very purpose of his life and the essence of his being here. Maybe he was supposed to make them and suffer from them on this earth.

Kindness and mercy is a need of the soul. The soul longs to love. Wilhelm has a fleeting sense of the soul's yearning when he is walking in the crowded underpass at Times Square.

> . . . all of a sudden, unsought, a general love for all these imperfect and lurid-looking people burst out in Wilhelm's breast. He loved them. One and all, he passionately loved them. They were his brothers and sisters. He was imperfect and disfigured himself, but what difference did that make if he was united with them by this blaze of love?

The blaze of love fades but he promises himself to remember.

> . . . I must go back to that. That's the right clue and may do me the most good. Something very big. Truth, like.

The tug comes again when Tamkin asks, "You love your old man?"

"Of course. Of course I love him. My father. My mother—" As he said this there was a great pull at the very center of his soul. When a fish strikes the line you feel the live force in your hand. A mysterious being beneath the water, driven by hunger, has taken the hook and rushes away and fights, writhing. Wilhelm never identified what struck within him. It did not reveal itself. It got away.

He may admit to Tamkin he loves his father, but Dr. Adler will neither love nor be loved. His father despises him and is ashamed of him and cares nothing for him. What does he want from his father? Money, yes, but more; he wants to ease his heart to him, to get what a son ought to get from his father, the primal gesture: He should "put his hands on me and give me his blessing." Not from this father. Dr. Adler advises his son to go to the gym, to take the baths, to cut down on drugs.

It was all he had to give his son and he gave it once more. "Water and exercise," he said. "You want to make yourself into my cross. But I am not going to pick up a cross. I'll see you dead, Wilky, by Christ, before I let you do that to me."

His wife freezes his heart with her cold aggression: "Are you in misery? . . . You have deserved it." The community he seeks to enter cannot be the community of fathers and wives. Wilhelm walks out onto Broadway and there, once again, he feels a surge of love for his fellow suffering human beings.

And the great, great crowd, the inexhaustible current of millions of every race and kind pouring out, pressing round, of every age, of every genius, possessors of every human secret, antique and future, in every face the refinement of one particular nature or essence—I labor, I spend, I strive, I design, I love, I cling, I uphold, I give way, I envy, I long, I scorn, I die, I hide, I want.

He believes he spots Tamkin under the canopy of a funeral parlor and moves forward with the pressure of the crowd and finds himself in the dark cool chapel.

Bellow always likes to hear anecdotes about family and I am sure many of his friends recognize in his fiction the choice stories they have told him. A good example of his gift for transformation is what he did with my anecdote. My father-in-law died in June 1952, and was "buried out of" Weinstein's on Devon Avenue in uptown Chicago. The funeral was scheduled for eleven o'clock and my father, coming from work by streetcar, arrived late. There were several "parlors" in the funeral home and he went quickly into the first one, got on line, and walked to the bier to pay his respects. Standing before the coffin, he looked down and saw a total stranger. As he told us later, "I knew it wasn't Kriesberg because this guy wore glasses and Kriesberg always had good eyesight." Many times I told my father that his mistake became one of the most famous scenes in contemporary American fiction. All he said was, "It's true. I didn't recognize anyone from his side. I couldn't find the old lady." And he struck a match to light his cigar and waited for me to pour him a cup of coffee.

It's Bellow who sees in such an experience a way to represent the apotheosis of Tommy Wilhelm.

> Presently he too was in this line, and slowly, slowly, foot by foot, the beating of his heart anxious, thick, frightening, but somehow also rich he neared the coffin, and paused for his turn and gazed down. He caught his breath when he looked down at the corpse and, his face swelled, his eyes shone hugely with instant tears.

Revelation and tears come together.

> He cried at first softly and from sentiment, but soon from deeper feeling. ... A man—another human creature, was what first went through his thoughts, but other and different things were torn from him.

He cried for himself, but then passes by his own troubles.

> The source of all tears had suddenly sprung open within him, black, deep, and hot, and they were pouring out and convulsed his body, bending his stubborn head, bowing his shoulders, twisting his face, crippling the very hands with which he held the handkerchief. His efforts to collect himself were useless. The great knot of ill and grief in his throat swelled upward and he gave in utterly and held his face and wept. He cried with all his heart.

Earlier, in the broker's office, Wilhelm hoped old Mr. Rappaport, with his two families, one in Williamsburg, one in the Bronx, and his chicken business in New Jersey, and his market ventures in New York, would give him some hints on the market. Rappaport gives him a different kind of advice.

> Finally old Rappaport did address a few remarks to Wilhelm. He asked him whether he had reserved his seat in the synagogue for Yom Kippur.

"No," said Wilhelm.

"Well, you better hurry up if you expect to say *Yiskor* for your parents."

While an organ plays in the funeral parlor, Tommy says *Yiskor* for himself and all parents.

> . . . the heavy sea-like music came up to his ears. It poured into him where he had hidden himself in the center of a crowd by the great happy oblivion of tears. He heard it and sank deeper than sorrow, through torn sobs and cries toward the consummation of his heart's ultimate need.

He has joined the community of man. Bellow remembered my father, too. At this extraordinary moment, so profoundly sad and bewilderingly ecstatic, Bellow interpolated the dialogue that ends the story.

> One woman said, "Is that perhaps the cousin from New Orleans they were expecting?"
>
> "It must be somebody real close to carry on so."
>
> "Oh my, oh my! To be mourned like that," said one man and looked at Wilhelm's heavy shaken shoulders, his clutched face and whitened fair hair, with wide, glinting, jealous eyes.
>
> "The man's brother, maybe?"
>
> "Oh, I doubt that very much," said another bystander. "They're not alike at all. Night and day."

"Distractions of a Fiction Writer"

From the perspective of the present time, knowing where Bellow has gotten to in his career of writing and prizes, we have accustomed ourselves to believe he has had only to publish to receive wide public praise. Not so. A glance at phrases taken from the reviews of "Seize the Day," the centerpiece of the collection of stories published in 1956, will disabuse us of the notion: "little more than a vignette," "little more than pathos," "a small success," "slight," "morbid social pathology," "smacks of a popular Manhattan brand of psychoanalysis wherein bored and shiftless people invent problems," "the third in Saul Bellow's mopery series," "not literature." Tommy Wilhelm is "perversely unheroic," a "composite of the weaker characteristics of Augie March, without Augie's ingenuity or ambition," "a middle-aged adolescent," "lost in an ecstasy of self pity," "a reversion to childhood," "finding release by sobbing hysterically at a stranger's funeral." Ray B. West, Jr., summed up the general response with a cynical observation:

> It seems likely that this is a volume put together and offered to the public, more to keep its author's name alive between more important projects than as a manifestation of Mr. Bellow at his best.[1]

Herbert Gold called the novella a triumph of perception, close to "The Death of Ivan Ilyich," and Alfred Kazin said it was a magnificent piece in which

Bellow creates for America "the uncreated conscience of modern man." But then, Gold and Kazin were personal friends of Bellow.[2]

The British reviewers were even less tolerant.[3] *The New Statesman and Nation* printed Walter Allen's wry judgment:

> "A mile further and all would have been marsh," wrote Yeats of *A Shropshire Lad,* and of "Seize the Day" it might be said a mile further and all would be William Saroyan.

The Spectator printed John Bayley's ironic assessment:

> Younger American writers today seem very taken up with the question of what it is to be *nice.* . . . Saul Bellow's latest hero, Tommy Wilhelm, now joins the ranks of the agreeable which include Chandler's Marlowe (a tough fellow as well as nice, but principally nice), the adolescent charmer of *The Catcher in the Rye,* and the brave little artist from the last Mary McCarthy. . . . Wilhelm remains a real and reverent hymn to niceness celebrated in Mr. Bellow's unemphatically distinguished prose.

London Magazine printed Francis Wyndham's opinion:

> "Seize the Day" is shorter, easier to read and less important than his brilliant but indigestible *Augie March,* an expanded short story, something more than a character sketch and less than a complete portrait . . . with an ending that is made to bear more significance than it can carry.

The *TLS* coolly dismissed the story:

> Mr. Bellow gives us a mere snack in "Seize the Day," but it is a snack recognizably prepared by the same chef. Yes, Bellow is a gifted writer but one is unable to grasp his precise meaning.

Within the year, Bellow began his project to respond to all reviewers and literary critics, not merely on his own behalf but in the interest of all writers. It seemed to him the so-called cultural elite, and he included the whole academic establishment in that "spurious elite," were guilty of a general attitude toward the writer that was not only debilitating to an artist but dangerous. At the request of Granville Hicks, who was putting together a collection of responses to the charge the novel was dead—or as was often said, useless, powerless, obsolete, finished—Bellow wrote "Distractions of a Fiction Writer."[4] He began the attack by asking himself a simple question:

> Why didn't you choose a different kind of work. . . . Why do you write fiction? . . . What makes you think it's wanted? What are you doing? . . . Only sitting here alone, oddly faithful to the things you learned as a boy. They taught you the Palmer method in school, so here you are still covering pages with words. You go on about men and women, families and marriages, divorces, crime and flight, murders, weddings, wars, rises and declines, simplicities and complexities, blessedness and agony, and it's all largely imaginary. Who asks you to write such things?

By the time he explained why a writer undertakes the task, the question has shifted to why people read books, and at the end of his contribution to the symposium, it is the critics who are dead and the poets, with their unique gift of a mysterious imagination, who live. Just as eros manages somehow to survive analysis, so imagination survives criticism. Out of the chaos of crude materialism and the awesome multiplicity of fact, which is unidentifiable reality, only the imagination of the artist can discover and impose order. The artist is the "intellectual, esthetic, moral genius of the human race." And critics?

> It's only natural that writers should have their enemies. It's the rule of life, among writers as among snakes, mice, and lice. The subtler creatures have subtler enemies. The subtlest enemies are those who get you over to their own side. You read the authoritative words of an eminent critic; they sound reasonable; you half agree, and then you are distracted and stiflingly depressed.

Bellow admits he has been depressed by disapproval of his calling before and remembers wistfully his family's bemused tolerance of a son's folly, as if he were a wayward child who could someday be brought to his senses, but what right did this pretender family, this commonwealth of power brokers, have to tell artists they were obsolete, finished, that they now had become no more than disruptive intruders? Why did the men who made their living by working the lodes of art disparage artists? Why wish them all safely dead?

> *Finished!* We have heard this from Valéry and from T. S. Eliot, from Ortega and from Oswald Spengler, and most recently from the summit of Morningside

Heights.* We are supposed to be done for. The great dinosaurs are gone; only vestigial Gila monsters remain. Oh, to have once more the unimportance of that poor poet whom Brutus and Cassius threw out! For every poet now there are a hundred custodians and doctors of literature, and dozens of undertakers measuring away at coffins.

In today's world, it is not enough to throw the artists out; they must be finished off. Novelists, Bellow says, are trained to take words seriously, and they believe the oracles, think they are hearing words of high seriousness saying "Obsolete. Finished." It may be the oracles who are the fakirs, however, their voices that carry the words of low seriousness.

Scholars and critics are often curiously like property owners. They have their lots surveyed. Here the property begins and there it ends. A conservative instinct in them, which every lover of order will recognize and respect, resists extension, calls for limits. And why not? Besides, it's awfully fine to be an epigone. It tickles one so in the self-esteem. But how odd it is that these words "obsolete" and "finished" should never be spoken with regret or pain. The accent is rather one of satisfaction. And this is all the more strange because if the critics are wrong their opinions will do harm. They are certain to be destructive.

    The students of literature line up with the epigones. "Thank God!" they say, "it's over. Now we have a field. We can study."

That same year, 1957, Bellow had another opportunity to address the scholars and critics. The editors of *The Nation* asked him to respond to their query: Are writers greatly harmed by teaching in the universities? He called the essay "The University as Villain," and began with his recollection of an encounter between himself and a prototype of the establishment.

In 1952, when I was teaching at Princeton, I met in New York a man I had known in Chicago in less happy times (for me) when he was connected with the University of Chicago, and I was connected with nothing. He had been one of Chancellor Hutchins' assistants; now he was near the summit of a huge advertising corporation in New York. We had always been fond of each other and we met with pleasure. He was dressed in such high style that I could hardly keep from touching his tweed. He had a fine red, conservative straight face and was smoking the biggest and shiningest pipe that Madison Avenue had to sell, so there was no need for me to ask how *he* was doing.

*Lionel Trilling was the reigning professor of literature, American and all the rest, at Columbia University, which stands on Morningside Heights.

"But what are *you* up to these days?" he said.

"Well," I told him, "you'll find it hard to believe, but this year I am teaching at Princeton."

It had never occurred to him that I might be connected with anything so classy, and because of his respect for higher learning, probably absorbed from the chancellor, he was upset. So I was very sorry, and I said, "It's only temporary."

"What do your academic colleagues think about this?" he said.

"Oh, it's probably a joke to them, but they still have most of the joint to themselves. What's the matter, Mack? Why does this bother you?"

"Well," he said, "writers have always come out of the gutter. The gutter is their proper place."[5]

"The gutter is their proper place." Were writers loafers and bums? Were they sneaking into safe harbor, under special protections, and, what may be worse, could they not fit into a world of truth and progress? Did they wander about in a childlike state of irrelevance? Or was it the professor who was safe and irrelevant?

> ... the professor of literature is likely to feel that the dull canal, all that remains of the once sweet Thames, is his only portion, and that he is foolishly watching the rats in the vegetation while he ponders the problem of Hamlet's uncle, unrelated to the gas tanks behind him and Sputnik overhead.

No, said Bellow, it is in the English departments of the universities that we find "discouraged people who stand dully upon a brilliant plane, in charge of masterpieces but not themselves inspired." Bellow concluded more temperately: no one can say where a writer may best thrive. Wherever they find freedom, wherever their spirit may prosper, that is the place to be. It is the quality of the spirit and not the nature of the place that signifies.

Often Bellow accepted invitations from elite colleges and large universities, public and private, and carried his attack into the heart of the country, where students read the great masters of modern literature under the tutelage of the despised epigones, where students wrote term papers analyzing the novel structurally, phenomenologically, symbolically, semantically, and what-all. On the college circuit, Bellow lectured on the sanctity of each individual's destiny and he everywhere declared unequivocally that because of their moral passion, their religious fervor, their awareness of human suffering, as well as by their artistic devices, writers speak for and to humanity. One such lecture still lies in manuscript in the archives of the Regenstein Library, in a file titled

"On Flaubert." He does not remember exactly where he gave this lecture and guesses it may have been the University of Chicago. It may have been Northwestern, but it did not matter. He was saying the same thing everywhere.

Written during the time he was at work on *Henderson the Rain King,* the lecture continued the attack on academia and also sheds light on Bellow's thinking while he was writing his fifth novel. Fiction, he said, is the enactment of human destiny, not an exercise in language. The writer should confront ignoble reality, not noble traditions. Received opinion and intellectualization are hostile to the blossoming of the human spirit. The imagination is the sole source of order; art is the work of the imagination and imagination is the instrument of the soul.

How, he asked the students and teachers crowding the hall to listen, how is a writer to accomplish a representation of the human heart? By abandoning the monologue of a Flaubert, of a Joyce or Proust, of a Gide, of all the writers so beloved in academia, but who are only talking to themselves; by refining instead the sense of dialogue, by representing people outside the self, people who speak to one another. The virtuosity of the suffocatingly limited internal monologue is not sufficient to represent what the psyche of every man knows. And, probably not looking up to see the consternation on many faces in his audience, Bellow went on to offer three suggestions, as much clues to his manner of writing *Henderson* as to his quarrels with the cultural establishment. The first is that we should see for ourselves what it is the human creature contains, and shun the error of thinking him to be ultimately knowable. The second is that writers turn away from all conventional perceptions of character and instead concern themselves with the search, the incessant search, for the unique attributes of the individual. Instead of types, create singularities. The third suggestion, which Bellow says he borrowed from his late friend Isaac Rosenfeld, is to know there is a light and a truth that can be discovered even in our phony and artificial age. A writer must be aware of what the living man really is in his life.

All three suggestions were about to lead to Eugene Henderson, the very image of *ur*-singularity, a garrulous, irrational character who searches for light and truth and cannot find it in the phony and artificial life of Danbury and Manhattan and must go to Africa to hunt it down.

There is an extraordinary consistency in Bellow. In 1979, so many years after his Flaubert lecture, he leaned back on his canvas chair on the lawn in Vermont, and said to me that the human, that which was human, is the key to objectivity. What counts is the experience of the heart, not intelligence, not reason, but feelings, passions. Bellow was pointing to his forehead, then dropped his hand and pointed to his heart.

He said that a writer must lay out the facts, without theories, without abstractions; just tell what is in the mind and the heart. Aesthetics? His aesthetics consisted, as I recall, of awareness. Of what? Of the wonder and the beauty—the ecstatic—in life. And no matter what is going on, no matter what, a writer has to remain always aware that there is a great beauty in the objective facts, in the day by day.

Indeed, it is the day-by-day details of the life of Eugene Henderson, combined with the imaginary details of a wholly improbable journey in Africa, that is the hallmark of the style Bellow contrived for his novel. True, the imagination of the artist perceives how a shaft of light reaches down from the sun or stars to illuminate the translucent wings of a fly, and the intuition of the artist perceives the presence of the source of light, but the observing eye of the artist is fixed on the fly. Henderson is just such a fly. Imagination cannot be bound by tradition. Bellow could choose, and he did so choose, to turn his back on all respectable literature, and the scholars and critics who believed in its sanctity, and write a novel that defied every tenet or principle or category or system of analysis.

Bellow was also turning his back on the respectable life he had chosen for himself, a life overrun with distractions, with duties and responsibilities and dull chores that swamped him. When his father died, Bellow had taken his share of the legacy and purchased a wooden manor house in Tivoli, New York, not far from Bard College, where he was teaching. There were acres of unkempt land, a huge old barn that needed shoring up, insulation, and heating if it was to serve as a studio; the rambling run-down house was much like the Hyde Park house of FDR, the Oyster Bay house of Theodore, a Rooseveltian house, with a ballroom with white-tiled walls and a marble floor on which fifty people years ago had waltzed around comfortably without crowding the musicians, and a kitchen that might easily have provisioned those fifty guests.

The house was in a constant state of disrepair, taking up time and money. There were students to meet and for whom to prepare classes. Bellow had a new son and a wife who chafed at the isolation and dullness of life at Tivoli, complaining, accusing, challenging him, spending his money carelessly and frivolously. To earn more, and always more, he interviewed the Chicago confidence man Yellow Kid Weil for *The Reporter,* took his "Illinois Journey" for *Holiday* magazine, wrote three book reviews and the essays on distractions and academic villainy. There was no time off. He hardly noticed his Ford Foundation grant, for which he never applied. And what difference could eight thousand dollars a year for two years make? He never saw it. His wife took it and spent it.

There were funerals to attend. A member of his family was dead;

Isaac Rosenfeld was dead; his publisher at Viking Press, Ben Huebsch, was dead. There were police stations and hospitals and lawyers' offices to run to. His friend Delmore Schwartz was in a dangerous state of collapse and Bellow organized a collection of funds to pay for Delmore's transfer from Bellevue to the Payne Whitney clinic. He was in contact with Josephine Herbst, who was sheltering Delmore's wife, Elizabeth Pollet, keeping her out of Delmore's reach. When Herbst wrote to report on Elizabeth's state of mind, she also asked him about Ford Foundation grants, and he sent Herbst a large sum of money, surprising her with his generosity. His friend Keith Botsford needed help with his first novel, *Summer Rain,* and asked Bellow how to find a way to get forty-five dollars a week. Botsford also wanted to discuss religious matters. The Newberry Library in Chicago asked Bellow to deposit his papers in their archives and he wrote to tell them he might, if they requested Rosenfeld's papers as well. The director of the Yaddo Foundation asked Bellow to serve as a member of the board and urged him to recommend writers worthy to be invited to live and work at the colony of artists. He hastily sent Elizabeth Ames the names of Arthur Miller and Ralph Ellison and, to have some peace and quiet, went himself for a short time.

In the summer of 1956, I was at Vassar College lecturing on the humanities for what was called a "Residential Seminar." Vassar was close to Tivoli and Bellow promised to visit. He wrote to me instead, on August 23, 1956, begging off because Sondra was not well enough for the trip, and Vasiliki Rosenfeld, who was visiting, should not be left alone. He, too, was trying to regain his equilibrium; Isaac's death had hit him hard. Also the house was a torment; Sondra was not good at this business and he wished only to know enough about such matters as to be able to write about them. He apologized for not asking me to visit Labor Day because there were too many repairs going on at the house, but he would be in New York, teaching at the New School, and we could meet then. Meanwhile, he was writing Henderson.

I had met Sondra at a dinner party and recall her telling me she was seldom bored. When trapped at a dull party, she amused herself by composing obituaries of the people in the room. From Reno, Bellow had written to me, asking if I had received the wedding announcement, saying he would let a Yiddish word speak for him: glücklich. "Lucky," he then was writing the dolorous "Seize the Day"; now, when everything seemed to be coming apart, in a state of turmoil and anguish and sorrow, he retreated to his cold, damp barn to write his novel of nonstop comedy. It had a plot like a Marx Brothers film, racing along from one zany situation to another, and dialogue that sounded like the one-liners from sitcom—"I am to suffering, as Gary is to smoke"—and merry descriptions of Henderson in the lion's den.

> I stood there half dead, half blind, with my throat closing and all the sphincters shut. . . . I could see myself chased all the way up [the stairs] and lying there with the animal washing its face in my blood. I expected the liver to go first, as with beasts of prey it is like that, they eat the most nutritious and valuable organ immediately. . . . She then moved off, returned behind us, came back again, and this time began to investigate me. I felt her muzzle touch upward first at my armpits and then between my legs, which naturally made the member there shrink into the shelter of my paunch. . . . I stole to the door, stepping backward, and when I reached it in very slow motion I wanted to continue through it and sit down outside to wait.

Bellow turned a deaf ear to the whirring noise of the new electric can opener and Sondra banging her saucepan down on the new stove, the unbalanced rasp of the new washing machine, and the ringing telephone; he turned his back on the plumbers and carpenters, the drillers and diggers. Exhorting his reasoning mind to leave him alone, he went off to his better world, where his imagination could do as it pleased: take him far far off to Africa, and place his ear against the belly of Willatale and listen to the rhythm of her steady old heart, talk with King Dahfu reclining on his old green couch and ministered to by his women. Better to place his hand on the flank of Atti. Bellow left behind, in the house in Tivoli, his hot shower and scented soap, his snappy hats and fine Italian shoes and Savile Row suits and became Henderson pulling on his green silk pantaloons over soiled underpants, clomping across the Hinchagara Plain in his old stinking boots with his socks rotting inside, wearing his pith helmet with his two thousand-dollar bills tucked inside the sweatband. In his barn, Bellow was total master of his house and he could sit down at his makeshift writing table and transform the annoyances to superstitions of the Arnewi, ridicule suburbia by comparing it to the affectations of the Wariri.

> With high ceremony the umbrellas were planted and an old bridge table was brought out by the amazons. . . . A silver service was brought, teapot, jelly dishes, covered dishes, and the like. There was hot water, and a drink made of milk mixed with the fresh blood of cattle, which I declined, dates and pineapple, pombo, cold sweet potatoes, and other dishes—mouse paws eaten with a kind of syrup, which I also took a rain check on. . . . I did my best to perform the social rigmarole with Horko. He wished me to admire his bridge table, and to

oblige him I made him several compliments on it, and said I had one just like it at home. As indeed I do, in the attic. I sat under it when attempting to shoot the cat. I told him it wasn't as nice as his.

Bellow sat alone, telling himself jokes about the desires and pretensions and ambitions of a Henderson who cries out "Truth! Justice! Mercy! Love!" and strives to outwit death.

"I am to suffering, as Gary is to smoke"

In "Distractions of a Fiction Writer," Bellow had said, "Out of the chaos of crude materialism and the awesome multiplicity of fact, which is unidentifiable reality, only the imagination of the artist can discover and impose order." He was writing a novel in which the chaos of materialism and the multiplicity of facts were juxtaposed with the single abiding inflexible aim of the spirit: to allow the fancy of the heart, the desire of the soul, to outwit death and so confront and transcend reality. He contrived a human subject, Eugene Henderson, who carried on a continuous dialogue with a collection of companions no Flaubert, no Proust, no Joyce would have had the audacity or, as some thought, the weakness of mind to conceive.*

The Chicago Jew—the naïve Augie March—and the New York Jew—the loser Tommy Wilhelm—become the uninhibited millionaire WASP from Connecticut; robust Eugene Henderson is another seeker, but one who will conduct the search in his own way, advised by no one. He stalks out of his house, leaving wife, children, farm, animals, habits, money, music lessons,

*Long after *Henderson the Rain King* was published, Bellow and his old friend David Peltz, a Gary contractor, went to Nigeria on a hunt for industrial diamonds. Cruising towards Murchison Falls, Bellow was deeply pleased to discover how near he had come in his story to the real Africa.

prejudices, and brutality behind and buys a one-way ticket to Africa. Henderson enters the nonexistent villages of the Arnewi and the Wariri, where in company with Romilayu, his guide, he strives to break his spirit's sleep.

"What made me take this trip to Africa?" Henderson asks the reader; after four chapters, he has still not answered the question. We do not find out until Henderson stands, pith helmet in hand, before Queen Willatale. Instead, we hear why Henderson married his first wife, Frances, why he married his second wife, Lily, how he became a pig farmer, why he plays the violin, why Lily is having her portrait painted, why he is afraid of an octopus, why he hates cats. By the time he boards the plane, we have enough facts about the man descending on the Dark Continent to follow his adventures. He is the only survivor of his family and has $3 million; he is fifty-five years old, six feet four inches tall, weighs 230 pounds, a graduate of an Ivy League university, a Purple Heart war veteran, twice married, with five children; and he is a hard drinker and a fast talker without good manners. By page four, the presentation of the facts of Henderson breaks down into an explanation of the truths of Henderson, events that occurred in the world of his soul. He has never chosen for himself, never done what he wanted, never known what that was. To please his father, he had married Frances, a woman "like Shelley's moon, wandering companionless." Frances had laughed at him when he told her his great ambition was to become a doctor. "That was the last time they ever discussed anything."

Lily, twenty years his junior, says, five minutes after they meet, "You ought to divorce your wife." Her mission in life is to marry him. He is a pig farmer because when he and Nicky Goldstein, lying under the olive trees at Monte Cassino, were planning what they would do after the war, Goldstein had said he wanted to have a mink ranch in the Catskills, and he said, "I'm going to start breeding pigs." Had Goldstein not been a Jew, he might have said cattle. He plays the violin because his father, sorrowing for the loss of the beloved son, Dick, who drowned in a river near Plattsburg—facts—played the violin in his declining years. Henderson, too, is sorrowing and hears a voice that says, "I want, I want," and tries to reach his father's spirit by playing the fiddle.

> . . . I didn't hope to perfect myself as an artist. My main purpose was to reach my father by playing on his violin. . . . I had felt I was pursuing my father's spirit, whispering, "Oh, Father, Pa. Do you recognize the sounds? This is me, Gene, on your violin, trying to reach you." For it so happens that I have never been able to convince myself the dead are utterly dead. . . . "Ma, this is 'Humoresque' for you." Or, "Pa, listen—'Meditation' from *Thaïs.*" I played with dedication, with feeling, with longing, love—played to the point of emotional collapse.

Once, while chopping wood, a chunk flew off the block and hit him in the nose. That was a fact. It was also a sign: The blow signified truth. But what truth? And once while staring at an octopus swimming in a tank in the marine station at Banyules in the South of France—all facts—he took that, too, for a sign.

> I looked in at an octopus, and the creature seemed also to look at me and press its soft head to the glass, flat, the flesh becoming pale and granular—blanched, speckled. The eyes spoke to me coldly . . . a cosmic coldness in which I felt I was dying. The tentacles throbbed and motioned through the glass, the bubbles sped upward. I thought, "This is my last day. Death is giving me notice."

The housekeeper who serves Lily and Gene each morning goes to the kitchen to get their boiled eggs, but she does not return. He goes to find her.

> I went into the kitchen and saw this old creature lying dead on the floor. During my rage, her heart had stopped. The eggs were still boiling; they bumped the sides of the pot as eggs will do when the water is seething. I turned off the gas. Dead! Her small, toothless face, to which I laid my knuckles, was growing cold. The soul, like a current of air, like a draft, like a bubble, sucked out of the window. I stared at her. So this is it, the end—farewell? And all this while, these days and weeks, the wintry garden had been speaking to me of this fact and no other; and till this moment I had not understood what this gray and white and brown, the bark, the snow, the twigs, had been telling me. I said nothing to Lily. Not knowing what else to do, I wrote a note DO NOT DISTURB and pinned it to the old lady's skirt.

He enters Miss Lenox's cottage and finds there a chaos of junk and this gathering of all the rubbish of life is the final sign.

> "Oh, shame, shame! Oh, crying shame! How can we? Why do we allow ourselves? What are we doing? The last little room of dirt is waiting. Without windows. So for God's sake make a move, Henderson, put forth effort. You, too, will die of this pestilence. Death will annihilate you and nothing will remain, and there will be nothing left but junk. Because nothing will have been and so nothing will be left. While something still is—now! For the sake of all, get out."

So, Miss Lenox went to the cemetery and Henderson went to Idlewild and boarded the plane.

This hyperactive, frenetic, mordant, neurotic, irrational man with a fluid mind, crowded with irrelevant details, clichés, commonplace phrases familiar only on the Eastern seaboard, recklessly unaware that no one outside America will have a clue to what he is talking about, this eccentric from Connecticut, will be outlandish when he carries his facts with him to visit the children of light and the children of darkness. All his memories— Frances's withering smiles and Lily's moral lectures, his army service, his boyhood, his bridgework, music lessons, taxicabs, train rides, newsprint—will be relived in the dark interior of a world that is outside history, outside civilization as he knew it. His mind wanders between present events and the bits and pieces of experiences from his past. His mind is like the rubbish in Miss Lenox's cottage.

> At night I would start a fire with my lighter, which was the type in common use in Austria with a long trailing wick. By the dozen they come to about fourteen cents apiece; you can't beat that for a bargain.

His mind scurries back and forth between the world he knew and the world he has entered. When Henderson meets the children of the Arnewi weeping for their cows, he becomes a Brooklyn cop.

> "Okay, okay, okay. All right ladies—all right, you guys, break it up. That's enough please. I get it."

He exchanges greetings with Itelo and speaks as if he was a neighbor on some Dogwood Drive in a town on Long Island, dropping in on a family at an awkward time.

> "How do you do?" I said. "And say, what's going on around here—everybody crying to beat the band? . . . This isn't a good time for a visit, eh? Maybe I should go and come back some other time?"

He must help the Arnewi get water. The American lend-lease expert takes charge.

> "So there must be something wrong with it? It's polluted? But look," I said, "there must be something you can do with it, strain it or something. You could make big pots—vats. You could boil out the impurities. . . . You'd be surprised, if you mobilized the whole place and everybody pitched in—gung ho!"

Frogs are swimming about in the cistern; that is the curse on the land. This Moses decides he will lift at least one plague. "Before long if this keeps up the town is going to be one continuous cow funeral. . . . Survival is survival." Itelo says it is forbidden. "Do you know why the Jews were defeated by the Romans? Because they wouldn't fight back on Saturday. . . . Live, to make another custom." Itelo has a more pressing custom to uphold. "When stranger guest comes we always make acquaintance by wrestle. Invariable." Like an old athlete, Henderson asks, "Can't you waive the rule for once?" No. "But I have the weight advantage on you." No.

> "Your Highness," I said, "I am a kind of commando. I was in the War, and they had a terrific program at Camp Blanding. They taught us to kill, not just wrestle."

Even as they begin to wrestle, Henderson chatters:

> "But in man-to-man combat I am pretty ugly to tangle with. I know all kinds of stuff, like how to rip open a person's cheek by hooking a finger in his mouth, and how to snap bones and gouge the eyes. Naturally I don't care for that kind of conflict. It so happens I am trying to stay off violence. Why, the last time I just raised my voice it had very bad consequences. You understand," I panted, as the dust had worked up into my nose, "they taught us all this dangerous know-how and I tell you I shrink from it. So let's not fight. We're too high," I said, "on the scale of civilization—we should be giving all our energy to the question of the frogs instead."

The fight is interrupted when he tells Itelo he is "really kind of on a quest." Itelo releases him as if he were "a sad sack." Irritated, Henderson says, "Okay, let's try it for real." "I gave him a butt with my belly (on which the name of Frances once tattooed had suffered some expansion)." When a bad blow smashes down on his vulnerable nose, he is elated. It's like the chunk of wood that struck him in his farmyard in Danbury. He has come to the right place. Here he will discover why truth must come in blows.

When he meets Queen Willatale, the woman of Bittahness—which means joy in Arnewi—and he sinks his face in her belly in proper Arnewi greeting, he feels her power in the calm pulsation of her heart and sees her person as a physical manifestation of happiness in merely being herself, and he asks himself whether truth must come in blows. What if it were a matter of simple contentment with oneself? What is the truth? "Which was *the hour that burst the spirit's sleep,*" the blow on the head or the rhythmic pounding of the heart, the awareness of pain or the awareness of joy, knowledge of death or knowledge of love?

When Willatale asks Henderson who he is and where he comes from, he stands oppressed and inarticulate, brooding:

> Who—who was I? A millionaire wanderer and wayfarer. A brutal and violent man driven into the world. A man who fled his own country, settled by his forefathers. A fellow whose heart said, *I want, I want.* Who played the violin in despair, seeking the voice of angels. Who had to burst the spirit's sleep, or else.

He must say something. Shall he ask her, "What's the best way to live?" Too abstract. He tells Itelo, "Now please tell the Queen for me, friend, that it does wonderful things for me simply to see her . . . it puts my soul at rest." He is overcome with a sense of love, this commando from Connecticut, and wishes Itelo to tell the primitive woman of Bittahness:

> "My soul is like a pawn shop. I mean it's filled with unredeemed pleasures, old clarinets, and cameras, and moth-eaten fur. . . . I am only trying to tell you how you make me feel out here in this tribe. . . . I love you. I love the old lady, too."

When Willatale asks why he has come all this way, across mountains and desert, Henderson replies,

> "Please tell the queen that I did it for my health. . . . Oh, it's miserable to be human. You get such queer diseases. Just because you're human and for no other reason. Before you know it, as the years go by, you're just like other people you have seen, with all those peculiar human ailments. . . . Who wants it? Who needs it? These things occupy the place where a man's soul should be. . . . Lust, rage, and all the rest of it. A regular bargain basement of deformities.

He adds, "Please tell the old lady for me that most people hate to meet up with a man's trouble. Trouble stinks."

"Trouble stinks." Even Henderson knows his words are not the right words. He will sing instead. He takes his text from the *Messiah*: "He was despised and rejected, a man of sorrows and acquainted with grief. For who shall abide the day of His coming and who shall stand when He appeareth?" It is the cry of his heart. Alas, he is an interloper, the wrong brother, the poor husband, the American among the Arnewi. Willatale, Mtalba, Itelo, and all the villagers listen respectfully.

"Oh, good show, sir. My friend," Itelo said.
"Grun-tu-molani," the old Queen said.

His booming voice has been answered by the primitive guttural sounds of "Grun-tu-molani." The question was Handel's; the answer lay in the words of the Queen: "Man want to live." "Yes, yes, yes! Molani. Me molani. She sees that? God will reward her, with one of those mutual aid deals." In gratitude, he promises he will rid the village of frogs.

That night, Princess Mtalba enters his hut silently and while he lies there planning how to construct the bomb, she licks him and kisses his fingers.

> If she knew what offences I had committed with those same hands, she might think twice before lifting them to her lips. Now she was on the very finger with which I had aimed the revolver at the cat and a pang shot through it and into my arm and so on through the rest of the nervous system. If she had been able to understand I would have said . . . "Beautiful lady, I am not the man you think I am. I have incredible things on my conscience and am very fierce in character. Even my pigs were afraid of me."

The hands of the Purple Heart veteran are better occupied fabricating a bomb. He politely refuses Mtalba's offer to buy him, in words that sound like a toastmaster's praise: "She's a grand person. A great human being." It would do no good, he knew, to tell her that he already had a wife. "It hadn't stopped Lily, and it certainly would cut no ice with Mtalba." Mtalba and Lily are women, savagery and civilization notwithstanding.

The bomb is constructed out of gunpowder from his bullet and from his flashlight case and shoelace. Preparations complete, the former commando tells Romilayu, "We ought to make arrangements to gather the dead frogs and bury them. We will do the graves-registration detail." Then he sets off for the reservoir, holding the bomb above his head, "like the torch of liberty in New York harbor." The villagers follow, but not all the way. "That was all right, too. In a crisis a man must be prepared to stand alone, and actually standing alone is the kind of thing I'm good at." The bomb works very well; Henderson is elated—he still has the touch—but when the retaining wall of the reservoir blows up and all the water disappears into the sands, he cries:

> "Itelo, kill me! All I've got to offer is my life. So take it. Go ahead, I'm waiting. . . . Use my knife if you haven't got your own. . . . Why for once, just once! couldn't I get my heart's desire. I have to be doomed always to bungle."

"What we do, sah?"

"We will leave, Romilayu. It's the best contribution I can make now to the welfare of my friends."

They walk back into the desert on their way to the village of the Wariri.

"What would the Wariri say if they knew who was travelling in their direction?"

"No know, sah. Dem no so good people like Arnewi. . . . Dem chillen dahkness."

Ten days of hard walking bring them to a terrain of stones. Ambushed by a company of tough tribesmen, they are conveyed by quick march to the Wariri village and placed under guard in front of an official building. Exasperated with being made to wait, Henderson bites down on a hard biscuit and breaks one of his dental bridges. There follows a history of his dental work. Bellow stops the action and, with another tall tale out of the past, Henderson remembers:

The first major job was undertaken after the war, in Paris, by Mlle. Montecuccoli. . . . Mlle. Montecuccoli had a large bust, and when she forgot herself in the work she pressed down on my face and smothered me, and there were so many drains and dams and blocks of wood in my mouth that I couldn't even holler. Mlle. Montecuccoli with fearfully roused black eyes was meanwhile staring in.

He sits, a captive of dangerous tribesmen, and recalls:

Her office was in a high building in the Rue de Colisée. The elevator was like a sedan chair and went so slowly you could ask the time of day from people on the staircase which wound around it.

The new dental bridge was uncomfortable. She said he'd get used to it soon and "appealed to me to show a soldier's endurance." The false teeth had been replaced in New York. Dr. Spohr was the dentist, and that reminds him of Klaus Spohr, the dentist's cousin, who is painting Lily's portrait. In the dark hut, he thinks sorrowfully of his teeth and of Lily; with both he has dismal prospects. His thoughts drift to his son Edward, to whom he would give zero in accomplishment. He recalls going out to California to reason with his dropout son.

"You should become a doctor. Why don't you go to medical school. Please go to medical school, Edward. . . . Go on and be a doctor, Eddy," I said. "If you don't like blood you can be an internist or if you don't like adults you can be a pediatrician, or if you don't like kids perhaps you can specialize in women. You should have read those books by Doctor Grenfell I used to give you for Christmas. I know damned well you never even opened the packages. For Christ's sake, we should commune with people."

But Eddy is in love with Maria Felucca from Honduras. So let him be. Henderson's associations drift from Maria Felucca to Clara Spohr, and thus back to the broken teeth—so much for unity in the writing of fiction, and so much for the stream of consciousness!

Henderson's recollections are interrupted by a dangerous-looking police official who asks him what was the purpose of his trip. Why had he come?

It was like the question asked by Tennyson about the flower in the crannied wall. That is, to answer it might involve the history of the universe.

Romilayu and Henderson are left alone. They open a packet of dehydrated chicken noodle soup, adding a stiffener of bourbon to the water, and then prepare to sleep. Romilayu begins his nightly prayers. "Tonight you want to make an especially good job, Romilayu." He turns aside and in the firelight he sees a smooth black body lying against the wall. The Danbury tourist says:

"They should have told us we were going to share it with another party. . . . Is he sleeping?"
"No. Him dead."

The man on quest reflects: "Why was I lately being shown corpses?" The commando drags the dead man out of the hut and chucks him into a ravine. He awakens at dawn and there, just inside the doorway, is the corpse, fetched back. The American soldier reflects:

I have seen dead men before this, plenty of them. In the last year of the war I shared the European continent with fifteen million of them though it's always the individual case that's the worst.

It is the day of the rainmaking festival and the village of the Wariri is coming to life. Henderson walks about observing the eccentric preparations. Horko, the King's uncle, arrives to escort him to the palace. They pass a scaffold from which a number of dead bodies hang upside down. "Seems to be a lot of dead people." No answer. "Dead people! I said."

> And then I told myself, "Don't ask for information with such despair." . . . I would have paid four thousand dollars in spot cash for Lily to have been brought here for one single instant, to see how she would square such things with her ideas of goodness. And reality.

Finally, he is taken before King Dahfu. The harem resembles, in temperature and closeness, a hatchery.

> I set my helmet straight and hiked up my short pants and wiped my hands on my T-shirt, for they were damp and I wanted to give the king a dry warm handshake. It means a lot.

The conversation proceeds amiably on both sides. Henderson admires Dahfu and feels at ease enough to ask him about the corpse and the inhospitality, but Dahfu interrupts the polite complaints with a direct question: "What brings you here to us, Mr. Henderson?" Henderson responds, "I am just a traveler."

He would like to say he is on quest, traveling to discover how to *Be*, as Whitman well knew, that he is in his soul weary of being taken up with *Becoming*, of always planning to live. The truth was, Becoming was beginning to come out of his ears. It was time to Be, to burst the spirit's sleep. He ends his silent reflections on his spiritual state with "Wake up America. Stump the experts." Jingoisms flow in and out of his thoughts as readily as colloquialisms color his speech. To Dahfu, he says only, "I seem to be kind of a tourist."

The tourist is uncomfortable as the King scrutinizes his body. Why does everyone take an interest in his physical self? Maybe "he has wandered into the wrestling part of Africa." He tries to talk himself out of the situation. Like many a middle-aged American would do, he tells this King he has not been in the best of health; if they are thinking of using him for a tribal sacrifice, they had better know a few facts: He runs a high temperature while pouring sweat; he broke his bridge; he has a pretty bad case of hemorrhoids; he is subject to fainting fits. It's like the chatter in an emergency ward to an intern taking a case history. The tourist is nervous.

I said, "what I have defies classification. I've been to the biggest men in New York with this, and they say it isn't epilepsy. But a few years ago I started to have fits of fainting, very unpredictable, without warning. They may come over me while I am reading the paper, or on a stepladder, fixing a window shade. And I have blacked out while playing the violin. Then about a year ago, in the express elevator, going up in the Chrysler Building, it happened to me. It must have been the speed of overcoming gravity that did it. There was a lady in a mink coat next to me. I put my head on her shoulder and she gave a loud scream, and I fell down."

He is like a late diner who has wandered into an empty restaurant somewhere in Suffolk County and realizes too late the cluster of men gathered around the far table are not eating but plotting.

I said in a loud voice, "Your Majesty, this has been a wonderful and interesting visit. Who'd ever think! In the middle of Africa! Itelo praised Your Majesty very highly to me. He said you were terrific, and I see you really are. All this couldn't be more memorable, but I don't want to outstay my welcome. I know you are planning to make rain today and probably I will only be in the way. So thanks for the hospitality of the palace, and I wish you all kinds of luck with the ceremony, but I think after lunch my man and I had better blow."

Bellow's comic style, still rooted in disjunction and disparity, now has gone beyond the catalogues and allusions, the tortured syntax and disharmonies between thoughts and actions, the expectations and realities in *Augie March*; Henderson is a good old boy, the stereotype of the ugly American on tour, a tough old braggart who sees no reason to leave his old self behind as he sets out to discover how to live the life of the spirit in exotic Africa. The children of light and the children of darkness do teach him—how to live in Connecticut. He does find a fate good enough. He is on his way to become a King.

Henderson enters the courtyard where the procession to the place of the rain ceremony is forming. He thinks:

I thought that this was like a summer's day in New York. I had taken the wrong subway and instead of reaching upper Broadway I had gone to Lenox Avenue and 125th Street, struggling up to the sidewalk.

When King Dahfu assures him the ceremonies will bring rain to a cloudless sky, he says:

"You know, Your Highness. My wife Lily subscribes to the *Scientific American* so I am in on the rain problem."

The ritual movement of each god in the pantheon of statues begins; the tourist Henderson shrieks encouragement to the fellow trying to move Hummat, the mountain god, in the words of a wrestling buff:

"Yay, yaay for you! You got him. You'll do it. You're husky enough. Push—that's it. Now up! Yay he's doing it. He's going to crack it. Oh, God bless the guy. What a sweetheart!"

Henderson is like the relative who runs up to join the band playing at the wedding reception.

Here was my chance, I knew I could do this. . . . I burned to go out there and do it. Craving to show what was in me.

He is like the third baseman on the bench pleading with his coach—Bellow's Casey at the Bat; except this Casey is trying to win a spiritual game.

To work the right stitch into the design of my destiny before it was too late. . . . "Here comes Henderson! Just let me get my hands on that Mummah, and by God . . . ! Sire, sire. I mean . . . let me! I must."

Henderson lays his cheek against the wooden bosom of the idol, and cranks down on his knees, and says, "Up you go, dearest. No use trying to make yourself heavier; if you weighed twice as much I'd lift you anyway." He carries Mummah the full twenty feet and sets her down in her new place among the other gods. His spirit is awake. He is bathed in light. Life anew! "He had the old grun-tu-molani." The rains do come and he is Henderson the rain king.
Stripped and covered with vines and leaves and given a whip and sent off to purify the ponds and wells, covered with the mud and slime of the cow pond, Henderson performs.

Yes, here he is, the mover of Mummah, the champion, the Sungo. Here comes Henderson of the U.S.A.—Captain Henderson, Purple Heart, veteran of North Africa, Sicily, Monte Cassino, etc., a giant shadow, a man of flesh and blood, a restless seeker, pitiful and rude, a stubborn old lush with broken bridgework, threatening death and suicide. Oh, you rulers of heaven! Oh, you dooming powers! Oh, I will black out! I will crash into death, and they will throw me on the dung heap, and the vultures will play house in my paunch. And with all my heart I yelled, "Mercy, have mercy!" And after that I changed my mind and cried, "No, no, truth, truth!" And then, "Thy will be done! Not my will, but Thy will!" This pitiful rude man, this poor stumbling bully, lifting up his call to heaven for truth. Do you hear that?

The reality and the appearance, the body and the spirit, the old self and the new self, the Yankee and the Sungo are so mixed up that the reader can only say, Yes. I hear that. What is going on with this crazy Henderson? Maybe he's not the WASP from Connecticut, the American, maybe he's Everyman.

King Dahfu's task is to capture Gmilo, a savage lion that roams in the wild, believed by the Wariri to contain his father's spirit; only then will Dahfu be confirmed in his role as King. "I too must complete Becoming." Henderson is extraordinarily excited. It's as if the King had heard Henderson's secret thoughts. "So tell me," he asks, "what do I illustrate most?" The answer thrills him.

> "Everything about you . . . cries out, 'salvation, salvation! What shall I do? What must I do? At once! What will become of me?'"

It is the same as Willatale had said: "Grun-tu-molani." Man wants to live. "You must understand," says Dahfu, "the Arnewi expression is only half the truth. Man wants to live, yes, but for what, why?" "How" must have a practical demonstration if Henderson is to complete his awakening; "How" must be learned in the world outside the Garden, not among the Arnewi but in the world of the Wariri. Dahfu must take Henderson to meet Atti the lion, the archetype of all reality instructors.

Across a long gallery, through a bolted door, down a long staircase, into a moldering darkness, Henderson follows, chattering:

> "What this calls for is a miner's lamp or a cage of canaries. . . . But okay, if I've got to go, down I go. One, two, three, and on your way, Captain Henderson." You see, at such a moment, I would call on my military self.

His soldierly training disintegrates when he enters the cave and sees he must traverse a long tunnel with a wooden door on the far side; he hears the low ripping sounds from behind the door and that door is ajar. He cannot budge. Captain Henderson from Connecticut trembles. "I cannot deny that there lay over my consciousness the shadow of the cat I had attempted to shoot under the bridge table. Not only the Wariri are superstitious." "I continued to entertain the obscure worry that my intended crime against the cat world might somehow be known here." His soul trembles. He was anxious about the hour that burst the spirit's sleep. He might have misapprehended the nature of it completely. How did he know that it might not be the judgment hour? "King, what do you need me here for?"

Dahfu chides Henderson. "You are still in fear." "It's a reflex." He places Henderson's hand on Atti's flank. Henderson sputters in a mixture of clichés wholly ludicrous in the situation: "Oh, Your Majesty, please. Not everything in one day." "Not many persons have touched lions." "I could have lived without it." "I don't know how much strain my heart can take." "How do you think she would behave if I keeled over?" Finally, the lion is locked in its cage and the two partners in the search for how to live converse. Grun-tu-molani is all very well, says Dahfu, but in what shape and form? "You need—" "Oh yes," Henderson breaks in,

> "Need is on the right track. . . . The form it takes actually is I want, I want."
> "Has it ever said what it wants?"
> "No . . . never. I haven't been able to get it to name names."*

All this high-class inquiry, by two such unlikely comrades engaged in a quest for the desire of the human soul, in a search for the principles of right conduct, is droll, whimsical—Bellow has always said *Henderson* was his favorite novel—and yet, why not? Henderson in a lion's den, Henderson in a harem, Henderson slinging mud at primitive totems is Bellow's parody of Bellow in the therapist's office learning how to love. Why not?

Dahfu explains the principle: Since the body influences the mind, and the mind influences the body, it makes no difference where one begins, whether through the flesh or through the intellect. The goal is unity, a process of dynamic interplay. The psyche is not a separate entity; it is the author of the body. The body, if it is strong and fearless, flexible and resilient, generates the spirit. A man is half-ass whole if he is one without the other. Not "either-or" but "both-and." Henderson believes it. So the practical Henderson will attend to his ritual duties as the Sungo, and the spiritual Henderson, quaking and yearning, will practice his physical exercises with a King and a lion.

*Part of the great mission of Senator Joseph McCarthy was to get fellow travelers to "name names." In 1956, Arthur Miller lived through the ordeal of testifying and wrote a letter to Bellow describing his experience before the House Committee on Un-American Activities. Miller refused to "name names."

Horko and the Bunam, enemies of the King, bring Dahfu's mother to plead with Henderson. The witchcraft must cease. The Bunam thrusts a horrible mummified head into Henderson's face to warn him. Again, death. Why can't he get away from death? Why is it always near him? He stares at the shriveled head with its "finished" look:

> It spoke to me as that creature had done in Banyules at the aquarium after I had put Lily on the train. I thought as I had then, in the dim watery stony room, "This is it! The end!"

That evening at prayers, Henderson exhorts Romilayu, his Virgil, to be especially fervent: "That's right, Romilayu," I said, "pray. Pour it on. Pray like anything. Give it everything you've got. Come on, Romilayu, pray, I tell you." He kneels down beside his guide.

Dahfu dismisses the warnings of the Bunam. Henderson must choose. Either he loses his fear of the lion or forfeits their friendship. Depart or agree.

> "You fled your world in order not to perish, with a hope of alteration, to resurrect your nobility, to become your best self."
> "Is there a chance for me?"
> "If you follow my directions."

This parody of the patient in Reichian analysis must purge himself of physical fear before any sense of the spirit's beauty can emerge. He must imitate Atti.

> What is this going to be, I thought, the Stanislavski method? The Moscow Art Theatre? My mother took a tour of Russia in 1905. On the eve of the Japanese War. She saw the Czar's mistress perform in the ballet.

He argues: Atti doesn't try to be human, why should I try to act the lion?

> "Are you afraid?"
> "I can't even bring my hands together to wring them."

Henderson does begin to walk. Then he is running, fast, but not brave. "King, King, wait, let me go in front of you, for Christ's sake." He falls and lies prostrate in the dust. Why, he asks, must he go through this? "Oh," he remembers, "high conduct, high conduct."

Henderson has scratched his hand. He licks his wound. It is only a small catlike gesture, but it is his beginning. Since he is down already, Dahfu suggests he remain on all fours and assume the posture of a lion. So he does. It's not hard to crouch. Not enough. He must also roar. Henderson moans. No, roar! He produces a kind of rumble in his throat.

"And glare as you do so. Roar, roar, roar, Henderson-Sungo. Do not be afraid. Let go of yourself. Snarl greatly. Feel the lion. Lower on the forepaws. Up with hindquarters. Threaten me. Open those magnificent mixed eyes. Oh, give more sound. Better, better," he said, "though still too much pathos. Give more sound. Now, with your hand—your paw—attack! Cuff! Fall back! Once more—strike, strike, strike, strike! Feel it. Be the beast! You will recover humanity later, but for the moment, be it utterly."

Dahfu, the parody of the Reichian therapist, is leading Henderson through the necessary steps to health. True, he tells Henderson, the body and face are painted by the spirit of man, but we bungle it by identifying ourselves with the wrong associates. "Think of what we could be if we used our imagination to change our nature, gay, brilliant, good, beautiful, noble. We have only to use our imagination to conceive ourselves as such, and so we will be." Alas, thinks Henderson, Dahfu is right. It wasn't to offend Goldstein, the Jew, that he had said "pigs" but because there was pig in his nature. Oh, can he replace his pig self with a self akin to the noble lion? Dahfu assures him he can. By imagining himself noble, he will become noble.

Imagination is a force of nature. Is this not enough to make a person full of ecstasy? Imagination, imagination, imagination! It converts to actual. It sustains, it alters, it redeems.

He knows it will take him a longish time because, as he says ruefully, he has the accumulation of a lifetime of pig. Meanwhile, his hair grows shaggy; when he coughs he grunts; he snorts. Is he still afraid of Atti?

"Damn right I am. I'd sooner jump out of a plane. I wouldn't be half so scared. I applied for paratroops in the war. Come to think of it, Your Highness, I think I could bail out at fifteen thousand feet in these pants and stand a good chance."

Henderson from Danbury tries to explain to his simple guide all that is happening.

"Americans are supposed to be dumb but they are willing to go into this. It isn't just me. You have to think about white Protestantism and the Constitution and the Civil War and capitalism and winning the West. All the major tasks and the big conquests were done before my time. That left the biggest problem of all, which was to encounter death. We've just got to do something about it. It isn't just me. Millions of Americans have gone forth since the war to redeem the present and discover the future. I can swear to you, Romilayu, there are guys exactly like me in India and in China and South America and all over the place. Just before I left home I saw an interview in the paper with a piano teacher from Muncie who became a Buddhist monk in Burma. You see, that's what I mean. I am a high-spirited kind of guy. And it's the destiny of my generation of Americans to go out in the world and try to find the wisdom of life. It just is.

Does Romilayu understand?

"Why the hell do you think I'm out here, anyway?"
"I don't know, sah."
"I wouldn't agree to the death of my soul."
"Me Methdous, sah."

The final episode in the novel is the lion hunt. Tame Atti only paces beneath the palace; Gmilo, "your dad, the late king," roams the bush. They leave the town in a hammock followed by the executioner, all calcimined in white, an omen of death. There is no weapon. "I didn't have so much as a diaper pin to defend myself with. . . . King . . . Hsst. Wait a minute. . . . Just like this? Are you supposed to catch this animal by the tail?" Dahfu must not wound Gmilo. A son may not harm his father. Henderson decides he will do the best he can with his helmet. They reach the hopo, a cone-shaped trap designed to capture the lion alive. Henderson lumbers along after Dahfu, who is now in a frenzy of power and will. Henderson, who had so carefully constructed his bomb out of flashlight batteries and a shoelace, is busy planning. "I could pull down these green pants and bag the animal in them." Loyal, faithful, he renews his covenant with the King: "King . . . you see these hands? It is your second pair of hands. You see this trunk? . . . It is your reservoir, like."

They ascend the hopo and reach a platform dangling some twenty-five or thirty feet in the air.

A sob came out of me. It must have been laid down early in my life, for it was stupendous and rose from me like a great sea bubble from the Atlantic floor.

Dahfu walks across a slender pole. With the grace of a tightrope walker, he balances a spinning net attached to the rope in his hands. He tests the pulley. Once the lion enters the hopo, he will drop the net for the capture. Only this? asks Henderson. Tradition! says Dahfu. "Can't there be an innovation? drug the animal . . . give him a Mickey." He is ever the man from Connecticut.

From the high platform, Henderson sees a small stone building hidden in the ravine.

> "Does somebody live there below? In our part of the country where farming has gone to hell, you come across old houses everywhere. But that's a crazy place for a residence."
> "It is not for living."

While they wait for Gmilo, Henderson, still the tourist, shows Dahfu photographs of Lily and the children, and his Purple Heart citation.

Suddenly, there is a rush of small beasts fleeing the approaching lion. Some enter the hopo. "They rushed the opening like immigrants." A hyena is the only animal to look up. It snarls at Henderson. "I looked for something to throw at it. But there was nothing with us on the platform to throw and I spat down instead." When the lion crashes in, Henderson takes one look and prays:

> "Oh my God, whatever You think of me, let me not fall under this butcher shop. Take care of the king. Show him Thy mercy." And to this as a rider, the thought added itself that this was all mankind needed, to be conditioned into the image of a ferocious animal like the one below.

With that rider, that one phrase, "all mankind needed, to be conditioned into the image of a ferocious animal like the one below," Bellow cut his attachment to orgone boxes and office visits and acting-out and seats of life force and everything else Wilhelm Reich would ever have to tell him.

The net to bag the lion is attached to a pulley; Dahfu, the rope on his arm, the rim of the net twirling, balances on the pole above. The pulley does not hold. The rope breaks and Dahfu falls. True, the treacherous Bunam has tampered with the ropes; true also, Dahfu has failed to drop the net with accuracy and caught only half the lion. No knife, no gun, no Mickey, Henderson, the loyal pledged brother, has only himself to throw into the pit to help. The old commando winds the rope around the hind legs of the lion a dozen times and captures it. The Bunam puts the muzzle of his gun to the temple of the beast and shoots it. Alas, the telltale ear is not the ear of Gmilo. This lion was not the father. Dahfu is dying and whispers, "The Sungo is my successor."

> "Your Majesty, move over and I'll die beside you. Or else be me and live. I never knew what to do with life anyway and I'll die instead. . . . The spirit's sleep burst too late for me. I waited too long. I ruined myself with pigs. I'm a broken man. And I'll never make out with the wives."

The king of the Arnewi and the man from Connecticut are placed in the house of death. Henderson weeps. "It's wasted on dummies." (Life is.) "They give it to dummies and fools." (We are where other men ought to be.) He is still the interloper, still the wrong brother to survive.* Henderson falls to the floor, bent double, and cries without limit. His clothes are stained with Dahfu's blood.

> Well, I thought, maybe this is a sign I should continue his existence? How? To the best of my ability. But what ability have I got? I can't name three things in my whole life that I did right. So I broke my heart over this too.

Like Tommy Wilhelm, his tears flow, for himself and the dead. Fifteen years later, Charlie Citrine will take Humboldt's gift as a sign he should continue the existence of Von Humboldt Fleisher. Henderson pauses in his lamentation: Maybe he does have royalty in him, maybe he should stay and rule in Dahfu's place, and service those women, start life over again, in a new place. But no. "I've gotten to the age where I need human voices and intelligence. That's all that's left. Kindness and love." Henderson decides truth, even if only barely perceived, must be tested in the real world; truth, if it remain an intellectual exercise, is useless. Henderson must return to his civilization.

Romilayu crouches in the side chamber. Beside the figure of the dead king, they find a lion cub tethered, and he tells Romilayu it contains the spirit of his friend. When they escape, they carry the lion cub in Henderson's pith helmet, feeding it a mash of worms and locusts.

When they arrive at the edge of Baventai, the old Henderson exults:

> The brown Arabs in their clothes and muffles watched us arise from the sterile road, myself greeting everyone with two fingers for victory, like Churchill. . . . "Get the band. Get the music."

*So Artur Sammler will think, reflecting on the death of Elya Gruner; so Citrine will think, reflecting on the premature death of Von Humboldt Fleisher.

When he tells Romilayu the meaning of their experience, it is the new Henderson who explains:

> "Is it promised? Between the beginning and the end, is it promised?"
> "What promise, sah?"
> "Well, I mean something *clear*. Isn't it promised? Romilayu, I suppose I mean the reason—*the* reason. It may be postponed until the last breath. But there is justice. I believe there is justice and that much is promised . . . the sleep is burst. . . . What I'd like to know is why this has to be fought by everybody, for there is nothing that's struggled so hard as coming-to."

Wandering among the villages of Africa, his old life had colored his reflections; now, understanding what he experienced in Africa, he is prepared for Connecticut. The King had been dishonest. "The king let me in for a lot of trouble, too, by allowing me to move Mummah. That he did." That King, like any commoner, lived under the omnipresent threat of death. So does every man. One forgives duplicity and betrayal and secrets. This same Dahfu had been his friend as best he could. Had he fallen, Dahfu would have mourned him, just as, he now realizes, had he died instead of his brother, his father would have mourned as much for Eugene. It's life. He will return to Lily. He believes she loves him. Even if she only seemed to love him, that, too, was better than nothing. "Either way, I had tender feelings toward her."

He gives Romilayu the jeep. "You have my address. Write to me. . . . Next time we meet I may be wearing a white coat. You'll be proud of me. I'll treat you for nothing." So back: to Khartoum, to Cairo, to Athens, to Rome, to Paris, to London, to Newfoundland. On the plane, he looks into the eyes of a Persian child, also traveling to America.

> Two smoothly gray eyes moved at me, greatly expanded into the whites—new to life altogether. They had that new luster. With it they had ancient power, too. You could never convince me that *this was for the first time.*

He steps down from the plane, onto the frozen ice of eternal winter, and he draws deep breaths of pure happiness.

How will it be for Henderson now that he has burst his spirit's sleep? One page before the end of the novel, Henderson thinks, "Lily will have to sit up with me if it takes all night . . . while I tell her all about this."

No one sat up with Bellow to listen.

Henderson the Rain King was published on February 15, 1959; the following November 11, Bellow had broken irrevocably with Sondra. By the time I went to visit the house in Tivoli, a couple of years later on my way up to Maine, she was long gone. Bellow sat writing at an old table placed in the center of the remodeled kitchen with its GE appliances arranged efficiently along one wall, with a large Anderson window installed to bring daylight to the new stainless-steel sink. The wooden cabinets, refinished and gleaming, were empty except for one cupboard half-filled with a neat stack of S. S. Pierce gourmet specialties—turtle soup, shrimp bisque, brandied fruit, seasoned vinegars. "My souvenirs." Bellow asked whether I would like some peanut butter and grape jelly on white bread. He was too busy to do much shopping. He was writing *Herzog.*

Violations of the Spirit

10

Well aware *Henderson* would meet with complicated interpretations, Bellow publicly cautioned his readers on the day after the book appeared in print, with an essay he wrote for the Sunday *New York Times Book Review*, flagged "Deep Readers of the World, Beware!" He began humorously:

> "Why, sir," the student asks, "does Achilles drag the body of Hector around the walls of Troy?" "That sounds like a stimulating question. Most interesting. I'll bite," says the professor. "Well you see, sir, the 'Iliad' is full of circles— shields, chariot wheels and other round figures. And you know what Plato said about circles. The Greeks were all mad for geometry." "Bless your crew-cut head," says the professor, "for such a beautiful thought. You have exquisite sensibility. Your approach is both deep and serious. Still I always believed that Achilles did it because he was so angry."[1]

Soon he became explicit; it was, he wrote, better to approach a book from the side of naïveté than from that of culture—idolatry. "Is modern literature scripture? Is criticism Talmud?" Much good it did; what journalist or critic approached anything from the side of naïveté?

What Bellow could not forestall was the negative response. On Sunday, February 22, 1959, the week after Bellow's warning appeared, the *Times* featured the first attack by Carlos Baker, a professor at Princeton

University. Professor Baker admitted *Henderson* was "a form of discourse to which the present reviewer is not strongly drawn," but, he promised the Sunday readers, he would try, and so he did, concluding that Bellow was forcing himself to be inventive, that the portrait of Africa was as far from reality as was Tarzan of the Apes, that Dahfu talked like a cross between Uncle Remus and the Emperor Jones, that the episodes of the novel read as if they had been taken out of Kipling's "Just So" stories.[2]

The New York Times usually accords important writers two reviews, one for its daily, one for its weekly readers, and Bellow was thus twice smitten. Orville Prescott said, on Monday, the novel was prolix and exasperating, an unsuccessful experiment, noble in purpose but dismal in result, so far from reality one half-expects to meet Tarzan, the adventures just silly, Henderson a bore, "cursed with the most embarrassing flow of fancy talk in a library of recent fiction, the apotheosis of fatuous egotism."[3] Thus the attack began; the novel was described everywhere as unclear, puzzling, unsatisfactory, long-winded, forced, awkward, flawed, sprawling, mumbo jumbo, heavy going, and insincere. Henderson was Daddy Warbucks trying to explain Spinoza; Henderson was a book with its belly hanging out of its trousers; Henderson was vague, abstract, metaphysical.

Commentary printed a long review by Richard Chase, a professor at Columbia University.

> We doubt whether Bellow should have sent him off so soon to Africa. We perceive that the author is not always able to make his highly imaginative Africa into an adequate setting for his hero. We fear that Bellow is in danger of confusing Henderson with another pilgrim to Africa, Hemingway. We feel that the book wanders uncertainly for a bad hour in the middle.[4]

Chase concluded with a remark that linked *Henderson* to all Bellow's earlier novels: "What is so far chiefly missing in Bellow's writing is an account of what his heroes want to be free from." *Atlantic Monthly* printed Charles Rolo's assessment that "Henderson, presumably a symbol of American unrest, is an attempted tour-de-force which has failed to come off—an impression of labored cleverness and stretches of pseudo-portentous mumbo-jumbo."[5]

Elizabeth Hardwick, the friend of the family of *Partisan Review*, wrote for them so harsh an assessment of *Henderson* that Dwight Macdonald, the friend who left the family and remained Bellow's friend for some thirty years, felt angry enough to send a letter of protest to *Partisan* and insisted the magazine print it in the same issue in which Hardwick's review appeared.[6] Hardwick called Henderson a kind of well-born, well-heeled beat-nik; said Africa was a joke Africa with whimsical tribes, fat native queens, and a faithful guide, a travelogue Queequeg, darkly devoted. She continued that the book was deliberately without any characters at all; that it was neither fantasy nor satire and not especially exuberant, that is, it was neither *Don Quixote* nor *Gulliver's Travels* nor *A Sentimental Journey*. She felt it didn't even have symbolic meaning: "the events have too little resonance for symbolic fantasy." She granted the book was not a falling off from Bellow's previous work; it was simply a "mutation." She concluded her piece with a sharp warning:

> This last novel is an incredibly secure piece of composition—profuse, splashy, relaxed. It is large and Bellow seems to want largeness, as though he felt his own position as an important American novelist imposed the responsibility for a large effort. He will not, knowing our artistic retreats, be guilty of "the refusal of greatness." But he may, eager courtier, travel too far in pursuit.

Dwight Macdonald defended the book and castigated the editors of *Partisan* for printing such a review. Why, he asked, did a critic as clever and witty as Miss Hardwick miss the obvious point about *Henderson* and maunder on about the lack of symbolic meaning? Why did a journal that purported to understand modern literature fail to recognize it when it appeared? He concluded his letter with an admonishment to Hardwick; Bellow, he said, was "pulling in his horns in order to penetrate deeper . . . giving up his ambition to be great in order to be good."

Writing for the *New Republic,* a month after *Henderson* appeared, Reed Whittemore reviewed the early reviews and counted four approvals, with qualifications, five disapprovals, with qualifications, and then he registered his vote and brought the tally to four and six.[7] Theodore Ross, writing for the *Chicago Jewish Forum,* could scarcely contain his indignation. Bellow's purpose, in writing *Henderson the Rain King,* was a wrong-headed, almost treasonous attempt to "Christianize the uniquely Jewish experience and uniquely Jewish spirit for the sake of transmitting that unique context into something vaguely acceptable to everybody under the sun."[8] Ross's comments on *Henderson* seemed only to be a spark for what Ross had always wished to say to Bellow directly: Never mind love, Bellow, you should have said Law; never mind art or great ideas, Bellow, you should have said faith and humility; never mind mankind, Bellow, you should have said the chosen people!

Fiction writers were more kind. Bernard Malamud wrote a personal letter to Bellow to say *Henderson* was wonderful; he described the pleasure he felt in reading such a wise and imaginative piece of modern fiction as a banquet for his soul.

Henry Miller wrote to Bellow from Paris to say he thought the book admirable and so did his friends; by coincidence Miller's agent also represented Bellow in France and when Miller was about to recommend the book to him he discovered negotiations to publish *Henderson* in Paris were already under way. Miller wrote again from Big Sur to tell Bellow all Europe was talking about *The Rain King* and his Italian publisher was interested.

Fiction writers and friends were not tastemakers. *Henderson the Rain King* had a disappointing sale and eventually drifted out of the public eye, falling into the panniers of the literary journals where serious interpretations were heavier and longer. Notions came to light year after year, redescribing the book as an allegory of Emersonian transcendentalism, as an allegory of the evolutionary destiny of man as his spirit and soul and imagination strive in their search for the meaning of life, as an allegory of the dangling American, of the alienated American, of the alienated modern man as a symbolic Jewish WASP.

In 1979, I asked Bellow about those early days, how he felt about the critical reception of *The Rain King*. He only meant, he said, to say in *Henderson* there is a distinction between complacent self-righteousness and the creative life of the spirit. "Oh well, I just write stories." Bellow knew there was a good deal more in the book, but he liked in casual conversation to talk as if he, too, were naïve, to say that he just writes stories. I asked him whether he seriously believed that just by saying he is only a writer of fiction, readers can forgive what he says in his fiction.

"Here you sit exposing our delusions about ourselves, telling us that beneath the veneer of civilized man there really is a vulgar brutal aggressor, and, you show us that beneath the scarrings and mutilations of the savage there really is a forthright, virtuous, and vulnerable human being—"

Bellow put up his hand in protest, saying the book was a comedy.

"True. That's true. *Henderson* is funny. But the writer, and that's Bellow, is telling us there are children of light and children of darkness in London and Paris and Rome and Danbury, there is a child of light and a child of darkness in every man, that, say, the octopus of foreboding death lays its face against the consciousness of each sleeping person and each dreamer struggles to wake from the same nightmare. Do you think you can say all that and arouse nothing but admiration of your skill? Do you honestly think you can say the whole world is obsessed with money, status, and power, and that we are all deluded, that we have all jeopardized our souls, without provoking hostility?" He replied that no one *had* to read what he wrote.

Bellow really expected people to play the game his way, to accept his premises. He stubbornly refused to admit that they weren't and that they wouldn't. However, he probably had no grief about the critics. It rolled off his back, especially since he had come into bad times then, was living through a hostile year. It was the year Bellow's cousin died and his nephew died and his wife Sondra asked him to leave.

When Bellow sat down to write *Herzog,* the innocent and naïve Augie March was long gone, the Grun-tu-molani man, Eugene Henderson, worn out. Asa Leventhal came back into focus as Moses Herzog, total victim, betrayed by his wife, Madeleine, and his best friend, Gersbach, betrayed, too, by the moral bankruptcy of America, a victim of realities far worse than Leventhal had surmised. Herzog is not innocent or ignorant of the duplicity and faithlessness in his private world, nor of the chicanery and hypocrisy of the public world.

Sitting on a garden chair on the lawn in Vermont in 1979, Bellow talked about the 1950s as if it were a week ago. He seemed frozen in time. The lover, the wife, the betrayal were as vivid to him as all had been when he wrote *Herzog* and would remain so in the stories and novels to come. Bellow probably never has revealed the whole truth about the affair between his wife Sondra Tschacbasov and his friend Jack Ludwig, and no doubt the wife and the friend would agree. What we see, however, reading Bellow's fiction as a whole, is Madeleine as a template of Bellow's characterization of women: the self-fulfilling prophecy of Thea Fenchel, who bewitched and betrayed Augie March; the mistress in Connecticut waiting irritably for Tommy Wilhelm. She will recur in Angela, the bizarre, coarse sexual animal who shocks Artur Sammler; she will return again as Renata, who prefers a screening of *Deep Throat* to high conversation with Charlie Citrine at the Plaza, and who absconds at the last with Flonzaley, the undertaker. Her scent will trouble Ijah Brodsky; and her violet eyes smolder on the beautiful mask that is the face of Matilda Layamon. Though she be at the last portrayed as a miniature woman, a tough little doll who prefers to follow her snowmobile salesman and live in his motor home, bringing baubles to flea markets rather than take Kenneth Trachtenberg for a husband, this Treckie will crave her sexual abuse and her secrets.

In my journal, I speculated that Bellow appeared more distressed that everyone except him knew what was going on, but I had already read *Herzog* and knew that Herzog had gone about from friend to friend, relative to relative, demanding they tell him when they knew about Gersbach and Madeleine. Ludwig lived not far from Tivoli with his wife, Leah, and his daughter, Susie. Sondra was the loyal friend of the Ludwig family. When

Bellow was offered a job at Minnesota that fall, Sondra insisted he take it. She wanted a winter away from Tivoli. She needed more action. Bellow must tell them he wouldn't go unless they hired Ludwig, too, and he did actually ask Ralph Ross, who was a member of a special humanities program at Minnesota, to take Ludwig. There was no chance Ludwig would be kept on at Bard, and Bellow was able to put pressure on Ross. He was the good friend with the power to work it out. Ludwig did go with the Bellows to Minnesota. Bellow told me it was after he rented a house and all the furniture was in place, that Sondra threw him out. It would be months before he understood what was going on.

Also a Canadian by birth, Jack Ludwig thought of himself as a writer, although he had only a few short stories to show. He had earned his Ph.D. at the University of California at Los Angeles in 1953 and went east as an adjunct teacher of literature at Bard College. I had met Jack Ludwig at a Halloween party years earlier, in the apartment that became the setting of "A Father-to-be"; it was a costume party, and there Ludwig sat in a huge black cape, a flowing black cravat, and a soft black fedora, leaning forward to balance on a heavy cane. He told us all he was Ivan Karamazov.

Bellow and Ludwig had long been planning to launch the literary magazine that would eventually become *The Noble Savage*, and while Bellow was off establishing residence in Reno for his divorce, Ludwig was seeking funds for the project. He wrote cheery letters of easy camaraderie combined with the down-home expressions of a family man. A letter dated October 7, 1955, is breezy, with quaint phrases and Yiddish expressions, joined with information about his efforts to secure money for *The Noble Savage*, unsuccessful efforts for the most part.

The Noble Savage was intended to offer an alternative to those dreary academic or commercial and slick or program-oriented magazines Bellow detested. He wished to create a showcase for new young talent. Eventually, Bellow convinced Meridian Books to publish and distribute the journal and provide some financial backing. He asked a young friend, Keith Botsford, to serve as the third editor and they began piecing together the first issue.[9] Ludwig and Botsford were not compatible co-workers, as a letter written by Ludwig on July 10, 1959, shows. Ludwig, who was in Canada visiting family, wrote to Bellow, spending his last summer with his wife and three-year-old son in Tivoli; Botsford was in Puerto Rico.

Ludwig began with a flourish and went on with an indignant report of Botsford's high-handed dealings with him, anger disguised as gaiety, spoof and satire, falling into Yiddish invective at the end.

After the Bellows separated, and obviously before Bellow was aware of betrayal, Ludwig remained at Minnesota for another year of teaching, meanwhile negotiating a new job elsewhere. On June 20, 1960, Ludwig wrote again to Bellow to complain about the progress of *The Noble Savage,* blaming Meridian for bad faith, suggesting that the journal find another backer.

Ludwig registered at great length his anger at Meridian's decision to limit the number of copies printed of the second issue of *Noble Savage* to six thousand. Ludwig blithely dismissed, with a single line, Bellow's complaint at Ludwig's editorial note which introduced the long and, at times, dull piece by D. H. Lawrence.* For Bellow's information, he described how busy he was, with his new hour-long TV show, on the air five nights a week, and his successful negotiations with Knopf to buy his contract from Viking, with good advances and nice royalty rates.

Bellow left Sondra on November 11, 1959. He put up briefly at Yaddo, briefly at Herbert Gold's apartment in New York, briefly back at Tivoli, and then took off for Poland and West Germany, ready to have a lecture tour anywhere, even one sponsored by the United States cultural affairs office. He had been dismissed by a wife who accused him of arrogance and selfishness and contempt, and worse. He took flight, but he was no Herzog climbing out the window of a friend's house on the Vineyard to escape her sympathy and heartiness.

In the archives there are letters from women in Aspen, in Serbia, in Chicago and London, pleas from Italy and Poland, from Indianapolis and San Francisco, reminders from Cannes and Paris, Dubrovnik and Yaddo. Two photographs hung on the wall in the "Color Room" of Kenneth's Hair Salon on Fifty-seventh Street in New York: One was of Marilyn Monroe; the other was Bellow.

He thrashed about as wildly from lectern to lectern. In the archives, there are letters inviting Bellow to lecture, to speak informally, to teach, to read, anything he cared to do—beckoning him to Northwestern University, to North Carolina State University at Raleigh, to Purdue, to Columbia College, to Barnard College, to Texas Technological College, to the University of California at Los Angeles, to San Francisco State College, to the Educational Alliance in New York, to a book club in Darien, to the First Methodist Church in Evanston. Some invitations he accepted gladly; others he dismissed politely.

It was not until months after the separation that Bellow learned of Sondra's long affair with Ludwig; the facts—reality!—came as a profound

---

*In every issue of *TNS,* under the heading of "Ancestors," there appeared a piece of fiction from the past. Lawrence's work was a preface to *Memoirs of the Foreign Legion* by Maurice Magnus, hardly fiction. It took up seventy-five pages of the second issue.

shock. After all the fireworks of his soul in search of a unique destiny, of a fate good enough, he was after all, in truth, the most commonplace of victims. His wife and his best friend, and he the last to know! To be dismissed unloved and unwanted was bad enough, but to be a fool? Moses Elkanah Herzog will become a lonely tearful man, recollecting, reflecting, justifying himself, and the story of his betrayal would become the basis for the plot of *Herzog*.

Because of legal contracts, it took a year to remove Ludwig's name from the masthead of *The Noble Savage* and replace him on the editorial board with Aaron Asher. Ludwig protested bitterly at the slight, at his being sent "to Coventry." Bellow retreated to a teaching job at the university in Puerto Rico. Undulations of the long grapevine finally reached him there. Exploding in indignation, Bellow wrote to Ludwig, criticizing Ludwig's performance as an editor, then hinting at the hypocrisy, the duplicity of the man, calling himself an idiot for having accepted friendship such as Ludwig offered. He closes by noting that Coventry was not the place to which he would consign him.

Lawrence Durrell and J. P. Donleavy wrote to Bellow offering to send something for *TNS*, but it was too late. Publication ceased after the fifth issue. Bellow alone paid the outstanding debts incurred by the experiment.

Ludwig left Minnesota for a permanent position at the newly established branch in Oyster Bay (later moved to Stony Brook) of the State University of New York on Long Island. Sondra and her son left Minnesota and moved on to bide some time in Skokie, Illinois. Eventually she settled herself in Great Neck, a ten-minute ride from Roslyn, where the Ludwigs, wife and now two daughters, Susie and Brina, were living. Bellow sat down, at wherever his kitchen table happened to be, and began the novel for which he would be voted the equal of Hemingway and Faulkner.

For a while, the table was in Puerto Rico; for a while in New York, when he stayed at his house in Tivoli; for the most part in his apartment in Chicago, where he lived with his third wife and third son. In 1961, Bellow had married Susan Glassman, daughter of Dr. Frank Glassman, a Chicago orthopedist. Susan does not enter *Herzog*—she is reserved for *Humboldt's Gift* and *More Die of Heartbreak*—but Herzog's "love-bandit," Ramona, is in part a borrowing of Rosette C. Lamont, a professor of comparative literature at Queens College.

Bellow had been writing a play—in all of this, Bellow was writing a play—and he had been invited by a newly formed group, "The Theater of Living Ideas," to give a reading. Rosette Lamont was brought to the gathering by Bellow's old friend, the Italian literary critic Paolo Milano. Years later, Professor Lamont wrote a review of *Mr. Sammler's Planet*, and in it she describes her first meeting with Bellow. By no means a dreary, suffering, withdrawn Moses Herzog, he impresses her as a thriving, sociable, ebullient, active man.

> We were all guests of Aaron Asher, [Bellow's] editor at Viking. . . . "Bellow reads with charm and humor," Milano had promised. "He likes to try out some of his work in progress on people he trusts." As I looked around the West Side living room of the Ashers, I recognized Mike Nichols, tall and surprisingly languid, the bird-like profile of Jules Feiffer, and the round, jolly face of the novelist Grace Paley. Bellow had not arrived; he was driving down from his house in Tivoli.
>
> The bell rang—I have since come to realize that Bellow makes a game of punctuality—and there was a ripple of laughter in the foyer. The man who entered the room had a shock of white hair, but the unlined, sun-tanned face was younger than the one I had seen in the newspapers, or on book jackets.
>
> As soon as hands had been shaken and old friends embraced, we sat down and roles were distributed. Bellow kept for himself that of his protagonist, the antihero Bummidge, Nichols volunteered for the part of the business manager, and Linda Asher, our hostess, interpreted all the women of the play. It was a spirited rendition, and the author often stopped his own reading to share in our merriment. He laughed at some of his own lines in that spontaneous, utterly natural way in which the truly handsome enjoy their own bodies.[10]

The first version of *The Last Analysis,* the manuscript he had taken to the Ashers, Bellow knew was far too long and he decided to put it aside for the time being and devote himself to *Herzog.*

Rosette Lamont visited Bellow that summer in Tivoli and they began to correspond, the letters traveling between Queens and Tivoli, between Queens and Puerto Rico, eventually between Europe—when she went abroad—and New York or Chicago; between, that is, wherever the two happened to be, Rosette telling him about her travels and the people she was meeting, and aglow with pleasure at the reception of her article on *Dr. Zhivago*, reporting that John Don Passos had read it and said, "This girl is a genius." She sent the article to Bellow, along with some advice. She had read his remark to an interviewer, when asked what he wanted to do most, that he wished only to be allowed to lead his own life and write. That, she said, was a strange thing to say. There were people in concentration camps who did not harbor such thoughts. After all, he was free, and the only person who did not allow him to live his life was he himself, at least that part of himself that would not let him exist as fully as it was in him to exist. She wanted him to become once again that Saul Bellow she had met a year before, the one who had arrived with his hat tilted over one eye, smiling, full of faith in the moment and in the future. Then she went on with her news of New York, describing her interview with Ionesco, her meetings with Marcel Duchamp and Elie Wiesel. She asked Bellow for his news.

While Bellow was in Puerto Rico, in his mail there also came letters from Susan Glassman, who fondly used pet names and sent him love. Rosette Lamont had lost. A letter from Herbert Gold to Bellow, dated December 16, 1961, congratulated Saul and Susan on their marriage. There are no more letters from Rosetta Lamont in the archives.

Long ago, in December of 1978, I came by train to Chicago to meet with Bellow. I wanted a long space of uninterrupted time to reread *Herzog*. We spent an hour or so at the Blackhawk, then taxied to his apartment on Sheridan Road. I asked Bellow why, after so demoralizing an experience with Sondra, he had rushed into marriage with Susan, who seemed to me a duplication of his second wife. Had he not recognized that? He admitted to me, so I recorded in my journal, that when he met Susan, she seemed intelligent, really smart, knew literature, and he was so worn out, so utterly weary, he was willing to believe her when she offered him total care, promised she would take care of everything, that he would not have to do anything ever again in the practical world. He hoped it would work out. He feared from the first it would not.

Bellow lived for a year at Tivoli with Susan Glassman and his third son, but Susan preferred New York, where she had a job teaching the seventh grade at the Dalton School, and so he also kept a small apartment in Manhattan. It was all temporary. In 1960, Alan Simpson, then Dean of the College at the University of Chicago, asked Bellow to teach a course in the modern novel. The winter quarter of 1962 seemed like a good time to get back to his city. Bellow gave the keys of Tivoli to Ralph Ellison, who wished to live in the country to work on his second novel without distractions, and went home. He told an interviewer at the time, "I feel I have unfinished business here in Chicago. I don't know what it is, but I'm trying to find out."

One piece of unfinished business was *Herzog*. Another was Susan Glassman. The third marriage took the least amount of time to collapse, but the legal quarrels, with their charges and countercharges, suits and countersuits, were to continue through *Mr. Sammler's Planet* and *Humboldt's Gift* and *The Dean's December*.

Bellow interrupted his conversation with me to stare in silence at the design in his carpet; then he studied the photograph of Rudolf Steiner that stood on his desk; he rose to stand for a moment before the medal given to him by the French government. Still on its velvet presentation tablet, the medal decorated a wall in the foyer.

His marriage lasted only three years. In my journal I wrote down his description of their return to Chicago, Bellow saw he had tied in with a different kind of political, social, and cultural crowd. Susan introduced him to a kind of upper middle class—Lake Shore Drive people—he never knew existed. Her father was a doctor and she seemed to know everybody who counted in Chicago.

It was true. I put myself through the University of Chicago working as a receptionist for two doctors who shared an office in the Monroe Building. In the morning, I worked for an eye-ear-nose-throat man, Dr. Benjamin Levee, the son-in-law of Moe Annenberg, who was in jail for income tax evasion. His wife was Polly, who wore a mink coat so heavy, I dropped it on the floor the first time she shrugged it off her shoulders into my hands. Her brother was Walter Annenberg. I remember Jake the Barber bringing his wife for treatment—two bodyguards standing in the waiting room—and there was old Mrs. Block of Inland Steel, with her silent companion; and once there was peppery, no-nonsense Jack Arvey. In the afternoon, the doctor was Frank Glassman, and he had a fluffy little daughter named Susie, to whom I gave lollipops and some coloring books and crayons for her to pass the time while she waited for her daddy. She grew up to become Mrs. Saul Bellow the third, and, in time, Dr. Layamon's wide-shouldered daughter, Matilda.

The Chicago to which Bellow returned was the third piece of unfinished business. When he went back to his city, he experienced the kind of culture shock a traveler may feel on arrival at Kennedy airport after a month in any country outside America.

Chicago had been the city to which Bellow's father took him as a boy. True, he had left it; he had lived in a dozen cities since, traveled in many countries; he had taken his father's legacy and bought a country house in New York; he had won prizes with his talk about reality and the imagination and the soul; but he had never given up trying to understand what had become of his past, the public world as well as his private world. Now he observed that his family and his old friends and acquaintances had grown prosperous and practical, some dissemblers, some frauds, and a few were not even trying any longer to bring Bellow to his senses. They seemed not to care much one way or the other. Those who cared were dead. Those who cared were creatures in his fictions. He observed that Chicago, which had nourished him, was now the most racially segregated city in the United States, with the largest black ghetto in the nation, and the most corrupt police force in the nation, and the most debased judicial system in the nation, with unethical judges and cynical lawyers, and a political leadership that had no patience with sentimentality and principle. Mayor Daley was the Papa Doc of Chicago. This Chicago was a reality far worse than any he had surmised, a Chicago threatening, duplicitous, faithless, like America.

When he sat down to write *Herzog,* he chose to depict a man not only striving to come to his senses but a man obsessed with the need to bring

America to its senses. That is the role of the letters that Herzog writes: to express his outrage at the betrayal of the immigrant's dream. In 1960, in 1961, in 1962 and 1963, Bellow was thinking as much of the disintegration of society as he was lamenting the collapse of marriage. His desire to love and be loved had ended in hatred and betrayal, but there was worse treachery to explain than killer wives and crafty friends. Chicago was a predator and Chicago was the simulacrum of America and America worked hard at the business of the world.

Bellow needed to understand how it could happen that Eichmann could be caught, taken to Israel to be tried and found guilty and be hanged, and his friends sit around arguing about the banality of evil. He needed to understand how it could be that Robert Kennedy wanted integration of the races and Malcolm X wanted separation of the races and the John Birch Society would agree with Malcolm X. He needed to understand how it could be that black activists would sit down to order coffee and doughnuts at a lunch counter and be served that coffee in jail; how 100,000 people could stand at the reflecting pool near the White House and listen raptly to Martin Luther King, Jr., say "I have a dream" and then all their fellow citizens could watch on their television screens the orderly progress of 3,000 soldiers escorting James Meredith into his classroom.

Bellow was well aware of all that was happening in America and the world during the years he was writing *Herzog*. The Berlin Wall rose between East and West Germany and Khrushchev was entertained lavishly in Hollywood. Alan Shepard rose 116.5 miles in space and whirled aloft for fifteen minutes, then Gherman Titov whirled about for more than twenty-four hours, and Gagarin orbited the earth once and John Glenn orbited the earth three times and Gordon Cooper went twenty-two times around, and the Russians sent up Valentina Tereshkova. Picard went seven miles down into the sea. Belgium said let the Congo go; Britain said let Nyasaland go; France would not let Algeria go. Africa was fragmenting into more than thirty independent states; Europe was unifying into the Common Market; France would not let England enter in. Castro took Cuba; China took Tibet; Ethiopia took Eritrea; and India took Goa. U.S. troops arranged to keep the peace in Vietnam; a U.S.S.R. missile base arranged to keep the peace in Cuba. It was CORE and DNA and RNA and ICBM and strontium 90. Pete Seeger sang "Where Have All the Flowers Gone?" Bob Dylan sang "Blowin' in the Wind." There were earthquakes, tidal waves, hurricanes, revolutions, guerrilla warfare, and galaxies were discovered to be moving away from the earth. Jacqueline Kennedy called the times "Camelot." America was dancing the Twist. Herzog would say sadly halfway through his recollections:

> I fail to understand! I fail . . . but this is the difficulty with people who spend their lives in humane studies and therefore imagine once cruelty has been described in books it is ended.

Herzog will reflect, pausing in the midst of his letter to the *Times*:

> Let us all dress in our shrouds and walk on Washington and Moscow. Let us lie down, men, women, and children, and cry, "Let life continue—we may not deserve it, but let it continue."

Herzog, haunted by private grief, is also Herzog haunted by public duplicity and moral bankruptcy. What do we have to say? What are we going to write about? Rosenfeld and Bellow wondered when they decided to become writers. In *Herzog*, Bellow knew what to say. His narrator no longer strives to break his spirit's sleep; he no longer seeks a fate good enough for himself alone; he would awaken the comatose spirit of all men and find for them, as well as himself, a unique destiny.

Bellow wrote a number of essays during the time he was composing *Herzog* and they give evidence of a writer fully cognizant of and appalled by violations of the spirit that came of the betrayal of citizens by the leaders of their society. In "The Sealed Treasure," in "The Writer as Moralist," in the Gertrude Clark Whittal Lecture delivered at the Library of Congress, afterward published as "Some Notes on Recent American Fiction,"[11] Bellow said yes, the world is overcome by Spam and beer, is covered with detergent lathers and poisonous monoxides, but that is not the only injustice in the world: There is injustice in the misuse of power, in the piety of the psychoanalytic understanding of violence, in the self-righteous justification of opportunism, in the dangers of bureaucracy, in the pretense of alienation, in contempt for the common man, in hostility toward thought and feeling and imagination and the soul. All this is as immoral as the cutting down of timberland and the feeding of hormones to chickens. He still clung to his belief, his optimism: In every heart, there is a sealed treasure, a hidden source of power, an innate intelligence, an intuition, oh yes, there is spirit and soul that generates the courage every heart requires to confront the rot and threat of experience.

So he said in his lectures and essays. Just as Bellow borrowed observations and memories from his own life to create his characters, and borrowed events from his own experiences to give those characters a story, so, too, Bellow lent his thoughts about society and culture and politics to Herzog so that Herzog can write his letters.

Letter writing was no happenstance device Bellow hit upon to use in his novel. Moses was a weeping man, isolated, reaching out to a world that ignored him. Bellow was not. Bellow was swimming hard, sometimes cold and tired, but swimming with strong strokes against a current of abuse and misuse. The world did not ignore him. During these frenzied years, Bellow was inundated by letters and he answered them all and put them in the mail.

> Send me your birth hour so that I can do an astrology chart for you.
> Push me at Viking.
> Join in our pilgrimage (World Federation of Bergen-Belsen Associates).
> Can we use your name to establish American Playwrights?
> Become a participant in our lecture bureau.
> Write a piece on Lyndon Johnson *(New Republic)*.
> Participate in a talk show (University of Chicago, BBC).
> Be on the board to choose outstanding faculty members for our Horace Gregory Award.
> Host a foreign writer (International Hospitality Center).
> Have you a Jewish short story for Faber & Faber?
> Write for our Literary Annual.
> Take a stand on Dr. Szasz's books.
> Read my article and tell me if I am right about Wilhelm Reich and Henderson.
> Do you want to rent your home in Tivoli?
> Write a letter supporting my application for a grant.
> Send my poems to Viking.
> Help me get that teaching job in Puerto Rico.
> Read my manuscript.
> Send us a manuscript.
> Join the Chicago Novels project.
> Join the Edinburgh Festival of the Arts.
> We are doing education films, will you participate?
> Write a piece for *Modern Occasions*.
> Do you know any American authors we should publish?
> Contribute an article for *Perspectives of New Music*.
> May I translate *Seize the Day* into Japanese?
> Help me to come to the United States.
> Speak out against Russian aggression.
> Write a blurb for Di Donato's *This Woman,* for Yves Berger's *The Garden,* for V. L. Cassill's *Clem Anderson,* for Walker Percy's *The Last Gentleman,* for Cynthia Ozick's first novel.

He corresponded with new young writers, accepting or rejecting their manuscripts for *The Noble Savage,* and when the journal folded, he read their typescripts nevertheless, and sent them advice. He corresponded with Lillian Hellman about his play, with Robert Lowell, Herbert Gold, Lawrence Durrell, George Elliott, John Berryman, John Cheever, and John Hawkes, with Ralph Ellison and Wright Morris, with Mark Harris and Norman Rosten. Leon Kirchner wished to compose an opera based on *Henderson*; Paul Heller wished to make a film of *Henderson*, Harry Horner to make a film of *The Victim*. Bellow wrote to his family, to old friends in Chicago, in Los Angeles, London, New York, and to new friends, well, to whoever wrote to him from wherever they happened to be. And all this time he was writing *Herzog*, and rewriting *Herzog*—up to the time he received the final galleys.

Bellow lent Herzog the literal facts of his own life, some left in, some left out, pushing a little this way or that, distorting, fusing, fragmenting, splitting. He borrowed his father, mother, brothers, sister, aunts, uncles, cousins, wives, mistresses, friends, enemies, his "archetypes," as he calls them, the figures who inhabit his psyche, not because they are universal prototypes but because in his life he knew them. He borrowed his memories and day-dreams, his humiliations, for he, too, is a remembered person demanding to be redescribed, contended with once more, assessed anew. He also lent Herzog his ideas and observations and judgments and warnings. Out of those turbulent years, he created *Herzog*, the book that remained on *The New York Times*'s list of best-selling novels for a solid year.

11

"Dear Mama, As to why I haven't visited your grave in so long . . ."

"Truth! Truth! Justice! Justice!" and "Mercy," too, was Henderson's cry. Now Herzog appeals for truth and justice—mercy is out of reach.

Henderson was well-meaning, loyal and loving, and when he left suburban life behind, he was confident his wife and children, house and pigs, would wait, tucked in place, while he, wearing his pith helmet with the nipple peak, went off to Africa on his mysterious quest for self-discovery. Then, on his way back, suffused with good intentions, wearing his new green velour hat with the happy feather, he thinks of Lily and says:

> Lily, I probably haven't said this lately, but I have true feeling for you, baby, which sometimes wrings my heart. You can call it love. . . . Dearest girl, everything is going to be different from now on.

What happened?

Herzog's kitchen, like the shabby cottage of Miss Lenox that had so frightened Henderson, is what happened.

> The kitchen was foul enough to breed rats. Egg yolks dried on the plates, coffee turned green in the cups—toast, cereal, maggots breeding in marrow bones, fruit flies, dollar bills, postage stamps and trading stamps soaking on the formica counter.

It is Madeleine, not Lily, who waits for Herzog, and when they quarrel, it is not about the neighbor's cat.

> Madeleine had come back from Sloan's Bath Shop with luxurious fixtures, scallop-shell silver soap dishes and bars of Ecusson soap, thick Turkish towels. . . . She brought home loads of groceries from the Pittsfield supermarkets. Moses was continually after her about money. . . . It was always something trivial that set him off—a bounced check, a chicken that had rotted in the icebox, a new shirt torn up for rags. "Where's all the dough going? I'm working myself sick." He felt black with rage inside.

Madeleine is more than a match for Herzog's anger.

> "Yes, I know, your darling mother wore flour sacks. . . . I suppose you'll start on my upbringing now—my lousy, free-loading bohemian family, and chiselers. And you gave me your good name. I know this routine backwards. . . . Spending your dead father's money. Dear Daddy! That's what you choke on. Well, he was *your* father. . . . Don't try to force your old man down my throat."

Herzog pleads for some order in their surroundings. She scoffs at his delusions.

> "You'll never get the surroundings *you* want. Those are in the twelfth century somewhere. Always crying for the old home and the kitchen table with the oilcloth on it and your Latin book. Okay—let's hear your sad old story. Tell me about your poor mother. And your father. And your boarder, the drunkard. And the old synagogue, and the bootlegging, and your Aunt Zipporah. Oh, what balls!"

The Lily who pursued Henderson, promising to save him from his melancholy sense of disconnection from life, has become Madeleine, who scorns Herzog's affectations.

> "But you gave me LOVE, from your big heart . . . yes, cured me of menstrual cramps by servicing me so good. You SAVED me. You SACRIFICED your freedom. I took you away from Daisy and your son, your important time and money and attention."

"Just think a minute," Herzog pleads.

> "Think? What do you know about thinking?"
> "I'm learning."
> "Well, I'll teach you, don't worry!" said the beautiful pregnant Madeleine between her teeth.

Herzog had thought things were improving. Madeleine slams the bedroom door, the bathroom door, the kitchen door, soon the car door. The dearest girl Lily had followed Henderson where he led. Paris? Connecticut? Good. Does he wish to go alone to Africa? She kisses him goodbye and waits. Madeleine refuses to be buried in the remote Berkshires; Herzog closes down the house in Ludeyville, abandoning books, English bone china, and new appliances to the spiders, moles, and field mice. They move to Chicago, where Madeleine slams the door on Herzog, finally.

> "We can't live together any more. It's painful to have to say. I never loved you. I never will love you, either. So there's no point in going on."

Glücklich is over. The fairy tale of his life is over.

> The husband—a beautiful soul—the exceptional wife, the angelic child and the perfect friends all dwelt in the Berkshires together. The learned professor is at his studies.

Thrown out of Madeleine's house, Herzog retreats to Ludeyville, where bones of dead birds lodge in the toilet bowl and only wasps and owls are present to hear him sort things out. His headquarters is that same kitchen.

The white paint was scaling from the brick walls and Herzog sometimes wiped mouse droppings from the table with his sleeve, calmly wondering why field mice should have such a passion for wax and paraffin. . . . A rat chewed into a package of bread, leaving the shape of its body in the layers of slices. Herzog ate the other half of the bread spread with jam. He could share with rats too.

Instead of Henderson's vague cry, "I want, I want," Herzog's heart's desire is to consummate his existence, to recognize truths that will free him to love others, and to learn to abide with the knowledge of death in full clarity of consciousness. He must confront the attributes of the Herzog he has been—a bad husband, a loving but poor father, an ungrateful child to his parents, an affectionate but remote brother, lazy in love, dull in brightness, an egoist to friends, an indifferent citizen, passive before power, evasive to his soul—and overturn them to become the Herzog he may yet be. He must retreat from the outside world to tell himself the story of his life, to recall the events that brought him to such bitterness and despair.

He roams within the boundaries of his twenty acres of hillside and woodlot, wanders from his mattress thrown on the floor, to the sagging Récamier couch, to the torn hammock, reliving his betrayal and defeat. The internal life is tough to confront. Reflections on his experiences become chaotic; the hard truths throw his mind out of gear, chronology gives way, memories attack memories, associations intrude on recollections, but still he must proceed. It is the only way he can restore himself. The prize will be the renewal of courage: to live, to try again to be Herzog.

He questions himself. Why had he accepted the right of his shrew of a wife to throw him out? Why had he traveled to Europe, so melancholy, so reckless? Why such horror when he discovered he had not been rejected but betrayed? Why such loathing that the love affair between Madeleine and Gersbach had been common knowledge? What need to go from one friend to another, from one member of his family to another, demanding they explain when they knew the truth? What difference did that make? *He* had failed to justify himself. They defended her. They called *him* the traitor. Who sympathized? Who understood? *He,* too, despised himself—more than he condemned Madeleine and Gersbach. They deserved each other. His revenge must be to restore himself—by himself. Does he have to go it alone? He can go it alone. A house and a man, decrepit and forlorn, can be reconnected. Only he can explain himself to himself. Only he can distinguish appearance from reality and teach himself essence.

At first he has not the strength, however. Herzog sits at his kitchen table writing letters.

> Late in the spring Herzog had been overcome by the need to explain, to have it out, to justify, to put in perspective, to clarify, to make amends. . . . Hidden in the country, he wrote endlessly, fanatically, to the newspapers, to people in public life, to friends and relatives and at last to the dead, his own obscure dead, and finally the famous dead.

The valise he has dragged along with him is crammed with notes to people he knows and knew, his son, his first wife, his mother-in-law, his psychiatrist, Madeleine's psychiatrist, her priest, his Aunt Zelda, his brother, old friends—Nachman, Sono, Libbie, Himmelstein, Asphalter—and new friends—Ramona, Wanda, Zinka—to his mother and to God. Now he sits immobile at the kitchen table writing to people in Washington and Chicago and Japan and Warsaw and Belgrade and Trieste and Beersheba and Paris, to people who are in the grave, who are in Heaven. He writes to tell them what has happened to him, to explain his defeat.

Is he a victim of Madeleine and Gersbach only? Has he not been betrayed by something worse than two such lovers? Herzog's mind slips and wanders and shifts while he writes his letters. He breaks off the letter he is composing to his psychiatrist to write a letter to Madeleine's doctor, Edvig, to inform him of the true character of his patient. He interrupts himself to write a note to Professor Byzhkovski, who gave him a copy of his book about the American occupation of West Germany; he must tell Byzhkovski he has overlooked the equally important occupation by Soviet troops of East Germany. Herzog suspends that in order to write to Dr. Beasley to suggest that, while his work with bums on the Bowery was all very well, he ought to realize that poverty on Third Avenue is related to moral poverty on Wall Street. Why doesn't Beasley do something about that? He writes to the credit department of Marshall Field and Company to say he is no longer responsible for the debts of Madeleine P. Herzog. He quits to address Dr. Hoyle, asking how the Gold-pore theory actually works. He decides, however, he had better write to Dr. Bhave and inquire about his plan for Utopia. Then he thinks he ought to deed his house and property to the Bhave movement. It will help with his taxes.

His briefcase becomes stuffed with letters written to public figures living and dead, to intellectual leaders, politicians and social activists, philosophers and bureaucrats—to Martin Luther King, Adlai Stevenson, Police Commissioner Wilson, his alderman, Mr. Nehru, Mr. Udall, Dear Willie the Actor, Dear Spinoza, Dear Herr Nietzsche—to anyone who maintains a position and offers a program. He has a need to set them all straight, to tell them they are wrong, to correct them. He judges their goals, their work, their theories, their politics. He writes a note to himself:

Dear Moses E. Herzog:
    Since when have you taken such an interest in social questions in the external
world? Until lately you led a life of innocent sloth. But suddenly a Faustian spirit
of discontent and universal reform descends on you. Scalding. Invective.

Herzog is as outraged at the way things are in the world as he is appalled at
himself. His anger and bitterness at his personal losses are matched by his rage
at the violations of integrity and morality in the public world. He scoffs at
his own errors and misjudgments; he challenges his own hypocrisy; he denounces his own spurious self. He scoffs at, he challenges, he denounces the
errors and hypocrisy of a world more spurious.

    Part Four is a good example of the way in which the public and the
private worlds collide in Herzog's mind. It is morning and he is at his letter
writing. His eyes narrow, he clears his throat, and begins a note to Monsignor
Hilton, who had instructed Madeleine in her conversion to the Catholic
faith. Monsignor should know the kind of person he baptized. Herzog's mind
drifts to her beauty and he asks himself, Was it her beauty he misses or is
he angry she dumped him for that "loud, flamboyant, ass-clutching brute
Gersbach"? He remembers his first wife, Daisy, also beautiful, and he recalls
his betrayal of Daisy, many times left, finally abandoned in Philadelphia while
he ran off to New York to be with Sono Oguki. He recalls his father's anger
at Moses's dissolute life, and remembers his own son, Marco. His mind shifts
to the long train rides between Philadelphia and New York, his reading
Kierkegaard, and he pauses now to argue a point Kierkegaard had made about
the death in life. That idea leads him back to his letter to Monsignor, not
to continue about Madeleine but to explain why the Roman Church cannot
serve these times, and he writes to say he is himself a specialist in intellectual
history and to his mind it is not a question of the defeat of Western religion
and thought but a question of the nature of ordinary human experience. "The
strength of a man's virtue or spiritual capacity is measured by his ordinary
life." His mind flits back to Philadelphia and he remembers sipping warm
milk, alone in his single room, and his memory lapses into a long reflection
on Madeleine's father, Pointritter, a charlatan, a sensualist, who asked, "Are
you in love with my daughter? Congratulations! Take her!" That memory
leads him to Madeleine's mother, Tennie. She, too, had said to take her. "You
won't hurt her, will you?" Ha! She wants Madeleine to have the best. Yes,
he had promised. And now Madeleine had returned her husband "like a cake
or a bath towel to Field's."

    His recollections shift to Madeleine in her apartment in New York;
he sees her again as she rose from their bed, a dewy naked girl, to dress and
become the prototype of a sober conservative woman of forty, fit to walk

down the aisle of a church for morning mass, to pray a little before going off to work. A true con artist. He returns to his letter, adds a phrase, then drifts back to remembering how they passed a fish store on their way to breakfast and he thinks of his mother, who came from the Balkans and loved fish. So the chapter proceeds, in fragments, in longer narrative passages, from private world to public world, from good friends to bad, from marriage to marriage, from his present broken self in New York to his childhood in Montreal. In the same manner, the entire book proceeds, leaping back and forth in time and place, breaking off one incident to describe another, jumping ahead, falling back, then further forward and further back, an illogical, inchoate rendering of Herzog's convolutions of thought and spirals of feeling. The reader must hold fast to the thread of the story of Herzog's struggle to restore himself to balance.

In a departure from Augie March's progress from mentor to mentor, arriving at last at a program for living that may justify his gift of life, Herzog is the reality instructor of Herzog and his memories and reflections are tangled, sometimes loose, sometimes taut, sometimes broken off and lost. To be sure, there has been flashback and free association juxtaposed with an ongoing narrative action before *Herzog*. However, in *Henderson the Rain King,* the recovery of the self occurred within a simple framework of travel, from Connecticut to the Arnewi to the Wariri and a return to Connecticut, but Herzog goes nowhere. He lies on his couch remembering, and when he finally pulls himself together, it is only to ride a few miles to the general store and back. For the single traumatic experience, akin to that of Tommy Wilhelm, Bellow devised a style far more complex, with incongruities that flow one into the other, juxtapositions with the borderlines confused, multiplicities of consciousness without demarcations, simultaneities of feelings without transition. Herzog's letters mingle, jump, switch, suspend; Herzog's cold judgments and sentimental outcries and frenzied appeals mingle, jump, switch, suspend. Out of all this disorder, Herzog nurses himself back to stability and coherence. His equilibrium arises out of chaos. He cries "I'm falling apart" at the beginning of the novel and declares at the end, "*I* am Herzog. I have to *be* that man. There is no one else to do it." He abandons, at the beginning, his treatise on Rousseau and Robespierre, Kant and Fichte, and at the end is eager to take up his new project, to write a cycle of poems for his little daughter June, and he fills his hat with rambler roses.

Herzog's self-discovery is an internal process; he goes over the ground of his life, again and again, to figure out where he went wrong, where he deflected himself from his own good common sense that always told him his primary need was to enliven his soul, to become a specialist in spiritual awareness. His leaps and shifts from private recollections to public issues, from memories and reenactments to notes and letters, show him that his compulsive need to redress his reputation was no more than self-indulgence, a way to soothe his vanity, to assuage his ego. He comes to realize (as Rosette Lamont had reminded Bellow) there are others who suffered more than he. There is no glamour in suffering, no status achieved by an individual who despairs. He shares a common fate and deserves no special dispensation because he is Herzog. Whatever he was, well, that was what he was; what happened, happened. More dangerous, far worse, more in need of redress, is society. In the public world, there are more gross departures from intelligence, as much evil and corruption and distortion and carelessness and irresponsibility as ever he need admit was present in his own heart.

So the private memories begin to be interrupted. For example, Herzog, lost in Ludeyville, recalls his wedding supper prepared by Phoebe Gersbach; he remembers how a tearful, dancing Valentin Gersbach toasted Madeleine and Moses. That leads him to a recollection of an older friend, a boy out of his childhood, tearful, too, not dancing, Nachman. He decides to write a note to Nachman:

> I know it was you I saw on 8th Street last Monday. Running away from me. It was you. My friend nearly forty years ago—playmates on Napoleon Street. The Montreal slum.

Vividly, that adult Nachman, the "stooped poet" who "took one look at Moses and ran away," appears before him. An older memory of Nachman in Paris intrudes, Nachman in despair at the loss of his wife, little Laura locked in an insane asylum. Herzog was not the only man to suffer.

From there, Herzog drifts into his long recollection of his childhood. "We did play on the street together. I learned the Aleph-bet from your father Reb Shika." He remembers the schoolroom, and his mind carries him back to his old house on Napoleon Street, to his father, to Ravitch the boarder, and the stories he had heard of his father's early life in Russia, of how he had come to Canada, struggled and failed, tearful and defeated, too. Herzog reaches further back, to his father's father, the old scholar, the scholar his mother hoped he would be, and there appears before him the memory of his mother, her gray hair, her toothless smile, her wrinkled fingernails, her endless labor, and he compares his beloved mother to his overbearing, pompous Aunt Zipporah, fat, rich, selfish, practical, a realist who wished to run the Herzog family. Herzog subsides into a mist of listening to the old quarrels, the plaintive cries of his father. No, not only Herzog suffered.

He stares down at his letter to Nachman. Why finish? He has no address for Nachman. His mother was dead. And Nachman's wife, dead. "Poor thing, poor thing—she too must be in the cemetery."

The pattern of interplay between letters and recollections pervades *Herzog*. In Part Two, there is another good example: Herzog begins a letter to his Cousin Asher in Beersheba, but decides to write to the President instead, to tell the President he is wrong to be so optimistic about his new tax legislation—it is discriminatory, will aggravate unemployment and lead to crime. He shifts to address Professor Heidegger, who is wrong about "the fall into the quotidian." "When," he asks Heidegger, "did this fall occur? Where were we standing when it happened?" He pauses to write to Strawforth of the U.S. Public Health Service, to tell him he is wrong about the Philosophy of Risk. Risk? Risk reminds him of the dangerous lunatic Field Marshal Haig, who drowned thousands of thousands of men in the mud holes of Flanders. And de Tocqueville, too, was dead wrong. Democracy had not produced less crime, more private vice. He tells de Tocqueville that as it turned out, there is less private crime, more collective crime. Herzog's mind shifts to Nietzsche, to Whitehead, and John Dewey and then he loses the thread altogether. A little poem about grasshoppers—his daughter Junie's favorite song—comes into his head and he smiles. He has a child, after all. Two children. Thus the turbulent man sunk in isolation and bitterness restores himself.

As Herzog reflects on public violations of integrity, the less evil do the private betrayals seem to be. The greater the hypocrisy and corruption of society, the smaller the treachery and villainy in the acts of Madeleine and Gersbach. The catastrophe of betrayal is soap opera and suds. His obsession is foolish and wasteful. What he ought to be doing is reconstructing himself, creating a character that will enable him to confront society, not the two jokers who deceived him.

He can do it. He has always had an intuition of what was really important. Herzog reminds himself of his visit to Poland: drab Poland, in all directions freezing, ruddy gray, the stones still smelling of wartime murders. Had he not scented the old blood? Gone many times to visit the ruins of the ghetto with Wanda, his guide? Herzog is tough on himself. He reminds himself, too, how he had turned his back on his own understanding, had shaken his head and shrugged, and kissed Wanda's knuckles and seduced her. It was the false Herzog, the little wounded man, who thought only of his betrayal by a neurotic wife and a gimpy psychopath. Is he still sitting here, writing his whining notes crying for sympathy? Dear Wanda. Dear Zinka. Dear Libbie. Dear Sono. He remembers Sono.

On Sono's bed, he had stretched out, dried and powdered, dressed in a kimono, drinking tea spiked with Chivas Regal, turning the pages of her collection of erotic scrolls. Oh yes, Herzog was the betrayer of Herzog.

> Is this really possible? Have all the traditions, passions, renunciations, virtues, gems, and masterpieces of Hebrew discipline and all the rest of it—rhetoric, a lot of it, but containing true facts—brought me to these untidy green sheets, and this rippled mattress?

"O mon philosophe, mon professeur d'amour!" Sono had cried. Yes, he was a philosopher, but not of love. It was true:

> [he] cared only about the very highest things—creative reason, how to render good for evil, and all the wisdom of old books. He thought and cared about belief. (Without which, human life is simply the raw material of technological transformation, of fashion, salesmanship, industry, politics, finance, experiment, automatism, etcetera, etcetera. The whole inventory of disgraces which one is glad to terminate in death.)

Oh yes, he looked and behaved like a philosopher. What then was he doing listening to Sono tell him how she bargained for a blouse on Fourteenth Street?

What then had he been doing buying a coat of crimson and white stripes and a new oval straw hat? He had said to the salesman "that in the Old Country his family had worn black gabardines down to the ground." He had stood before the mirror and seen another Herzog reflected in the glass.

> . . . he looked like his father's cousin Elias Herzog [who] wore a skimmer like this one, set on this same head of hair shared also by *his* father, Rabbi Sandor-Alexander Herzog, who wore a beautiful beard as well.

What then had he been doing "groomed, scented, and his face sweetened for kisses," lying on a bed waiting for his beautiful mistress Ramona to appear? He, the reasonable Herzog, was capable of thoughts of modern man in this century, of transition and mechanization, of man pressured, devalued; he, the intelligent Herzog, could think of the chapter of his book, wondering how best to proceed with his discussion of Rousseau, Kant, Hegel. Why then was he at the same time listening to Ramona's whining Egyptian record, staring at the bathroom door?

> At this moment Ramona appeared. She thrust the door open and stood, letting him see her in the lighted frame of bathroom tile. She was perfumed and, to the hips, she was naked. On her hips she wore the black lace underthing, that single garment low on her belly. She stood on spike-heeled shoes, three inches high. Only those, and the perfume and lipstick. Her black hair.

What was he doing here? Proving to Madeleine he could make it with women?

> End this grief, this idleness you suffering joker! Sexual struggles and paltry sexual pleasure is not the goal of your vague pilgrimage.

Herzog's notes to himself begin to admonish *him*, advise *him*, demand that *he* weigh, reason, take himself on his way.

> For Christ's sake, don't cry, you idiot. Live or die, but don't poison everything.

What was the use of telling his story over and over again? He recalls going in despair to his old buddy and his Chicago lawyer, Sandor Himmelstein. How could Himmelstein help him?

> "Come, settle down in Chicago and sell the dump in the Berkshires, get a housekeeper or a girl who survived the concentration camps and we'll lead the good life, we'll go to the Russian baths and find ourselves an orthodox shul and track down a good *chazan.*"

While Himmelstein talked, had not Herzog been thinking of the general conditions of common people, of their great need, of their hunger for good sense, clarity, and truth? What could Himmelstein tell him? His craving for help and confirmation and justification was useless. Unclean really. He was not the only one to struggle with unhappiness. Why should he demand justice for what a Madeleine and a Gersbach did to him?

> Most of mankind has lived and died without—totally without it. People by the billions and for ages sweated, gypped, enslaved, suffocated, bled to death, buried with no more justice than cattle.

And you, he chastizes himself, you, Moses E. Herzog, are bellowing at the top of your lungs to have justice?

Social organization, for all its clumsiness and evil, has accomplished far more and embodies more good than I do, for at least it sometimes gives justice. I am a mess and I talk about justice.

He judges himself harshly. He is too weak, too self-absorbed.

True, personal life is a humiliation, and to be an individual is contemptible, but what goodness can we hope to achieve, and how can we exercise our benevolence and love alone, being so emotional and passionate, so much a creature of deep peculiarities, such a web of feeling intricacies and ideas, never independent, never able to understand it all through the intellect, never holding on to it through the heart.

The dream of a man's heart cannot be reduced to living out the fairy tale of a happy life on the farm or in the suburbs.

The dream of a man's heart, however much we may trust and resent it, is that life may complete itself in significant pattern. Some incomprehensible way. Before death. Not irrationally but incomprehensibly fulfilled. There is always, for every man, another chance, even if it is a last chance, to know justice. Truth.

He grows more and more excited by his comprehensions and new resolves. He writes to Smithers, an academic administrator:

O Smithers, my whiskered brother! What a responsibility we bear, in this fat country of ours! Think what America can mean to the world. Then see what it is. What a breed it might have produced. But look at us—at you, at me. Read the papers if you can bear to.

He writes to an old boyhood friend, now become an academic killer, a hack, an intellectual cheat. He castigates Shapiro, not for his phony pretentiousness, his fancy talk, his leering at Madeleine when he came to visit them in Ludeyville, but for his phony ideas and his bankrupt morality.

Are all the traditions used up, the beliefs done for, the consciousness of the masses not yet ready for the next development? Is this the full crisis of dissolution? Has the filthy moment come when moral feeling dies, conscience disintegrates, and respect for liberty, law, public decency, all the rest collapses in cowardice, decadence, blood? . . . Commonplaces of the Wasteland outlook, the cheap mental stimulants of alienation, the cant and rant of pipsqueaks about Inauthenticity and Forlornness. I can't accept this foolish dreariness. We are talking about the whole life of mankind. . . . A merely aesthetic critique of modern history! After the wars and mass killings. You are too intelligent for this. You inherited rich blood. Your father peddled apples.

Herzog is healing himself. True, he leads a muddled intellectual life, and he is, he admits, a poor soldier of culture, but, he tells himself, he has not lost his human sympathies; he, with his memory, has custody of all the dead: "I am the nemesis of the would-be forgotten." His work is awareness, "extruded consciousness was his line, his business. Vigilance." Thus Herzog is able to explain to himself what he ought to be doing in his life. Yes, he is Herzog who practices the art of circling among random facts, but he is Herzog who can swoop down on the essentials. He has eyes, nostrils, ears. Let him hear, smell, see. He has intellect and heart. Let him consider. He recognizes, too, he is Herzog, a throb-hearted character.

But I am. I am, and you can't teach old dogs. Myself is thus and so, and will continue thus and so. And why fight it? My balance comes from instability. Not organization, or courage, as with other people. It's tough, but that's how it is. On these terms I, too—even I!—apprehend certain things. Perhaps the only way I'm able to do it. Must play the instrument I've got.

To "play the instrument I've got" requires he turn his back on Gersbach and Madeleine. Yes, he has cause enough to hate the man—Gersbach has spread the rumor that Herzog's sanity has collapsed; Gersbach has stolen his wife—but what was he, after all, a moral megalomaniac, a radio announcer, a disc jockey, a man with a wooden leg, a dandy with the eyes of a prophet, a *shofat*, yes, a judge in Israel, a king, who lectured to Hadassah women on Martin Buber, a frequent weeper of distinguished emotional power, a misuser of Yiddish expressions, so booming in conversation, so emphatic in style, so impressive in his glances, you forgot to inquire whether he was making sense. A Goethe, a poet in mass communications; a Gloria Swanson; an Emil Jannings; a Czarist general; a family man. Kill Gersbach? It was sheer theater to think it. How could he be broken by such a man?

Or such a woman? He takes a long final look at this Madeleine when she arrives at a police station to collect their daughter. He stares at her blue eyes, straight Byzantine profile, the small lips, the chin that pressed on the flesh beneath.

He thought he could make out a certain thickening in her face—incipient coarseness. He hoped so. It was only right that some of Gersbach's grossness should rub off on her. Why shouldn't it? He observed that she was definitely broader behind. He imagined what clutching and rubbing was the cause of that.

Yes, she was masterful, efficient, but too severe, too proud, too much a mixture of "pure diamond and Woolworth glass." "Sweet as cheap candy." What did she know of him? Nothing. She would never have power over him again. "I'm out of this now. Count me out. . . . I withdraw from the whole scene as soon as I can. Goodbye to all."

So Herzog's eyes begin to shine, not with tears but elation, sitting at his kitchen table in Ludeyville. He will paint an old piano a bright apple green for June. It is responsibility and love that make a man human, that enable a man to live a good life. Weakness or sickness is copping a plea. Monstrous egoism is vanity. Herzog has become the man who may now write a letter to God:

Dear God:
   How my mind has struggled to make coherent sense. I have not been too good at it. But have desired to do your unknowable will, taking it, and you, without symbols. Everything of intensest significance.

He is ready, at last, to finish his letter to his mother, for that was where he began his journey to health. His first letter had said, "Dear Mama, As to why I haven't visited your grave in so long . . . ," but then he had stopped. Five days of self-scrutiny told him why he had not visited her grave. Now he can write a letter that is free of self-pity, the words of a man on the track of truth.

Dear Mama:
   The life you gave me has been curious . . . and perhaps the death I must inherit will turn out to be even more profoundly curious. I have sometimes wished it would hurry up, longed for it to come soon. But I am still on the same side of eternity as ever. It's just as well, for I have certain things still to do. And without noise, I hope. Some of my oldest aims seem to have slid away. Life on this earth can't be simply a picture. . . . I may turn out to be not such a terrible hopeless fool as everyone, as you, as I myself suspected. I want to send you, and others, the most loving wish I have in my heart. This is the only way I have to reach out—out where it is incomprehensible. I can only pray toward it. So . . . Peace!

Not with a letter of self-justification but with a declaration of his will to live, Herzog reaches out in love to join the human race, writing to his mother, long, long ago lowered into her grave.

The "love bandit" Ramona has traced him to Ludeyville. He invites her to dinner. The electricity is turned on, the range and refrigerator reconnected, the house cleaned, and he places two bottles of wine in the spring to chill. He picks some flowers for the table. And yes, it is now he fills his hat with rambler roses, like Henderson in his Tyrolean hat with the feather.

In 1985, Bellow told his audience—an overflow crowd, so large a crowd the Ethical Culture Society, under whose auspices Bellow came to New York to read, had to borrow the auditorium of the neighboring YMCA—what he intended to say in *Herzog*:

> *Herzog* as I was writing it was really a big joke to me. It's what a professor does when his wife leaves him—he sees what Spinoza would say. I really meant the book as an attack on higher education in America.

The audience laughed and Bellow laughed. Did he believe it? Bellow cannot resist a put-down. So be it.

There is a good deal more to *Herzog* than his reading Spinoza. For one thing, Bellow had found a way to write that would carry him all the way through to *Humboldt's Gift* and *The Dean's December,* and his later short tales and *More Die of Heartbreak.* He had found a narrative style to represent flux and process and concurrence. Out of the gladiatorial struggles of his life, he had created a demonstration of what it means to be human. That there is a disparity between the thinking man and the sensual man is not an irony but a truth. That there are two modes of thought, two areas of concern—no, three, five, ten, there are as many modes of thought as there are experiences to reflect them—is not an irony but a truth. In *Herzog,* Bellow found a new way to say what he has long believed, when he sat at his bridge table writing *Dangling Man,* when he sat at his café table writing *Augie March,* when he sat in his cabin in Reno writing "Seize the Day," and in his barn writing *Henderson the Rain King:* The fragmenting of the imagination is not merely a flow but its essence; there is treason and error but there is also a mysterious power of faith; optimism and belief may exist side by side with betrayal and falsehood; reason and the senses, spirit and the soul coexist as well. Bellow demonstrated again the truth of not "either-or" but "both-and."

Joseph and Asa Leventhal and Tommy Wilhelm were sober men. As Bellow's life became more and more tormented, his comic style emerged. Like Henderson, suffering, weeping, lamenting, crying out "I want, I want," while shooting off his snappy one-liners, lumbering along on his ludicrous experiments, boisterous, ebullient, so the melancholy Herzog, on his way into and out of chaos, submerged in grief, is comical. Wry jokes interrupt furious quarrels; irreverent comments deflate intellectual discourse. Herzog goes to visit Phoebe and notices the small bloodless marks on her face: "As if death had tried her with his teeth and found her still unripe." Herzog visits his stepmother, Tante Taube. She is slow, slow, taking a long time to walk and talk. She was, Herzog thinks, "a veteran survivor to be heeded, had fought the grave to a standstill, balking death itself by her slowness." Taube was formerly the patient widow Kaplitzky.

> She had good reason to mourn Kaplitzky. "*Gottseliger* Kaplitzky," she always called him. And she once had told Moses, "*Gottseliger* Kaplitzky didn't want I should have children. The doctor thought it would be bad for mine heart. And every time . . . Kaplitzky-*alehoshalom* took care on everything. I didn't even looked."

Himmelstein tells Herzog he ought to buy a large insurance policy and says, "You'll be glad to think of your death, then. You'll step into your coffin as if it were a new sports car."

Perhaps it was the audacity of the writer who chose to depict a turbulent man sunk in grief, disconsolate, hopeless, and healing himself by means of a do-it-yourself encyclopedia; perhaps it was the zaniness of the writer who saw no reason not to have that man, writing a treatise on Rousseau and Robespierre, stare at a Merry Widow corset; perhaps it was true that readers were more interested in lechery than in the soul; whatever it was, *Herzog* received the National Book Award. *Herzog* was called "the best book by the best writer in the U.S.A.," was called bold, brilliant, extraordinary, profound, an act of literary transcendence, honest, magnificent, the paradigm Jewish novel, a modern Milton, a Leopold Bloom brought up to date in New York, inexhaustible, lovely, vibrant, filled with compassion and empathy, with sensuous vigor, an original imagination, Bellow's best book, and his best book, and again, his best book. There were negative reviews, of course—by Richard Poirier and Leslie Fiedler and Maxwell Geismar—but this time they were driftwood on the dunes.

In February, 1965, a few months after the publication of *Herzog*, Ludwig published a long review of the novel in *Holiday*, describing it as a work of unparalleled complexity, "a kind of summing up, fictionally, of everything Bellow has written since his first novel entered the world." He said *Herzog* was like Thomas Mann's *Dr. Faustus*; the unsent letters were a "curious modification of Joyce's interior monologues in *Ulysses.*" Ludwig also lectured often on the novel as a fine example of Bellow's skill in the writing of fiction.[1]

At the December 1965 conference of the Modern Language Association, Ludwig was scheduled to speak on *Herzog.* I remember it well. My friend Professor Sallie Sears was first on the program of what was announced as a "Topics in Modern Literature" session. She was prepared to talk of Virginia Woolf to a small audience of no more than thirty-five members. She was aghast to discover the session had been moved to the main ballroom, and while she read her paper, she noticed people were constantly filtering in, until by the time she ended, there was standing room only. Five hundred scholars had gathered to observe Professor Jack Ludwig speak on Saul Bellow and *Herzog.*

In a letter to Bellow, written in 1968, Sondra declared the score was even between them. He had certainly profited from their divorce, while she had suffered years of embarrassment and pain from the phenomenon of *Herzog.*

12

"Life and death are

two slopes under me"

On September 21, 1964, *Herzog* was published. A week later, on September 29, *The Last Analysis* opened on Broadway. *Herzog* was an astonishing success. *The Last Analysis* closed in twenty-eight days.

On the Sunday before opening night, the theater section of *The New York Times* printed Bellow's account of how he came to write his play:

> A writer must consider himself equal to any demand in his line. He is tradition-ally the anti-specialist. . . . I, myself, was quite prepared to become a dramatist, and was not taken by surprise when, about five years ago, Lillian Hellman suggested that I write a play. In a short time, my play was ready. Miss Hellman found it amusing and estimated it would run about eight hours without Wag-nerian orchestration. She offered valuable advice, much of which I could not use because it required the collaboration of experts, the serious interest of a theater. So I put my Utopian project away and turned again to fiction.[1]

When he was invited by the "Theater of Living Ideas" to give a reading, he took a long look at his manuscript, cut it down to size, as he thought, and arrived confident and excited. He was pleased at the reaction of his friends gathered to listen. Then, on the eve of a public showing, Bellow was less sure.

Ask a writer what he thinks of the American theater and he will tell you that it has no language, that it lacks rhetoric or gesture. Ask any professional in the theater what is wrong with plays written by novelists and he will answer that they don't know the difference between the page and the stage. On this matter it's still a bit early for me to express any opinion worth considering. What I am aware of now is the limit placed on the authority of the writer by the theater. It intrigues and amuses me to recognize how independent the habits of a novelist are.

In print, Bellow was polite, even jovial, perhaps stiffening himself for the attack he expected on Monday.

Alone with his page, between four walls, he is compensated for his solitude by a high degree of autonomy. In the theater, he discovers the happiness of collaboration . . . in the theater you see living faces, you feel yourself part of a company, your heart opens to the actors, even to the squalor of West 44th Street. . . . The price of all this delight is a reduction in one's exclusive powers.

In truth, Bellow was badly rattled by the experience of seeing his play through production.

Sitting alone, within his four walls, he had no qualms about carrying both his novel and his play to completion. As fifteen and more drafts of *Herzog* accumulated on one shelf, as many revisions of *The Last Analysis* piled up on a shelf nearby. He saw no reason why the dolorous night-school teacher Herzog and the clown Bummidge could not both restore themselves to health simultaneously. Wife, mistress, family, and friends of Herzog seemed to Bellow easy to recast into their slapstick counterparts, harassing Bummidge. He did not realize that Herzog, freely wandering across the range of his memories, had no one but Bellow to stop him, whereas in the theater, Bummidge had to conduct his self-analysis on a stage, eventually, as Bellow called it, the gloomy stage of the Belasco Theater, where actors, directors, stage managers, set designers, lighting experts, and costumers all had advice to give and the right to give it. Bellow negotiated, compromised, altered, wrote new dialogue, scrapped old dialogue, but suspected he was party only to the dismantling of his play.

When Zero Mostel withdrew from the cast and Sam Levene was given the role of Bummidge, Bellow knew the whole project had slipped from his hands. Levene did not understand what Bellow was getting at in his text, and Joseph Anthony, the director, did not know how to explain. Wearing his jaunty hat and a loud "Broadway" jacket, sporting a cane, Bellow went from the grueling rehearsals to a nearby tavern to drink whiskies and brood. "I tried," he said in the *Times*, "to put ideas on the stage in what is possibly their most acceptable form at this time, the farce." He hoped, he said, Bummidge would manage "to stand on his own feet, and even to dance a bit."

The Last Analysis did not dance. The reviewers did. Some blamed Bellow, some the production. Barry Hyams called it an unwieldy play; unfortunately, only conventional means were summoned to make it wieldy.[2] Harold Clurman called Bummidge a gigantic effigy, a puppet, a figment of verbiage without a truly dramatic existence. The play lacked the right director and the right Bummidge.

> All might have been saved if the production had a style . . . what we see at the Belasco is a hodgepodge that shifts from an attempt at vaudeville exaggeration—badly accomplished—to a prosaic "sincerity." This includes a setting of cluttered and unsightly realism with hardly anything of the boisterous imagination indicated by the speech and idea of the text.[3]

Time magazine defended Sam Levene:

> . . . part Jewish-family comedy, part psychoanalytical cliché, part spoof of psychoanalysis—and all claptrap. . . . On opening night Sam Levene tried valiantly to assist *Analysis* by sweeping some of the dialogue under his tongue. The trouble is that Bellow has given him more bad lines than he can possibly throw away.[4]

Robert Brustein defended the play:

> There is an awful lot of noise issuing from the stage of the Belasco these days, but the loudest explosion of all can be heard only with the inner ear: it comes from the head-on collision of a gifted writer, Saul Bellow, with the crassness and incompetence of the whole commercial theater system. Since this has been an accident with no survivors, and since the vehicle being driven was smashed beyond repair, it will probably never be known that *The Last Analysis* was, potentially, a remarkable play, or that its protagonist, Philip Bummidge, was among the most flamboyant comic characters ever written for the American stage.[5]

Vogue blamed the production:

> Neither the ending nor Sam Levene's prosaic playing of Bummidge did full justice to his inspired pseudo-intellectual lunacy. The production seemed not to

have found its proper style and the inconsistency of the acting tended to distract from the main issue. This is not necessarily a closet drama, but only a witty play that was made to seem like closet drama.[6]

Certainly Bellow was disappointed. He wrote to his friend Norman Rosten, describing the protests at the Belasco Theatre when Sam Levene told the audience the play was closing. It survived for another week.

Bellow, too, blamed the failure of his play on its production. In a letter to another friend, Thomas McMahon, written three months after the play closed, Bellow was still outraged, and complained that the profession of the theater was anything but a profession.

Determined to stand Bummidge on his feet, Bellow revised the text and published *The Last Analysis* in 1965. In a front note, he said: "The present version makes use of some of the timbers of that shipwreck, but much of it is entirely new."* Whatever its fate in its first month of life, Bellow wished to preserve *The Last Analysis* as a significant piece of writing from his hand.

With the play in print, we can read it in tandem with its twin, the novel, and discover that Bummidge crystallizes what Herzog was all about, and what is more to the point, *Herzog* and *The Last Analysis* taken together illuminate what Bellow thought then that he was all about. Both announce a turning point in Bellow's career, a shift that he explained in *Herzog* and confirmed in *The Last Analysis* and would soon demonstrate in the novel *Mr. Sammler's Planet.*

Instead of the seedy couch in the dilapidated house in Ludeyville, Bummidge reclines on an old barber chair in a loft in a warehouse in Manhattan. "Near the sofa is a bust of Sigmund Freud." Bummidge is resting in preparation for a demonstration of his method of *Existenz*-Action Self-Analysis. He is sponsoring himself in an appearance on closed-circuit television before an invited group of psychiatrists, artists, comedians, and a member of the clergy, gathered at the Waldorf to observe. An old-time comedian, Bummidge has grown

---

*Marilyn Stasio, in her book *Broadway's Beautiful Losers,* 1972, gives an interesting account of the revival of *The Last Analysis,* this time at the Off-Broadway theater Circle in the Square. Despite the replacement of Sam Levene with Joseph Wiseman in the role of Bummidge, and Theodore Mann directing instead of Joseph Anthony, the play opened June 23, 1971, and closed five weeks later, a prey once again to "a misconceived production." Wiseman was too refined, in no way convincing as a comedian, and Mann was simply weak in his direction, conventional, and fearful of imaginative staging.

In 1981, Bellow was again revising the play, planning to bring it out in a new version. He has not done so yet.

sick of the sound of laughter, tired of the mask of the comic. Now he wants insight, values, to get off the surface of life, to achieve a life of the spirit. "I'm hampered, hindered, held back, obstructed, impeded, impaired," he cries. He must cleanse himself of two sources of pollution, his past life with all its neurotic fears, guilts, and traumas that stunted his growth, and his present life with all his predators, the blood-sucking vultures—his family and associates—who force him in the wrong direction.

Act One is a parade of Bummidge's manipulators. One by one, they arrive for the broadcast: his cousin Lawyer Winkleman, contemptuous of Bummidge's search for self-knowledge, predicting he will end up "waiting in an alley for a handout of dried eggs from Federal Surplus"; his old pal Mott, a leech demanding five thousand dollars to pay the rental fee for the technical equipment he has brought; his sister Madge, the matron from New Rochelle, who refuses to lend him money: "Don't make a poor mouth," Bummy says to her. "You took your diamonds off in the street. I can see the marks." Bummidge's son Max comes to prevent the waste of his inheritance on a television production: "Artist?" asks Max. "Feet of clay, all the way up to the ears." Bella, his former wife, hurries onstage, still greedy for money, still jealous of his paramour, Pamela, who comes onstage to bring her lover to his senses, to see that he gets back into the big time. Bummidge would rather have her diamond ankle bracelet returned to him: It cost fourteen thousand dollars at Tiffany's. Aufschnitt, the tailor, arrives with the Nehru jacket Bummidge has designed to wear for his broadcast. He, too, demands to be paid. Only Bertram, an old pal, formerly a rat catcher, and his pretty little secretary, Imogen, believe in Bummidge. "He's done great things for my mental development. He saw more than these externals," Imogen says, pointing to her breasts and the curves of her hips. "I think psychology is worth every sacrifice. I love it more and more."

To get into the right mood for his performance, Bummidge must do some "couch work" before the broadcast. He reenacts a session of self-analysis, taking the roles of both patient and doctor. "Why can't I live without hope like everybody else?" asks the sick man. "The Id will not release you to the Ego, and the Ego cannot let you go to the Id. Try laughing. Laugh as you face the void of death," answers the healer. The patient confesses he dreams of his father and recalls how the death of that mighty hero shocked him. The analyst says no, that Bummidge was glad. Bummidge insists he loved him. The analyst says no, so Bummidge admits:

"My father couldn't bear the sight of me. I had adenoids, my mouth hung open—was that a thing to beat me for? I liked to hum to myself while eating—

was that a thing to beat me for? . . . But I fought. I hid in the cellar. I forged
your signatures on my report card. I ate pork. . . . Well, you grim old bastard,
I made it. You're dead, and I'm still jumping. What do I care for your grave?
. . . Down goes the coffin. Down. The hole fills with clay. But Bummidge is still
spilling gravy at life's banquet. . . . I put a rose bush on Mama's grave. But Papa's
grave is sinking, sinking. Weeds cover the tombstone."

Such thoughts overcome him. The analyst asks Bummidge about his mother
and Bummidge admits his oedipal longings. He feels worse; analysis suceeds.
His brain is like a sea of light. He pays himself twenty dollars, and allows his
memories to flow out: He is a boy of eleven opening his sister's bureau drawer,
fondling her silk underwear; his father beats him for stealing a piece of candy;
he loses his galoshes and trembles. While Bummidge practices his analysis,
Aufschnitt fits the coat of the liberator of India on the liberator of the self.
Bummidge interrupts Bummidge to ask: "You call that a buttonhole?" A
makeup technician comes to work on Bummidge's face: "Emphasize the
serenity of my brow." Meanwhile, all the sycophants quarrel, pushing, demanding to get into or out of the act. Bummidge breaks into their clamor
with a violent shout:

> "Stop! Why are you here? I am your food, your prey. You have filled my life
> with stench and noise; dogged me night and day; lived on me like green fungus
> on pumpernickel. But you won't be happy till I'm crucified? You, a Roman
> crowd? I, an Asiatic slave?"

He asks Imogen to staple the cuffs of his jacket to the wall, and when he is
satisfied he is the very image of human suffering, he says, "Forgive them,
Father, for, for . . . what comes next?"

In Act Two, the broadcast will take place. Bummidge provides each
predator with a symbolic costume—to Pamela, a burlesque stripper's outfit;
to Madge, a flapper's dress with fringes; to Max, a shopkeeper's apron; to
Bella, a bridal gown; to Tante Velma, the midwife who brought him into the
world, a hat trimmed with fruit. An infant is rented off the street to represent
Bummidge, newborn. To symbolize civilized man in chains, humankind in
bondage, Aufschnitt is given threads to wind around his fingers. Now Bummidge can present each person from his significant past; he can probe the
causes that underlie his problems and so cure his disease of "Humanitis" or,
as he calls it, the "Pagliacci gangrene":

> "Caused as all gangrene is by a failure of circulation. Cut off by self-pity.
> Passivity. Fear. Masochistic rage. . . . Disease is trying to infect me. Time waits

> to consume me. . . . I become like an ancient Mongolian idiot, old, wrinkled, yellow. I run and hide, steal, lie, cheat, hate, lust."

Bummidge leaves the scene to televise an exhibition of charts and diagrams he has prepared in his library. He returns to reenact his career, mingling snippets from his comedy routines with a sketch of the circumstances of his marriage. To show the danger of such a wife and such a family, he requires someone to throttle him, for that is the life he has known; a messenger wanders onto the stage and is happy to oblige. Bummidge is pleased at the authenticity of the throttling: "Suffering and agony can be repressive forms of gratification. From top to bottom, each man rejects himself, denies what he is." Max, too, playing Bummidge's father, is happy to hit Bummidge so violently he bleeds and must withdraw from the performance. Aufschnitt steps into the breach, and so the common man speaks:

> "Ladies and gentlemen, my name is Gerald Aufschnitt. I was born in Vienna, also the home of Mr. Freud. I am now Mr. Bummidge's tailor for thirty years. What a wonderful person. He helps me with my troubles. My daughter's troubles, too. I make his costumes in my little shop on Columbus Avenue. He asked me to play in his show. I was just man, in the grip of relentless suppressions. I was never in a show before. How do I look?"

Winkleman pushes him aside and takes the spotlight:

> "Good evening. Yes, we are relatives. Were playmates. My cousin is a man of genius. Without him, my life would have been very empty. It is becoming rare for any person to need any other specific person. I mean, usually, if death removes the one before you, you can always get another. And if you die, it might be much the same to the rest. The parts are interchangeable. But Bummidge is *needed—*"

Bertram pushes Winkleman aside, but he can only talk about rats, and so Pamela comes forward to do what she can do best: She wriggles, does bumps and grinds. Now Bummidge returns, ready to reenact his primal scenes—his conception, his gestation, his birth, and finally his rebirth. He tells his audience he can no longer continue as a clown. A comedian cannot dispel injustice or eliminate suffering.

> "I chose to serve laughter, but the weight of suffering overcame me time and time again. As I rose to my unsteady feet I heard the sins of history shouted in the street."

The only way to regenerate his empty heart is to identify himself with universal suffering and share the common status of mankind. He describes the moment of his illumination:

> "Armistice Day, nineteen eighteen. From the abyss of blood, the sirens of peace. I have a vision of bandaged lepers screaming, 'Joy, joy!' Twenty million mummy bundles of the dead grin as the child, Philip Bummidge, intuits the condition of man and succumbs for the first time to Humanitis, that dread plague. Being human is too much for flesh and blood."

Overcome by the memory of his trauma, he sinks down in emotional exhaustion. Imogen and Bertram step forward to read the lines Bummidge has prepared, should he falter. The bunny girl and the rat catcher chant Bummidge's compendium of the history of the twentieth century—totalitarianism, social disorganization, Freudianism—and arrive at Bummidge's decision to devote himself to the civilization that is to come. He will, henceforth, direct his weapons of wit and comedy to the moral struggle and teach individuals how to achieve the manhood "we are born to inherit." He will establish "a center, an academy or conservatory of comic art based on the latest psychological principles." Bummidge returns to the stage just in time to act out his rebirth. He is Lazarus rising from the dead and there the telecast ends.

The guests at the Waldorf are deeply impressed; the impresario, Fiddleman, races over with a new contract and a fistful of checks. No. The Top Banana meant what he said. He has quit show business. Bummidge tears up the contract and the checks and dismisses Fiddleman. Next, he orders the removal of all the leeches and tarantulas and vultures of his present life—his mistress, his marine sergeant wife, his useless son, and all the rest. Bummidge will join the fellowship of man. He puts on a toga and arranges the folds carefully, ready to pursue the sublime, to teach "the poor, the sad, the bored and tedious of the earth" how best to live. He rises, his brutal life behind him, to enter the real world, taking with him his suitcase filled with money, his playgirl and his sidekick, and departs for the Trilby, an old theater he will remodel into a new center for *Existenz*-Self-Analysis.

> "I must reach everyone. Everything. Heart, reason, comic spirit. I have something tremendous to say. The enterprise is bigger than me, but there's no one else to do it."

"There's no one else to do it" is exactly what Herzog told himself at the end of his self-analysis: "*I* am Herzog. I have to *be* that man. There is no one else to do it." Yes, Bummidge is kidding his audience and his actors, deriding old-fashioned notions of loyalty and newfangled notions of psychoanalysis, but Bummidge is also poking fun at the pretensions and needs and longings of a Moses Herzog. Herzog had said his work was awareness: "I am a specialist in spiritual self-awareness, or emotionalism, or ideas; or nonsense. Perhaps of no real use or relevance except to keep alive primordial feelings of a certain sort." Herzog had said that "extruded consciousness was his line, his business. Vigilance." Herzog declared he "practiced the art of circling among random facts to swoop down on the essentials," that he "often expected to take the essentials by surprise, by an amusing stratagem." Bummidge is the amusing stratagem. Bummidge is the grotesque specialist in spiritual self-awareness, the victim of emotionalism. Bummidge, too, assesses his career and says much the same as did Herzog:

> "I am the instrument of a purpose beyond ordinary purpose."
> "I act out my past life."
> "I formed my own method. I learned to obtain self-knowledge by doing what I best knew how to do, acting out the main events of my life, dragging repressed material into the open by sheer force of drama. I'm not solely a man but also a man who is an artist, and an artist whose sphere is comedy."

There is more to Herzog and Bummidge than that they sound so alike. Suppose we read the lines again from the point of view of Bellow. In Herzog and Bummidge taken together, we may hear the voice of Bellow reflecting on his art, curiously, Bellow explaining his purpose as well as the method of his fiction. Herzog, the poor soldier of culture, the aging scholar who has led so muddled an intellectual life, taken such pride in his lacerated heart, swelled so often with human sympathy, and served so long as the custodian of the dead, joined with Bummidge, the aging Comedian, enacting the role of analyst and of patient, of confessor and interpreter for the common man, for everyman, using his wit and his comic sense to tell the truth not only of the individual but of society, together sound very much like Bellow's view of himself. It is Bellow who has the great Utopian project, to be the artist who understands reality, who tells the truth and expects to be believed. Despite that, Bellow is mocking Bellow.

When the family and friends of Bummidge deride the old comedian's pretensions, it sounds very much like Bellow, ironically assessing himself.

Bummy's lawyer-cousin Winkleman says:

"You lost your touch. They stopped laughing. And you're going to cure the ravaged psyche of the mass? Poor cousin! . . . Earnestness has been the ruin of my cousin. Highmindedness. The suckers had their mouths open for yucks—he fed them Aristotle, Kierkegaard, Freud. Who needs another homemade intellectual? One more self-nominated boring intellectual sick with abstractions? . . . Bummy wants to dump his friends, to try to make it as an intellectual."

Bummy's son says: "An obsolete comedian? His generation is dead. Good riddance to that square old stuff." Bummy's secretary Imogen says, "They insist on treating you like a hambone comedian. They don't know how profound you are." His sister Madge says, "He turned solemn, boring, a Dutch uncle, a scold." His old pal Mott says, "Here goes the poor-childhood routine again." His estranged wife Bella says, "Some people fade or subside, but not him. He'll go through every agony."

To be sure, all these accusations sound like the charges leveled against Herzog, but they are also Bellow's reflections on his writings, not only on his narrators—Herzog, Tommy Wilhelm, Augie March, all the way back to Leventhal and Joseph—but on his own pretensions as well, his own heart's desire. Bummidge says: "Ultimate reality. That's what we want. Deep, deep and final. The Truth which daily life only distorts." Bummidge says in a few lines what Herzog said in a series of long rhapsodic recollections and revaluations:

"Life and death are two slopes under me. I can look down on one side or the other. What was I before? I'm not the person I was. Something has happened. . . . I am drenched with new meaning. Wrapped in new mystery.

Like Herzog, who heals himself by turning his back on predators such as Madeleine and Gersbach, so the comical parody of the heartsore twin recognizes there is a higher truth, a more significant reality; he, too, seeks an ultimate reality. "The soul! I feel life drifting into me. I have attained rebirth. I am in a pure condition which cannot be exploited." Mott asks, "Is he serious? Is that Bummidge the comedian? He's lost his marbles."

Bellow was giving his public notice he would enter a new phase in his career. He had found his marbles and was going off to play a new game on another curbside. Herzog and Bummidge are turning their backs on the world they knew and intend to begin all over again. Bellow was planning to write *Mr. Sammler's Planet*. Artur Sammler will peer with one sightless eye into himself, and with his undamaged eye, will scrutinize the real world, the world outside the four walls.

To compress 340 pages that leisurely record the transformation of the spirit from humiliation and suffering to regeneration into two acts of slapstick that render the same drama of suffering and reversal may have been an error of judgment, a misconception of the capacity of the New York stage to represent such intellectual and spiritual discoveries: perhaps farce is not so good a vehicle for the exploration of ideas, but then Bellow thought *Herzog* was an intellectual comedy and was surprised at the solemnity with which it was received.

It is the phenomenon of the simultaneity of conception despite the disparity in execution that counts here. Both are the public record of Bellow's transformation, the externalization of his internal sense that he had changed. *Herzog* looks back on and writes *finis* to a past that he interprets as humbug and false humility and self-indulgent sensuality, a past in which he sees himself as a participant in duplicity. Herzog's bookish cures for emotional upheavals, his unmailed letters challenging political and social hypocrisy, and Bummidge's decision to live a new life, to create for himself a future in which he would be neither exploited nor exploiter, not whining or laughing, tell us that Bellow was about to write a new kind of novel. Artur Sammler will mail Herzog's letters. In the Academy of *Existenz*-Self-Analysis, Sammler will explore existence in the real world.

13

"Duck the bricks or field the bouquets"

Tom Prideaux, who saw *The Last Analysis* and read *Herzog* in October 1964, wrote amusingly about Bellow's perplexity for *Life* magazine:

> This must be a confusing fall for Saul Bellow. His newest novel, *Herzog,* and his first Broadway play, *The Last Analysis,* both clocked in at practically the same time, and both drew a richly mixed assortment of reviews. Bellow could hardly know from day to day whether to duck the bricks or field the bouquets.[1]

The close of 1964 and the year 1965 were indeed a confusing and strident time for Bellow; 1966 and 1967 were worse. Nineteen sixty-eight and 1969? Nadir it would seem, and Prideaux might have said again, "Bellow could hardly know from day to day whether to duck the bricks or field the bouquets."

Take, for example, the year 1968. In October, Bellow published a collection of short stories, *Mosby's Memoirs and Other Stories*; the book was generally dismissed, if noticed at all, by reviewers who complained that too many of the stories were old; the new ones were unsuccessful or boring; the appearance of the stale collection was nothing more than a publisher's ploy to keep Bellow's name before the public. Robert Lasson called Bellow a "graduate anthropologist," and asked:

> But is intelligence enough? Or rather is it possible to be too intelligent? . . . To paraphrase what Mrs. Walter Lippmann has to keep telling her husband when they're on vacation: "Saul, stop thinking!"[2]

Charles Thomas Samuels said categorically Bellow had never written a successful novel, his ideas and imagination simply did not mesh, and added:

> On the whole, the short form simply does not provide him with room sufficient for the flexing of mental muscles, and the most recent stories in this new collection seem undernourished versions of his longer works.[3]

Only Tony Tanner raised a lonely voice in defense of the book:

> Bellow's main question is existence; he strives to understand the central experience of the realization of mortality; both "Mosby's Memoirs" and "The Old System" are moving toward a lonely encounter with the ultimate mysteries.[4]

In 1968, B'nai Brith announced it would confer its Jewish Heritage Award on Bellow, and the French government invited him to go to Paris to receive its Croix de Chevalier des Arts et Lettres, and Bellow, long inured to critical slings and arrows, as he liked to say, arrived smiling and gracious to receive his prizes.

The years between the publication of *Herzog* and *Sammler* were years of good decisions and bad, of ambivalence and certainty, a time of rant and silent reflection.

In 1966, Bellow came to New York to deliver the keynote address to the PEN Congress, a gathering of internationally concerned writers and compassionate academicians.[5] Deeply saddened by the collapse of Delmore Schwartz, angry at what society does to its poets, Bellow was in rare form. Professors, he said, had miseducated the young. Critics were promoters of culture that suited them. Novelists allowed themselves to be recruited to meet the chic requirements of the manipulators of received opinion. Art only pretended to cognition. Imagination had accepted service to the masters of intelligence.

Two unpublished lectures are in the archives, in folders identified as "1967 Deposit," one, titled by hand, "The Modern Religious Novel," the other, "The Next Necessary Thing." Bellow does not recall the occasions for which he wrote them or the universities where he delivered them. But he thought they had been sharp; he had said what he wanted to say.

In "The Modern Religious Novel," he challenged those who lamented the failures of modern civilization. Lamentation had become fashionable in the sixties, he declared. On every side we hear that the great ages of faith are gone and what is left, they say, is waste and loss and alienation. Alas, Bellow said, all *we* have left is the commonplace and the ordinary, too contemptible to care about.

In "The Next Necessary Thing," Bellow attacked the publicity industry. Why should it assume to itself the responsibility for making up the rules and setting the standards? Why should we believe them when they tell us what we want, what to buy, what to do? Why do contemporary writers cater to these manufacturers of taste, these manipulators of the public heart, and believe them when they tell us what we need to learn and what we ought to say? Why should writers not have a good word for any social institution? Why should they only lash out and condemn?

Week in and week out, during 1966 and 1967, Bellow's third wife, Susan, had been urging him to take her to live in New York, to assume, as she said, his proper place in the intellectual center of the world. She had not bothered to read his essay, printed in 1967, "Skepticism and the Depth of Life,"[6] a diatribe against spurious and corrupt New York, nothing more, he said, than the business center of American culture. New York intellectuals were mandarins. Writers who immersed themselves in the New York world did little more than substitute art behavior for art, practiced a lifestyle, not art.

> Money, production, politics, planning, administration, expertise, war—these are what absorb mature man. . . . Radical destructiveness has replaced human standards and ideals. All is gesture, excitement.

All was manipulation, rackets, power struggles, infighting, bluster, vehemence, swagger, fashion, image making, and brain fixing. He caught his breath to say that English departments had become the Paris substitutes of young literary men and that universities had no such thing as a unified intellectual life. He permitted himself only one or two humorous sentences in eighteen pages of unrelieved assault, concluding that skepticism was an attitude generated by self-dislike, the contemporary form of misanthropy, and wondering why everyone had simply agreed that the depth of life was gone. He asked:

> If it is no longer where it used to be, where has it gone? Where can it go? If you drain a lake, the water must run somewhere. If some wicked engineering

genius invented a way to steal Lake Michigan, he would have to find a place to store it.

Like all of Bellow's prose pieces of this period, published and unpublished, "Skepticism and the Depth of Life" is forthright; he denounced, exhorted, and accused without disguise—no unmailed letters, no antics of a clown.

Bellow's earnest reminders that there are values, there is a depth to life, there is love and duty, family, beauty, heroism, the precious self, seemed only to separate him from his audiences. When he finished, he heard only polite applause. Sometimes a few courageous souls asked him questions, but not many cared to risk his caustic reply. No one found much to say to him at the receptions that followed and he often left early to avoid the awkward silences.

Many listening to Bellow in 1967 found him uncomfortably conservative, distastefully anti-American. Those who read what he had to say thought there was too much Jewish pedantry showing in Bellow—or not enough—or dismissed his arguments as bombast, nothing more than the cosmetics of middle-aged weariness. Some, gathered to hear him in 1968, refused to listen. In October, Bellow went with his lecture carefully prepared to San Francisco State College and he began to read in his quiet voice, peering from time to time at the hundreds of students before him. There seemed to be a stir among them. Instead of the respectful silence that usually hung over a Bellow lecture, he heard catcalls and groans and whistles; then the flow of his argument was interrupted by shouts and questions from all sides of the hall. Finally, he returned his papers to his portfolio, clicked the lock, walked off the stage, and left the hall. Nobody stopped him.

Bellow described the fiasco in a letter to Mark Harris, a writer and a professor who had changed jobs, leaving San Francisco for Purdue, and had been urging Bellow to accept an invitation to speak.[7] He had felt grossly offended by the groans and catcalls, the ribald insults challenging his manhood, by the name-calling and laughter of those in the audience; he had felt affronted by the silence of the faculty members present. No, he would not accept Harris's invitation to speak, thank you.

Mark Harris wrote back to Bellow to explain what he believed had happened, calling the students disappointed young men who wished they were writers, and agreeing with Bellow that the professors ought to have risen in Bellow's defense. Harris concluded with assurances he was fond of Bellow though he too sometimes felt intimidated by Bellow's wit.

Bellow did go to Purdue to deliver the major address at the Annual Literary Awards Banquet, a speech later reprinted as "Culture Now: Some Animadversions, Some Laughs."[8] Indeed, Bellow was on the attack:

I'm not sure that what we have *is* a literary situation; it seems rather to be a sociological, a political, a psychological situation in which there are literary elements. Literature itself has been swallowed up. In East Africa last year I heard an account (probably sheer fantasy) of a disaster that had overtaken one of three young Americans who had parked their Land Rover under a tree for the night. A python had silently crushed and swallowed the young man. In the morning his friends saw the shape of his body within the snake and his tennis shoes sticking out of the creature's mouth. What we see of literature now are its sneakers.

Bellow identified the publishing industry and academia and literary critics, taken all together, as the hungry python; contemporary writers as the sneakers. He said calmly, reading from his text to the young aspiring writers at Purdue, that William Phillips, the founder of *Partisan Review,* wrote worse than did Eleanor Roosevelt in *My Day*; that Phillips was a dry old stick who was afraid he might not make it with the New York crowd because he feared he might be hopelessly out of it. He said that Richard Poirier, then the editor of *Partisan,* had turned that magazine into "a butcher's showcase [of] pink, hairless pigginess," adorned by Poirier "with figurines of hand-carved suet which represents the very latest in art, literature and politics." He called Leslie Fiedler the "coroner of criticism," who wanted only more obscenity, more of the mantic, more of the mad and the savage. He said outright that reading Fiedler "promptly and strongly brings fascism to mind." And, standing in the auditorium at Purdue, Bellow said universities were the "sanctuary, at times the hospitals of literature . . . a bureaucracy with its own needs and ambitions and its own orthodoxy." He told that audience—gathered to award its students—that Ph.D. programs in literature had given us "apocalyptic clichés; a wild self-confidence, violently compact historical judgments, easy formulas about the cancellation of the world." Art had become a toy, a wardrobe for the misconduct of life; literature was nothing more than a scenic background; and modernism had fallen into the hands of demagogues, dunces, and businessmen.

Many listening to Bellow knew he had accepted a permanent appointment on the faculty of the University of Chicago.

So much for the public outcries of Bellow. It was as if *The Last Analysis* had jumped the gun. Recall Bummy's son Max: "His generation is dead. Good riddance to that square old stuff." Recall his sister Madge: "He turned solemn, boring, a Dutch uncle, a scold." Recall Mott: "He's lost his marbles."

What of the private life?

In 1967, Bellow turned his back on Susan. Instead of going with her to live in New York, he retreated from her into a couple of furnished rooms on the South Side of Chicago and sat down to write a novel about New York. His third marriage was over but the quarrel had just begun. Fifteen years later, Bellow would still be entangled by lawsuits, liens, settlements, renegotiations, recriminations, affidavits, disclosures, fines, and fees, and Bellow would come to know all the trappings of uncharitable judges, sharp lawyers, threatening bailiffs, hearings in private chambers, harassment by a windstorm of paper. He had been sad to see his father's legacy dwindling away in Tivoli; what would he say to his own fortune blown away by Susan's lawsuit? He would say it in *Humboldt's Gift* and again in *The Dean's December*. At the time, he was reading *A Year in Treblinka* as background for his novel in progress: Artur Sammler would be a victim of the Holocaust.

When the Six Day War between Israel and Egypt broke out, Bellow flew to Israel to report on the war for *Newsday*; his three articles, printed on June 12, June 13, and June 16, distressed his readers, for Bellow did not write of the aspirations of the State of Israel but described violence and death in the Sinai.

> What good are these traditional dignities? No good at all if they lead to the Sinai roads with their bloated Russian tanks, the black faces of the dead dissolving and the survivors fighting for a sip of brackish water.[9]

Artur Sammler will take a seat in a plane and ride to the desert in a jeep to report on the Six Day War for the readers of a Polish newspaper; Sammler will be disgusted by his Israeli son-in-law, Eisen, one of the vulgar custodians of Israel.

Nineteen sixty-eight was perhaps a worse year. In 1968 Jack Ludwig published a novel, *Above Ground,*[10] in which there was a second account inspired by the same affair that inspired *Herzog,* now seen through Ludwig's eyes. Mavra is a nymphomaniac, an egomaniac, a jealous, predatory woman, a mess of tears, saliva, and stale effluvia; Louie is her husband, whining, selfish, vulgar, a violent playactor, a failure, untalented and irresponsible. Louie and Mavra pursue the noble, loyal, loving, wise, sensitive, erudite, good family man, Joshua, who is apparently based on Ludwig.

Bellow thought Sondra had lent her hand to the making of the book. Although she tried to assure Bellow that she had not seen a word of the Ludwig manuscript beyond the first third, if he was revolted by the vulgarity and ugliness of the writing, could he imagine what she must have felt thinking she was loved and respected and honored? To her, *Above Ground* was a vicious crucifixion of the humanity of everyone involved.

Ludwig had used the device of letters, so successful in *Herzog*, to carry forward the plot and characterize the actors in *Above Ground*, but imitation was not enough to enable the novel to reach any rank on a best-seller list.

Why had Ludwig written such a book? Perhaps he was tired of hearing that Bellow was a far more sensitive and elegant man, with a keener intellect and a finer talent. Maybe it was his need to justify his treatment of his wife all these many years, and therefore Ludwig had to portray himself as victim, the seduced rather than the seducer. So the character derived from Bellow was portrayed as a basketcase, so the character derived from Sondra was portrayed as a degenerate. I do not believe, although all of Stony Brook was aware of it, that Sondra suspected Ludwig still lived with his family, that each night when he left her he was returning home. Ludwig kept a rented room in Oyster Bay, and that, whoever asked him, was where he spent his nights—writing fiction.

In 1965–66 the Ludwigs rented my house in Roslyn, Long Island, while my family and I went off for a Fulbright year in India; they remained in Roslyn on our return. It was curious to me to listen to Leah Ludwig's description of her situation, telling me as she formed the little dough packets for her verenikes, or tossed the crepes for her blintzes, that she really didn't care about Sondra and Jack, or *Herzog* and *Above Ground*; she had a fine house, lovely children—so she did—a good income, and what did Sondra have? Jack.

I met Bellow in Great Neck around this time and he asked about Ludwig at Stony Brook. I said he was a popular and prestigious member of the English Department, driving a showy Jaguar, sort of moving and shaking students, faculty, and administration alike. Bellow sighed. He had probably paid for the Jaguar. "Oh, don't complain, Saul, you have the best of it. How long has *Herzog* been on the best-seller list? Spend the money and enjoy it." I remember Bellow pulled out a gold watch and swung it on a long and heavy chain and smiled.

A letter from Robert Penn Warren to Bellow, sent to thank him for his kind remarks about Warren's poems, suggests Bellow's feelings in 1969. Warren assures Bellow he is confident that although Bellow tells him he is distraught, his mind turbulent, he will live happily too, for after all, he is Bellow.

And a letter from Bellow to Jean Stafford,* dated April 22, 1970, at the close of this period, provides a good picture of his frenzied activity. He

---

*Jean Stafford (1915–1979) was a novelist. She had been married to Robert Lowell in the forties, and to A. J. Liebling, from 1959 until his death in 1963.

apologized for not writing sooner; he had been traveling—to Kenya, Uganda, Ethiopia, Texas, and Florida, to De Kalb, to Lafayette, Cincinnati, and St. Cloud. He cannot explain his restlessness. He would like to buy a house and settle down. He is sending her a copy of his speech at Purdue, soon to be in print, thinking she might want to read about some of their mutual acquaintances.*

What of the interior man? What was going on inside his heart? What was the melodrama of his spirit? For that, we have his stories, the two he wrote during the time he was creating Artur Sammler: "The Old System," a wistful melancholy recollection by Samuel Braun of his family, that first community that no one can choose to join; and "Mosby's Memoirs," an account of a friendless, withdrawn Mosby, who lives alone in Oaxaca, writing of his past life. Both narrators are isolated, lonely, reflecting on their past, speculating on their character, engaged in a quest for self-identity, trying to discover from what they emerged so that they may reenter the world.

Braun has no project for putting the world in rational order; his project is for himself. He hangs limp between being and not being. His quiescence is emptiness, not harmony. How can he restore his vitality and emerge from his state of torpor? Braun knows it has been said of him he loved no one, could not love, but he defends himself by reflecting on the accusation. It was only partly true. He loved unsteadily, his instability the surge and ebb of his soul. To prove to himself he is not detached, Braun decides to think affectionately of someone, and like so many Bellow heroes, Braun chooses to reflect on his beloved dead. That may enable him to identify the longings of his spirit. Oh yes, he did love his family. "Who did I ever love as I loved them?" Herzog had asked.

He remembers that as a boy, he had lived among his relatives, his Aunt Rose, his Uncle Braun, Cousin Mutt, Cousin Isaac, Cousin Tina, and out of that immigrant family, "descended from the tribe of Naphtali," Braun selects two, the obese businesswoman, Cousin Tina,† and her brother, the orthodox businessman, Isaac (identifiably Herzog's relatives, identifiably Bummidge's sister and cousin). Braun, like Herzog, listens to "the dead at their dead quarrels"; he hears their voices from Vancouver. Tina and Isaac had gone from Europe to Canada and then to New York—the Mohawk Valley and Albany—where they had grown rich, Tina in real estate, Isaac in

---

*The essay was the Purdue Awards Banquet speech, about to be reprinted as "Culture Now: Some Animadversions, Some Laughs." See note 8 on page 360.

†Obesity, for Bellow, is usually an endearing quality; we recall Queen Willatale, and in *The Bellarosa Connection* Sorella Fonstein, with whom the narrator would like to spend the rest of his life, is "a mountain of lipids."

contracting, building shopping centers and housing developments, masking their love in endless arguments, in tricks and deceits, making their way in the public world with the same tenacity and strength with which they sustained their private quarrel. Each believed the other was a betrayer; each accused the other of theft, of cheating and snobbery. Neither, however, was able to turn away from the other; both backed into a relationship of imperishable love and hate. Ought Samuel Braun to love as they did, under the old system? What is the good of such excess of emotion? Perhaps his cold eye was better. Why not look with equanimity on life, on death? Emotions create uproar, a crude circus of feelings. "Oh these Jews—these Jews! Their feelings, their hearts!" Braun had been right to end such turbulence.

> For what came of it? One after another. You gave over your dying. One by one they went. You went. Childhood, family, friendship, love were stifled in the grave. And these tears! When you wept from the heart you felt you justified something, understood something. But did you understand? Again *nothing!* It was only an intimation of understanding. A promise that mankind might— *might*, mind you—eventually, through its gift which might—*might* again! be a divine gift, comprehend why it lived. Why life, why death.

As Albert Corde would do fifteen years later, Braun stares into the black darkness of the infinite sky, at the stars alight there. Fires: "These things cast outward by a great begetting spasm billions of years ago." Begetting spasm. That is as far as Braun can reach in his effort to understand the purpose of feelings and hearts. Braun's ambivalence will be ended by Sammler, who justifies the need for detachment, accepts the hiatus between being and not being, and affirms Braun's suspicion that love is an anachronism, a shard on the rubbish heap of the old system.

Willis Mosby lives alone in a small cottage below the main building of a resort hotel, writing his memoirs, the record of his progress as adversary and gadfly. He had been a radical in Spain, a government man in Paris, a professor at Princeton, always on the attack, attack on Franco, on Harold Laski, on Lévi-Strauss, on FDR, on the Stalinists, on Hitler, Sartre, UNESCO, Dean Acheson, Truman. He, too, knows what others have said of him, that he was too abusive of left-wing dunces and right-wing predators, too intolerant of slovenly intellectuals, too merciless in his censures of academic mountebanks. Then Mosby realizes he ought to interpolate some vitality into his memoirs, "to relieve the rigour" of his account of that fearful sequence of his mental wars. He decides to recall something comical and chooses his old friend

Lustgarten to divert his brooding thoughts from the way the world has turned.

Lustgarten was an old-time Marxist who eventually married Klonski's sister and now ran a laundromat in Algiers, proudly displaying photographs of his children. Was Lustgarten really so funny? Mosby discovers, instead, a man betrayed, cheated, manipulated, abandoned by his first wife, doomed to "gaping comedy." Then what of himself? Was Mosby wise? Was he not just another such fool? What was he doing touring the ruins of Mitla in company with two Welsh women and a fat-faced Mexican guide? What has he done with his survival?

Mosby was going once more through an odd and complex fantasy. It was that he was dead. He had died. He continued, however, to live. His doom was to live life to the end as Mosby. In the fantasy, he considered this his purgatory. And when had death occurred? In a collision years ago. He had thought it a near thing then. The cars were demolished. The actual Mosby was killed. But another Mosby was pulled from the car. A trooper asked, "You okay?"

Yes, he was okay. Walked away from the wreck. But he still had the whole thing to do, step by step, moment by moment.

Here Mosby was, under the hot Mexican sun, tottering at the head of a steep stairway that would carry him down into an excavated tomb. What was the good of a Mosby, like a Lustgarten, a "cogitating, unlaughing, stone, iron, nonsensical form." He tries to convince himself that he has made himself ready, having disposed of all things human, to encounter God. Would he? "What God was there to encounter?" Mosby feels faint, oppressed, afraid, paralyzed. Nevertheless, he descends, and once inside the tomb, he refuses to accept his loss, his death. Whatever he has been or is now become, he is not ready to concede. Whatever remains to be done, he will have to do it above ground.

Stooping, he looked for daylight. Yes it was there. The light was there. The grace of life still there. Or, if not grace, air. Go while you can.

One task is left to him. He will return to his cottage, sip mescal, and write his memoirs. Comic or tragic, understood or misjudged, wise man or fool, he will write his memoirs.

Sammler, too, will wonder what he, a Polish Jew, who once lived in Bloomsbury, who once was made to stand before a firing squad, and who crawled out of a mass grave, is now doing on a Broadway bus worrying about a pickpocket. Sammler, too, will reconstruct in his mind the fearful sequence of his mental wars and end up with a prayer to God, with an exhortation to himself to find the strength to continue to live.

Bellow was leaning over the table of his rented cottage on Nantucket Island, or whatever desk he could find, revising, reworking, and revising again the manuscript of *Mr. Sammler's Planet*. He was transforming the rhetoric of his lectures and speeches into the jeremiad of Artur Sammler, who is first seen moving about quietly in his furnished room, drinking his grapefruit juice, grinding his coffee beans, watching the water come to a boil.

14

"If in—in. No? If out—out. Yes? No? So answer"

Everyone knows an old man like Artur Sammler who walks with a cane in a crowd of strangers, always feeling left out, wondering what has come of it all, why he is still alive when so many lost out, and being alive, what he ought to do with the rest of his days. Sammlers tolerate the aches and pains of old age, faithfully taking their tablespoons of brewer's yeast each morning, visiting old friends, talking about old times, remembering the old days, reviling the new.

All during my childhood, on Sunday mornings, old Uncle Asher from Coclán in Grovna Gubernya in Lithuania waited on the back porch for someone in our family to wake up and open the door. He would take the Western Avenue streetcar to the Lawrence Avenue line and walk from Kedzie Avenue to wherever our house happened to be, on Sawyer Avenue or Carmen Avenue or Whipple Street. He wanted his breakfast and someone to talk with about what used to be. Each time my father found him looking through the kitchen window, he said to my mother, "And they shot a man like Lincoln!" but he always let him in. My father was born in Coclán but to him gone was goodbye. "What is, is. What was, was." Still, he liked to hear Uncle Asher tell the old stories. My father-in-law, a furrier in Chicago, was born thirty kilometers from Coclán. When he came to visit us in New York, we thought he would like to see the Lower East Side and eat at Ratner's, but he stopped on the corner of Orchard Street and said, "Get me away from here. Why do you bring me here? Who cares? It's gone. I worked all my life to get out of this. What was so good about it? They killed us in the old country. A man can live and raise a family, be clean and maybe rich in Chicago. What do I need to come here for?" Always, however, when old Kriesberg came to visit old Mike Miller, before he took off his coat, he sang out the first lines of a Yiddish song, changing "Rumania" to "Gubernya"— "Gubernya, Gubernya, Gubernya, oh that was a good land, a sweet land and beautiful." And my father would answer with the chant of the *Shma:* Hear O Israel, the blessed God is one God.

Bellow knew such old men—his own father, his uncles, the fathers of his friends. Artur Sammler was not the commonplace immigrant survivor, however. He was Bellow himself, the kind of man that Bellow, gazing through the far end of binoculars, imagined he might be in twenty years, just such a withdrawn dissociated old man. Suppose, Bellow reflects, I was to focus the lens on Anita and Sondra and Susan, and all the women I have known; how will they appear to me in twenty years? He saw Sammler's dead wife, Antonina, and Sammler's niece, Angela Gruner, the Jewish American Princess with the "fucked-out eyes" playing switch with her Wharton Horricker, and tedious Margotte, chirpy and cheerful huntress, and Sammler's demented daughter, Shula. And what of my brothers? Bellow peered down on two images and they fused together into Elya Gruner, a friend of Zionism, an abortionist for the Mafia, vain, sending for a manicurist on his deathbed, nostalgic, sending for Sammler to talk about the old relatives, the people on "the old system." What of my lost friends, Isaac and Delmore and Oscar Tarcov? Taken together, Bellow saw the dead Ussher Arkin, a "good man," missed, regretted, mourned by Sammler. And what of my present friends and cousins and associates? He changed the position of his binoculars, diminishing and magnifying them as they push and pull at Sammler—the officious busybody, unreliable Lionel Feffer, the whining Wallace Gruner, the crafty pretentious ruffian Eisen, the pompous little academician Govinda Lal. And what of my writings? How will they appear in twenty years? Will all my books end up as Govinda Lal's manuscript of new life on the moon, irrelevant, true, with no one but a Sammler to turn the pages? Will the writing I may still do become Artur Sammler's project for the memoir of H. G. Wells?

Bellow lent to Sammler fragments of his personal experience, the fiasco of his lecture at San Francisco State, the hurried trip to Israel to report on the Six Day War, the spells of tachycardia, a visit to an art gallery, a wait outside the hospital room of a sick friend, and soon Sammler borrows from Bellow—"the book takes over and leads me where it wants to go"—Bellow's reaction to Hannah Arendt's theory of the banality of evil, Bellow's distaste for New York, his unwillingness to think of himself as a Jewish writer, his perceptions of women, his judgments of youth—"The children were setting fire to libraries. And putting on Persian trousers, letting their sideburns grow." Sammler borrows the accusations and protests and recriminations of Bellow's prose pieces, the charges that twentieth-century America, once a model, has become a mockery of Western culture, lapsed into romanticism, the higher standards and the great ideals abandoned.

Artur Sammler sits alone in his room speculating, remembering, brooding—unquiet, fearful, outraged.

> Fits of rage, very rare but shattering, laid [Sammler] up with intense migraines, put him in a postepileptic condition. Then he lay most of a week in a dark room, rigid, hands gripped on his chest, bruised, aching, incapable of an answer when spoken to.

When Sammler walks out, he enters a world fallen into the hands of an elegant pickpocket who unzips his trousers and arrogantly waggles his penis in the old man's face. He stands in a world fallen into the hands of his Israeli son-in-law, Eisen, who carries a bag of bronze medallions and swings it full force into the face of the pickpocket. Disciplined and smiling, murderous, Eisen tells Sammler:

> "You can't hit a man like this just once. When you hit him you must really hit him. Otherwise he'll kill you. . . . If in—in. No? If out—out. Yes? No? So answer."

Answer.

Artur Sammler is half in and half out of his present world. He is made to listen to others, friends and family who seek him out as if he was a priest or doctor. They want to confess, to ask him to explain and analyze and judge, but he has lost all patience for their small troubles. Peevish, he tries to be kind. Bored, he tries to hear them. For what reason? He can set nobody straight. He can tell Angela to make it up with her father; he can tell Wally Gruner to make it up with his father; he can tell Shula not to steal; he can say to Bruch, the survivor of Buchenwald, weeping because of his erotic fixation on women's arms, "I'll pray for you." He tells half-truths; they half-listen.

Sammler has lost his wish to cure human perversity. He is too old to be on any quest for transcendence. He has strength enough only to daydream and reflect. He has strength left only for one project. He needs to be left alone to explain to himself the meaning of history. History, too, may be an organic being, with the cycles doomed to the same conditions of mortality, as if arising and thriving, the cycles of history also must disintegrate and die and become nothing more than a memory.* Where was that polite and cultured world of England? Where was that dangerous world of Poland? Dead. Dead memories in the imagination of the dying. Sammler needs to analyze his own troubles, to judge, to set himself straight. He is warped: too much rage and contempt and snobbery and rebuke and incoherence; too much intellectualizing. What has happened to him? He has gotten off the track, but what, after all, can he do? This fate, his life, is as good as he will get. He has led all the significant life he has been allotted. He must make it up with himself, heal himself before the next stage of his life begins. Next stage? After life? Sammler walks with an erratic step, weary, heartsore, grieving. He imagines his soul skimming across the shallow waters of reality, plunging through death, to what may or may not be eternal life. Sammler fears the street, he fears the desert, he fears the grave.

Herzog restored himself to sanity and was poised to climb back into his life; Bummidge proclaimed he was reborn and was poised on the stair of his life. Sammler is that Lazarus still; hands on the ladder or hands on the fire escape, he does not know. He is halfway in life, halfway in death. Blind in one eye, Sammler looks out on the hypocrisies and injustices of the public world; his darkened eye stares into his private world. He cannot take any step, up or down, until he discovers the design of his past life. It was accident the storm troopers missed him, animal cunning that preserved him in the Zamosht forest, the good heart of his nephew that brought him to America. He had nothing to do with that. What can a Sammler do now, with this second life? He can choose to think. A man in his seventies can prepare for his final entombment, discover for himself some meaning before he is struck down. An old man requires spiritual truth. Wrestling with facts is over. The only turf on which he wishes to wrestle is the greensward of truth—before the earth is dug up for him a second and final time.

While the recollections of the old man span decades, the literal narrative of *Mr. Sammler's Planet* is compressed between two consecutive mornings. On the first day, Sammler rises, dresses, takes his breakfast, and goes off to address a gathering of students at Columbia University. They don't

*In Bellow's most recent novella, *The Bellarosa Connection*, 1989, the narrator is the founder and director of the Mnemosyne Institute.

want to hear about British life in the thirties, or his scheme for "Cosmopolis," and he is jeered by the audience. "What you are saying is shit." "His balls are dry. He's dead. He can't come." No one defends him. He slips out a side door. In the lobby of his apartment building, he is cornered by the pickpocket he had seen working the passengers on a Broadway bus. Safely back in his room, he finds a manuscript by Govinda Lal, who writes about the moon as the future home of man. Such ideas interest Sammler and he reads it. He goes off to visit his nephew, Elya Gruner, in the hospital. Gruner is asleep after surgery. Sammler waits in the dayroom with Wally, who wishes Sammler to ask his father where he has hidden his hoard of cash, money Wally believes his father received for performing abortions on demand for the Mafia. On his way home to rest, he meets Feffer, who informs him Lal is distraught at the loss of his papers and Sammler realizes his daughter Shula has stolen the single copy, because her father, writing his memoir of H. G. Wells, ought to read it.

Wearily, he goes to Shula's apartment and exhorts her to return the manuscript to Lal. Back in his room, he bathes his feet, rests briefly, then, after sending Margotte to find and placate Lal, he returns to the hospital. Elya sleeps; now it is Angela with whom he waits. She wishes him to intercede with her father on her behalf. Angry at her wild eroticism, he may be frittering away her inheritance out of spite, for he is still playing the stock market from his hospital bed. Shula's estranged husband, Eisen, arrives to visit Gruner; his purpose is to sell the dying man medallions designed in Israel for rich Americans to collect. After a brief visit with Gruner, Sammler and Wallace climb into Elya's Rolls-Royce, on their way to New Rochelle—Sammler to find Shula where she has fled with Lal's manuscript, Wallace to search for the money. It is a grand suburban mansion. Margotte arrives with Lal in tow, and Shula is there, but without *Life on the Moon.* She has placed it for safekeeping in a locker at Grand Central Station. While the women prepare dinner, Sammler and Lal have a long conversation, Sammler at last speaking aloud his own views—a diatribe against intellectualization, against the playacting of being human, against the pretense of personality, spurious liberalism, the denial of the true purpose of existence, the nurture of the spirit. Lal half-listens, his eyes following Margotte's quick little body, moving about the room. Wallace, searching in the attic, breaks a pipeline he expects to be stuffed with dollars. Water flows down the back stairs across the white plastic Pompeian mosaic tiles. Sammler walks alone in the garden and finally sleeps.

The next morning, he strives to return to the hospital to say some final words to his nephew, who lies near death. The Rolls-Royce is halted near Lincoln Center; Eisen, in company with Feffer, is clobbering the pickpocket on the head with the sack of medallions. Sammler stops the fight and drives on. Elya's bed is empty. Sammler waits with Angela, speaks by telephone to Shula, who, good scavenger that she is, has found Elya's money, thousands and thousands, stuffed in a hassock. The good doctor has indeed performed illegal abortions. What shall he say to Elya? Nothing now. Elya is dead. Sammler goes down to the morgue, uncovers his nephew's face, and the words he has come to say, he can say only to God.

That is all the action of the book. Through the nightmare rush of two days, Sammler remembers his past, the old events and lost emotions and useless arguments intruding on the present, out of sequence, confused and meaningless. His history and the history of the times mingle together, disordered and incoherent. H. G. Wells in Bloomsbury, and his wife, Antonina, and King Rumkowski, and Cieslakiewicz in Poland, and Hannah Arendt and Meister Eckhart and the Negro pickpocket and the Mafia and Eisen and Soviet tanks and the King David Hotel in Israel. What design was there, what significance can he find in his metamorphosis, the Sammler of Bloomsbury, the Sammler of Poland, the Sammler of America? The evolution of history has brought him, and humankind, to the 1960s.

> And he was supposed to be the remarkable thing; he who was sitting on this glazed slipcover felt under him the tedium of its peach color and its fat red flowers. . . . No Antony bestriding the world like a Colossus with armies and navies, dropping coronets from his pocket. He was only an old Jew whom they had hacked at, shot at, but missed killing somehow.

Even granted two lives, what has he learned? If there were a covenant between God and man, to become what is promised humankind will take another billion years. He has only a year or two left to fulfill what has been pledged between God and Sammler. He has only a day or two in which to discover a principle of coherence, a verifiable truth, so that he can comfort Elya Gruner on his deathbed. What can Sammler find to say to his nephew? How can he tell Gruner the truth of love and brotherhood and responsibility and progress and pride and hope as such principles have become manifest in the world?

Sammler considers love. What can he say of love? He gazes at women with his one blind eye and sees error and default and crime and neurosis, the uncleanness of the world all caused by women. He remembers his wife, Antonina, and Gruner's wife, Hilda, both dead. Antonina, the social climber with a passion for membership in English society, ended in a mass grave. Hilda, greedy for wealth and status, nagged Gruner to perform abortions—she was the real criminal. Women are not capable of love, only of manipulation. Intelligent, thoughtful Ussher Arkin had been diverted from serious ideas by his wife, Margotte, who demanded he service her with erotic inventions. Poor harmless Walter Bruch was a victim of the lascivious curves and dimples of a woman's arms. Was H. G. Wells, that "horny man of labyrinthine extraordinary sensuality," to blame for his failure of reason?

He recalls Arkin's wife, Margotte, who fancied herself a political theorist, a social reformer, boundlessly, achingly, hopelessly on the right side, the best side, of every big human question—for creativity, for the young, for the black, the poor, the oppressed, for victims, for sinners, for the hangdog hungry. Sammler listened to her chatter and observed her legs in their black net stockings, her underthighs attractively heavy. He sighs at his recollection of Arkin, who said of his wife, "She was a first-class device as long as someone aimed her in the right direction."

Women? Daughters? He recalls Angela, Gruner's daughter, who said all a woman wants is "a Jew brain, a black cock, a Nordic beauty." Angela, with the green ribbon tied around her hips, is representative of the sexual sophistication of the times.

> Cheeks bursting with color, eyes dark sexual blue, a white vital heat in the flesh of her throat, carried a great statement to males, the powerful message of gender.

Sammler translates the message: "transgression and pain and sex; lust, crime, and desire, murder and erotic pleasure." Angela had described how she bathed with her playmate Wharton Horricker:

> "Oh, a woman is a skunk. So many odors, Uncle," she said. Taking off every-thing, but overlooking the tights, she fell into the tub. Wharton was astonished and sat on the commode cover in his dressing gown while she, so ruddy with whiskey, soaped her breasts. Sammler knew quite well how the breasts must look. Little, after all, was concealed by her low-cut dresses. So she was soaped and rinsed, and the wet tights with joyful difficulty were removed, and she was led to the bed by the hand. Or did the leading. For Horricker walked behind her and kissed her on the neck and shoulders. She cried "Oh!" and was mounted.

Sammler thinks of his daughter, wigged, bedizened Shula. In New Rochelle, he found his daughter cowering in the tub. He switched on the bathroom light and with his one good eye he saw her.

> In the light he saw Shula trying to cover her breasts with a washcloth. The enormous tub was only half occupied by her short body. The soles of her white

feet, he saw, the black female triangle, and the white swellings with large rings of purplish brown. The veins. Yes, yes, she belonged to the club. The gender club. This was a female.

With his inner eye he reflects:

> This woman with her sexual female form plain in the tight wrapping of the woolen robe (especially beneath the waist, where a thing was to make a lover gasp) . . . this woman, unhinged, wavering-witted daughter with higher aims . . . by extravagance, by animal histrionics, by papers pinched, by goofy business with shopping bags, trash-basket neuroses, exotic heartburn cookery . . . was *kulturnaya,* Shula was so *kulturnaya.* . . . in her nutty devotion to culture she couldn't have been more Jewish.

Females cultured? Spiritual? Capable?
Sammler listens to Wallace Gruner explain women to his uncle and he does not argue with Wallace.

> She's [Angela] a female-power type, the *femme fatale.* Every myth has its natural enemies. The enemy of the distinguished-male myth is the *femme fatale.* Between those thighs, a man's conception of himself is just assassinated. If he thinks he's so special she'll show him. Nobody is so special. Angela represents the realism of the race, which is always pointing out that wisdom, beauty, glory, courage in men are just vanities and her business is to beat down the man's legend about himself. . . .
> I often think a man's parts look expressive. Women's too. I think they're just about to say something through those whiskers.

No. Fulfillment of the destiny of humankind cannot be found in the love of women.
Then what of brotherhood? Are men clean, kind, wise? Sammler thinks of Feffer and Eisen: not kind, not wise. He thinks of Wallace. Clean? ". . . a bit careless perhaps in his toilet habits, [Wallace] often transmitted . . . a slightly unclean odor from the rear. The merest hint of fecal carelessness."
Perhaps because Sammler is too old to touch, and half-blind, and the sounds of the urban world are only the gabble of conversation or the roar of machinery, it is the sense of smell that is left as the instrument of perception. That may be, but Bellow has associated odors with decadent physicality from the time of raunchy Thea and careless Lily and fetid Madeleine and soiled Allbee and defecating Einhorn and Ravitch with the *dreckishe* pants and

rancid Gersbach. The odor of the erotic life cannot be disguised with the attar of roses: Mtalba arrived in the perfumed night air; harmless, bargain-hunting little Sono laved Herzog with scented soap; Ramona withdrew to undress and scent her body; and even little June was washed and rinsed and powdered by Gersbach.

What would Sammler have been able to tell his dying nephew about brotherhood and free will and the truth of human nature? Sammler has learned in his two days that the silent exposure of the princely black man's penis, and the thrust of a sack of medallions, aimed at the head, were demonstrations of the truth.*

Not love, not brotherhood, but power has the metaphysical warrant for victory. Can such truths, such understanding be relevant to Elya on his deathbed? Can Sammler find no better understanding for himself before *he* departs from *his* life?

At forty years of age, Sammler fell into a grave beneath a mound of corpses of the old world, the played-out world of culture and tradition, with its old answers buried. He crawled out, a man of action, hiding, fighting, killing to reach the new world of America, where his second chance to find answers waited. For thirty years, he observed the operation of new answers, reading, watching, and interpreting. With his one good eye, he has seen all there is to see of reality. With his analytical damaged left eye, he has found no coherence in history. He has found no traces of the sacred in the progress of civilization. Perhaps the earth as a planet had beauty, but what have we made of it? Sammler has found nothing honest in the life of the intellect, nothing honest in politics or society, nothing honest in the human heart.

Despite all his mental labors, Sammler had no sign, no talisman of comfort, for Elya Gruner. He peered into the darkness of the past, with his one blind eye, and saw anomalies and contradictions, sophistries and illusions. He peered with his one good eye out the window of the hospital room and saw a condemned building across the street, a large whitewash X painted on each window. What did it signify? That there was no one there to look out? Nothing to see in? Empty on both sides? Could that be the truth?

Sweet Augie is long gone. The good-natured blustering Henderson is long gone. Herzog and Bummidge, with their faith in the human spirit, are memories. Sammler stands on a ridge, wavering, uncertain how to advance or retreat. He has a poor blunt knife with which to make his way—no suitcase, no valise, not even a new hat, old shoes.

Unlike the devout nun who might say at the end of her life, "I have

---

*The truth comes in blows, Henderson lamented.

nothing. Everything worked out very well," Sammler, poor, dependent, half-blind, reflects that he knows nothing; nothing has worked out very well. Without the piety of the cloistered nun, he is on the point of departure, not yet composed for his final transformation. To be disinterested, to turn away from creaturely needs, from involvement of every sort, to cease all action but patient waiting is all that is left for preparation to swim out on the currents of death and join the larger community, the genuine convocation of souls. However, how can one prepare for death if one does not understand life? He wished to bring answers to Elya and has brought only questions.

If history repeats and repeats itself, how can one know the purpose of civilization? If one counts for nothing, what is the use of the individual? In the crowd, what is the use of the unique personality? If one can do nothing to alleviate the grief and suffering of one's fellow, what is the use of striving? What is the significant life? What is it to be human? In this present world, is there a cure for the sickness we have created ourselves? We have a body that tires of itself and longs to be restored, cell by cell, to its original matter. We have a mind that observes the evidence of reality and refuses the demonstration. We have a soul that cherishes the possibility of spiritual unity with God but trembles at the advent of the sublime. We have an imagination that evokes the possibility of eternity and immortality but whites out the place of honor that awaits us. Sammler would be glad to pick up his marbles and go home—if he had some marbles; if he knew where there was home.

How does he know there is an afterlife? If I sleep will I wake? If my soul exists, can I transcend death? Am I promised immortality? Who made the promise?

The WASP Henderson sang in his quavering voice the words from Handel's *Messiah*: "Who shall abide the day of His coming?" The old Jew, Sammler, whispers to himself disjointed phrases from the Requiem Mass: *"Timor mortis conturbat me. Dies irae. . . . Quid sum miser tunc dicturus?"* Yes, the fear of death disturbs me; yes, the days of wrath. And yes, death is natural, death is an organic part of life, but the shallow grave may be the only reality. How do I know the freed soul shall dwell in the deeps of the cosmos? How do I know the sacred life remains to be lived after death? Is death oblivion or transition?

Sammler has found no healing power in Scripture, none in great books. He has verified only isolation and meaninglessness and mediocrity and facticity and does not delude himself: Society is disintegrating; history is a tail chase. Imagination is a slender cane to guide him on his quest for transcendence, a feeble tap tap tap on experience. What can he say to Gruner?

"There is a bond." "There is a bond." These are all the words he can bring. He can say only that the single soul is unique and it is at the same time a bond. That is the great mystery. That is the sustaining grace. Life, Elya, is a skimming of the surface. Death, Elya, is a penetration through the surface. We have no proof there is depth under the surface, but we have no proof there is not. And there is God. Whether God is or is not, Sammler believes in God. When he read Meister Eckhart, he agreed with the words of the mystic: "But if nothing can comfort you save God, truly God will console you." Then and now, the words are true. God gave every man a spirit. Why? So that he may continue.

> Something that deserves to go on. It is something that has to go on, and we all know it. The spirit feels cheated, outraged, defiled, corrupted, fragmented, injured. Still it knows what it knows, and the knowledge cannot be gotten rid of. The spirit knows that its growth is the real aim of existence. . . . Very often, and almost daily, I have strong impressions of eternity.

Sammler accepts, even welcomes, his dissociation from man; he refuses to be dissociated from God. Perhaps that is the plan. Despite society and history, the sacred life remains. Despite the horror and pain caused by the ego, despite the desire of the personality to be unique, despite the destructive will, the spirit may thrive. The soul can nurture itself and refine itself and make ready to go outward.

Sammler asks himself, Is this too great a demand on human consciousness or human capacity? Can he, by himself, create himself to be a human being of stature? Well, what else is there to do? It is not much of a message to take to a man who may have only a few minutes left in which to regenerate himself, to refine and prepare himself.

In fact, there is no time left at all. Gruner's bed is empty. He lies a corpse on a slab in the morgue. The nephew has gone without the benefit of Sammler's inner eye and outer eye and spiritual imaginings and cosmic probings. It is Gruner who has left the message for his uncle: "Goodbye." Sammler must give his message to God.

> The attendant pointed to the wheeled stretcher on which Elya lay. Sammler uncovered his face. The nostrils, the creases were very dark, the shut eyes pale and full, the bald head high-marked by gradients of wrinkles. In the lips bitterness and an expression of obedience were combined.
> Sammler in a mental whisper said, "Well, Elya. Well, well, Elya." And then in the same way he said, "Remember, God, the soul of Elya Gruner, who, as willingly as possible and as well as he was able, and even to an intolerable point, and even in suffocation and even as death was coming was eager, even childishly

perhaps (may I be forgiven for this), even with a certain servility, to do what
was required of him. At his best this man was much kinder than at my very best
I have ever been or could ever be. He was aware that he must meet, and he did
meet—through all the confusion and degraded clowning of this life through
which we are speeding—he did meet the terms of his contract. The terms which,
in his inmost heart, each man knows. As I know mine. As all know. For that
is the truth of it—that we all know, God, that we know, that we know, we know,
we know."

When Sammler lay in hiding in the Mezvinski tomb in the Polish cemetery,
he sustained himself with similar thoughts, at that time hateful to him and
overwhelming.

You have been summoned to be. Summoned out of matter. Therefore here you
are. And though the vast over-all design may be of the deepest interest, whether
originating in a God or in an indeterminate source which should have a different
name, you yourself, a finite instance, are obliged to wait, painfully, anxiously,
heartachingly, in this yellow despair. And why? But you must! So he lay and
waited.

By now, we recognize this act of waiting, the watershed of experience described by so many narrators of Bellow's stories. To overcome the yellow
despair is to reflect on the past and discover some pattern, some design, some
meaning that may enliven the spirit with energy enough to cope again. Now,
near the end of his second life, in the presence of the dead man who precedes
him, Sammler seeks to understand what it means to be human before he is
released from his human state, to strive thereby to learn what may be the
nature of life after death. So he reflects on the dualism of the unique soul
and the congruent soul.

God offers life but God has made no contract for a good life on earth.
What a man does with his life in the real world is his own business. The aim
of existence while on earth is to nurture, as well as one can, the progress of
the spirit. Despite its innate flaws, the spirit must grow beyond the conditions
of the real world. Oppressed, dragged down, intimidated, the spirit must
remain obstinate in its refusal of mediocrity. Thus, each unique soul is by its
nature akin to each unique soul of his brother. That is the bond between man
and man. Each soul, however, belongs to God. Each man must pay for his
life with his death. That man belongs to his fellowman, and that man belongs
to God, is not paradox but polarity. Both are true. Does God guarantee
transcendence? Maybe. Maybe not. What we may become in life is in our
keeping; what awaits us after we dip through the surface of life, we can only

perceive by intuition. We know. We know. It is a deeper knowledge hidden in one's inmost being, whispered on the primary instrument of the human heart: the imagination.

Bellow has always rendered possibilities, and, from *Dangling Man* to *Mosby's Memoirs,* his readers have always been urged to contemplate alternative ways to fulfill themselves as individuals and as citizens. Few readers of *Mr. Sammler's Planet* would care to choose among the alternatives presented: a middle-aged man who lies dying and an old man preparing himself for his death, among such wives and children, such friends and associates.

Bellow may have believed he was peering through the convex lens of a magnifying glass, viewing himself as he might be twenty years hence, but his lens rotated under his hand from time to time and magnified the Bellow of the sixties. He was staring at himself, cheated, disappointed, rejected, abused, misunderstood, friendless.

He knew that to cling to the old standards and storm against the new, to try to reform the world as his brother and father had tried to reform him was as useless an endeavor as to refuse to age, to refuse death. He knew his rage and rant against the America of the sixties was as much a rage against the loss of his state of the beloved child of his mother, as much a rage against the women who betrayed him. How could he not recognize his own myths? That he had been beloved was as much a myth as that the old standards were better. His desire to live a life of the spirit was as fragile in his hands as it was in the hands of any person on earth. Perhaps Bellow himself came to dislike his pontificating old man Sammler, for he turned his glass often on Sammler's child Shula, the demented scavenger of other people's castoffs. "In her nutty devotion to culture she couldn't have been more Jewish." A paragraph describing her may very well be Bellow's reflection on his own anima.

> Shula, like all the ladies perhaps, was needy—needed gratification of numerous instincts, needed the warmth and pressure of men, needed a child for sucking and nurture, needed female emancipation, needed the exercise of the mind, needed continuity, needed interest—*interest!*—flattery, needed triumph, power, needed rabbis, needed priests, needed fuel for all that was perverse and crazy, needed noble action of the intellect, needed culture, demanded the sublime. . . .

It makes a good deal more sense to read the words as a wistful reflection of Bellow on Bellow, for there is no precedent for such a Shula, no aftermath of such a Shula.

Still, he did publish *Sammler* and could kid Robert Manning of the *Atlantic Monthly*—who wrote in 1970 requesting a piece for the magazine—saying his book was doing well but not as well as *Herzog* had. So, he broods, betrayal and divorce are more interesting than apocalypse.

In 1979, Bellow and I were talking of Emily Dickinson and it was the man who had written *Sammler* who told me he felt very close to her. I was surprised to hear his assessment of her, but as I read his words in my journal, his empathy with the nineteenth-century poet made sense. He thought her a great heroine of the solitary, one who knew and experienced and accepted the solitary life like no other writer, more than Thoreau, more than Melville and Whitman and Emerson and Poe, who, yes, did withdraw but not for her reasons, not with such a totality. What Bellow seemed to me to admire most was that Emily Dickinson saw it through. He found that very attractive, although he could never do it. I said: "For all your living in the big world as you seem to do, you are as solitary as Emily Dickinson. In your heart, you know that no one hears you, no one listens to what you say. Running about the world as you do, you still live in isolation, in a kind of dejection of the heart, not by choice but by nature."

He broke in to say a rift existed between him and all the others, a rift he could not pass. I went on, however; I would say now, blithely on.

"I think your wives, the women you knew, are only one part of the story. There are the relatives and the old friends, so many gone, lost, dead, and the new friends you pick up and leave and pick up and leave, always wondering what happened. You hunt for connection, to find someone who will listen, someone you can trust." I was thinking of all the fiction I had read and was not prepared for his pausing to tell me facts, about his view of marriage as a way to capture connection, about his abiding love for his family, about his disappointments with the women he had tried to love.

He pulled his chair out of the sun, sprayed himself with more mosquito repellent, and began to tell me about a woman he had once admired. They had taken a trip to San Francisco together and she had told him he had to go with her to see a wonderful picture, *M*A*S*H*—well—*M*A*S*H*! She had gone on and on explaining to him what the movie was all about. As he had sat there in the theater, he had said to himself, My God! What am I doing here?* He looked at me, offering the Cutter's spray can, and smiled,

---

*In "What Kind of Day Did You Have?" published in 1984, Trina remembers a mistake she had made with Wulpy: "She got into trouble in San Francisco when she insisted that he see *M*A*S*H*. 'I've been to it, Vic. You mustn't miss this picture.' Afterwards he could hardly bear to talk to her, an unforgettable disgrace. Eventually she made it up with him, after long days of coolness."

shaking his head. He said that the most important thing in his life were his books and no one seemed to care at all about them. I thought the wear and tear showed on him.

When *Mr. Sammler's Planet* was published the last week in January 1970, it was received with the divided opinions that always greeted Bellow's fiction, with the exception of *Herzog*. *The New York Times*, with its daily and Sunday papers, pointed in an either-or direction: Christopher Lehmann-Haupt, on Monday, called Sammler a long-winded bore, the book monotonous and drifting, filled with interminable discussion; Anatole Broyard, the following Sunday, called the book a success and welcomed Sammler as the character who at last embodied Bellow's ideas, saying Sammler was human, a man of grace, the ideal antihero.[1]

Robert Kiely, in the *Christian Science Monitor*, called *Sammler* Bellow's deepest, most reflective book, an elegy, a lamentation. John Bayley, writing for *The Listener*, was wholly negative, dismissing Sammler as too predictable, contrived and leaden. "We are not moved."[2] Irwin Stock, in *Commentary*, called it a book "beautifully adapted to Bellow's middle-age," Sammler a ripe intelligence, each episode of his experience a representation of the current zeitgeist. He praised Bellow for his great emotional power, for re-creating the very experience of thought.[3] In *The Nation*, Beverly Gross called *Sammler* in every respect an old man's book. Crotchety old Bellow had foregone the art for the sake of nasty caricature. She said that the book was reductive, the action no more than an erratic counterpoint to ideas. "It is Saul Bellow conducting a graduate proseminar. The faltering design of this book cannot bear the burden of such self-indulgence."[4] L. E. Sissman, in *The New Yorker*, said *Mr. Sammler's Planet* was Bellow's chef d'oeuvre, and praised "the humor, the terror of the book, and its constant revelation of character through the development of its characters."[5]

Often the critics were themselves ambivalent. If there was respect for Mr. Bellow, there was dismay for Mr. Sammler, but usually it was a matter of dismay at both. Alison Lurie, writing for *New Statesman*, began with an acknowledgment that Bellow was one of the best writers anywhere in the world today and that in this book all his characters and events were perfect dramatic renderings of the situation of the "Now Scene," but she said finally the novel was a conservative book, the conclusions stoical and pessimistic.[6] Raymond Sokolov, writing for *Newsweek*, admitted the novel rivaled anything Bellow had done for sheer splendor of prose, but then went on to complain that Sammler's cerebral rage was hard to take seriously. The farce of the stolen manuscript was creaky, he felt, the tone too bitter, and the mockery desperate. He continued that Bellow was the "grand rabbi of the postwar Jewish renaissance in fiction," but in the case of *Mr. Sammler's Planet*, Bellow and Sammler were far too close and Bellow was overreacting to the times.[7] In the *New Republic*, Charles Thomas Samuels acknowledged the book as "middling Bellow" but admitted that middling Bellow approached the zenith of contemporary fiction. Before long, he pointed out that the characters in the novel were egomaniacal enemies of the human community that Bellow relentlessly criticized. He believed the action proved the presence of vice, the rhetoric argued for virtue, but no connection was ever achieved between action and ideas. One was a parody; the other, unconvincing angry meditation.[8] Alfred Kazin, in *The New York Review of Books*, began with praise, then subtly moved to his negative position, saying Bellow was penetrating, with an unparalleled ability to express the extraordinariness of the Jewish situation, but he was not a dramatic novelist. When Kazin pointed out that Bellow was Sammler, unequivocally, then went on to condemn Sammler as too intelligent, uncharitable, drifting into moral arrogance, that Sammler disliked everyone, disapproved of everyone, that Sammler appeared always to be right, was world weary, indulged in austere dismissive jeremiads, was too haughty and contemptuous of women—well, of everyone and everything but himself—then what have we but a harsh judgment of the man who wrote the book?[9]

"I read the book with a recurring frown," warned Edward Grossman, writing in *Midstream*. He found *Sammler* verbose, the irony sour, the action faltering, the comic episodes grotesque and horrible, and at the last, he discovered the novel was bitter and bleak, and stood against all the political, intellectual, and social values of the times. Since he could find no way to distinguish between Sammler and Bellow, he determined it was Bellow who was hostile, and there was no doubt in his mind that Bellow had with this book taken himself out of the establishment. He had canceled his membership. "Bellow's fashionable reputation reached its epiphany with *Herzog*. By now it cannot be said any longer that he is central, that he is considered the favorite voice of a self-confident group. He now stands outside and his constituency is not being renewed."[10]

Between one critic saying Sammler was a "sophisticated Portnoy, complaining," and another asking "Why is Bellow writing like Arthur Hailey?" Joseph Epstein had to come forward to close the circle. *The New York Times* printed, in May of 1971, a long essay in its book review section, assessing Bellow's work and reputation.[11]

Saul Bellow is the premier American novelist: the best writer we have in the literary form that has been dominant in the literature of the past hundred years.

He has come to his eminence not through the mechanics of publicity, self-advertisement or sensationalism, but through slowly building up a body of work, an *oeuvre,* that with each new novel has displayed greater range, solidity, penetration and brilliance.

In his work perhaps alone among that of living American novelists it is possible to trace a clear line of development, to find a steadily increasing confluence of intellectual power with the more sheerly joyous aspects of narrative art. From the skeletal *Dangling Man* . . . to the masterwork that is *Mr. Sammler's Planet,* Bellow has advanced from being a promising writer to an interesting writer to an exciting writer to a major writer, which is where he is today.

By the time Epstein spoke out, Bellow had already gone off with his National Book Award, his three honorary doctorates, one from Harvard, one from Yale, one from New York University, where he sat beside his sponsor, Mrs. Vincent Astor. He had carried home his Academy of American Achievement Golden Plate Award and his Formentor Prize and the honor of induction as a Fellow of the American Academy of Arts and Sciences.

Who would choose to be a writer? Bellow had no control over his critical reception or his readers or on the bestowers of prizes. He had control over only his pen and his papers and not always over his pen, that wand of his imagination, as he called it, his prompter, his transcriber of so mysterious an inner voice, he himself was both exalted and grieved. However, he had so chosen. All he could do was to sit down and begin again.

Sammler, standing in the garden in New Rochelle, observes Shula talking to the flowers, and he thinks:

It would be too bad if the first contact of plants were entirely with the demented. Maybe I'd better have a word with them myself.

The Well-Worn Map

Denise, Charlie Citrine's former wife, warns him of the danger of Renata, his present mistress: "Your mental life is going to dry out. You're sacrificing it to your erotic needs." She launches into an assessment of the products of his mental life:

> "Well, you wrote a few books, you wrote a famous play, and even that was half-ghosted. You associated with people like Von Humboldt Fleisher. You took it into your head you were some kind of artist. *We* know better, don't we."

Citrine reflects on her charge:

> She said I was writing stuff that made sense to no one. Maybe so. My last book, *Some Americans*, subtitled *The Sense of Being in the USA*, was quickly remaindered. The publishers had begged me not to print it. They offered to forget a debt of twenty thousand dollars if I would shelve it. But now I was perversely writing Part II.

That book, *Some Americans*, subtitled *The Sense of Being in the USA*, is an ironic reference to *Mr. Sammler's Planet;* Part II, which Citrine is perversely writing, is *Humboldt's Gift*.

Once before, as if he was enjoying a private joke on himself, Bellow had disguised his fiction as the prose works of his narrator. In *Herzog*, the night-school teacher thinks:

> His reputation is good. His thesis had been influential and was translated in French and German. His early book, not much noticed when it was published, was now on many reading lists, and the younger generation of historians accepted it as a model of the new sort of history, "history that interests *us*"—personal, *engagée*—and looks at the past with an intense need for contemporary relevance. . . .* His first work showed by objective research what Christianity was to Romanticism. In the second he was becoming tougher, more ambitious. . . ."

Herzog's "early book," the "objective research" into the relationship between romanticism and Christianity, was *Henderson the Rain King*; his second, the book he was now writing, the "tougher, more ambitious" work—Kant, Hegel, Robespierre, Rousseau—was *Herzog*. Long ago, Bellow himself had referred to *Dangling Man* and *The Victim* as his master's thesis and dissertation; that model of the new sort of history, in fact on many reading lists, certainly a model for a good deal of contemporary American fiction produced by the young seekers of the sixties, was *Augie March*.

In Part I *(Mr. Sammler's Planet)*, Bellow had imagined how his world and the events of his life would seem to a man of ripened consciousness; in Part II *(Humboldt's Gift)*, Bellow recounted again the story of his life, reflecting on how he appeared at that time to his friends and lovers and family, and above all to himself. *Humboldt's Gift* is an intensely felt and unequivocally personal book. Formal interviews, prose essays and lectures, and speeches seem now to be part of a carefully conceived public display; reminiscences on a garden chair in Vermont and conversations in his quiet living room high above Lake Michigan are less candid than what Bellow tells himself while sitting at his dining room table, with no person on a chair nearby to listen. He talks best and more honestly to himself and transfers what he hears to his manuscript. The fiction writer is the most reliable character witness.

Writing *Humboldt's Gift*, Bellow looked back on all his losses: the defeat of the journal he tried to publish, *The Noble Savage*; the failure of the play, *The Last Analysis*, which ran only a month on Broadway; the laconic acknowledgment of his collection of short stories, *Mosby's Memoirs*; the

---

*Remembering his quarrel with the Existentialists, Bellow ironically coupled "personal" and "engagée."

negative reception of his seventh novel, _Mr. Sammler's Planet_; the tangles and disentangles of three wives; the dwindling away of family, the deaths of his friends; the waste of his money; the erosion of his status. He lent his failures to Charlie Citrine. Charlie recalls the accusations brought against him by his ex-wife, Denise, and her charge sheet reads like an overview of Bellow's career. What is the matter with him? Denise asks. Isn't he the man who has had all those wonderful insights? Isn't he the author of all those books? Isn't he respected by scholars and intellectuals all over the world? Hasn't he lectured at the great universities and been given fellowships and grants and honors? Didn't de Gaulle make him a Knight of the Legion of Honor and didn't President Kennedy invite him to the White House? All this is literally true of Bellow. And why, asks an exasperated Denise, why is Charlie still in Chicago, hanging around with his old Chicago school chums? Such freaks! Why has he chosen to commit mental suicide? It's a death wish, this refusing to have anything to do with really interesting people. Why does he not enter the real world, move to London or Paris or New York? What is so great about this deadly, ugly, vulgar, dangerous Chicago?

Denise asks the questions and she answers them. Her explanation is Bellow's suspicion about himself: He is at heart still a kid from the slums; he cannot, he will not, forget the old West Side gutter out of which he came. Bellow's decision to live in Chicago baffled his wife Susan, puzzled his friends, amused his enemies, and irritated his relatives, all of whom had scattered except for his brother Samuel.

What difference, Bellow said, does it really make where he hangs his hat? It's not where he lives but who he is. The question was and still is, who is Bellow? Where is he in spirit?

With a modest subterfuge and perhaps some share of ambiguity, Citrine comes as close as Bellow can to telling the truth about himself. The facts and the feelings of Bellow as he reflects on his purpose as an artist, assesses his progress and defeats, explores his efforts to live a life of the spirit, his backsliding as he acknowledges his erotic attachments, his cravings to stabilize his belief in the soul, his longing to penetrate the mysteries of the afterlife, his testimonial of the value to him of Rudolf Steiner's principles of anthroposophy—all this is part of the subject matter of the fiction.

Citrine uses the well-worn map of Bellow's past life, the old routes still marked, the same mountains and valleys, the paths of ascent and descent, the dangerous ridges, the seductive meadows. Citrine walks where Bellow walked and climbed and fell back and found caves in which to hide. All Bellow's personal archetypes reappear wearing new disguises, borrowing bits and pieces from one another, as well as from Bellow's memories—the good mother, the stern father, the lame man, the con man, the good fool, the

Liliths and Jezebels and Esaus. Transformed into the characters of *Humboldt's Gift*, they are encountered anew by a tenacious Citrine, whose purpose is to "Vacate the personae!" Bellow's purpose, too, in writing *Humboldt's Gift* is to "Vacate the personae."

Like Citrine, Bellow did play a good and steady game of paddleball, and learned to stand on his head to relieve his arthritic neck, and, like Citrine, Bellow did get into an argument on a subway train when a passenger made a snide remark about old geezers and their young chicks. Once Bellow had been proud of it; now Citrine scoffs, calling himself "an old troubled lecher taking a gold-digging floozy to Europe." Bellow's purpose in undertaking his project of *The Noble Savage* was a high-minded act of literary citizenship; now Citrine is involved in a project to publish *The Ark*, the title alone a sad admission of the pretensions of that enterprise. Mike Schneiderman, a gossip columnist, probably Irv Kupcinet of Chicago, says to Citrine: "Now I remember. Somebody said you were going to publish some kind of highbrow magazine. When is it coming out? I'll give you a plug." Citrine recalls: "In *The Ark* we were going to publish brilliant things. Where were we to find such brilliancy? We knew it must be there. It was an insult to a civilized nation and to humankind to assume that it was not. Everything possible must be done to restore the credit and authority of art, the seriousness of thought, the integrity of culture, the dignity of style." Renata taunts Citrine when she asks: "Who needs this *Ark* of yours, Charlie, and who are these animals you're gonna save? You're not really such an idealist—you're full of hostility, dying to attack a lot of people in your very own magazine and insult everyone right and left." She calls him arrogant.

Many personalities in *Humboldt's Gift* are a pastiche of recognizable counterparts in reality, as well as characters familiar from Bellow's fiction. Bellow's associate editor, Keith Botsford, with some of his defunct coeditor, Jack Ludwig, added to the portrait, is lent to Citrine to be his partner in the enterprise; he is Pierre Thaxter. Denise is created out of Sondra Bellow and Susan Bellow, as well as out of Madeleine and Lily. Renata wears the miniskirt of Angela, and is a mingling of Madeleine and Ramona; in Renata, pursuer and pursued, some of Rosette Lamont reappears. Naomi Lutz is like a Daisy, a Mary, and I believe she reaches all the way back to Bellow's first wife, Anita Goshkin. Alec Szathmar, like an earlier Sandor Himmelstein, is based on Sam Freifeld; Flonzaley, the Valentin Gersbach from *Herzog*, is derived from Jack Ludwig; brother Julius—Ulick—has appeared in Bellow's fiction since *Dangling Man*; he is Maurice Bellow.

Readers familiar with Bellow and his world can recognize references to Harold Rosenberg, Meyer Shapiro, R. P. Blackmur, Gordon Ray, Richard Stern, Dwight Macdonald, James Laughlin, David Peltz, Sidney Harris,

Oscar Tarkov, Isaac Rosenfeld, Delmore Schwartz, John Berryman. Readers without direct knowledge of Bellow and his circle are at no disadvantage; they can recall the fiction. Citrine, forced into the cab by Cantabile, thinks of John Stuart Mill as did Herzog in the depths of his despair think of Spinoza; that reading is useless has been lamented in *Henderson*, in *Herzog*, in *Mr. Sammler's Planet*. The conversations on boredom and sloth in *Humboldt's Gift* reach back to Augie in his lifeboat. The TB ward and the Russian baths on Division Street are long-familiar sites, well known to readers of Bellow. Citrine seeks answers to questions raised long ago by Joseph, and asked again and over again by every Bellow hero. Which one did not wonder about the nature of reality, or the "death question" as Citrine calls it, the nature of the soul, the survival of the death of the body? Well before Citrine studies Rudolf Steiner, Henderson admitted he was "highly mediumistic and attuned" and believed corporeal bodies were images of the spiritual, that visible objects were renderings of invisible objects. It was Henderson who said, as he gazed into the eyes of the Persian child with him on the flight to New York, "You can never convince me that this was for the first time."

Herzog, ten years earlier, sought the rebirth of his spirit: "Figuring will get me nowhere, it's only illumination that I have to wait for." Sammler, five years earlier, studied the writings of a mystic. Now Charlie Citrine reads books on the Consciousness Soul given him by Professor Scheldt, who instructs him in the manifestations of unseen beings, whose fire and wisdom and love created the universe and continue to guide the universe. Bellow, too, visited regularly with Professor LeMay, who lived on the South Side of Chicago. LeMay, a man immersed in the esoteric subjects of anthroposophy, gave Bellow books to read about etheric and astral bodies and instructed him in the practices of Rudolf Steiner, the "Scientist of the Invisible." Citrine accepts the program of metaphysical meditation because it can lead him to mental and spiritual clarity. So did Bellow. Citrine says:

> I want it to be clear that I speak as a person who had lately received or experienced light. I don't mean "The Light." I mean a kind of light-in-the-being, a thing difficult to be precise about, especially in an account like this, where so many cantankerous erroneous silly and delusive objects, actions and phenomena are in the foreground.

Citrine reminds us:

> And this light, however it is to be described, was now a real element in me, like the breath of life itself. I had experienced it briefly, but it had lasted long enough

to be convincing, and also to cause an altogether unreasonable kind of joy.
. . . I knew long ago what this light was. Only I seemed to have forgotten that
in the first decade of life I knew the light and even knew how to breathe it in.

So Bellow described the flashes of insight he experienced when reading
Steiner; so Herzog felt, so Bummidge felt, so Uncle Benn Crader will appear
to Ken: Benn has "the magics." Benn will have the faculty of seeing: "the
light pries these organs out of us creatures for purposes of its own. You
certainly don't expect a power like the power of light to let you alone."

It is clear that the relationship between Charlie Citrine and Von Humboldt
Fleisher is the analogue of the long and troubled friendship between Bellow
and Delmore Schwartz. It is a fact that Bellow met Schwartz in New York;
that Schwartz did buy a house in rural New Jersey, in Baptistown, so sure was
he of a permanent appointment at Princeton. Professor Sewell, who agrees
to hire Citrine to assist Humboldt at Princeton, is R. P. Blackmur; and
Langstaff of the Belisha Foundation, to whom Citrine speaks on behalf of
the poet, appears to be based on Gordon Ray of the Guggenheim Foundation. Delmore Schwartz did attack Hilton Kramer, the art critic, whom he
accused without any evidence, of seducing his wife, Elizabeth Pollett, and he
sued poor Kramer for $150,000. Kramer is Magnasco; Elizabeth is Kathleen.*
It is a fact Bellow did try to move Schwartz from Bellevue to Payne Whitney,
and he did try to collect money from friends who knew Schwartz and would
be willing to help. Bellow wrote to James Laughlin in 1957 and Laughlin
responded to Bellow's request for money to establish a fund for Schwartz.

September 23, 1957

Dear Saul:
    The enclosed came in the mail to me from Germany, with a long piece about
"Augie" and I thought you might be interested in seeing it.
    I am terribly depressed about poor old Delmore's predicament. I certainly
am glad that you and Miss Carver are looking after him.† I haven't tried to visit

---

*When Humboldt tells Citrine of Kathleen's father, he exaggerates the faults
of the old man; but a similar father appears in the novel *A Family Romance,* written by
Elizabeth Pollett. Humboldt says, "Yes, the old guy was supposed to be just a pleasant
character . . . but he was an international criminal, a Dr. Moriarty, a Lucifer, a pimp, and
didn't he try to have sexual relations with his own daughter?" The central trauma of the
narrative of *A Family Romance* is incest.
    †Catherine Carver had been employed at *Partisan Review* during the 1940s and
remained the friend of Schwartz and Bellow.

him at the hospital, as I thought it might just upset him—there having been a bit of friction now and then—but if you think it would cheer him up in any way, I would be glad to.

I had a letter the other day from Arthur Mizener up at Cornell, in which he asks for news of Delmore. I guess he had not heard about this recent illness. I shall be writing him, but I thought perhaps you or Miss Carver might want to approach him if additional funds were needed.

I saw Ted Morrison the other day up in Vermont and asked him whether he knew of anyone around Cambridge who might be interested in helping, but he didn't think so.

With best wishes, As ever,
James Laughlin

When Citrine meets Orlando Huggins, the executor of Humboldt's estate, they talk affectionately of their old friend. Citrine says, "We still have one bond, anyway. We both adored Humboldt." They talk of the decline of the poet and Huggins says, "Enough to make you cry when you think how viv-viv, how fresh, handsome, wonderful and what masterpieces."

James Laughlin, appointed to be the executor of Schwartz's estate, contacted Bellow when *Humboldt's Gift* was about to be published; he thought it a good time to bring out a collection of Delmore Schwartz's writings, published and unpublished, and asked Bellow to write a few words of introduction. Bellow said he would if he found the time, acknowledging that to be sure he had been thinking of Schwartz when writing *Humboldt's Gift*, but only in part. The failed poet is a composite person—Delmore, yes, but also Isaac Rosenfeld, and also John Berryman, and a significant fragment Bellow himself.

In *Humboldt's Gift*, Humboldt is a composite person; the failed poet is Delmore Schwartz but only in part. Part is also Isaac Rosenfeld and John Berryman. The more significant part to me to be Bellow himself.

Bellow and Rosenfeld had published their first novels almost together, *Dangling Man* in 1944, *Passage from Home* in 1946. *Dangling Man* received a good deal of notice if not universal praise, but Bellow was welcomed as a writer to watch by Irving Kristol, Mark Schorer, Edmund Wilson, Diana Trilling, Delmore Schwartz, George Mayberry, Peter DeVries, John Chamberlain, Kenneth Fearing, and Herbert Kupferberg. When Rosenfeld's turn came, *Passage from Home* received brief notice—a few short reviews that were reserved but respectful, from Elizabeth Hardwick in *Partisan Review,* Diana Trilling in *The Nation,* Marjorie Farber in *New Republic,* Richard Sullivan in *The New York Times,* and Richard Match in the *Herald Tribune.* [1] Irving Howe wrote at nicer length for *Commentary;* he approved the book because Rosenfeld passed no adverse judgments on his Jewish background, because he explored sensitively the relationship between father and son, between Jewish immigrants and their Americanized children, between old-world tradition and contemporary alienation. For Howe, that was all to the good. However, the novel, he was sorry to say, was immature, muddled in point of view, unsophisticated, and lacking in literary skill.[2]

In 1947, Bellow published his second novel, *The Victim,* and again it was widely reviewed: "surely one of the most complexly moving books of the past ten years"; "part of the great theme of European literature, the dilemma of urban man"; with "the tone of E. M. Forster"; and "as good as Graham Greene."

In 1951, Rosenfeld's second novel, *The Enemy,* was completed; the manuscript, rejected by one publisher after another, was returned to more and more grubby addresses. In 1951, Bellow received his Guggenheim Fellowship; in 1952, he received a National Institute of Arts and Letters Award; in 1952–1953, he was a creative writing fellow at Princeton, and the following year went to Bard College. *Augie March* was formally published on a Friday—mid-September 1953—and that weekend there were reviews to greet it in the *Chicago Tribune,* the Sunday *New York Times,* the *Herald Tribune,* the *New Leader,* the *Saturday Review. Time* magazine caught up as soon as it could. In all the literary circles in the United States and England, there was extravagant praise, as well as attack, but no one ignored the phenomenon of *The Adventures of Augie March.* Bellow was publicly declared to be the peer of Malamud and Mailer and Salinger and Updike and Roth, all of whom had successful novels published during those years. In 1955, Bellow had a second Guggenheim, a contract with Viking Press to edit, with Delmore Schwartz, a collection of pieces to be called *What the Great Novelists Say About Writing the Novel,* and an assignment from *Holiday* to write a travel sketch on Illinois; Granville Hicks, putting together a book in defense of the novel, asked Bellow to submit an essay. Nineteen fifty-six was the year that "Seize the Day" established Bellow as a significant voice in American fiction.

In 1956, Rosenfeld had retreated to his hometown. He was writing what proved to be his last piece, a weary and wistful contemplation of Chicago for *Commentary* magazine.[3] A page or two before his overview of "Life in Chicago" was halted, there was the following sentence: "There has been some talk of starting a quality review, fortnightly or monthly, but nothing has yet come of it. (Interested parties please get in touch with me.)"

Isaac died alone in a furnished room on Walton Place on Chicago's Near North Side. Cartons of manuscripts were sent to his wife, Vasiliki.

Always loyal to Rosenfeld, Bellow often declared they were hearts' companions and believed Isaac was the more intelligent and wiser man. In

1977, when we were driving to the University of Chicago to pick up a copy of the Jefferson lectures, he told me Isaac once had a room on the South Side, and showed me the building, a dilapidated brick tenement. We stood staring at it for a while and then walked on. A few years ago, Rosenfeld's diary came to light and Bellow was startled to read there the hidden, often cruel, thoughts of his friend. All Bellow said, simply and sadly, was that he had discovered Rosenfeld hated him, and Bellow loved him, and that's all there was to it.

Delmore Schwartz had an extraordinary success when he published "In Dreams Begin Responsibilities" in 1938. Such success never came again. *Genesis,* Schwartz's long autobiographical poem, failed, and *The World Is a Wedding,* a collection of short stories, failed, and *Vaudeville for a Princess,* a collection of poems, failed. Like Berryman, Schwartz was in and out of mental wards, on and off whiskey and drugs, irrational, vain, consumed with despair and hatred and suspicion. Delmore collapsed in a dismal hotel off Times Square and died in Roosevelt Hospital; his body lay unclaimed in the morgue for two days. Suitcases filled with manuscript were found in Schwartz's dollar-a-day room.

John Berryman, too, seems to have been much on Bellow's mind while he was writing *Humboldt's Gift.* Berryman had been at Princeton the year Bellow and Schwartz had their temporary appointments. Eileen Simpson, in an account of her life with Berryman, recalled Bellow at a party in 1951:

> Saul, whose dark good looks had made the heart of more than one Princeton matron beat more rapidly—it was generally agreed among them that Bellow was a "dish"—greeted us with an open-mouthed smile which made one smile in reflex. He seemed to be the only person present who was in a genial mood.[4]

She went on to say Bellow was the only one among them who was "sane."

> Ted [Roethke] was not in his right mind. Cal [Robert Lowell], in Salzburg, had gone clear out of his again. Delmore had changed so heartbreakingly one could no longer use the word "crazy" in the old innocent way when talking about him. Saul was sane. The "ease and light" Cal had found in John's company in Damariscotta John now found in Saul's. Until December the two men had met only in the company of other people, on campus, at the seminars, with Delmore, at the house of mutual friends. Returning from a Sunday walk down by Lake Carnegie with Monroe Engel and Saul, John said to me, "I like Bellow more each time I see him. A lovely man. And a comedian. He threw a log he found

at the edge of the lake into the water and, with a gesture of command, said, 'Go. Go be a hazard!' "

A few days later John came home with a typescript of Saul's new novel and said, "I'm going to take the weekend off to read this." . . . When he finished, "Bellow is *it.*"

To Berryman, fame came tardily, with the publication in 1956 of "Homage to Mistress Bradstreet," and his reputation as a first-rate American poet was enhanced by the issue of *77 Dream Songs* in 1966—for which he received the Pulitzer Prize—and by more *Dream Songs* in 1969, and *Sonnets* in 1967. For Berryman it was too late, however. He could not ride out the severe criticism that also greeted each new publication of his poems. He could not dry out, could never calm down for long. His frequent hospitalizations were respites, not cures, from alcoholism, his uncontrollable aggression, promiscuity, and fear of dwindling power. Bellow always tried to help Berryman. The last time he saw him was at a reading arranged at the University of Chicago. Berryman arrived drunk and shabby, was inarticulate, finally degradingly sick in a taxi. Berryman retained no memory of the fiasco of his nonperformance.[5]

In 1971, writing to Bellow from Minneapolis, Berryman announced joyously the birth of his daughter, christened Sarah Rebecca, and then went on at great length about the novel he was excitedly writing—a supposed fiction of his confinement in a hospital to cure his drinking and depression—sure it would be "hot as a pistol" though not as good, perhaps, as *Herzog* or *Moby Dick*. He was also excited about Bellow's progress on his new novel, *Humboldt's Gift*, and said, "Let's join forces, large and small, as in the winter beginning of 1953 in Princeton with the Bradstreet blazing and Augie fleecing away. We're promising." He tells Bellow he has finished his long nine-part poem, "took all winter and all but ended *me,*" a poem on the Divine Office, *Opus Dei,* and reported that Robert Giroux had taken back to New York the complete manuscript of *Delusions,* which was planned for spring publication. Berryman enclosed the three latest lyrics that Bellow had heard in Chicago.

Delusions was published posthumously.* Berryman climbed the railing of a bridge and flung himself into the Mississippi River.

In Bellow's deeply sad and moving tribute to "John Berryman, Friend," he explained the death:

John had waited a long time for this poet's happiness. He had suffered agonies of delay. Now came the poems. They were killing him. . . . Inspiration contained

*The title was changed to *Recovery.*

a death threat. He would, as he wrote the things he had waited and prayed for, fall apart. Drink was a stabilizer. It somewhat reduced the fatal intensity. Perhaps it replaced the public sanction which poets in the Twin Cities (or in Chicago, in Washington or New York) had to do without.

And at last it must have seemed that he had used up all his resources. Faith against despair, love versus nihilism had been the themes of his struggles and his poems. What he needed for his art had been supplied by his own person, by his mind, his wit. He drew it out of his vital organs, out of his very skin. At last there was no more. Reinforcements failed to arrive. Forces were not joined. The cycle of resolution, reform and relapse had become a bad joke which could not continue.

In *A Margin of Hope,* published in 1982, Irving Howe remembered them all: "Berryman, Schwartz, and Bellow formed a haughty young aristocracy of letters, devoted to the stress of their temperaments, bound together by a fraternity of troubles." John Berryman was the most "violently original" and Bellow, "not quite so famous yet," was acknowledged as "the virtuoso." Isaac Rosenfeld "was our golden boy . . . *a Wunderkind* grown into tubby sage," radiating "a generosity that melted the crustiest New York hearts," with a purity that made the circle of New York intellectuals hope wildly for his future. Alas, said Howe, Isaac did not fulfill the hope.

> . . . he never quite found the medium, in either fiction or essay, to release his gift. . . . Profligate with his being, his time, his thought, he lacked only that cunning economy that enables writers to sustain lengthy careers.[6]

That could be said of so many poets of Bellow's circle. The judgment of the wistful memorialists of the eighties seems harsh.

William Barrett, in *The Truants,* recalled:

> An evening at the [Philip] Rahvs . . . tended to be a more sedate, careful and calculated affair; and depending on the particular guests, one sometimes had to tread warily. The late Isaac Rosenfeld—a young and promising novelist and critic who, sadly, died before his promise was realized—was an occasional guest until Rahv decided he was on the skids and was no longer a "winner."[7]

So were they all on the skids, except Bellow, the writer destined to fulfill the promise, the writer, as Barrett remembered, with the chip of self-confidence on his shoulder, the writer whose strategy was self-protection, the self-appointed contender, as if to have faith in himself was an affront to intellectuals and New Yorkers.

Bellow, looking back on himself, sees something quite different: this Bellow of the forties, beginning; this Bellow of the fifties, winning and winning; this Bellow of the sixties, frenetic, restless, and angry, also abandoned, also friendless, but still in the fight, was still seeking the way to rekindle his spirit.

For all his wistful sense of loss of this sad group of friends, Bellow continued to wonder why they had never been able to put aside their debilitating focus on Me! Me! Me! Why had they allowed themselves to be sucked into the confessional mode, living under the foolish illusion that there was a "Next Necessary Thing" to which they must adhere? Despite their lip service to Whitman, they had willfully neglected the larger concerns, issues of society, public events, questions of the progress of history, of the human dilemma. Could they not have taken refuge in the realm of myth, which for Bellow was the provenance of the soul?

Bellow had no quarrel with personality as a subject matter, but he wondered why they could not see that personality, with all its flaws, was an ill-fitting suit of clothes, to be changed by will, by character that required of itself right action, not submission and self-doubt. If the critics looked down their noses at them, his friends fell apart. Why could Schwartz or Rosenfeld or Berryman not choose to attack the judges instead of themselves, attack their sterility, castigate their crippling of students, denounce their indifference to art, their lack of moral passion, and go on with the trade of poetry, nurture their imagination, the wellspring of art? Why choose instead to pollute their bodies and prostrate their souls? Why should any poet envy Robert Lowell, or Eliot or Pound for that matter, and disconnect from the spirit of Whitman?

Bellow disentangled himself from these friends who were losing and taught himself to walk, many times wounded; but who is not wounded? He found himself on a road of prizes and awards and medals and enormous sales, but he knew the reward was not success but, rather, the power to create beauty, the power to create art. He understood he was not Schwartz, not Berryman, not Rosenfeld, but himself, uniquely the self. And who was that, finally? The explanation of that self occupies the whole field of vision of *Humboldt's Gift.*

Recall that Herzog begins a letter to his old friend Nachman:

Dear Nachman, he wrote. *I know it was you I saw on 8th St. Monday. Running away from me.* Herzog's face darkened. *It was you. My friend nearly forty years ago.*

Herzog abandons the letter, asking himself how was he to reach Nachman? He had no address. "He would do better to advertise in the *Village Voice*." Ten years later, Charlie Citrine writes a long long letter to Von Humboldt Fleisher, the failed poet—it is this book, *Humboldt's Gift*—and Citrine, like Herzog had done before him, lays aside his reflections on Humboldt to address himself; Citrine, too, is faltering and would like to run away from himself.

So Bellow lends to Humboldt his own irritation at the practice of academics. It is Humboldt who says, "For them the whole purpose of art is to suggest and inspire ideas and discourse. . . . Their business is to reduce masterpieces to discourse." These were exactly Bellow's words spoken in his keynote address to the PEN Congress in 1966. Bellow lends to Humboldt his own dismay at the savagery of critics. It is Humboldt who says, "Lots of people are waiting for me to fall on my face. I have a million enemies. . . . if [an artist] makes a ritual mistake the whole crowd tears him to pieces." This is Bellow's recurrent question: "Why should poetry make you a million enemies?"

Bellow knew well that at the outset of his career he, too, had been arrogant, confident, smart, ambitious, excited by his early success, wildly exuberant at his possibilities; Humboldt had disappeared but Citrine lives to lament it is he who has no foothold, he who is the instrument that dismantles his world, he who has lost faith in the possibility that any truth can be known, he who is the failure. Bellow, too, has had the bad reviews, the silent friends, the jeering audiences, the tumult of a domestic life ending in betrayal and vengeance.*

I am suggesting that Von Humboldt Fleisher is early Charlie Citrine and, more to the point, early Bellow. The Citrine who narrates the tale represents Bellow of the seventies, assessing what he had once been, what he

---

Herzog had made a great deal of money for Bellow, but much of it was lost in his divorce settlement with Susan. The figure of $250,000 was arrived at by a judge who heard the charges and countercharges, the appeals and counterappeals. The lawyer who represented Susan Bellow was well known in Chicago. Every woman contemplating a divorce wanted Jerome Berkson to handle her case. Five years after Bellow's divorce, a law was discovered that said if one enters into a property settlement in a divorce case and does not make a full disclosure of income and assets, the aggrieved spouse may go into court and vacate the decree and reopen the case. Bellow's award of the Nobel Prize was accepted as evidence of his nondisclosure and his case became a test of the application of that law.

Ready to go to jail for contempt of court, Bellow refused to pay, but he was prevailed upon at the last to place $200,000 in escrow while he dragged and was dragged through appeals and countercharges, further appeals, renegotiations and settlements, upsets and reversals. So Citrine will be beset by lawyers, judges, and wives.

is now, and then explaining what he would like to become. We will encounter this odd device of a splitting apart of the narrator into a young man and an older man in dialogue with each other when we get to *More Die of Heartbreak*. There, however, it will be young Kenneth Trachtenberg (early Bellow) who tries to figure out why older Uncle Benn Crader (late Bellow) went wrong. *More Die of Heartbreak* goes over the ground again—eroticism, frenzy, confusion, a man of light and spirit betrayed, manipulated, preyed upon, and, because it is Bellow writing, restored, regenerated.

I think of *Humboldt's Gift* as another turning point in Bellow's career and this has nothing to do with Nobel Prizes. When Bellow left old man Sammler reconciled to his final task, attending to the growth of his spirit, twenty-five years of Bellow's search for how to lead a significant life in the real world had come to an end. From *Humboldt's Gift* on, Bellow will tell his story again and over again—*The Dean's December*, "Cousins," "Him with His Foot in His Mouth," "What Kind of Day Did You Have?", *More Die of Heartbreak*— but the narrator, from Charlie Citrine on, will no longer be a man betrayed solely by others, but by himself. Young Ken will be betrayed by his Uncle Benn; that is, the illuminated man will betray the man on quest. The war between the external world and the internal world will recede and the war between Eros and Logos, staged in the heart of the single man, will come to a full boil.

Charlie Citrine, speaking to his readers—"Dear friends, I'll tell you how I saw it"; "But I'm getting ahead of myself"; "But I have another thing to tell you"; "I interrupt to observe"—discloses the truth about himself. Neither the world nor history but, rather, he himself was to blame for the fall of his soul from innocence to error; only he precipitated his decline from virtuous joy to corruption and hypocrisy; only he, Citrine, allowed his own aggressiveness and prodigality and vanity and eroticism to fog and blur and all but extinguish the radiance of his spirit. As harsh with himself as ever Sammler was harsh, gazing at America, Citrine peels off layer after layer of lies, and his recollections reveal he was not pure in the morass of unrighteousness, not a Saint Sebastian, but an enthusiastic member of the sect of the Prince of Darkness. Mrs. Harscha had been right.

> "So this is Joseph . . . *Er ist schön.*"
> "*Mephisto war auch schön,*" Mrs. Harscha answered.
> Joseph thinks, "She had seen through me . . . and, where others saw nothing wrong, she had discovered evil."

Sammler whispered to himself that the only covenant in force was the covenant between the soul and God; the only way to live the good life was to prepare for death. Now an anxious middle-aged Citrine strives to prepare his soul to enter the next stage of his life, to restore himself to spiritual clarity before he pays his death. It may take a billion years to ameliorate human nature; Citrine has only a few months to discover how to transcend the appearances of reality.

Citrine's "Consciousness Soul," in company with memory, must reexamine the life already lived and by a process of reflection—meditation—reconstruct each stage of experience. If he has the courage to be honest, he can reach the very essence of his nature and thereby restore his soul to tranquillity before it is consigned to the cosmos. Citrine renews an old commitment—to fulfill the life of the spirit:

> The job, once and for all, was to burst from the fatal self-sufficiency of consciousness and put my remaining strength over into the Imaginative Soul. As Humboldt should have done.

This was something Augie tried to do, that Henderson strove to do, that Herzog said he would do, that Bummidge promised, that Sammler prayed he might still do. It was an old responsibility, this mission to communicate the truth of the life of the spirit. Von Humboldt dead? Citrine survived. While he had memory and imagination, he would restore Humboldt and himself to consciousness.

16

"I speak as a person who has lately received or experienced light"

Bellow's style—the rendering of simultaneity, the interplay of present events and associates with the events and associates of the hero's past life, with now and again extrusions into the life he hopes to lead—serves well for the narrative of *Humboldt's Gift*. The great shift in the meaning and purpose of Citrine's recollections is the startling surprise. No longer do they arise to justify Citrine, helpless among predators, a victim of twentieth-century amorality and decadence; Citrine reflects on his past in order to judge himself, accuse himself, condemn himself. He is the one to blame for the dimming of his light, for his melancholy and instability, and yes, for the waywardness of his present life. The design of the book is Citrine's progress in the uncovering of errors, the gradual discovery of truth about himself, and the gradual restoration of faith in the spirit. A man's character is his fate, Augie March had said, quoting Novalis before him, and now Citrine explores his character to find a way to change his fate. What were the flaws? How may they be healed? That is the form of *Humboldt's Gift*.

The present experiences out of which Citrine will recall his past are no more melodramatic than the events in Sammler's few days of activities: having his Mercedes wrecked, meeting the small-time hood Rinaldo Cantabile in a Turkish bath, losing his shoe while dining at the Plaza, going with his old friend Thaxter to a jeweler's shop, calling on his old girlfriend Naomi Lutz in Queens, dropping in on Humboldt's Uncle Waldemar at a nursing home in Coney Island, going off to Texas to visit his brother Julius, who is about to undergo open heart surgery, waiting for Renata in Madrid, losing Renata to his rival Flonzaley, retreating to a pension, accepting Humboldt's legacy, arranging a funeral. Probably such commonplace actions disquiet those Bellow critics who relate him to Dostoevski and Kafka, but so it is. And, just as all that Sammler saw and heard, sitting on hard chairs, stuffed chairs, bus seats, leaning on windowsills, standing against the walls of corridors, walking about the streets of New York, generated memories so that we learn what happened to Sammler in his sixty-odd years, so Citrine remembers, lying on his couch, on a bed, sitting in a latrine, drifting out of his present into the past. Sammler recalls wars and concentration camps. Citrine recalls poets and women.

Sammler's memories evolve out of the contrast between old age and youth, reason and action, a dying Europe and a decadent America, aspiration and moral bankruptcy; Citrine's memories reconstruct a past interpreted as a chronic war between himself and himself, and he is deliberate in his meditations, reaming his mind to be rid of the nonsense of wives, lovers, mentors, spurious ideas of art and American society, but above all, his purpose is to face his own lies, his own wastes, his own impurities, to discover how the connection between himself and Divinity had been broken. He acknowledges that he is the loser, not of status or money but of joy in his spirit. "I had no heart at all, only a sort of chicken giblet." No one has done this to him. He performed his own disintegration. Tranquillity, too, may be achieved by an act of his will; his soul can free itself from distraction and waken itself from its dreaming sleep. He can restore radiance to his soul.

Like Sammler, Citrine fears he is running out of time—death is going to catch him "off base on the racquet-ball court or on the Posturepedic mattress of some Renata or other." His plan to achieve mental and spiritual clarity had better come into operation at once. If "light-in-the-being" is to be regained, he must learn the exercises in meditation described in Steiner's *Knowledge of the Higher Worlds and Its Attainment*; he must learn how to leave his present world and observe and reflect on the internal world that consists of memories; he must trap the evidence of his own participation in his erosion. Steiner teaches him how to will his imagination to focus on some object or incident or person in the past and recapture all the evanescent thoughts and feelings generated by these memories. "If this was what transcendence took it was a cinch. I could do it forever."

Bellow can indeed do it forever. The people, incidents, and thoughts that will enable Citrine to meditate are ready to hand, waiting to emerge out of Bellow's past. Remembering, however, is not the sole task, neither of Citrine nor of Bellow. The purpose now is to snare the self in all its duplicity.

Steiner instructs his pupil to imagine a bush covered with roses, dense with tiny garnet flowers and fresh healthy green leaves.

> I visualized the twigs, the roots, the harsh fuzz of the new growth hardening into spikes, plus all the botany I could remember . . . attempting to project myself into the very plant and think how its green blood produced a red flower. . . . I concentrated all the faculties of my soul on this vision.

The plant, according to Steiner, expressed the passionless laws of growth. Human beings, aiming at higher perfection, are burdened with instincts and desires. A man takes a greater risk with passions, but if the man is willing to chance emotions in the surety the higher powers of the soul can cleanse him, he may transform his passions and be reborn into a higher manifestation. Citrine is eager to take the risk of the next exercise. Steiner recommends the contemplation of a cross wreathed with roses, but "for reasons of perhaps Jewish origin," Citrine prefers to contemplate a lamp post, like the old black iron lamp post he saw outside his bedroom window when he was a boy and crept out of bed to stare at in the night. Citrine meditates.

Always the shape of a man appears beside the rosebush, under the lamp post. Von Humboldt Fleisher is the luminous apparition. His earliest mentor, his oldest friend, the poet of radiance, fallen into decay, consumed with neuroses, pomposities, and falsehoods, it is Citrine Humboldt has come to warn. Humboldt forebodes not death but the danger of leaving the earth empty-handed, with no true or clear word to say before the soul leaves the earth. The human day must not end in falsehood.

Citrine reconstructs long-past events so that he may discover how and why he allowed business and bureaucracy, politics and society, eroticism and artificiality, ostentation and sanctimony to pollute his soul. Citrine forces himself to remember and face the truth about himself.

When a young man, filled with optimism and idealism, an innocent sentimental youth, Citrine believed in the life of the mind. Like Humboldt, Citrine believed the life of poetry, of art, was the life of the highest order.

It was a delusion; it was inevitable that Humboldt should fail. Who could think Citrine had succeeded? He, too, had been sidetracked into a life of the body; the distractions of success had led him too into error, entangled him with gangsters, lawyers, judges, awarded him a vindictive wife, false friends, and he, too, was sunk in a quagmire of money and court cases, sensuality, showmanship and vanity. Sleaze as well as art was as much an attribute of his character as was his faith in the life of thought. What was the reality of his present life if not a "melting" into affectation, sham, and desolation? His art, too, had suffered. "The agony is too deep, the disorder too big for art enterprises in the old way."

Yes, Humboldt had had an early success in the thirties when he published *Harlequin Ballads*; yes, Citrine came to New York to meet the great man with whom he could talk of literature and significant ideas. He remembers their teaching together at Princeton, Humboldt in rural New Jersey with his schemes for presiding as a reincarnated Goethe, bringing Weimar to Washington, once Adlai Stevenson is elected. He remembers Humboldt's decline into failure and madness, his shambling appearance on a side street in Manhattan. Citrine remembers, too, his own beloved young mistress, Demmie Vonghel, who died in an airplane crash while on a mission with her father in South America, his ex-wife, Denise, with her "huge radial amethyst eyes in combination with a low-lined forehead and sharp sibylline teeth," this Denise who sued him in collusion with corrupt lawyers and corrupt judges in the corrupt Chicago courts. Citrine remembers taking off Naomi Lutz's blue terry-cloth pajamas just after he had helped her father, a foot doctor, swab the sores on the legs of a lady who worked at the National Biscuit factory. He remembers the sofa bed at the Plaza, his taking off Renata's plastic raincoat and finding her naked, drunk, passed out.

How can he pride himself on Logos? On loyalty? He had locked himself in a men's room to weep after reading Humboldt's obituary notice in the *Times*. But he had run away from Humboldt. Was it out of compassion for his old friend, whom he would humiliate by his manicured well-tailored presence? Or had he been angry at that old friend who bilked him out of seven thousand dollars, who picketed the theater when *Von Trenk* was playing to standing room only? Was it contempt for the womanizer? How free was he, Citrine, from neurotic erotic attachments? When Humboldt lay dead in the hallway of the Ilsecombe, Citrine admits he lay in bed with voluptuous Renata at the Plaza. How pure was he? How radiant his spirit in pursuit of how significant a fate?

Citrine recalls the first time he saw Renata. The door of an elevator had opened, and although he heard no voice that said "My Fate!" he had pursued her as if she was. He knew this Renata, this erotic engine who generated erotic satisfaction, who took off his shoe and placed his stockinged foot between her legs and masturbated, hidden by the tablecloth while they dined with Thaxter at the Plaza, then, leaving them to talk of higher matters, hurried off to make the late afternoon showing of *Deep Throat*; this Renata who flattered him: "You're in terrific shape, Charlie. You're not a big fellow but you're sturdy, solid, and you're elegant also." He needed to hear that. He knew he looked good, his belly was flat, he was always well-dressed, his cholesterol level was low, he had money. Yes, his strong legs were agile enough for him to outrun a mugger. Ah yes, the thought intrudes, those same flexible legs had taken him off to hide behind a car when he had seen Humboldt, seedy, a "gray stout sick dusty man eating a pretzel stick." Admit: This Renata had value for him. She impressed George Swiebel, who fawned in admiration of his old friend Charlie who could still keep up "an active erotic and vivid fluent emotional life." Admit: She has greater value for him. She tells him the truth about his noble self: "You're full of hostility, arrogant. Nobody makes the grade with you." All that he does, she scoffs, is to invent relationships with the dead he never had when they were living. "You create connections they wouldn't allow, or you weren't capable of." She was right. He cannot deny it. "You're like a mandolin player. You tickle every note ten times. It's cute, but a little goes a long way." Renata's words are the judgment he can never bring himself to say. Well, now he will say it.

Citrine thinks of Thaxter, who has phoned to say he is in New York and will stop in to see him at the Plaza. Thaxter, he knows, is a fop, a phony, a swindler, on blacklists of country clubs, a con man with every shade of larceny in his heart. Yet he believes he has always loved Thaxter. Why? Because he is like Thaxter. His diverse interests were also little more than "cultural nosiness," his scope and dash also nothing but ostentation and caprice—worse. Citrine suspects he likes to bask in Thaxter's flattery, in Thaxter's respect for his serious desire to improve mankind, in Thaxter's confidence that Citrine will write interesting and important "high level analyses" of American civilization, the true chronicle of Chicago. Citrine is the phony; he loves the sycophant.

Citrine thinks of his brother, who always required to have a fortune under his control. Citrine has always prided himself on his disdain of money but has he not, like his brother, believed money to be a vital substance like blood? Why has he pretended all these years to have contempt for his brother? Why, if money is base, is he angry because his brother cheated him out of money? Maybe he was not so very different from that brother, whose mustache mitigated the greediness of his mouth, a strutting, heavy, graceful, rapacious man, somehow connected with the underworld. Yet he believes he loves Ulick. Why? Because Ulick has always told him the truth. Ulick has his number.

You poor nut, you overeducated boob. . . . I can't read the crap you write. Two sentences and I'm yawning. . . . Pa should have slapped you around the way he did me. It would have woken you up. . . . You were always a strong-willed fellow and a jock. . . . You're a sexy little bastard, never mind your big-time mental life. All this fucking art! Your scribbles.

Ulick was right. Charlie was the phony. Charlie was the pretender. He has no wisdom or solace to give a man about to risk heart surgery.

Why does he sneer at Cantabile? Was it only because Cantabile cheated him at cards? He had been there, had he not, playing poker? He had not even noticed Cantabile palming cards because he had been too busy showing off how smart he was, talking, quoting, spouting ideas. Citrine admits he likes to appear to have all the answers, to seem smart to everyone, to anyone, to shine even for a Cantabile. He likes the small-time gangster because Cantabile, too, has his number, tells him to his face he is a dude, a sexpot, and dumb. "When are you going to do something and know what you're doing?" He is the phony, Cantabile the honest man.

Another fantasy intrudes into Citrine's meditations. He should have married a woman like Naomi Lutz: "Fifteen thousand nights embracing Naomi and I would have smiled at the solitude and boredom of the grave. I would have needed no bibliography, no stock portfolios, no medal from the Legion of Honor." However, that lie also gives way before the growing power of his judgment. No, he requires the erotic life. Like Augie, like Henderson, like Herzog, Citrine defends himself: He needs the swelling heart, the tearing eagerness of the deserted, "the painful keenness or infinitizing of an unidentified need." What is that unidentified need? It is to outwit aging, to deny his own mortality. Naomi looked so comfortable in her slippers, smiling in her kitchen, her fat arms crossed. To have slept with her for forty years would have defeated death itself. But no. Citrine interrupts his fabrications. He could not have borne it. He has grown fastidious with the passing years. And Naomi doesn't look so tasty now. He is, as Naomi tells him outright, an old chaser and he does not deny it. Worse is true. He is not trying to improve the Renatas of the world. He is in erotic bondage to this Renata, and there will be Renatas always. Why? Because she was in the biblical sense unclean and has made his life richer "with the thrills of deviation and broken laws." And with enough Renatas he can then break the law of human destiny. With no Renata, he stands on the edge of the grave.

Naomi offers him a sop: At least he cherished his family—"you people all loved each other." "Yes." He grasps at the memory. "I never lost this intense way of caring," and he pulls himself up: "No, that isn't so, I'm afraid. The truth is I did lose it. Yes. Sure I lost it." His illusion of old-time family love must be revised. He had only pretended. Why? "I required it."

It was the same with his love of women. Nothing more than appearance. "For women," he admits to Naomi, "I had this utopian emotional love aura and that made them feel I was a cherishing man. Sure, I'd cherish them in the way they all dreamed of being cherished." Naomi says it for him. "But it was a phony. You didn't cherish." He does not deny it.

At the last, it is Naomi who faces him with the major deception. It is the whisper of the wife in "The Wrecker," across the years, of Marcella Vankuchen in "A Wen," sitting alone at a coffee table. Casually, she says, "I never really knew what you were talking about." She asks him to give her an example of his important thoughts and he complies, willingly, easily, glibly. He slips back, becomes the old Citrine, preening himself, and offers Naomi a long interpretation of sloth. After which she says:

> "Is this really a sample of your mental processes? . . . Oh, Christ, Charlie," said Naomi, sorry for me. She pitied me, really, and reaching over and breathing kindly into my face she patted my hand. "Of course you've probably become even more peculiar with time. I see now it's lucky for us both that we never got together. We would have had nothing but maladjustment and conflict. You would have had to speak all this high-flown stuff to yourself, and everyday gobbledygook to me. In addition, there may be something about me that provokes you to become incomprehensible. . . ."

So much for his beloved fantasy that he communicates with the common man. How different was his pipe dream that he had business on behalf of the human race from Humboldt's scheme to bring Weimar to Washington? "I never really knew what you were talking about."

Citrine loves all these people, not only because of who they are but because they tell him the truth about himself, the truth he always suspected but never had the courage to face. It is as if he needs to hear the words on the lips of others, as if once he realizes his true self is known to others, known outside his room, he can no longer fall into self-justification, weep with pity for himself, defend himself to himself. When he hears what others think of him, he must close off his shabby retreats. Is he then not brave? Not a man of honesty and courage to write his own arraignment for all the world to hear? Is he not heroically writing Part II?

To emancipate the ego, one must separate from the old self. To become a significant individual, Charlie must face the truth about his past life. And when we consider it is Bellow, emancipating himself from the old Bellow, we must pause in wonder at the revelations he seemed driven to put down in print. Citrine or Bellow, it scarcely matters which, admits he was weak, dependent, his sensitivity a mask, his naïveté spurious, his knowledge a disguise. At heart, he is a snob. Citrine challenges himself: Had he left Denise because she denied the Light? Well, well. It sounded good. Admit: His mission had been to lay her low. "In fact it was one of my cherished dreams and dearest hopes. To lay them all low." And not one of them, no one at all, had gone down. He alone lay prone.

"Writing books is no proof that you're smart," says the old señora, Renata's mother. "Any little Polish girl on confirmation day knows more than you, with all your books and prizes," says Cantabile.

What then of Humboldt, now gazing down at him from the other side of the circle of eternity? Had not Charlie genuinely believed in his responsibility to carry on for certain failed friends like Von Humboldt Flei-sher, who had never been able to struggle through into higher wakefulness? Was it not true he loved Humboldt, spread out somewhere, "his soul in some other part of the creation, there where souls waited for sustenance that only we, the living, could send from the earth, like grain to Bangladesh." Citrine knows he has no wheat. He is the one who is starving.

Citrine refuses Humboldt's gift of the scenario. From Cantabile's lips fall words that are true. "You don't want to hear any more about your pal. . . . Why, because he blew it—he goofed? This big jolly character with so many talents caved in, just a fucking failure, crazy and a deadbeat, so enough of him?"

It is so. Citrine admits the truth about Humboldt: a malicious, scheming, crazy, dishonest man, a slanderer, a suspicious man who brutalized his wife, a paranoid, a thief, soaked in gin, spaced out on drugs. How could he have ever hoped Humboldt would drape the world in radiance? He was the mere figure of a poet. No. America does not destroy its poets. The poets destroy themselves. However, he loved Humboldt. Why? The reason is the same as it has been throughout his meditations. Humboldt, too, had assessed Citrine correctly, laughed at his dark ingénu eyes and his nice midwestern manners, recognized the sharp, ambitious, aggressive Citrine and told him the truth, finally slamming the door on his refuge into isolation:

"You're too lordly yourself to take offense. You're an even bigger snob than Sewell. I think you may be psychologically one of those Axel types that only cares about inner inspiration, no connection with the actual world. The actual world can kiss your ass. . . . You leave it to poor bastards like me to think about matters like money and status and success and failure and social problems and politics. You don't give a damn for such things . . . you stick *me* with all these unpoetic responsibilities. You lean back like a king, relaxed, and let all these human problems happen. There ain't no flies on Jesus. Charlie, you're not place bound, time bound, goy bound, Jew bound. What *are* you bound? Others abide our question. Thou art free! . . . you can't pay attention. You're always mooning in your private mind about some kind of cosmic destiny. Tell me, what is this great thing you're always working on?"

When Citrine reads Humboldt's final letter to him, he weeps, but not for Humboldt, who says:

> I always had it in for you because you thought I was going to be the great American poet of the century. But I just could not do it. The original fresh self isn't there any more.

He weeps for himself.

> I haven't made it here, Charlie. Be sure that if there is a hereafter, I will be pulling for you. . . . You are lazy, disgraceful, tougher than you think but not yet a dead loss. In part you are humanly okay. We are supposed to do something for our kind. Don't get frenzied about money. Overcome your greed. Better luck with women. Last of all remember: we are not natural beings but supernatural beings.

Alas, Humboldt was right—on all counts. He has been shut up for years trying to reach an understanding with all representatives of the modern intellect. He has read all the books and learned nothing he needed to know. What has come of it? Humboldt had not become the great American poet of the century; has Citrine any chance? Has he any original fresh self left?

Sitting in the cold latrine in the boardinghouse in a run-down neighborhood in Madrid, wearing the black cloak lined in red that he bought for Renata, Citrine cannot warm himself. He is reflecting on the final reality of his character; it has arrived in a letter from Renata, who will never come to Madrid. She has married Flonzaley. You missed your chance, she says.

> You turned me into a sex clown. There are too many zig-zags in your temperament. I don't want to get involved in all this spiritual, intellectual, universal stuff. I prefer to take things as billions of people have done throughout history. You work, you get bread, you lose a leg, kiss some fellows, have a baby, you live to be eighty and bug hell out of everybody, or you get hung or drowned. But you don't spend years trying to dope your way out of the human condition.

His own lawyers have cheated him; settling the case with Denise has wiped him out. Thaxter has cheated him: There is no arrangement with a publisher to live abroad at their expense, no contract to write a literary guide to Europe. Friends and enemies have wiped him out. Compared to the Denises and Renatas and señoras of the world, the Ulicks and Thaxters and Cantabiles and Von Humboldt Fleishers of the world, Citrine "might have been buttoned into a suit of Dr. Denton's Sleepers." He has succeeded in nothing in the real world. He cannot change the past. Can he at least change himself? His soul is anesthetized. How can he do anything to help his spirit burst from its mental coffin? How can he transcend himself?

He has written the bill of particulars against the apparent Charlie Citrine. Can he, having peeled off layer after layer of appearances, find any self left? Meditating on his own accomplishments and failures he has destroyed the false categories, rid himself of his sex obsessions, his money obsessions, his compulsion to explain. Something more is needed. Now his task, as Sammler had come to know, is to enter the final zone of his mortality and learn simply how to *be*. Being is also a form of knowledge; more, it is wisdom. It may be inevitable that the life already lived remain unrevised, unrefined, unimproved, but now, again, it is up to him:

> It was up to me to do something, to give a last favorable turn to the wheel, to transmit moral understanding from the earth where you get it to the next existence where you needed it.

There, he trusts, "all the right human things would—at last! happen." A man can reach a more correct way to think of his death. That is his significant future.

To heal himself, Citrine turns to the life of the soul. "Now we must listen in secret to the sound of truth that God puts in us." His spirit can restore itself to its natural light if he listens to the voice sounding in his soul, the murmur of essence, and that voice will teach him how to step out of his old self and find new meanings that will enable him to connect with the angels of the dead, the spirits that are immortal. Rudolf Steiner, with his exercises in meditation, will guide him in the way to reconstruct his life.

Citrine returns to Chicago to settle his affairs. He visits Uncle Waldemar and shares Humboldt's gift with the old man. He arranges to remove Humboldt from his pauper's grave and rebury his remains in a fine new coffin in a nice cemetery on the other side of the George Washington Bridge. Then he will remove himself to the Goetheanum, where Steiner established his school of spiritual science, and begin a new life in the environment of Dornach.

Citrine stands at the graveside of Humboldt, his old companion in the search for the significant life. Their film script was at this hour entertaining the public from Third Avenue to the Champs Elysées, piling up dollars; together they had filled theaters, and people were rocking with delight, hundreds of thousands, millions of spectators, shouting with laughter. Their film taught nothing, clarified nothing, prevented nothing. Let it be. Who can understand fate? The meaningful life now is to prepare for immortality.

The heavy coffin is deftly lowered by a yellow machine working a little crane, into a concrete case where it will rest. Citrine watches it disappear under the soil. So one deals with Humboldt. What of Citrine?

> How did one get out? One didn't, didn't, didn't!
> You stayed. You stayed!

He has gone as far as he can alone. He had better go to Dornach and take further instruction.

17
Enrolled in
Theosophical
Kindergarten

Had it been left to the New York literary establishment, *Humboldt's Gift* would never have found its way into the display case of Sweden's King Carl XVI Gustaf. When Bellow rose at the Friday night banquet after the awards ceremony, he said:

> I need not worry too much that all men will speak well of me. The civilized community agrees that there is no higher distinction than the Nobel Prize, but it agrees on little else, so I need not fear that the doom of universal approval is hanging over me. When I publish a book I am often soundly walloped by reviewers, a disagreeable but necessary corrective to self-inflation.

The establishment had a good track record for soundly walloping Bellow. Norman Mailer had said of *Herzog:*

> There is a mystery about the reception of *Herzog*. For beneath its richness of texture and its wealth of detail, the fact remains: never has a novel been so

successful when its hero was so dim. Not one of the critics who adored the book would ever have permitted Herzog to remain an hour in his house. For Herzog was defeated, Herzog was an unoriginal man, Herzog was a fool—not an attractive God-anointed fool like Gimpel the Fool, his direct progenitor, but a sodden fool, over-educated and inept, unable to fight, able to love only when love presented itself as a gift. Herzog was intellectual but not bright, his ideas not original, his style as it appeared in his letters unendurable—it had exactly the leaden-footed sense of phrase which men laden with anxiety and near to going mad put into their communications. Herzog was hopeless. We learned nothing about society from him, not even anything about his life. And he is the only figure in the book. His wives, his mistress, his family, his children, his friends, even the man who cuckolds him are seen on the periphery of a dimming vision. Like all men near to being mad, his attention is within, but the inner attention is without genius. Herzog is dull, he is unendurably dull—he is like all those bright pedagogical types who have a cavity at the center of their brain.[1]

Christopher Lehmann-Haupt wrote of Sammler in *The New York Times:*

Despite Mr. Bellow's wonderfully civilized intelligence, there is no growth or discovery in Mr. Sammler's mind, and he slowly flattens out into a long-winded bore. As a fatal consequence, Mr. Bellow's planet grows unstable. As it hums along, it gradually flies apart. First, the language comes unstuck, peels away, and slips off like so much decoration. Then the plot breaks up into a series of unfunny but odd coincidences. Then the characters hurtle off into pointless eccentricity. And we are left at last with Sammler, turning and turning, droning on monotonously like a toy top.[2]

Alfred Kazin's corrective to self-inflation was tendered in the course of his review of *Mr. Sammler's Planet* for *The New York Review of Books:*

The protagonists of Bellow's novels are generally the voices of his own intellectual evolution from Joseph the dangling man in 1944 to old Artur Sammler in 1970. If an anthology is ever put together from his novels, it will take the form of a breviary, an intellectual testament from protagonists whose most felicitous brilliancies were expressed not to other characters but in diaries, letters to public men and dead philosophers. . . . Sammler's opinions are set in a context so uncharitable, inordinately arrogant toward every other character in the book but one, and therefore lacking in dramatic satisfaction, that the book becomes a *cri du coeur* that does not disguise the punitive moral outrage behind it. . . . The unsatisfactory thing about Mr. Sammler is that he is always right while most other people are usually wrong, sinfully so. . . . [His] moral haughtiness becomes as audible to the reader as sniffing, and is indeed that.[3]

Contemporary reviews of *Humboldt's Gift,* on record by the time Bellow arrived to collect his prize, registered universal disapproval. Richard

Gilman, writing for *The New York Times,* began and ended his review with displeasure. Bellow, he said, was the prototype of the rabbi "(no beard or black suit)," representative of "an ancient Jewish tradition of alarm wedded to responsibility." *Humboldt* and *Sammler* were books marred by too much commentary on the crises of our times, were nothing more than case histories of locally stricken souls. True, he continued, *Humboldt's Gift* was more relaxed, more open, more ingratiating, less literary than *Mr. Sammler's Planet,* but the large themes of the present novel "pull and tug like insecurely moored balloons, crossing each other's paths, and its 'solutions' to the dilemmas it poses are arbitrary, lacking in weight and rigor."[4]

For *New Republic,* Daniel Aaron departed from conventional prose and wrote what he believed to be a more lively review, constructing it in the form of a series of marginal notes for the reader, the writer, the book. One gloss noted the ideal reader of Bellow was a man in his middle fifties; another, that the theme of *Humboldt's Gift* was Bellow's old favorite, the "well-trod passage from spiritual torpor to insight"; another, that Citrine was a nonstop talker with a bald spot, who searched for answers to Big Questions, and eventually linked up "with Creation"; Von Humboldt Fleisher, "named after a statue in Central Park," was the object of Citrine's "deepest longing." Finally, Aaron recorded his aesthetic judgment in parentheses: "(Reader: you either like this sort of thing or you don't.)"[5]

John Updike began his assignment from *The New Yorker* with words that warn where Updike would go: "Bellow's great gifts deserve great indulgence." In his judgment, events in the novel pulled away from the issues; confusion replaced conversation; everybody sounded like Citrine; Madrid was tenuous; there were too many characters, not enough surprises; and by the time he got to the end of the story, the reader would probably be asleep. After comparing *Humboldt's Gift* to *Dangling Man,* Updike concluded *Dangling Man* was better.

> *Dangling Man,* though in snippets, merged earth and air, whereas *Humboldt's Gift,* washed up on our drear cultural shore like some large, magnificently glistening but beached creature from another element, dramatizes, in its agitated sluggishness, the body-mind split that is its deepest theme.[6]

Roger Shattuck began his review for *The New York Review of Books* by declaring *Humboldt's Gift* was strikingly different from all Bellow's other books, a vast distance from *Dangling Man,* a change on all levels. Whether the alterations were good or detrimental was another issue, and Shattuck urged the reader to proceed with caution. He felt the whole second half of the novel was ambivalent; the images of sleep might be confused with a state of higher consciousness; the colorful writing was often overloaded and fussy, descriptions overblown, too many digressions, and the transitions between a present event and a flashback were too casual. There were too many characters; Citrine did not need to go to Texas; there ought not to have been two film scenarios; Citrine did not need two alter egos; Steiner and anthroposophy split the book apart. He believed Citrine's interest in Steiner was a "search for a higher selfishness," his decision to go to Dornach was in pursuit of a "rest cure." Citrine was desultory and sardonic, static, concerned only with his own survival, and worse, Citrine was too close to Bellow to fill out a fully extruded novel. "In the characters of Augie March, Henderson, Herzog, and Sammler, all in some degree projections of himself, Bellow employed devices to create an adequate distance from himself. In *Humboldt's Gift* Bellow gets in his own way." Shattuck comforted himself finally: "His awaited masterpiece of exuberant intelligent fiction is still to come."[7]

Negative as Shattuck was, he at least did take notice of Citrine's experiments in anthroposophy. Few reviewers did, dismissing Bellow's interest in Steiner as spoof or irony or an error in judgment.

What did the anthroposophists think? In their *Newsletter* and their *Journal,* public thank-yous were accorded the world-famous novelist for bringing forward his interest in anthroposophy without ridicule, in sincerity, in good taste:

> It is encouraging that a writer of Bellow's stature has the moral fortitude to imbue his fictional character with such a testimonial to anthroposophy, thus risking possible ridicule and criticism himself. Anthroposophists can only welcome such an attitude and wish Mr. Bellow much success in his further studies of spiritual science.[8]

Alan Howard in the *Anthroposophical Quarterly* was gently remonstrative: Anthroposophists "pursue their studies in a somewhat less erotic atmosphere." Howard was grateful, nevertheless:

> Whatever else others may think of it, the book is another instance of what is becoming noticeable in the Western world, that Rudolf Steiner and anthroposophy are being looked into with seriousness and understanding by competent and representative people. It can be confidently expected that many more who have never heard of either will want to know more about both as a result of reading this book.[9]

Nick Lyons, writing in the *Journal for Anthroposophy,* was glad that the long quest for the axial lines that began in *Augie March* was happily ended with

Citrine's discovery of anthroposophy. True, Citrine was only doing meditation exercises, but it was a good start.

> Though the Anthroposophy is a bit lumpy in the novel, and the novel is somehow too discursive (there's *so* much talk—and *must* Citrine have an affair with Scheldt's daughter and take that tiresome trip to Texas?), even prolix, what we have is brilliant and honest.[10]

Lyons was glad Bellow was sincere in his movement toward a spiritual life.

Paul Margulies printed a letter to Saul Bellow in the spring *Newsletter,* recording his gratitude to Bellow for interesting people in Owen Barfield, who had not been able to get many of his friends to read Steiner. However, Margulies suggested, Bellow ought not to have distorted Steiner's views on the supernatural. To have said, in the words of Humboldt, "we're not natural but supernatural beings" was wrong. Steiner would have said, "We're both physical and spiritual beings." Margulies believed that made a vast difference, for if you said "supernatural" you entered the realm of mysticism and encouraged a split between the material world and the spiritual world. He said that anthroposophists bridged the gap.

> I love you, Saul Bellow, for opening the door to Anthroposophy a little wider. I can't wait for your next book when Charlie's had the chance to get his thinking saturated with feeling and down into his free and loving everyday willing right here on Earth.[11]

The next book turned out to be *To Jerusalem and Back,* and, worse for the opening of the door to anthroposophy a little wider still, Paul Margulies would have to settle for Albert Corde, supersoaked in the realities of Chicago and Bucharest, unfree, and not so loving, unanthroposophical in *The Dean's December.*

I met Owen Barfield in 1985 and asked Bellow a few weeks later whether Steiner and Barfield had been of much use to him during those years of turmoil, between the publication of *Humboldt's Gift*—the triumph—and *The Dean's December*—the clobbering.

Bellow replied no. He was less involved in anthroposophy since the friend with whom he had had long discussions had died. Professor LeMay was gone.*

I told Bellow I had met Barfield:

*Professor LeMay, a dedicated anthroposophist, died in 1983.

"Well, the elegant old man Barfield is still alive. He came out to Stony Brook to give a lecture on poetic license. I met him. He's very serious. Serious, serious, about everything, his diet, his reprints, his audience, the affection of his follow-ers. I met some of them. Nice people from New York who came all the way out to Stony Brook, never minding they had already heard that lecture."

Bellow had been out of touch with Owen Barfield for several years. Barfield had never liked Bellow's fiction. At a small dinner party in my house, just before the lecture, while my friends feasted on roast beef and Yorkshire pudding—my gesture to the British anthroposophist, Barfield accepted only some mashed potato, a boiled egg, and red jello—I had the chance to hear Barfield's view of Bellow's fiction. The books, he said, puzzled him and bored him, but then he smiled and admitted, "I don't like novels in general." One has only to read Barfield's comments on language to understand why.

In Barfield's *Saving the Appearances,* which Bellow had indeed been reading carefully while immersed in writing *Humboldt's Gift,* there is a paragraph on representation in language—in common terms, metaphor and simile—and Barfield's words, placed beside a few examples of Bellow's use of figurative language, show why Barfield could have no feel for what Bellow was writing.

If I know that nature herself is the system of my representations, I cannot do otherwise than adapt a humbler and more responsible attitude to the representa-tions of art and the metaphors of poetry. For in the case of nature there is no danger of my fancying that she exists to express my personality. I know in that case that what is meant, when I say she is my representation, is, that I stand whether I like it or not, in . . . a "directionally creator" relation to her. But I know also that what so stands is not my poor temporal personality, but the Divine Name in the unfathomable depths behind it. And if I strive to produce a work of art, I cannot then do otherwise than strive humbly to create more nearly as *that* creates, and not as my idiosyncrasy wills.[12]

Interwoven with Charlie Citrine's most serious reflections on the notions of anthroposophy are "representations" from a directionally free creator who writes exactly as his idiosyncrasy wills. Bellow's figurative language would certainly have puzzled the English "historian of consciousness," as Barfield calls himself. Citrine's daughter says, "Daddy you look like a million dollars— green and wrinkled." Of Humboldt's house in Baptistown, Citrine says, "It was all pauperized. The very bushes might have been on welfare." Of Hum-boldt's car, Citrine says, "The windshield was covered with white fracture-blooms. It had suffered a kind of crystalline internal hemorrhage." Of the barrier to higher consciousness, Citrine thinks, "The painted veil isn't what it used to be. The damn thing is wearing out. Like a roller-towel in a Mexican men's room." Charlie's attention is directed to the Beautiful by Renata, who is "linked with Beauty." This Renata is a "floozy," as "full of schemes and secrets as the Court of Byzantium," and she is "certainly not one of those little noli me tangerines."

Citrine, the practitioner of Steiner's exercises in meditation, allows his Consciousness Soul to evoke the memory of one "natural man" he has known, Orlando Huggins, a poor temporal self unable to find transcendence, lost in ephemeral social and political questions:

> It came back to me that more than twenty years ago I had found myself at a beach party in Montauk, on Long Island, where Huggins, naked at one end of the log, discussed the Army McCarthy hearings with a lady sitting naked and astride opposite him. Huggins was speaking with a cigarette holder in his teeth, and his penis which lay before him on the water-smooth wood, expressed all the fluctuations of his interest. And while he was puffing and giving his views in a neighing stammer, his genital went back and forth like the slide of a trombone. You could never feel unfriendly toward a man of whom you kept such a memory.

Citrine goes to visit Uncle Waldemar in a nursing home on Coney Island:

> I thought he would cry, he sounded so shaky. So little stood between him and death, you see. On the bold harsh crimson of the threadbare carpet, a pale patch of weak December warmth said, "Don't cry, old boy." Inaudible storms of light, ninety-three million miles away, used a threadbare Axminster, a scrap of human manufacture, to deliver a message through the soiled window of a nursing home.

To connect with the angels of the dead is the supreme goal of meditation. Citrine succeeds in connecting with the angel Humboldt. And when Humboldt's spirit disperses and drifts away, Citrine bids him farewell: "Oh, kid, goodbye. I'll see you in the next world."

What could an Owen Barfield make of this burnt-out case, who has enrolled himself in theosophical kindergarten, this Charlie Citrine who locks the door of the latrine so he can talk to the dead without distractions?

When I met Barfield at Stony Brook, he offered to send me Xerox copies of his correspondence with Bellow, and their exchange of letters will dispel any notion that Bellow had not been genuinely interested in anthroposophy. The letters suggest, too, how their friendship rose and subsided. Bellow made the first approach. He was on his way to Dornach, after which he planned to take a holiday in Spain. Bellow asked, on June 3, 1975, to meet with Barfield, declaring himself to be an earnest reader of Barfield's books, especially *Saving the Appearances* and *Unancestral Voice*. [13] Admitting he was no philosopher, that he was unwilling to engage in controversy over abstract issues such as rationality and irrationality, reality and unreality, he wished nevertheless to question Barfield about the powers of darkness, what Barfield called the Maggid. He and his wife planned to be in London between the 10th and 15th of June.

Barfield and Bellow did meet and Bellow wrote, on July 15, 1975, to thank him for his time, impressed with his patience and kindness, pleased that Barfield should have travelled to London to talk with someone he had never met. Bellow assured Barfield he was continuing to study *Unancestral Voice*, acknowledging that such condensed, perhaps abstruse, material was difficult for him but worth pursuing. When Bellow hinted that he himself has had glimmerings of the experience of illumination, his words presage what he would say in an interview with Jo Brans some months later; he admits to her he has experienced clairvoyant powers. "I have sometimes definitely sensed that it's a little more than a natural process. Something beyond positivistic, rationalistic, common sense or the clear light of day."[14]

Writing to Barfield again, on July 24, 1975, two weeks after their meeting in London, Bellow indicated that he has indeed visited the Steiner Center although he did not remain to take instruction, feeling uncomfortably an outsider at the Athenaeum. He thought it more important to discuss anthroposophical matters directly with Barfield. He hoped that on his return from a vacation in Spain they could carry on their conversation before Bellow returned to America.

Meanwhile he would go on reading and pondering *Unancestral Voice*, acknowledging that in Barfield's study of Romanticism he has come to understand how any representation in modern times is bound to fail. Present-day fiction, maybe some of his own books, are derived from atrophied memories. As Bellow had said in his occasional pieces, for example as long ago as "The Sealed Treasure" and the Hopwood Lecture, "Where Do We Go From Here?," individuals are conceding that they are no longer interesting, losing their power, their sense of significance and identity.

If Barfield did not grasp exactly what Bellow was saying, he could have found the same notion articulated in Bellow's published "An Interview With Myself." Bellow, speaking of contemporary fiction, asks himself if an individual who is the hero of a novel can compete with the prevalent interest in corporate destinies. He asks himself: Have we become so politicized we lose interest in the individual? And he answers himself: "Exactly."

This question of what interests the reader, Bellow's readers, lingered on. Speaking to William Kennedy in an interview held years later, in 1982, Bellow says he felt moved on behalf of humans and believed there was a need to recover the power to experience. "A question that bugs me all the time is what really is interesting? What is it human beings long to think about, read about, see or feel?"[15]

Near the end of his letter to Barfield, Bellow touched on what for him was an old concern, the failure of psychoanalysis as a way to nullify ignorance, to mitigate despair. Psychoanalysis, he said, directed us to turn our attention to the unconscious, but for Bellow this won't do. He used the same metaphors to make the same point he would in a later interview to Jo Brans when he explained his antipathy to psychoanalysis:

> The fact is there are other deeper motives in human beings which I don't like to call unconscious because that's a term pre-empted by psychoanalysis. . . . Now I know that psychoanalysis has found a natural preserve for poets and artists called the unconscious. A writer is supposed to go there and dig around like a truffle hound. He comes back with a truffle, a delicacy for the cultural world. . . . I don't believe that we go and dig in the unconscious and come back with new truffles from the libidinous unknown.

Bellow sincerely wished to understand what Barfield knew and practiced.

Barfield was puzzled but flattered by Bellow's interest; he refused the role of mentor, although he felt responsible for Bellow as word got around in anthroposophical circles of the internationally famous writer's interest in their society. On January 5, 1976, he wrote to assure Bellow he would protect him from intrusions, saying too he was surprised by the publication of *Humboldt's Gift*.

> . . . .
> You did not mention, when I saw you, that *Humboldt's Gift* was in the pipeline and near its mouth, and I had not then seen the "Newsweek" article, with its very generous allusion to O.B. I was very glad to see the enthusiastic welcome the book received over here, as well as in the U.S.A.
> I hope all goes well with you—both exoterically and esoterically.
> Kindest regards,
> Owen Barfield

Rare for *Newsweek*, the article was indeed filled with praise for Bellow and *Humboldt's Gift*.[16] Five pages of tricolumns and photographs gave Barfield a good overview of Bellow's life and career, of which Barfield knew next to nothing, and it placed on record Bellow's discovery of Steiner through his encounter with *Saving the Appearances*, "by Owen Barfield, a remarkable British writer who now lives in retirement in Kent after a long career as a lawyer."

Bellow did not respond to Barfield's letter for many weeks. On February 25, 1976, he pleaded confusion rather than enlightenment, with only hints of clarity, but assured Barfield he was continuing to practice Steiner's exercises, those especially found in the "I Am, It Thinks" meditation. He described his visit to Israel when he accompanied his wife to Jerusalem. She had been invited to lecture on Probability Theory at the Hebrew University and he had planned only to tour, rest, and visit old friends, but he found himself caught up in the political and social conflicts in Israel and was writing a small book on the problem. Bellow, we know, was researching, by reading and conversations, the documentary narrative soon to be published under the title *To Jerusalem and Back*, a project that would engage him in as much controversy as had his interest in anthroposophy.

Bellow did pick up on Barfield's reference to *Humboldt's Gift*, but lightly, saying he had neglected to mention it because he knew Barfield was not much interested in fiction, and he feared this novel would displease him.

He apologized once again for his inability to change quickly and easily from an old self to a new self and reassured Barfield of his respect.

Now it was Barfield who apologized and, thinking to ease Bellow past his well-known touchiness, told him he had at last a copy of *Humboldt's Gift* and proceeded to describe his reaction to the novel.

March 17, 1976

Dear Bellow,

(I feel uneasy with "Mr." but have never got comfortably acclimatized to the contemporary practice of jumping straight from there to first names.)

I was glad to get your letter. Would it be an exaggeration to add "and a little relieved"? I'm not sure. . . . I did get hold of Humboldt's Gift and may as well confess that I couldn't get up enough interest in enough of what was going on to be held by it. If it's any comfort to you—and the possibility that you don't particularly need comforting ought not to be altogether ruled out—I had very much the same experience with the Lord of the Rings. Later I met a man who for some reason had typed out all the references to Steiner and Anthroposophy and he lent me his extracts. I read them through and then sat back and asked myself what exactly you had *got* from Anthroposophy; and I found I couldn't answer. Your literary mind is so active—or perhaps *agile* is the word I really want—that it was like trying to catch a flea!

To mitigate his harsh words, well-meant as honest but hurtful nevertheless, Barfield offered Bellow some serious advice on his progress in meditation.

Because it evoked certain rather deep-seated and arcane vibrations, I was especially struck by a sentence on p. 293: "For me the deciding argument was that the impulses of higher love were corrupted by sexual degeneracy."* One should not forget that the correlative to *corruptio optimi pessima* is *redemptio pessima optima*. Only, of course, it has to *be* redemptio, and that is something I fancy even Blake never managed to get quite clear about.

The *I am: It thinks* meditation has meant much to me too before now. By the way I don't think I ever asked you if you are familiar with the "Foundation" meditation (given at the founding, or refounding, of the World Society in 1923). You have probably come across it somewhere, but in case not, as I typed it out for someone years ago and kept a carbon I don't want, I am enclosing it. It is central to everything. If you haven't already got it, perhaps it will make amends for a maybe rather trivial letter. I daresay you noticed, during our two conversations, that, whatever I may have somehow managed to write in some book or other, I am not personally much at home in a "wise old Dr. Barfield" role.

Let me know some time, if you feel like it, whether you are engaged on another book and how you are getting on with it.

Kindest regards,
Barfield

Wise old Dr. Barfield had dismissed *Humboldt's Gift* and compared Bellow to Tolkien. And had forgotten that Bellow had explained his new project, that he was indeed engaged on another book, an overview of the politics of crisis in Israel.

Bellow knew Barfield had said some curious things about Jews and Jewish literature and the Jewish nation in *Saving the Appearances*. [17] In the course of his survey on the evolution of thought, Barfield wrote: "Now the Jews, as we have seen, were not interested in phenomena. They were interested in morality." Jews had converted the fountain of life, which Barfield equated with the world of nature, into a system of laws. He contrasted Greeks and Hebrews:

> Suddenly, and as it were without warning, we are confronted by a fierce and warlike nation, for whom it is a paramount moral obligation to refrain from the participatory heathen cults by which they were surrounded on all sides; for whom moreover precisely that moral obligation is conceived as the very foundation of the race, the very marrow of its being.

Instead of realizing the inwardness of the Divine name—a consummation to which their whole history had been leading—the Children of Israel turned

---

*The sentence appears on page 294 of the first edition of *Humboldt's Gift:* "For me the clinching argument was that the impulses of higher love were corrupted into sexual degeneracy."

aside, cut themselves off from the accumulated wisdom and insight of the past. Thus Barfield understood "the history and literature of the Jews," which ought to have culminated in Christianity. Some instruction from Bellow should have proved useful to Barfield.

In exchange for the "Foundation" meditation Bellow would send him his book on Israel, on contemporary Israel. In a letter dated August 13, 1976, after the usual assurances that Bellow is continuing to train himself in Steiner, practicing his morning meditations, Bellow devoted a long paragraph describing his motives for writing his book on the plight of the Jews, as well as the stressful six months of work he had devoted to the project. Promising to send Barfield a copy when it was published, he referred him meanwhile to the attenuated version printed on July 12 and July 19 in *The New Yorker.*

Then Bellow took up Barfield's reference to *Humboldt's Gift,* saying only that he thought the book would displease him. Perhaps, he admits, he ought not to have located a spiritual quest for truth in a comic setting, but although Barfield might not approve, as an experienced writer he had so chosen.

Barfield did not respond to the gift of *To Jerusalem and Back;* instead, he sent Bellow an article by Seymour Epstein, "Bellow's Gift," which he had found in the *University of Denver Quarterly.* [17]

One wonders why Barfield wished to make sure Bellow would read such lines as:

> . . . and the failure of Western Civilization to sustain the individual would appear to be Bellow's theme; but mixed with that theme is so much self-indulgent clownishness and cultural detritus that it practically forms a sandbar connecting the old mainland of unifying themes to the island of anomie where so many of Bellow's contemporaries have exhibited themselves.

The seashore imagery modulates to plumbing at the close of the essay:

> Indeed the whole novel seems more a dramatic *theory* of a life than a dramatic presentation of one. The clownishness and cultural detritus has finally clogged the fictional pipeline, and it wouldn't be too unfair to assume that this has come about through a general debilitation of the theme's vitality. The push is no longer strong enough to wash it all through.

In between Epstein switches to a metaphor of eating:

> Charlie Citrine is an ageing Augie March, still the Chicago boy sitting down to the feast of life; but now the exotic dishes are all familiar, and instead of the marvellous appetite that stimulates the early Bellow *fressers* there's a definite dyspepsia souring the many pages of *Humboldt's Gift.*

Finally, Epstein gives the unkindest cut of all:

> Bellow—or any novelist—owes us no answers. . . . But the novelist who has raised important questions owes us the integrity not to trivialize those questions by repetitive improvisations on a theme, no matter how adroit.

Six months elapsed before Bellow wrote to Barfield, on February 5, 1977. Of course he thought the article offensive, but instead of his usual disclaimer that he never read the critics, he characterized this article as a product of the powers of darkness, that is to say, Epstein's words were vulgar, riddled with sophistry, and he hoped Epstein was wrong.

He observed, much as he had said to me years ago, much as he always replied when accused of this and that, that he was above all a comic novelist, a writer of fiction was all. But, he pointed out, he had been wholly serious in *To Jerusalem and Back,* and although it generated severe attacks, he welcomed criticism.

Having begun with the usual account of his efforts with Steiner, he closes with the usual chat about their meeting again.

Eager or not, Bellow did not stop off to see Barfield when he next passed through London; nor did Bellow see Barfield when Barfield came to lecture in America.

Bellow wrote again on September 29, 1977; he began with an apology for not having been able to find the opportunity to come to the Midwest to hear Barfield lecture. He had been spending his time at Brandeis University in the East. But, he assured Barfield, he was continuing to read and study Barfield, although it was difficult. Writers of fiction do not take easily to reading epistemology.

To lighten the tone of his letter, he shared an anecdote with Barfield. Recently he had received a letter from a woman anthroposophist who was sitting in the front row among her associates at the Bracenose College lecture. She upbraided him for failing to bring an important message: He had wasted their time with reminiscences of becoming a writer in Chicago.* He should, she said, take further guidance from Owen Barfield. Bellow shrugged off the accusation—after all, he was invited as Bellow the writer, not Bellow the man

*The lecture seems to be a version of Bellow's Jefferson lectures.

of wisdom—but as to allowing himself to be taught by Barfield, she was surely correct. The letter ended conventionally with a hope they might meet.

A year later Bellow wrote on a far more personal note, describing the horrors he was experiencing with his debilitating lawsuit and then probably startling Barfield by his request: Bellow offered to send a hundred pages of a manuscript on which he was hard at work. Knowing full well the difference between the theoretician and the novelist, the novelist solicited the theoretician's opinion.

When I questioned Barfield, he could not remember any manuscript nor did he confirm that he had received anything. On the contrary, he had sent Bellow a book by C. S. Lewis.

Bellow's letter, dated September 19, 1978, opened with the formulaic reference to his unswerving interest in the writings of Barfield and went on to describe a seminar at the University of Chicago in which two texts were read, *Saving the Appearances* and *Worlds Apart.* [19] So unusual was the seminar, the *New York Times* printed a news item describing the course. Bellow acted as the leader; participating were Professor Wayne Booth of the department of English, Professor Wick, of the department of philosophy, whose field of expertise was Kant, a colleague of Bellow's wife, Zabel, and two doctoral students. Booth was curious and admired Barfield's writing style; Wick thought they all needed a year or more studying Kant.

Bellow closes his letter with an appeal to Barfield's kind heart, hoping it would allow him to accept some manuscript from Bellow.

By August of 1979, Bellow had been to Rumania and back; he had taken a hard look at some realities in the concrete world, and he wrote to reassure perhaps himself as well as Barfield that he was still interested in Steiner and in anthroposophy.

Writing on August 15, 1979, Bellow described briefly his experience in Bucharest, all of which would find its way into *The Dean's December:* the death of the aged mother, the entanglements with Rumanian officials, the grief and subsequent illness of the wife, and so on. Then he came forward with what was really on his mind, his reaction to Barfield's attitude toward his writing. He was distressed by Barfield's harsh judgment. To be sure, Barfield was not bound to like his books, but why should he dismiss them as false? Barfield doesn't have to like novels in general, but that has been Bellow's sole profession for four decades. To make his point, Bellow evoked one of his favorite metaphors, that of the juggler who comes before the icon of Mary and in an ecstasy of worship does what he can do best—he juggles.*

Finally Bellow quoted Steiner for the edification of Barfield, provid-

---

*The allusion appeared in "Starting Out in Chicago," published in 1974, and the juggler will appear again in *More Die of Heartbreak,* in 1987.

ing him with the page reference (page 202 in *Anthroposophy: An Introduction*) so that Barfield could check him out: "... if a man has no ordinary sense of realities, no interest in ordinary realities, no interest in the details of other's lives, if he is so 'superior' that he sails through life without troubling about its details, he shows he is not a genuine seer." The letter concluded with assurances of unaltered affection.

Barfield's lengthy apology arrived finally at a bantering remark about Bellow's status as a Nobel Prize winner, a jest not likely to have restored camaraderie.

August 23, 1979

My dear Saul:

I was very pleased to get your letter. I had been wondering a little at having heard nothing especially as the last time you wrote you had suggested sending me some pages of your current work and I had (I thought warmly) welcomed the suggestion. But I put it down to your being submerged in personal preoccupations—a supposition which appears to have been roughly correct though the preoccupations have been of a rather difficult sort—much sadder and more violent—than anything I may have been imagining. . . .

. . . I doubt if you have been much more troubled by anything I have said about your novels than I was by what you say about its effect on you. You speak of me judging them. I thought I had made it clear that I do not feel confident enough to do anything of the sort. . . . I imagine you regarding it as something of a joke that, in spite of all we have philosophically and spiritually in common, my personal levitations (you know I was born in the reign of Queen Victoria) prevented me from seeing in *Humboldt's Gift* what nearly everyone else sees plainly enough. Evidently I was much mistaken but I still do not understand how you can have got the impression that I found anything "false" either in *H.G.* or anything else I read. Not the shadow of a dream of anything of the sort.

Maybe you have not fully realized what a Nobel prize winner feels like from outside. I wrote as lazily as I did because I supposed that any lack of appreciation from this quarter could do about as much damage as a peashooter will do to an armoured car. . . . Actually you had not asked me for an opinion, and I only recorded—not an opinion, but a frank statement of my reaction because I felt it would be somehow disingenuous to make no reference at all to the novels, the more so as they were much in the news at the time.

When all that is said I remain feeling unpleasantly guilty in the light of your letter. . . .

With all this I nearly forgot to thank you warmly for the generous paragraph on my forthcoming little book, of which the Wesleyan University Press have sent me a copy.

I suppose there is no chance of your attending a conference in East Lansing from October 11 through 13?. . . .

Affectionately,
Owen

Barfield did not see Bellow in East Lansing.

It was on his lecture tour to the States in 1985 that I met Barfield, in Stony Brook. He took me aside to confess he had never been able to understand Bellow or his writing, or modern writing or novels either, for that matter. He was working on his poem *Orpheus,* [19] a poetic drama he had written over forty years before, and was then revising in hopes that it would be of interest to a new generation. A few lines from *Orpheus* are enough to show the distance between the novelist and the poet, this novelist, this poet.

Orpheus
      Chides him!
Other sages chide their pupils
For neglect to learn the lesson,
But Eurydice the tyrant
Scolds them when they learn too well!
She is "otherwise"!
      Eurydice,
Praise me not for voicing nature!
When the Whole speaks through me,
I am not. The languid urchin
Vibrates to the moon-thrilled sea
But, abiding not, is nothing.
He who says: Lo, what I gaze on
Is the same as even now,
He abides and knows and loves it,
Clinging: steadfastness is all.
Once you sighed: What is a lover?
From yourself I learnt the answer:
Seeing less, he sees more clearly,
Knowing less he knows more nearly,
Steadfastness is all. Unending
Is the might of constancy.
Through the part, the little wicket,
Shines the glory, burns the Whole,
And Orpheus, finding new earth, air and sea,
Still hymns them all, hymning Eurydice!

Writing on November 11, 1979, Bellow admitted he was pleased by Barfield's warm letter, adding that perhaps his reading so deeply in Steiner has had its effect on him—now he was more able to perceive the kindness and humility in a man of such stature as Barfield. He assured him he would have come to East Lansing had he been able, but must content himself with reading and rereading Barfield's books.

    There was little likelihood that Barfield would reread Bellow's books, and there the matter ended.

* * *

I am not yet able to satisfy myself about the degree to which Bellow was provoked by negative assessments of his work. True, he has often said he never read the stuff, yet he was well aware of all the excitement generated by *Humboldt's Gift*, praise perhaps outweighing the old remonstrances by diehard Bellow detractors. I know he was outraged by Louis Simpson's attack when it appeared in *The New York Times* magazine on December 7, 1975.[20] Simpson accused Bellow of resenting "any sign of intellectual pretension in other people." That said, he warned the readers of the Sunday *Times* against Bellow's view of the poet as expressed in *Humboldt's Gift.* "It is dangerous to make generalizations about the life of the poet in America."

Citrine had reflected on poets:

> The ordinary sensual man looks at the life of the artist and says to himself, "if I were not such a corrupt, unfeeling bastard, creep, thief and vulture, I couldn't get through this either. Look at these good and tender and soft men, the *best* of us. They succumbed, poor loonies."

Simpson interpreted Citrine's thoughts to mean that Bellow believed art struck the middle class as an aberration, as a kind of insanity. Well, conceded Louis Simpson, himself a poet, "some poets have hastened to conform, accepting the role assigned," but how did Bellow dare to say that if poets do not survive it is because they are weak? "Bellow's view of poetry and the arts isn't fundamentally different from that held by the cynical people he has been explaining." He continued that to Bellow art was out of date. He thought Bellow was telling poets to give up writing poems and to compete instead with RCA and IBM. For Simpson, Charlie Citrine merely gave voice to Bellow's cynicism disguised as philosophy.

Underlying the review was Louis Simpson's indignation that a novelist should presume to make statements about poets. Certainly such a public lambasting of his book, to say nothing of Simpson's distortions, upset Bellow. He wrote a furious letter to me on January 23, 1976, in which he castigated Simpson's piece as cruel and low. He declared he was surprised that Simpson should have even bothered about Bellow or what he wrote since he had never taken any notice of Simpson, neither of the man nor the poetry. He wondered why the *New York Times* should print so destructive a piece, giving national and international coverage to such muck.

Perhaps it was Simpson's declaration at the outset of his article that aroused the wrath of Bellow:

> Charlie Citrine, who tells the story in the first person, bears a striking resem-
> blance to Saul Bellow. Indeed, there are times when Bellow's fiction seems closer
> to fact than Bellow's publicity . . . he has trouble imagining a character who is
> not like himself. . . . Some scenes from life appear almost unchanged in Bellow's
> fictional life of the poet.

Perhaps it was the conclusion of his essay that enraged Bellow:

> I have thought that the flowering of the Jewish novel, the writing of Bellow and
> Malamud and Roth, owes something to Delmore Schwartz. . . . Schwartz
> . . . may have been the first to approach Jewish life in America imaginatively.
> . . . He perceived that Jewish life in the United States could be as rich in poetry
> as the life of the past.

Bellow's outcry, in his letter to me, that he was only a writer, a novelist who
strove to amuse his readers, is much the same that he had said to Barfield.
But why should he be so villified for writing a book? It is Citrine's question:
when Humboldt said "Lots of people are waiting for me to fall on my face,"
Citrine asks, "But why should poetry make you a million enemies?"

On February 22, 1976, I replied to Bellow's letter, describing a
dinner party I had attended at the house of Siv Cedering Fox, married to
David, a multi-million-dollar container-cartage man. Among the many guests
were Hillel Daleski, a professor of English at the Hebrew University, and his
wife Shirley Kaufman, a poet recently emigrated to Israel, both of whom
Bellow had met in Jerusalem. And Louis Simpson.

We were all shown the underwater lighting of their swimming pool.
Around the huge dinner table a strident argument was carried on between
Simpson and Daleski about *Humboldt's Gift*. Simpson said Bellow had no
right to make statements about poets, "Poets are——, poets are——," and
since Bellow was a novelist, and a successful one, how could he know what
the failed poet experiences? That was his main point. And, not every poet
fails. Daleski was eloquent in Bellow's defense.

Simpson leaned back to allow the maid in her crisp black uniform
and her white lace cap and apron to spoon another helping of soufflé onto
his dish. Miss Cedering rose to make her way to the sideboard and said, "Oh,
I find poverty so boring," and her husband, who knew no one around his table
except his wife, said aloud to nobody in particular, "None of my family lived
past fifty."

18
"The man
with no foothold"

The memory of what followed Bellow's triumph in Sweden always rankled. Bellow was elated and grateful, that goes without saying, and there were many friends who were highly pleased for him and told him so, but he remembered more vividly the friends less effusive in their praise. In 1980, my journal records Bellow's recollections of that time. Everybody sent him messages, everybody congratulated him, but always there was a snide comment; some fatherly advice from one not to turn into a grand old man, another cautions that he's not Homer, just an American James Joyce, and in these times, given what was to be recorded, he might be adequate to that. One old friend dismissed all the novels together as piffle, and another said Bellow could have been *the* major American writer but missed out. Bellow thought everyone seemed to have missed entirely what he was saying. In *Humboldt's Gift*, he had to pretend—the comedy—but, in fact, he had been dead serious in the Jerusalem book, Bellow knew it would generate a storm of controversy in Israel, predictably, many quarrels. He welcomed attack, especially when those who took issue with him were inflexible or malicious.

However, face-to-face with the critical reception of *To Jerusalem and Back*—Bellow was called eccentric, cruel, patronizing—he tormented himself with self-doubt and disguised his bitterness with some pretty severe castigation of his own, which crystallized in *The Dean's December*. What did *To Jerusalem and Back* say?

Accompanying Alexandra, who was invited to teach at the Hebrew University, Bellow found himself with three months free in Jerusalem, and never a good tourist, he chose to spend his time learning everything he could about the complex dilemmas of the Jewish state. He read a dozen books, a score of articles, interviewed government leaders, and held long conversations with old friends and new acquaintances, and by the time he returned to Chicago, he had the materials for his long commentary, not analysis but reactions to the analyses of others. "My most unprofitable conversations have been with the people who presumably had most to say." Published first in *The New Yorker*, Bellow expanded the report into a proper book in hardcover—all this within a year of the appearance of *Humboldt's Gift.* He worked rapidly; as he said, "No one is at ease in Zion."

The mingling of fact and fiction has been a mode of writing for Bellow throughout his career; not only are there mixtures of actual events experienced by identifiable persons in the stories that emerge from his imagination, he often switches from fiction to direct discourse, writing reports on travels, essays and speeches, where fantasy plays no part. In *To Jerusalem and Back,* Bellow shifted focus from poets in America to Jews in Israel; observations of the real world and reflections on his reading that pertain to that world are offered without disguise.

The book was organized chronologically, proceeding from his flight on El Al through a series of meetings with friends and public figures, accounts of what he read, interpolations of a few old memories, and confessions of his state of mind, concluding with his departure and a brief trip to California, to Washington, "to gain clarity," coming to rest in Chicago.

To Jerusalem and Back is the book that generated all the talk about Bellow's so-called neoconservatism, his lack of understanding of the true state of affairs in the world of politics, his ignorance of Israel, of the history of Zionism, the history of Islam; it would be useful, then, to see to whom he did talk, what exactly he read, how much of Israel he came to know.

Bellow spoke with newspaper people: Michael Tatu, the editor of *Le Monde;* Mahmud Abu Zuluf, editor of *El Kuds;* Jay Bushinsky, of the *Chicago Daily News;* Joseph Alsop, retired then but known the world over— it seems to me the model, in part, for Dewey Spangler in *The Dean's December*—and Terence Smith of *The New York Times.* He included no Israeli journalists.

He met with public figures and government leaders: Mayor Teddy Kollek; the Armenian archbishop; the Greek patriarch; a Mr. D. of the foreign ministry; David Farlie, advisor on Arab affairs to Israeli authorities on the West Bank; Shimon Peres; Abba Eban; Israel Galili, a minister without portfolio; Prime Minister Rabin; Meyer Weisgal, moving spirit of the Weizmann Institute; Yuval Ne'eman, a physicist who entered politics; and Kissinger—when Bellow traveled to Washington on his return from Israel. Relying on reports on Orthodoxy in Israel by friends and acquaintances, Bellow spoke directly with no Israeli religious leaders; he met no militant radical leaders, no grass-roots opposition leaders.

He lunched, dined, and took tea with professors from the Hebrew University: Joseph Ben-David (sociology); Shlomo Avineri (history); Shalom Kahn (English); the elite, devout Zvi Werblowski (philosophy)—and Jacob Leib Talmon (history). Only Harold Fisch (English) was from Bar Ilan University. Bellow encountered no one from Tel Aviv University, Haifa University, Ben Gurion University, or the Technion.

He met with personal friends, mainly writers and poets: David Shahar, A. B. Yehoshua, and Amoz Oz—novelists; Dennis Silk and Harold Schimmel—poets; Chaim Gouri—poet and journalist. On their kibbutz near Caesarea, he visited his friend John Auerbach, a writer—to whom Bellow would dedicate *The Bellarosa Connection*—and his wife, Nola Chilton, who was in theater. He briefly attended a master class held by Isaac Stern and Alexander Schneider. He met some of Alexandra's friends, mathematicians from the university, especially Eliahu Rips, a "genius algebraist" who had set himself on fire to protest the Russian occupation of Czechoslovakia. He was happy and astonished to find his brother Sam and his wife at his door one morning. Cousin Nata Gordon came down from Tel Aviv. Bellow talked with a taxi driver, the old barber at the King David Hotel, Moshe Feldenkreis, the masseur, and Dr. Z., a gynecologist. He browsed in Stein's bookshop, had a look at the President's house and Montefiore's Windmill, wandered through the *Souk,* and stopped off at a Yemenite synagogue. Three months is a short time in which to hold long conversations and so he did not talk with anyone connected with music, art, archaeology, industry, or business; no one who ran the museums or theaters; no one from the multiplicity of agencies engaged in running the country—medicine, unions, settlement, the economy.

Instead, he read: books and articles, for the most part recent publications. Citations and quotations abound in *To Jerusalem and Back,* packed with views for and against the Palestinians, for and against the Zionists, for and against American and Russian intervention in Middle Eastern affairs: Elie Kedourie, Jakov Lind, Lev Navrozov, Herman Kalm and B. Bruce Briggs, Sinyavsky, George Steiner, Professor Tzvi Lamm, Professor David Landes, Professor Yehoshafat Harkabi, Professor Malcolm Kerr, and Mikhail Azursky, Henry Fairlie, Raymond Aron, Laura Riding Jackson, Marshall Hodgson, Alvin Cottrell, Walter Laqueur, Noam Chomsky, James R. Schlesinger, and Sartre and Sartre and again Sartre, and Kissinger, Kissinger, and again Kissinger. Thus Bellow reflected throughout his book on Kissinger's duplicity and Sartre's anti-Semitism coupled with his counsels of violence. Indeed, as Bellow said, "I am simply an interested amateur—a learner." He learned of the DP camps, of the attitudes of the Arab countries toward the Palestinians, of the attitude of the Jews toward the Arabs, of terrorism, of military strategies and weapons, and of the wars—the War of Liberation, the Six Day War, the Yom Kippur War, the ferment of violence in Lebanon.

On his return to Chicago, he sought out his old friend Morris Janowitz, a colleague at the University of Chicago, one deeply concerned with the fate of Israel, hoping with him to arrive at some clarity.

To what conclusions did Bellow come? He arrived at highly interesting ones, considering that he had to withstand attacks from all sides on his Jewish sympathies, on his indifference to issues that affected Israel, on his rising conservatism, on his despairing nihilism.

Bellow admitted that for all his study, he was infected with disorder; he had no way to resolve the opposing factors: Islamic history, Israeli politics, Russian ambitions in the Middle East, and American problems, foreign and domestic. What, he asked, was the root of the problem? The Arabs would not agree to the existence of Israel, period. All the Jews wanted was a Jewish State, period.

His sympathies for the Israelis are profound. After reading *To Jerusalem and Back,* no one can accuse Bellow of anything but empathy and commitment. "These people (Israelis) are actively, individually, involved in universal history. I don't see how they can bear it." True, he leveled accusations at Israel for intransigence, refusal to compromise, but his remarks were directed at self-serving government servants and feckless political leaders. Bellow understood Israelis who said it would be better to prepare to fight, who cried out against American domination and tampering, outright manipulation of Arabs and false promises tendered the Jews. Bellow agreed that Jews dared not trust their destiny to the patronage of America. Israelis do live under the threat of extinction, it is no fantasy that literally survival is at stake; there is danger. The threat of anti-Semitism, a madness, an insanity, is real, not only growing but thriving.

Bellow lamented his inability to come to any clear resolution and in the passage that follows, he sounded a cry that would resonate in *The Dean's December,* and reverberate on the pages of *The Bellarosa Connection.* Bellow said in *To Jerusalem and Back:*

> With us in the West wakefulness, for some mysterious reason, comes and goes. Our understanding fires up briefly but invariably fades again. Sometimes I

suspect that I am myself under a frightful hypnotic influence—I do and do not know the evils of our time. I experience or suffer this alternate glowing and fading in my own person. . . . I am familiar with the history of World War I and of the Russian Revolution. I know Auschwitz and the Gulag, Biafra and Bangladesh, Buenos Aires and Beirut, but when I come back to facts anew I find myself losing focus.

In *The Bellarosa Connection* he would say:

I didn't want to think of the history and psychology of these abominations, death chambers and furnaces. Stars are nuclear furnaces too. Such things are utterly beyond me. A pointless exercise.

The critical response to *To Jerusalem and Back* was oddly mixed.

Christopher Lehmann-Haupt, writing in the daily *New York Times*, was bored: too much talk; too much theory; no unifying perspective. He said Bellow was overwhelmed, stumped, bewildered, lost his aesthetic sense in political preoccupations.[1]

Anthony Burgess wrote cunningly in the *Spectator*, taking the publication of *To Jerusalem and Back* as an occasion to comment on Bellow's receiving the Nobel Prize. It was certainly proper, said Burgess, to confer the award on Bellow, for he was a long-settled, totally achieved artist from whom no surprises would come and so, of course, he deserved to be placed now in the company of Romain Rolland and John Galsworthy and Matilde Serao. Then Burgess interrupted himself to say he wished to continue with some thoughts he had long ago presented in his remarks in "The Jew as American" (1966). Then he had said the modern American hero is a contrivance of Jewish writers, that prewar Jewish writers had a death urge, were neurotic, obsessed, self-pitying, and paralyzed; then, he wrote that postwar Jewish writers were urban immigrants crammed with neuroses and dialectic, witty and compassionate, but without muscular vitality. Now he could add that Bellow deserved his prize for he was an American, his works were disfigured by neither scandal nor experiment, and, moreover, "he is a Jew, and the American novel . . . may be regarded as more or less a Jewish monopoly." Now he could say, American Jews were the great urban experts and the stuff of the modern novel had become therefore urban experience, and Bellow had all the qualifications for writing important fiction. He was from Chicago, complex, anxious, inhibited, and given to speculation and dialectic.[2]

Burgess was not interested in fact so much as he was in rhetoric. When he dismissed *Dangling Man* as the mere fruit of Bellow's having lived in France, and declared there had been no new line of development since *Herzog,* no one thought such errors important enough to take issue with; but, then, neither did anyone come forward to object to Burgess's elite anti-Semitism in these two articles. Jewish partisans were busily engaged with their own attack on Bellow.

Irving Howe, writing in *The New York Times Book Review,* called *To Jerusalem and Back* an impassioned and thoughtful book, but sometimes an exasperating one, a sharp if patched-together picture of contemporary Israel.

> Writers are often drawn to this loose form, since it allows them to dazzle and flee, shift tones at will, evade the labor of transitions. Yet a reader may find it frustrating, if only because one expects from a writer like Bellow more sustained argument, deeper probing. We don't get it.[3]

He said Bellow left out too much; he shifted ground too often, had too many "ideological seizures."

Irving Saposnik, writing in *Judaism,* asked why had Bellow said to Jerusalem and *Back?* Why keep himself so much outside the homeland? He felt Bellow, like all Americans who tour Israel and return, diminished the validity of Israel's territorial significance, and violated the core of the Zionist idea.[4]

Sarah Blacher Cohen, writing in *The Modern Jewish Studies Annual,* explained why Bellow felt so ill at ease in Jerusalem. She thought he was an absentee caretaker, apprehensive about what he had left behind, that he should not have bought a round-trip ticket. What could he learn in three months in the holy city?[5]

Louis Ehrenkrantz, writing in *Midstream,* explained "Bellow's curious amalgam of insensitivity to the Jewish experience and his ensuing neutrality in the Middle East controversy" as no different from Bellow's fictional characters who refuse to be committed to anything. Bellow was too intellectual to be stirred by two thousand years of history, too rational to be committed: "One cannot discount the possibility that Bellow represents the stereotype of the Jewish intellectual who tries to please those with whom he would assimilate." Throughout the book, he felt Bellow was condescending; that he should not have made fun of Teddy Kollek.[6]

Who could have foreseen the strange taking of sides in the critics' response to *To Jerusalem and Back?* The Jews for the most part condemned; the Christians, for the most part, were effusive in their praise. Peter Prescott, writing for *Newsweek,* called the book the most "precise reading I know of the psychological climate in Israel today."[7] *Time* flagged its review with "Tour de Force" and greeted Bellow's book as a successful evocation of an emotional landscape, as an account filled with quicksilver insights; Bellow was adept at political analysis and brisk invective, a man of talent, conscience, and grace.[8] Paul Johnson, writing for the *Times Literary Supplement,* called Bellow a superb writer, with a mind unusual and sharp, so that when it flickered from one topic to another, we were quite happy to follow, knowing we would be entertained and enlightened. "What impresses me is the skill and delicacy with which he poses his unanswerable questions," "the mannerly persistence with which he forced at least one reader to think." He has taken us to the human heart of Israel.[9] Amanda Heller, in *Atlantic Monthly,* said Bellow examined the country with an artist's eye; few other writers had brought to the subject the exacting intelligence, the sense of style, and the presence that were Bellow's.[10] John Hollander, in *Harper's,* was delighted with a book so filled with rewarding asides and extraordinary energy, at first glance seeming almost irrelevant, on literature and politics and the life of the mind, but finally unified by the author's personality and insight and sensibility.[11] Roderick Nordell, writing in the *Christian Science Monitor,* called it a gleaming book, in which he took his readers with him to the human heart of Israel behind the media images of Middle East diplomacy and conflict.[12] Carlos Baker, in *Theology Today,* acknowledged that Bellow was no propagandizer for anything except humanity; his sharp-eyed witty observations of the land and the people offered substance to Jews and Christians who had not visited the Holy Land.[13] Henry Fairlie, in *New Republic,* titled his remarks "Epistle of a Gentile to Saul Bellow." He exuded praise and bore witness to a shared concern for the ultimate conviction within ourselves that the defense of Israel was a moral imperative from which we could not escape without a moral disaster for our civilization from which we would never recover. He said this book of high integrity had the power of individual art.[14]

Bellow may or may not have read the reviews of *To Jerusalem and Back,* or of any other of his works. What would they have taught him? To persist or to quit his job?

We know he did listen to the statement of reasons read aloud by a member of the Swedish Academy when he received his citation in Stockholm from the hands of King Carl XVI Gustaf. Bellow heard unequivocal praise for his "human understanding and subtle analysis of contemporary culture" so felicitously combined in his work.

Bellow's style, the statement went on to say, had gone through two distinct stages, the first representing an emancipation of American writing from the "hard boiled" but increasingly "routine" style of the 1930s, the second representing Bellow's improvement on himself. In *Dangling Man,* *The Victim,* and "Seize the Day," Bellow refocused American literature on the ordinary inner agonies and joys of the central characters in his novels. In *The Adventures of Augie March, Henderson the Rain King, Herzog, Mr. Sammler's Planet,* and *Humboldt's Gift,* "Mr. Bellow added to his gifts for introspection a new set of weapons: exuberant ideas, flashing irony, hilarious comedy and burning compassion." Bellow had created his own mixture of the "rich picaresque novel and subtle analysis of our culture, of entertaining adventure and drastic and tragic episodes in quick succession, interspersed with philosophic conversation with the reader."

Henderson the Rain King was singled out as his "most imaginative expedition," the novel showing, as did most of his works, a fascination with a variety of settings as well as a continuing lively interest in his most identifiable subject, "the man with no foothold." What gave Bellow's anti-heroes "their lasting stature" had been their courage, the courage of a man who "keeps on trying to find a foothold during his wanderings in our tottering world, one who can never relinquish his faith that the value of life depends on its dignity, not its success."

When asked by an interviewer what he would do with his prize money, $160,000, Bellow said, "I don't have any plans for the money. At this rate—considering the publicity and attention—my heirs will get the money in a day or two."

Bellow might have been highly pleased had he taken the trouble to glance at the essays or chapters in books and festschrifts and monographs written on the subject of Bellow in the seventies and continuing on in the eighties.[15] The younger critics, unknown to Bellow, the very pupils in academia he so reviled, had no interest in the ancient controversies over Bellow that engaged *Partisan Review, The New York Review of Books,* and the *Commentary* crowd, with their old questions of the novel, alive or dead, the Jewish writer real or fanciful, the intellectual engagée or alienated. They were now discussing him as an artist, talking of significant craft and style, as well as metaphysics and social criticism, tracing his progress, not in contrast with Malamud or Roth or Updike but in comparisons drawn between early works and late, ranging through his canon from *Dangling Man* to *Mr. Sammler's Planet,* eventually to *Humboldt's Gift.* Younger scholars were examining Bellow's work with loyalty to critical principles, not factions. Had Bellow known of the shift in critical writing on his work, he might not have been so quick to dismiss every effort to interpret his work by using his well-used quip about himself as a temple tree, told once again to the writer William Kennedy in an interview for *Esquire* to mark the publication of *The Dean's December:*

"I don't mind becoming an industry," he said. "In Japan people go to the Buddhist temple and buy a long strip of paper with their horoscope on it, and with Japanese efficiency they roll the papers up and tie them to shrubs by the temple door, so the shrubs have more horoscopes than they do leaves. And I suppose the Saul Bellow industry makes a shrub of me by the temple door. It's all right as long as they don't come and tear off my blossoms."

He would have been less vulnerable in an encounter with John Updike between sessions at a PEN Club meeting in New York, when Updike told Bellow, during a friendly chat, that the novel as a form belongs to a Christian literary tradition; less vulnerable when he flew into New York on April 25, 1979, to attend the memorial service for his friend Harold Rosenberg. Sitting in his assigned seat in the small auditorium of the New York Public Library, he listened to the eulogy delivered by Mary McCarthy. She began with the following words:

> For me, Harold's death was the conclusion of a series, which began with Heinrich Blücher, went on with Philip Rahv, Nicola Chiaromonte, Edmund Wilson, Hannah Arendt, and finishes with him. He was the last tall pine in the forest to go down. There is no tree left standing in that noble array to look up to or mourn for; the axe has fallen on a generation, mine, of intellectuals and bold thinkers; *consummatum est.* And reviewing the scene through the present flat perspective, I cannot help feeling that in those days there were giants in the earth.[16]

I met Bellow that same afternoon. He was still fuming at Mary McCarthy, who had had the audacity to say, with such people in the audience as Dwight Macdonald, Willem de Kooning, and Saul Steinberg, that all the great men were gone, that the last pine in the forest was gone. There were so many there, none of them very healthy themselves, sitting there and listening to her say the great ones were all dead. It was true, Bellow reflected, Edmund Wilson was gone, and some of his early work was respectable; he had had some intelligent things to say in *To the Finland Station,* but, Bellow said, *Axel's Castle* was only a syllabus for a course in world literature.

During these years, and these are the years surrounding the writing of *The Dean's December* and reveal his state of mind when he opened his manuscript book to begin his ninth novel, Bellow felt himself—knew himself—to be under siege from all sides. Restless, out of temper, quick to take offense, he accepted invitations to speak that would provide him with opportunities to rise to an attack—provided they were class-A invitations, for there were to be no more debacles such as he had experienced at San Francisco State. In 1977, he read the major address to the Emerson-Thoreau Society, sponsored by the American Academy of Arts and Sciences; a month later, he read his Jefferson lectures before audiences present by invitation only; he went to Brasenose College at Oxford and read a revised version of his Jefferson lectures to a gathering that was a model of decorum; in 1980, his keynote address to the Conference on Creativity was delivered in the hall of the secure Library of Congress.[17]

When Bellow rose to accept the Emerson-Thoreau award, he held an address in his hands entitled "Why Not?" To the Americanists, the specialists in Americana, he said, "Critics often enjoy bringing down the glittering axe of European high culture on the heads of Americans." To the elite community of scholars and critics, the well-established practitioners of Arts and Sciences, he said:

> Of course it is better to be big in Washington than to be an afflicted poet, or, even more profoundly afflicted, a pedant digging blindly in the stacks, mole-wise, under the roots of masterpieces. . . . Even megalomania is better than a lobotomy performed by high-culture surgeons.

He directed his serious attention to young artists, few or probably none of whom were in the audience, and appealed to those outside the establishment to remain outside, to refuse to surrender their intellect to the intelligentsia, exhorting those outside the doors to trust to their intuitions of genuine morality, for that would strengthen them and give them courage to turn away from "the adversary culture," whose representatives were seated before him. Artists must rid themselves of the rubbish of clichés, dismiss what they have been taught, and, if they were to be artists—and "Why Not?"—they must accept their unique task, which was to reunite imaginatively what has been put asunder by history. No matter what the literary pundits or the sociologists or technologists say, there can be no meaningful life without art. It is the artist who is necessary to life and can find "a more beautiful way to be."

Such were the words of Zetland when he cried out to Lottie from his sickbed: "What really frees you from these insulating social and psychological fictions is the other fiction of art. There really is no human life without this poetry." But in the story, Zetland has his Lottie, who is all for him: "But, honey, you don't have to do anything you don't like. Switch to something else. I'll back you all the way." Bellow had no Lottie to help him become anything he liked. He had already become the husband, the citizen, the moral man, the writer, without support, without approval, and he was not so sure any of it had worked out.

The first Jefferson lecture was given on March 30, 1977, a month after "Why Not?"; the second, a couple of days later on April 1. "Why Not?" seems now to have been a revving up for the jeremiad he launched against the ladies and gentlemen, the gentle wives and accomplished husbands, the literateurs and patrons of the arts, in a word, the National Cultural Elite, invited to hear Bellow.

On the podium, Bellow was a cool unflappable man, and after the greetings and the first applause ended and there was silence in the hall, he launched into his enraged indictment of contemporary times with the demeanor of a weary don, impeccably tailored, smiling, rarely raising his voice. He began with a quiet reflection on the jeopardy in which the artist finds himself; by the time he concluded, he had described the disintegration of his Prairie City, the dehumanization of America, and the likelihood of the dissolution of the human species itself.

The members of the audience may not have been familiar with the Chicago he described, but Bellow was a Chicagoan and he seemed to have the facts: the school system was disintegrating, the welfare system an unbelievable mess, the courts, hospitals and health clinics a shambles. They believed him when he said even the good old slums were ruined, fallen into the hands of a violent subclass of hookers, pushers, rapists, thieves, demons of sexual violence and drugs and vices. He was no doubt right when he said a large part of Chicago's black population was armed, and sexual abuse of children was common.

The audience may not quite have followed Bellow's discourse on the Bitch Goddess of Success, who has been replaced by the Goddess of Rebuke, but there was no misunderstanding of where he placed the blame for the present state of affairs: nay-saying intellectuals whose nattering criticism undermines the creative artist. The artist, the man who seeks beauty in life, must struggle with irrelevancies, noises, fakes, and brutalities.

At the conclusion of his diatribe, Bellow offered his startled listeners small comfort: that which is given us is our spirit, our free spirit, with its single most powerful if delicate instrument, the imagination. That which is taken away is our courage to assert our right to live a life of the spirit in America.

Bellow and his wife went home to their Sheridan Road apartment and the audience went back to the suburbs.

In the second Jefferson lecture, Bellow reminisced once again about his beginnings in 1939, when he had been immersed in ideas of beauty, harmony, love, goodness, friendship, and freedom. There were probably members of the second audience who had different memories of their state of mind in 1939, but they had come to hear Bellow, and so they sat. He told his listeners he had felt disconnected from reality; he had felt detached.

Why? Because he could not agree with a D. H. Lawrence who told him the way to find meaning in life was to separate the self from society; neither could he agree later with a Sartre who instructed him in the necessity to become engagée, because the engagement required him to embrace a cause of violence and cruelty. Bellow, again wearing his tuxedo, confided how he had longed for community, for warmth, order and continuity, for meaning and essence. He would have liked, he said, to follow Whitman, to free himself, to become a free man in resplendent America. But how, he asked the audience—the men in formal attire, the women in long gowns, perfumed and coiffed—how could he engross the spirit in Depression Chicago? How could the son of immigrants leave family, friends, lovers, the old home, the old street, and take to the Open Road to cultivate dignity and joy? Yes, the soul required attachments, the soul said join, and he had wished he could, like Whitman, embrace his fellowman, but how, he asked the faces attentive in the great hall in 1977, how could Whitman have known the kind of fellowman to whom Bellow was supposed to hold out his hand in the world of the 1940s? He described the prototype of the American to whom he was supposed to reach out.

The audience may or may not have recognized themselves in the archetypal American Bellow described, but if they had read Bellow's fiction, they could have recognized his narrators, and indeed half the characters in his stories and novels, and some in the audience would remember Bellow's words that night when they sat down to read *The Dean's December:*

> But the leap towards the marvellous is a possibility he still considers. In fact he is peculiarly qualified by his experiences to make it. He dreams of beating the rap, outwitting the doom prepared for him by history.

Bellow confirmed the pact he made with himself in 1939; he would reject the fate of separation and isolation; he would retain his belief that the leap toward the marvelous was still the only possibility he considered.

The conclusion he reached in his talk was familiar Bellow, for this Jeremiah always gives way to an Isaiah, and his words warmed the hearts of all who would aspire as did he to live well—he as an artist, they as best they could: always to seek the marvelous in life and to find it, to participate in it through the wonder that was art.

Then Alexandra's mother suffered a heart attack followed by a stroke and Bellow and his wife flew to Rumania.

In Bucharest, Bellow faced a reality of oppression and criminality and terror, an omnipresent bitterness that outdid anything he had seen in Chicago. Mayor Daley was a piker compared to a Communist secret police colonel. What Lawrence, what Sartre, what Whitman? It is Albert Corde who asks whether art can still pretend it may connect to the wayward inner longings of so meek a man to whom securing a spoon of jam to spread on a piece of bread has become the victory. Can the artist invest the particular with resonant meanings when the particular is a raggedy fake fur coat, a half glass of slivovitz, a pack of American cigarettes? Longings? Can art comfort so destroyed a woman that her eyes ask only that the plastic tubes be pulled from her veins and the smoke of her body be released through a chimney flue into the sky? Art? How can art generate awe and beauty out of such muck?

When Bellow rose to speak to the audience at the Conference on Creativity in 1980, he had come back from Rumania and had reentered his spacious apartment on the twelfth floor of his high rise by the lake, with its four baths and two studies, with its barricades of walls lined with books. In his keynote address, Bellow began again with a description of his early life in Chicago—it was like touching home plate before he began to run—but his nostalgia soon gave way to an eyes-front, face-front, long hard look at his present-day city, his Chicago against which no protection, no insulation, was possible. The landmarks were gone; the buildings boarded up; the old park was now the scene of riots; drug pushers sprawled on the benches where once garment workers read their poems in their mother tongue, Yiddish, to one another, and on the corner of Potomac and Rockwell Streets, the city's largest narcotics market thrived. On his old turf, murders were now daily occurrences. There was arson, stabbings, depravity, desolation, illiteracy in and out of the slums, and media pollution.

Facing the participants in the dialogue on creativity, peering at those who had agreed to set aside a day or two to think about creativity, Bellow described the old system, looking back to fifty years before when he first conceived his mission to write books, but he soon shifted his attention to the environment of the present day. The new Chicago was an enclave of immunity and privilege, indifferent to the outlying despair, the rapes and killings, and the new politicians were only simulations of integrity, piety, sincerity, dependability.

However, it was a conference on creativity, and so Bellow turned to himself, to confide how much he chafed at the public distrust of the writer. He recalled waiting in an office in the Sears Tower in Chicago, met with smooth executive courtesy, but as he reported it, with irritating curiosity about what this aesthetic dreamer, this literary professor, could be up to in the city of broad shoulders, sharp elbows, and greased palms. In two years time, the professor would become Dean Albert Corde; five years after that, he would become the botany professor, Benn Crader, staring at the Illinois State Building, called "the Ecliptic Circle Electronic Tower."

It was 1980. *Humboldt's Gift* and *To Jerusalem and Back* were in all the bookstores: The Nobel Prize had been awarded by a fairly respectable and responsible committee; and Bellow was standing under the light in the auditorium of the Library of Congress, saying to a gathering of the leading intellectuals of the era that intellectuals were sycophants to those who ruled society. It was nothing new. Over the years, in his essays and speeches, in his interviews, Bellow had called intellectuals literary mandarins, culture-bureaucrats, Philistines, pampered children, small Daedaluses, custodians of culture, ideological package-makers, truffle makers, French-chocolate makers, epigones, pseudo-learned swamp-makers, crisis chatterers, mind defectives, high-culture surgeons who perform lobotomies, technological achievers, the enemies of the past, oblivion-makers, pedants digging blindly in the stacks of libraries, mole-wise, pythons, ivy league sodomites, and figurines of hand-carved suet. Now, in this time and this place, he called intellectuals ruling reptiles.

Bellow's wife was watching the audience; she saw a tweedy gentleman in the front row bite the stem of his pipe clear off when he heard these words. Bellow was reading his speech and did not notice. What, he was asking, can the artist do? He fixes nothing. He offers no theories on the best way to live. Art is the work of the spirit. Art can release a man from his prison or from his madhouse in which he sits alone, isolated from nature and his fellow man. With the quiet aspiration of a man reaching the end of his rope, Bellow said he was grateful that in art there were still sightings of the truth about reality.

About this time, I visited Bellow in his not such a prison, not such a madhouse. Bellow was dressed to inhabit this posh apartment, with its emerald-green velvet couch and muted rugs, not thick-piled Orientals, no, no, more like kilims, and the neatly placed chairs near graceful side tables. He wore a low-keyed brown plaid suit with a vest, a beige shirt, all having the effect of a monochrome, and like a flag, a strong print tie of hard blues and chrome yellows. Dapper and clean. So clean. We went to sit on the balcony, not so cut off from nature, for there was all of Lake Michigan below us. He was gleeful about the effects of his talks and wished he had said more of the truth. He had been interviewing people in high places and low for the book he was planning to write on Chicago, a nonfiction account of the real city, and he had been visiting courtrooms, hospitals, housing projects, bureaus of this and offices of that, gathering evidence for the kind of record his city was guilty of making. Everything in Chicago, in America, seemed to him to be done under the guise of moral virtue. What was distinctive about Chicago, America, was its great mixture of business and high moral sentiment, of law and politics. What distressed Bellow were the lies, always the bare-faced lies under the guise of virtue. He would be given long explanations of higher truths and higher virtues, but at bottom he knew no one would tell him the truth. He met all these people in Chicago and they would see him and talk to him, but their faces were frozen and their eyes half-closed, and they lied.

And he? He was afraid, he said, to talk about the single most important thing about the self, the death in life. This sober thought was interrupted, not by me, for I could find nothing to say, but by himself. What, he seemed to me to be asking himself, what if I do it the wrong way?

A cheerful, gracious Alexandra brought out a tray of tea and light biscuits and then left us to attend a lecture. We remained through the long afternoon, Bellow musing, talking; when the chill could no longer be disregarded, we went into the living room and Bellow drew the curtains against the sad gray light of Chicago and took the frosty bottle of aquavit from the freezer and we settled down, taking small sips, sparingly.

In my journal, I tried to recapture his mood and remember his words, but he shifted focus often, veered around from one subject to another, one idea to another, with thoughts intruding and silences hanging. Bellow tacked from how can we tell each other the truth, if the truth is that we are weak, to living as a sexual being bringing a man closer to inevitable death, to his belief in the soul and his intermittent spiritual experiences, to his inability, his reluctance, to tell his wife he learns about the spirit by looking at trees— this wife who jumped up and down clapping her hands like a child with a new toy when she solved a mathematical problem. He ranged from a description of his working hours, his scribblings, his trying out new things, to his reading, his long drives down to the university, his playing racquet ball to keep his body from going stale. He returned to the subject of his wife, who never read poetry or fiction, who seldom read his stories and if she did had little or nothing to say. He discussed his problems as a writer unable to find the metaphors, the images, for what he wants to say; his loss of his comic sense and his unwillingness to come out raw—straight—with the tragic. He came to a stop at last, quickly rising from his chair and going to a bookshelf to take down a book by Owen Barfield, thrusting it at me, telling me to take it home and read it. It was *Unancestral Voice* and before I could ask "What's there?" he put it down on the coffee table, saying Barfield was theoretical, intellectual, Barfield could not get past that. And he? He was a writer, a novelist. Playing the intellectual was not for him. He told himself to do some light writing, something that would be fun. He could not do that, either.

He was trying to write an exploration of his life, an account of all he did, but he could not bring himself to examine that life. He would get to sleep at eleven or twelve o'clock and get up again at two and lie awake all night thinking. Talking to me, sitting there in his living room, was one thing, but to put it all before readers, to make it all public, well that was something else. He was hedging, holding back, fooling around, avoiding getting to the real truths, playing around with details that didn't mean anything, unable to find the objectivity he needed. He knew that novels require form, a style, a design that would lead him on, in, it had always worked that way, his books took over, but this time he could not do it. The instruments of his craft had left him.

Bellow had not yet begun to write *The Dean's December;* he seemed truly to have forgotten he had ever written *Humboldt's Gift;* but then, as I have found, it is always the next book that claims him. The next book had not yet manifested itself to his vision. Done is gone.

He told me he was writing a story about a man called Rude, who is in Reichian analysis, and discovers his animal nature, that sexuality and violence go together. He was writing about Rude, who brings an ugly tart into his house to act out his brutal sexual fantasies with her, about Rude in a fit of rage going to his psychoanalyst and killing him, and returning to his house and killing the prostitute and himself. Dear God!

I hoped he would feel better in Vermont. That summer, one weekend in August, I took the Port Jefferson ferry across to Bridgeport and went up to Montpelier and turned off for Brattleboro. I found him much more cheerful. For the first time I saw Bellow in what he would probably call sports clothes, comfortable full-cut trousers, cotton twill, with large flap patch pockets, front and back, below and above the knees, and a short-sleeved shirt to match. What might he need to carry in so many pockets? Money? Knives? Fishing gear? A compass? Pencils? Notepads? Who knows? An L. L. Bean sportsman would know. And leather running shoes.

There was Alexandra, a wonderful person for him, beautiful, warm-hearted, caring, I thought, enjoying him and his wit and his stories, genuinely curious about his immigrant past, comparing it with her own childhood in Rumania, admiring, if a little wary of the literary world he inhabits, contrasting it with her isolation as a mathematician, with no more than twenty people in the world working on Banach spaces.* Both were émigrés into the life of

---

*Stefan Banach (1892–1945): mathematician born in Poland; died in Lvov, the Ukraine. His work led to theories of topological vector spaces and orthogonal series; his major contribution lay in functional analysis. According to the *Encyclopaedia Brittanica,* a Banach space is "any real or complex normed vector space that is complete as a metric space, under the natural metric $d(x,y)=\|x-y\|$ induced by the norm." I made my way through two reprints by Alexandra Ionescu Tulcea, "An Application of Number Theory to Ergodic Theory and the Construction of Uniquely Ergodic Models," and "Probability on Banach Spaces." Mme. Bellow works on linking geometric theory and probabilistic results, the characterization of a probabilistically significant category of spaces by convexity conditions.

the mind. He enjoyed her and was as solicitous of her, charmed by her ways, and wary, too, of her theory of probability and geometric space.

She gave us a bite of lunch, crackers, some cheese, a tomato, and tea. The dinner was simple. She was careful of his health and removed the least thread of skin from the chicken breasts; she prepared a light sauce, while Bellow tore the salad greens and mulled the salad dressing. She warmed a small garlic bread and cut the melon slices for dessert; he chilled and served the wine. All the tasks were shared. He set the table; she cleared. She loaded the dishwasher; he scrubbed and dried the pots and pans. The whole scene, I thought, was like something out of Bonnard: the retired ship captain's house set down among farms, sheltering in a valley; nearby flower gardens; farther off birdcalls and the splashes of frogs going in and out of the pond; in the distance, hills with their pine cover; and over all, the serene blue sky. Then I remembered, from *Herzog:* "The husband—a beautiful soul—the exceptional wife, the angelic child and the perfect friends all dwelt in the Berkshires together. The learned professor is at his studies." No, this was Vermont. And we, all we did was go to the post office to pick up the mail.

Jacqueline Onassis had sent him the manuscript of a novel written by a friend of hers. He carried the box, which once held a ream of paper and now held the ream of the novel, and placed it on the chair near his desk. "You are going to read all that?" I asked. He replied that one didn't ignore a request from Jacqueline Onassis. He opened a letter received from a young woman, not known to him, asking whether he would like to meet and talk with her about literary subjects. A photograph was enclosed. He asked me what I thought of it. She was a pretty young woman wearing a short skirt and a tight red sweater; she was perched on the arm of a chair, shoulders twisted to the right, knees crossed, pointing to the left, the eyes in her smiling face looking squarely into the camera at whoever would stare at her picture.

"You'll keep that?"

Why not? He thought it was a good picture. He looked at me with as much wonder as I was looking at him. Why should he confine himself only to bills and lawyers' letters? He carried it to the coffee table in the living room and during the evening I saw him pick up the letter from time to time, but mostly he studied the picture.

We sat outdoors before dinner. I told Bellow what I was finding in the Regenstein archives, about all those letters, with everyone using him, pleading, soliciting. "They want, they want," I said. He had never realized it. He knew something was happening but did not know what.

"The letters always begin with a paragraph or two of flattery: Bellow, you're the most respected man among American writers today; Bellow, no one can touch you for wit and wisdom; Bellow, you're such a generous man; and then zing! the pitch! please write a blurb for this, for that, write a recommendation for a prize, a teaching job, a publisher, a grant, write a preface, a foreword, an afterword, everybody, all the time, endless and shameless."

Bellow seemed to me to be excited by what I was saying. Yes, he knew he was in the middle of something, but he had been so scattered, so easily distracted. He always thought, he said, he was supposed to do what everybody said was the right thing. He was afraid any suspicions were paranoia.

"Oh, it was real enough. There is a pattern to all those letters. And it was not just America. Letters came from England, Italy, France, Germany, Japan. Wherever you were going, they always knew and were waiting."

He wanted me to tell Alexandra this. When she listened to him, she thought he was making it all up, that he did not trust people because of his own character.

"No. How you survived it all beats me. And that, with all this going on, plus wives, plus children, plus lawyers, you wrote your books is a miracle."

That may be, he said, why he never wrote his books the way he wanted to, and then he wondered whether the book he had started to write was the right book for him. It might be his last book. He had to think of things like that now. Should it be this book on Chicago or should he come at the real thing now? Get it said. Should he tell what the yonder side of reality is? He had only glimmerings. He did not really know how to do it.

Alexandra came out on the lawn and sat down for a while before we all went inside to prepare the dinner. She sat stiffly on the edge of the old lawn chair and listened to Bellow. He told me Alexandra had had a very bad time of it. Her father had been the first minister of health in Rumania after the war. He had been imprisoned for defection, they said defection, and he died and her mother took over. Her mother had been the second minister of health. She had been a child psychiatrist specializing in retarded children. Then they had brought her down, too. They had accused her of "cosmopolitanism," too much Westernized thought. He said that in the iron curtain countries, there was no such thing as retarded. They believed everything stemmed from the society and in their society nothing bad could ever occur; there couldn't be any such thing as retarded.

Alexandra interrupted. Her mother had had an assistant, a very good younger woman assistant who had taken over for her. Her mother had not been allowed to practice or keep any job, but the assistant, who was consulted by the very same officials who had accused her mother, would go and ask the assistant, as intermediary, her mother's advice and treatment. She would give it. Of course. They were sick children. When her mother died, there was not a line about it in the newspapers. It was as if she had never existed. And yet so many people went to the funeral—hundreds. It was very brave of them to do so.

At dinner, Saul pressed Alexandra to tell me about her emotional upset that afternoon. A testimonial to her parents, soon to be published, had come in the mail and she discovered in it things she had never known.

Alexandra was reluctant to talk about it, despite his urging her to articulate her miseries. It was Saturday night, very quiet. Mostly we sat in gaps of conversation. There was only one telephone call, from Meyer Shapiro to tell Saul he was ill and to apologize for not being able to get together. It was very depressing for Bellow. Bernard Malamud was sick, too.

Alexandra said she wished to excuse herself. She wanted to say good night.

"No, no, my dear." They addressed each other as "My dear," very formal. I never once heard her call him Saul, or him say Alexandra. I, too, in that house was "my friend" or "dear friend" or "my dear friend," never Ruth. We were not going to talk seriously, he assured her. Then he admonished her, saying she made him nervous jumping around like that. He asked her to sit down and relax for a short while, to just be with us.

"Would you like something to drink, my dear?"

"Yes, my dear. I'm very thirsty."

We chatted over tea. So I began to tell Alexandra about the letters in the archives. It did not fly very high off the ground we were suddenly on. She said she has this experience. People would meet her once and then send her a letter, flattering her, yes, saying how nice it was to have met her, and then would enclose a manuscript for her to read, hoping she would give it to her husband. I asked Alexandra what kind of book she thought I should write, what would be good from her point of view. She laughed and said she knew nothing about literature. "Nothing."

Bellow interrupted to say I should assume an absolutely Martian distance, look at his career as a novelist from a Martian point of view.

I reminded him, "At one time you said because I have known you for so long I could tell the story from up close." However, I knew Bellow did not mean me when he talked of Martian distance. It was I who excused myself and left them both sitting there.

Early the next morning, I found Bellow in the kitchen. He looked ghastly, worn and grim. "What's the matter?" I asked.

He had not slept well. He finally had to take a pill, Dalmane, I think he said, but it had not helped at all. He had read half the night. Did I want some coffee? "Sure." Did I want an egg? He would make me an egg. "Okay." And a bagel? "Yes. I want breakfast," I replied.

He did not feel like working that morning. While he fiddled with the radio, trying to tune in some classical music broadcast on the local station, he told me it was hard for Alexandra, being stuck away in Vermont with only him to talk to. She really missed her own friends and her people. Whenever

Alexandra got into difficulties, she called a Rumanian friend and they had a heart-to-heart talk in Rumanian. He could not do that. He did not know her language.

Alexandra joined us for breakfast. "Do you want an egg?" "Yes." "Take this one." "No. I'll make my own." "Take this one and I'll make another." "No, my dear. Did you grind the coffee beans fine enough?" "Yes, my dear." "Did you warm the milk?" "Of course, my dear." "I will have tea." Refusing the bagel, she took slices of toast and a lot of butter and jam. Silent. Bread and jam. Silent.

Saul finally got up and asked me to please go outdoors for a while; he wished to have a few words with Alexandra alone and would come outside later. Half an hour passed. He came out on the lawn and sank down on a chair facing the house, telling me to look at the view. He wanted to talk, but not about the literary establishment as we had planned.

He told me that when Alexandra's mother had been ill, he had dropped everything and had gone to Bucharest and taken hold of the situation there. He had dropped his life entirely. When they had returned to Chicago, Alexandra had just gone into the apartment, taken off her gloves and coat and hat, and had gone into her room and sat down at her desk and began to work. For ten days, she had done nothing but her work. They had lived like strangers in the same house. When she had gotten sick, he had nursed her and done everything, everything, and she had not acknowledged what he was doing for her. She had taken no interest at all in what he was doing.

A couple of days ago they had driven out to look at a house for sale in the area. When they talked about it after they got back, she said no, no, she did not want the responsibility. She had not even asked Bellow what he thought. That rankled him more, that she had just decided. He said, ruefully, that she was looking out for herself. After all, it was true, he was so much older than Alexandra and perhaps she could see that she might be left with it on her hands. She did not need that.

I said, "Maybe she was testing you. Maybe she wanted to know if you would buy her a house like Tivoli. Would you give her as much or more than you gave your other wives? Once it's clear you would, that and more, it's all she needs to know."

He said, it seemed to me, wistfully, he would build her a house ten times better than that New York Tivoli and right here in New England.

And why had they quarreled after I left them the previous night? She was angry at how he had treated her in front of me, insisting that she stay with us after she had said good night. Perhaps it was rude of him, Bellow said, to speak to her as he did; perhaps he should not have talked about her private affairs in front of a stranger. He had known she resented violations of her privacy. And so he had to listen to her calling him sardonic and self-centered and oblivious of her feelings. And so on and so on.

Two hours later, I was back on Route 9, on my way to Route 91 and 95 and 495 and 347 and Nicholls Road and 25A, which led into Port Jefferson. Bellow put aside the story of Rude and the chronicle of Chicago and began *The Dean's December*.

"Can't go through it on the old iambic pentameter"

More than thirty years ago I received a letter from Bellow telling me kindly but firmly I missed the boat in my essay on Ralph Ellison's *Invisible Man.* [1]

I might have expected his reaction, knowing well by then his attitude toward close explication of texts as a type of literary criticism practiced by the Chicago School of critics. What had I done wrong? I had not taken into account the quality of the parts of the book, mistakenly thinking it was enough to analyze the structure, forgetting the significance of the creative act, dwelling on meaning and interrelationship, on form, to the exclusion of judgment.

Why meaning and creation were opposed eluded me then—it is Bellow's distinction between intellect and imagination—but what he went on to say, in 1955, about meaning in fiction will surprise any reader of *Mr. Sammler's Planet* and *Humboldt's Gift,* and astonish if not bewilder the reader of *The Dean's December.* A major flaw in novels published in America, and he pointedly included his own, is the chasing after meaning; the wrong-headed goal of the American writer was to give instruction, to push morality, not feeling. Meaning, as such, truth as such, ideas, have no place in a work of art. Vision has, perception has, reality has. Instead of all this complicated analysis of what incidents signify, I should have judged the disparate parts of *Invisible Man* as some false, some authentic, have seen that the parts on the Brotherhood, the hospital, the seduction were commonplace, present to expand or continue Ellison's argument, and the sweet potato seller, the eviction, the riot were far, far superior because they stemmed from Ellison's perception of how things were, not what they ought to be. Writing should be simple, not a convolution representing fixed ideas.

Bellow had recently published *Augie March* and was at work on *Seize the Day*. Perhaps when he wrote to me he was regretting the interpolation of the Mexican episode into *Augie March*, the frenetic piling on of episodes. His exhortation that works of fiction should be simpler surely had something to do with the compression and focus of *Seize the Day*. Who would believe, reading Bellow's fiction from *Henderson* on, he had once thought writers should not run after meaning, be so earnest, so intent on preaching?

I was reminded of this letter when I read William Kennedy's interview of Bellow in *Esquire* magazine. The occasion was the publication of *The Dean's December* in 1982. Bellow told Kennedy outright his purpose as an artist was to tell the truth: ". . . If I didn't think I was speaking to people's souls, I would not write anything. If I didn't have a true word to speak to them, I'd keep my fucking mouth shut."

I dug out my old letter and reread it and decided that was then, and now is now. If there is a difference between what a man says and what he does, that is no hanging matter. Bellow, a man born suspicious of all programs, contemptuous of all fixed visions of reality, his own representation of alternatives among them, is also the writer who devoted thirty-five years to his search for the truth. *The Dean's December* brings it to forty years.

It seems a century ago that Bellow described to me that earliest of his memories when, as a child, he stared into the gutter and saw beneath the oily surface reflections of truths generated by the light above. It was his need to talk about that, the light, which, though it caused his chest muscles to contract and made him anxious, he always chose to do. Now Albert Corde, in the December of his life, reflects on the oily muck on the surface of life and penetrates below the surface, stares at the dirt, the slime, the debris of reality, and fears he has lost the strength to lift his head to contemplate what "that" was. Even the light may be a delusion.

Since Bellow began his career as a writer, his main concern has always been the individual, the safekeeping and maintenance of the unique self. Whatever the circumstances, the hero is on quest for a fate good enough and that is always understood to be the fulfillment of the longings of the spirit.

The soul of the hero seeks to confront the ubiquitous threat of annihilation—in the real world: betrayal, misunderstanding, disdain, contempt, rejection, abandonment; and in the natural world: decay and death. At the outset, the Bellow hero is young, strong-willed, suffused with hope and determination, energetic; gradually, the Bellow hero sags, grows older, wears down in flesh and limb; his heart is fractured and his spirit falters, but despite the stress of years and the disputes and conflicts, the sport of the soul continues.

That was until *The Dean's December*. With this book, it seems as if Bellow had come to a dead stop. Despite all the fireworks of the novel, the action and reaction, the double line of events present and events past, Albert Corde stands still. "Can't go through it on the old iambic pentameter" is the way Corde puts it.

In a video interview with Melvin Bragg on the occasion of the publication of *The Dean's December* in England, Bellow called the book his *cri de coeur,* his cry of outrage and frantic indignation when, after forty years of practicing his trade as a writer, he took a new look at the city where he had spent most of his life. Thirty years earlier, Augie March had challenged "that sombre city," describing Chicago as a city on the make, with no sense of what it ought to become. Then, the immigrant boy, mooning of art and culture and the significant life, imagining his anecdotes of integrity, saw a prairie city, oiled at the joints, in constant motion, conniving for profit, corrupt, taunting America with its restless schemes. Now Albert Corde has something further to say and by the time he concludes, Chicago is described as the "contempt center of the United States," no "Darwinian jungle but a city dump," with its evils and stinks and "ectoplasmic darkness," infected with mental disturbances, terrorism, barbarism, cultural degradation, with its savage and subsavage citizens living side by side, its ethical values wholly lost and justice unobtainable; Chicago is no longer a place but a condition; like the South Bronx, Cleveland, Detroit, St. Louis, from Newark to Watts, it is "all the same noplace." Corde's Chicago is America, the degenerate descendant of Europe.

When Melvin Bragg suggested *The Dean's December* was a tale of two cities, Bellow agreed; he had fully intended the comparison with Bucharest. Corde finds in that city of feeble melancholic light, as much dreariness, danger, toughness, poverty, violence—"if emigration were permitted the country would be emptied in a month"—as much ignorance, as much loss of reasoning, as much loss of spirit, as much indifference to the fate of as large a class of people who were equally expendable. Corde realizes in both there is an underclass consigned to damnation; in both, people are wholly passive in their acceptance of their affliction. Bucharest has been at it a longer time.

Bucharest is the inheritor of Oriental brutality and Byzantine despotism. Bucharest is the Europe of wars and revolutions, bombings and camps and terror and the Gulag. But what, after all, was the difference, now, between the Party in Bucharest and machine politicians in Chicago? Corde sees the plastic covers on the obelisks in the Bucharest cemetery and remembers the plastic covers on sofas and morris chairs in Chicago. There is hard nihilism in Bucharest and soft nihilism in Chicago and neither has the advantage over the other. The disappointment of a Valeria, who, with her husband, both Marxists, had "gone into the streets with roses to greet the Russians" is not so different from the disappointment of Albert Corde, who, driven out of his classrooms and libraries, comes down onto the streets of Chicago to see.

In the interview, Bellow was polite; Bragg was polite; the camera treats us to the sight of a warm, gentle, reflective man, neatly groomed, holding his book in his hand, reading passages from time to time in a quiet, thin voice, or talking, leaning his head on his hand, fingers stroking his temple or cheek, explaining patiently why he had written *The Dean's December*. "It would be wrong of me to wrap myself in my honors and lie down quietly. I couldn't bear to do that." He has been impassioned only by his desire to be understood as a writer and an artist with the right to call attention to the dissolution of society. "I'd always sympathized with Hemingway, who said if you're looking for a message, try Western Union." Now, Bellow told Bragg, he knew if the artist did not tell the truth, who would? Someone must write it without generalizations and disguises. Who else is there to do it? The social workers? The politicians? The sociologists? The media? No. The artist alone has the language, the independence, the freedom to speak, and only the artist can compel people to realize they are individuals, human beings, not statistics or types.

All of this is effectively impressive on screen. Bellow had been given the opportunity by the media he so deplores to explain to Bragg why he wrote the book, to say he was compelled to penetrate below the surface of appearances, driven to ask himself, Can all this be as it appears to me? "The real job of the writer is to penetrate with his own transforming power, to find what is essentially human under all these disguises, these appearances. . . . it is my business to penetrate with my being into their being."

"What," asked Bragg, "was besetting you when you wrote the book?"

"For forty years I've been an observer, asking myself, can it be they are what they appear? Can it be that they are no more than what they appear to my superficial observation? Where is the depth level? It's one of the themes of the book." When the sympathetic interviewer asked the fiction writer, "Do you see yourself in the process of writing the book like Corde as you describe him?" Bellow replied, "He refuses to—as I have refused in my life—to be bound by surface appearances."

In 1980, Bellow wrote an exploration of his life that told the truth and allowed his findings to be made public. He represented himself as Albert Corde, a man of two personalities, the private man, husband, artist, uncle, brother, and the public man, the college dean who wrote two scathing articles for *Harper's* magazine exposing the disintegration of Chicago on all levels, who involves himself in bringing to justice the black hoodlum who murdered a white graduate student. Speaking through Albert Corde, Bellow neither hedges nor holds back; he plays around with details—Chicago, Bucharest—and gets to the truth, not only the truth of the dissolution and decay of culture, East and West, but the far more significant truth of Bellow.

The ostensible action of the book consists of the immediate events of Corde's few weeks in December in Bucharest; the depth level of the action is the unfolding of a series of recollections of Corde's life in Chicago, the gradual disclosure of Corde's discovery of his own reality. The substratum of *The Dean's December* is the depth level of Bellow. Notwithstanding all the disguises he uses, all the masks he puts before his face, we recognize that the man consumed with anxiety, the man examining his own past, reflecting on his mistakes, his ambivalences, the injuries inflicted on him by fate and his own false steps, is Bellow. Corde seeks the depth level of his friends, his family, his acquaintances, even his enemies, and the depth level of the city, the inner city, but it is the inner slum of the human heart, mainly Bellow's heart, his spirit, his soul, that he discloses.

To miss this dimension of the novel is to miss the insight Bellow offers on Bellow, for what he thinks of his wife and family, his friends and fellow writers, his own career and his art, is as important as Bellow's attitude toward Chicago and the United States and Russia, toward society and politics and science and history and culture. Without perceiving that Bellow, whether consciously or not, has stopped at the apex of his life and turned around to take a backward glance over his main traveled roads as his respected Whitman had done in 1889, without realizing this is what is happening in *The Dean's December,* the novel on first reading will seem to be an irascible outburst, a conglomeration of yoked-together parts with disparate recollections of long-past confrontations and old conversations intruding into unlikely events and improbable meetings colliding with old bits of prose writings and newspaper reports.

We may be confused—some may be annoyed or saddened—by the reappearance of old images in new contexts. Corde does "real philosophy, not the grovelling stuff the universities mainly do." Corde is flirting with a delusive philosophy, serious in secret about the reunion of spirit and nature, divorced by science. Corde says, "I felt my weakness as I approached the business of the soul—its true business in this age." He recollects, "He wrote about whirling souls and became a whirling soul himself, lifted up, caught up, spinning, streaming with passions, convulsive protests, inspirations." He acknowledges, thinking of Charlie Citrine and his forays into anthroposophy, "He never did get around to explaining how we must reconstitute ourselves."

The childhood friends are back, the old buddy become a frayed and frazzled lawyer, the old buddy become a pretentious journalist, and we read again of the swindler brother, the lamented mother, the harpy former wife; but now there is a sense of despair, of sadness, a concession of defeat inherent in Corde's judgment that the early life is dead, the immigrant past, the Chicago neighborhoods, the wheeling and dealing, the erotic life, even the spiritual life and the desire to attain cosmic communion are all played out— gone.

The trial of Lucas Ebry for the murder of Ricky Lester is a fiction; Corde's two articles, one an exposé of the county jail, the second an exposé of the county hospital, are a fiction. What Corde saw in the real Chicago— grotesque, violent, corrupt, dehumanized, the paradigm of a society that may very well signify the future of America—is not a fiction. All this Bellow learned as he chased about Chicago interviewing for his projected book. Corde's presence in Bucharest, observing the sickness unto death of his mother-in-law, Valeria, observing the iron fist of impassive bureaucrats, the spite and envy and contempt, the poverty, the dehumanization of the citizens of Bucharest, is not fiction. Bellow was there. He saw it: just as he described it on his return to Chicago, when he rose to speak at the Conference on Creativity; just as he represented it in his novel.

In the disguise of Albert Corde, it is Bellow who is the writer with the tearing need to find out the truth, and despite all the antagonism and anger he will surely arouse, he is compelled to make public the truths he discovers. It is Bellow who must "recover the world that is buried under the debris of false description or non-experience." Bellow is the man of words, so distraught that his words may be, may always have been, words of the wrong kind, who knows, with his "radar-dish face" he has been "picking up signals from all over the universe, some from unseeable sources," Bellow who "in a mad flight of clarity" would say "incomprehensible, ungraspable, glassy, slippery and finally, terrible harmful things."

With the character of Corde, Bellow is using fiction to look back on his life, on his marriages and divorces and lawsuits, on his family and friends, on his goals and failures and successes, on his career, his novels and speeches and essays, on all that has been said of him, done to him, on where he has been, intellectually, spiritually, morally, ethically.

When the Japanese go to the temple to tie their strip of paper to some auspicious tree nearby, on that paper they have written down a miniature record of their misfortunes, and they leave their misfortunes hanging there for the deity to dispel. That is the meaning of the practice, not a horoscope as Bellow mistakenly said, not a request for redress or good fortune, but a plea for the turning aside of evil thoughts or deeds or the injuries of fate. *The Dean's December* is the long scroll of Bellow's misfortunes tied to his own temple tree. He is the deity who observes the life that is recorded on the scroll, the deity who will explain all, judge all, but alas dispel nothing.

For the most part, Corde is confined in a cold dark room in a shabby apartment in Bucharest with a cyclamen for company. He stands staring out the window, sits drinking slivovitz, huddles under a blanket for warmth, thinking, always thinking, recollecting the experiences left behind in Chicago, reflecting on the experiences of this place, this time, this December. Like the telephone ringing in a play, serving to communicate information, Corde reads his mail forwarded to him by his secretary, Miss Porson, and each letter generates a flashback; he leafs through the articles he had long ago sent to Valeria, noting her glosses and checks and underlining, remembering what had led him to write as he did. His memories and observations are like a force field of contending places and events, old conversations and new exchanges, incidents and persons and feelings. Pulsating with "inflammation and deadening," galvanized and passive, outraged and defensive, he is at the center of a system of satellites; everything is in flux, unsteady, mysteriously oscillating, drifting. The Dean, too, throbs with agitation, vibrates with disorderly harmonies and discontinuous connections as he engages in his efforts to discover exactly what he had been and what he has now become. Nothing falls outside the pull of his vision; everything bears the imprint of his consciousness. Chicago and Bucharest become the Jerusalem destroyed, and he, a Jeremiah lamenting, prophesying woe and calamity.

When he leaves his room, he is in a state of panic, turbulent, cold, disoriented. Corde describes again and again his sense of being on the edge of an emotional outburst. "Everything seemed to move him now." "He was strongly agitated." "Is there something wrong that I'm so liable to get agitated?" That deep old woman, Valeria, probably knew his worst thoughts; Corde credits her with knowing his instability and weakness, his vices and "how near to an emotional eruption." Corde is obsessed by his mental disquiet, whether at Valeria's bedside or in the lawyer's office in Chicago or in the ambassador's office in Bucharest, or in a restaurant drinking and talking with Dewey Spangler, his journalist friend, or on the street, walking, talking with his wife's friend Vlada, in the heat of the crematorium, staring at the punt coffin on the conveyor belt, "trying by shallow breathing to keep out the corpse smoke," or at the Palomar observatory, in the lift ascending on its curved course moving along the arch, trying not to breathe in the killing cold. Corde is always out of balance, askew, tilted.

At the opening of the novel, Corde describes himself as a man displaced, six or seven thousand miles from his base. In the small closetlike office of the suspicious KGB colonel, Corde "loosely sat there in wrinkled woolen trousers and sports jacket, the image of the inappropriate American—in all circumstances, inappropriate, incapable of learning the lessons of the twentieth century; spared, or scorned, by the forces of history or fate or whatever a European might want to call them." At the end of the novel, Corde, back in his own world, stands in an iron cage and what he sees is a sky tense with stars, "but not so tense as he was, in his breast." Between the beginning and the end of this novel, there is no progress to illumination, no alleviation of agitation and turbulence, no metaphysical lift to transcendence. The agitation that grips Albert Corde at the start transforms only to outrage and passion at the end.

While writing the novel, Bellow suffered from the same fitfulness, the same sense of isolation, the same tearing apart of his spirit. It was not solely the calamity of Chicago and the menace of Bucharest, not only his despair at a deranged America and fear that humanity itself was endangered; there was more. There was the reality of himself. Bellow was well aware he had antagonized his friendliest well-wishers when he created Artur Sammler observing the decadence and violence and weakness and hypocrisy of America through his one observing eye; that he had aroused ironic disbelief when he created a Charlie Citrine practicing the exercises of Steiner; that he had generated outrage and dismay with his *To Jerusalem and Back;* that he had angered every member of his audiences listening while he read his Academy of Arts and Sciences address, his Jefferson lectures, and his talk at the Library of Congress. Bellow knew he was called elitist, snob, crank, querulous, offensive, alien, spinsterish, dreamy, muddled, wrong-headed. The melancholy, heartsore, agitated Corde will listen to the same charges.

Corde's sister Elfrida says he thinks too much, he is too sensitive, too emotional—"her moved and distracted brother might fall into one of his theorizing fits." Corde's brother-in-law Max Zaehner says Corde is on the "wicked side," he is self-destructive, disloyal. Corde's nephew Mason Zaehner thinks his premises are all wrong, he is prurient, privileged, "out of it," a racist. Lydia Lester thinks he has a fervent pity in him, yes, but "he seemed to carry an indignation load." She does not trust him. His old friend Dewey Spangler calls him regressive, pathetic, reclusive, not ambitious enough, "crazy with rage." He is too earnest, too moralistic; he does not even know that he has offended everyone; the obscurity of his language may have protected him, but his "poetry," his so-called poetry, his theorizing, has never been understood by anyone at all. Being a professor was a mistake. He is off base, out of line.

Everyone attacks Corde for his articles on Chicago, for his unmitigated and unrelenting attack on Chicago. Alec Witt, the university provost, thinks him a fool, a troublemaker and wants him off the faculty—out. O'Meara, a ninety-year-old union man, tells him he is "a punk journalist who called himself a professor." Rufus Ridpath can't make Corde out, just tolerates him, maybe, hopefully, because he likes him. Varennes, the public defender, is puzzled but respectful and asks Corde what he is after. Tante Gigi wonders whether he is stable, can he be trusted. His mother-in-law, Valeria, is mute; he puts in her eyes the plea that he not harm or betray her daughter. To his wife, Minna, Corde is suspect: "There's one of your troubles. You still want to say things to any lost soul." She is suspicious of his so-called good intentions, of his paranoia and contempt; there is too much of the freak or crank about him.

No one is cheering on Albert Corde. What does he think of his detractors? Corde gives as good as he gets. Throughout his reflections, there are hints of what Corde thinks of all his assessors and their judgments. Mason Sr. is a special kind of highly intelligent top-grade barbarian. He resembles Goering. Mason is a weak kid, insolent, aggressive. Detillion is a man in despair, in erotic collapse, a liar, a cheat; "he took a course in boneheadedness and idiocy." If Max had been ultrarich, all his psychopathic suffering "would have been safely embalmed. . . . nobody would have noticed how stupid or cracked he is." Spangler, once "a pale vinegar worm," now a pundit, is still a vain and greedy child. "Big time deportment had not subdued the struggling punk." Even his faithful secretary, Miss Porson, comes in for a drubbing. Miss Porson doubts his motives for helping people. What does he say of Miss Porson?

> You confided in people, you *had* to. From this came dependency, and then unwanted intimacy, and presently you discovered—horrifying!—that though Porson listened and nodded and looked as clever as Alexander Woollcott (whom she strongly resembled) and as melting as a mother, that though you moved her to tears, she was an exasperating dumbhead, and a lustful old frump.

Yes the Dean is angry.

Corde reflects on his reputation: "At first I was suspect, and presently

I was distrusted and afterwards disliked. Finally by my own sincere efforts I worked my way down into the lowest category—contempt." Or, as he says later, in more poetic terms, "now the wind is from the north, with rain and harsh water." As did Bellow, Corde wonders has he communicated nothing? Are there no contemporaries left for him to talk to? What has he done, after all? Written some books? Described death—of King Dahfu, of Elya Gruner, of Von Humboldt Fleisher, of Ricky Lester, of Mrs. Sathers; described violence—Nazis, Israeli zealots, armed blacks; described the truth? What else? How else? Where was the sin of such disclosures? Corde feels he is helpless, torn between good and bad, shrouded in mute heartaching numbness, living in a vacuum. "His controls were not in dependable working order." He feels his slippage, his aging, his looseness; perhaps it was true: He was out of it; he had "an on the shelf effect." He was like Voynich, the old man who spent many years in solitary confinement. He was closest of all to Valeria, who is near "to that strict blue zero and simple ice." He, too, wished to be free of "badgering perplexities, intricacies of equilibrium, sick hopes, riddling evils, sadistic calculations"—life.

Has he read too much? Was he working with a set of foolish assumptions? Were his concerns destroying his essential self? Has he, with his unwanted and misplaced high-mindedness, lost not contact but sympathy with human beings? It is so. Corde—like Bellow—experiences spiritual loneliness. He understands nothing. He is unteachable, out of step, blocked. "He had publicly given himself the fool test and he had flunked it."

Gradually, Corde begins to justify himself, for it is not only a question of what everyone thinks of him but what he thinks of himself. As the detractors are demolished, the individual begins to lift his head.

Yes, "there was a sort of anarchy in the feelings with which those sketches were infused," but also an uncontrollable flow of poetry, "the truth passion he had taken into his veins as an adolescent." Where, he asks himself, was the control of deeper experiences? There wasn't any. Maybe so. He ought to have "another go at the thing. To do it right next time."

Like Henderson who cries out his need to break the spirit's sleep, like Charlie Citrine who has been in "a snooze for twenty years," Corde assesses himself as hanging in the dark too long, going bad, "spoiling in suspension." He has been right about Chicago. It was all true. Why mind that to the liberals he was reactionary, to the conservatives he was crazy, to the urban sociologists he was hasty? He has been right about the universities, too. He became a college professor in order to cure his ignorance, to learn why his "modernity was all used up." But the Great Books, the good ideas don't work anymore. The intellectuals talked jargon; they discoursed on humanism, materialism, and eroticism instead of reflecting on the soul, on the unique self. From intellectuals, all we get are concepts. They prefer their ideas to be abstract, stillborn, dead. He wrote the articles and he had been right. It was his karma. Why should he look to anyone to spare him? He does not need to be spared. There may be some who are willing to let people be ruined, decay, die. Not he. He cares. If he sacrifices his sense of the truth, he sacrifices himself.

However, perhaps all he had said in his speeches and articles, in his public talks about the slums, political murders and bloody murders, of art and pollution had been mere abstractions, just reportage, not nearly strong enough. He has to make a new start. He will say it all again, but this time, on "the second go," he will be concrete. *The Dean's December* is the second go, and it would not be only "two, three, five chosen deaths being painted thickly, terribly, convulsively over all his organs, but a large picture of cities, crowds, peoples, an apocalypse, with images and details supplied by his own disposition, observation by ideas, dreams, fantasies, his peculiar experience of life." Like the sisterhood of women who stand together against the onslaught of assaults and betrayals, he, challenged, will challenge. His loyalties torn apart, he will put back together.

Bellow did not put off his project to observe Chicago in a nonfiction book akin to his report *To Jerusalem and Back;* he gathered together all the material he had found in books about Chicago, in old newspapers and magazines, and all he had said in his Jefferson lectures and Creativity Conference address, and all that he had thought and written and said in *Mr. Sammler's Planet* and *Humboldt's Gift,* and gave the whole to Albert Corde. Bellow lent Corde Bellow and wrote *The Dean's December,* a meditation on his career.

He lent Corde a fragment of a childhood friend, perhaps Sidney J. Harris, as well as a fragment of a public acquaintance, Joseph Alsop, named here Dewey Spangler, to question Corde on his choices and his career. The interplay between Corde and Spangler is very much like the running controversy between Von Humboldt Fleisher and Charlie Citrine in *Humboldt's Gift.* Bellow, as we know, had said he was thinking as much of himself as of Delmore Schwartz when he created Von Humboldt, and here, too, we can find a good deal of Bellow in the challenging friend "Screwy Dewey," who asks Corde why "he blew it," why, when he had made such a good beginning and could have gone, as a competent and entertaining journalist, right to the top, he ruined himself. Bellow also acknowledged he was thinking of Walter Lippmann when he decided that Spangler would be an internationally known journalist who can interview world leaders. Thus a concrete representative of the media, a specialist in communication, can interview the artist who has achieved some notoriety of his own.

The two old buddies meet for a drink in the crowded bar at the

Intercontinental Hotel; they sit cramped and uncomfortable, each wary of the other, reaching out and drawing back. Corde had known Spangler at Lakeview High School; his father had been a peddler. He is kin to the pompous Shapiro to whom Herzog writes a letter, pausing to remember "Your father peddled apples." Spangler says, "What would you say to taking stock, or doing an inventory?" Corde agrees. "Where would you like to begin?"

> "Let's look at the curve of your career for a minute. You started with a bang."

Remembering the bang—*Augie March*—Bellow remembers *Sammler's Planet* and *Humboldt's Gift*, too, when Corde says:

> "I was thrown a curve, but I stayed in the ball game, and caught the next pitch and hit me a home run and that's all there is to it."

And then Spangler summarizes Corde's career in terms that are familiar to us from our having shared Corde's acerbic reflections on himself.

> "Then you settled down on the *Herald Tribune* doing lighter cultural features, very good, no special world perspective. All of a sudden, in your mid-forties, you head back to Chicago and turn into a professor. . . . is it a kind of retirement? You're reading books, talking to academics, trying to get the right handle on things, I presume. Then all at once it's Bam! Here is how things look. Is there any salvation for this order? The harsh things of the soul, what do we do about them in America? You hit Chicago with everything you've got. . . . It was when you got apocalyptic about it that you lost me: the dragon coming out of the abyss, the sun turning black like sackcloth, the heavens rolled up like a scroll, Death on his ashen horse. . . . You were hell-bent from the beginning to unfold your special sense of life. You were blocked. Then, all of a sudden, it all pours out. There's a passionate but also a cockamamy flowering. You still haven't had a complete deliverance."

To have a complete deliverance, to deliver himself from his trepidation before the negative assessments of his motives and personality, made by all his associates, family as well as friends, enemies as well as his beloved wife, and more than that, to deliver himself from his own self-doubts is the central goal of Dean Corde. He stares at Dewey Spangler, who came toward him from a past as remote as a former life on earth. Corde reflects:

Were these the boys who had mooched through Lincoln Park with poets and philosophers tucked under their sweaters; who bought caramel corn in the zoo and lounged against the replica of the Viking Ship and made themselves at home with Socrates in the *Phaedrus* or with Rilke in Paris? . . . Since then each of them had died at least three or four times. . . . What would this wonderful palship of two old boys from Chicago look like if we brought it up to date? . . . Each of them had been spoilt, humanly, but in very different ways.

Dewey has become a mere talking machine, "living in a kind of event-glamor," bogus and grotesque, "there was no real experience in it, none whatever." As Corde stares at the lost friend, he reflects "with stormier objectivity" on himself.

Well, Albert Corde had illusions comparable to Dewey's, notwithstanding that they were in different fields. Look at him—an earnest, brooding, heart-struck, time-ravaged person (or boob), with his moral desires and taking up the burdens of mankind. He was, more or less in secret, serious about matters he couldn't even begin to discuss with Dewey. There was, for instance, the reunion of spirit and nature (divorced by science). Dewey (Corde happened to have caught this in one of his columns) was rough on writers who talked about "spirit," intellectuals in flight from the material realities of the present age. Corde could name you ten subjects on which they could never agree. And if he himself had been thoroughly clear in his mind, if the subjects had been cleanly thought out and resolved, there would be no difficulty in discussing them. So it was evident that Albert Corde was a spoilt case. Dewey pressed him about his motives for writing those *Harper's* articles. What was the real explanation? Again, the *high* intention—to prevent the American idea from being pounded into dust altogether. And here is our American idea: liberty, equality, justice, democracy, abundance. And here is what things are like today in a city like Chicago. Have a look! How does the public apprehend events? It doesn't apprehend them. It has been deprived of the capacity to experience them. Corde recognized how arrogant he had been.

By the time Corde returns to Chicago, Spangler has published his account of their meeting. In Spangler's public account of Corde, Bellow placed on record all he had ever read of himself and his career; it is a list of all the charges leveled against him by critics, known and unknown, and by friends, supposed and true. Corde was: an inordinately bookish high school kid, a gifted but mysterious individual hostile to psychoanalysis, a clever observing journalist type with no background in history or world politics, with a talent for observation, hypersensitive but inexperienced, engaged in unpleasant infighting, with an adolescent refusal to accept prevailing standards, temperamentally tender-minded but incapable of grasping the full implications of world transformation, misunderstanding the growth of a new technology for managing human affairs, a delicate spirit, yes, a genuinely reflective person who retreated into the academy and on coming out again to have a look at the present sociopolitical scene went into shock, a sensitive, emotional, private observer appalled at the transformation of his native city, as unlike his fellow Americans as he can be, an unwitting alien, so obscure in his language none of his fellow citizens can follow his argument.

How can Corde say, asks Spangler, our cultural poverty has the same root as the frantic and criminal life of our once-great cities, and blame the communications industry, academics, and intellectuals for our flight from humanism? "It was too bad," writes Spangler, "that he was carried away by an earnestness too great for his capacities, because he was a very witty man."

So Dewey Spangler betrays Corde, but it is Bellow who is asking himself, Have I been wrong to write as I did? Have I been on a false track? Was I out of kilter? In a burst of anger, with a cry of righteous self-justification, he answers himself: "*His* patience was at an end. *He* had had enough. *He* was now opening his mouth to speak. And now, look out!" What he should have said, he will say now. He will view America and Europe, Chicago and Bucharest, and the underclass and the overclass, the taunts and the glamour, the spoilage and the dream, as with an "anguish beyond the bounds of human tolerance." And it will not kill him. It may very well save him. Despite all his common, practical, responsible sense, he wrote the *Harper's* articles; now he has found the "words, lesions, cancers, destructive fury, death" and he feels called upon to make a special exertion, "to interpret, to pity, to save!"

He knows it is stupid, insane. His reflections bring on a wave of depression. It is as cold inside him as it is out on the Bucharest street in the snow.

> But oddly enough, when the wave of depression returned from its far low-down horizon it brought back the idea of having another go at the thing. Do it right next time.

Bellow lent Corde Chicago and Bucharest and committed himself to "the second go." *The Dean's December* would take it all the way home. He would say it and never mind whether Chicagoans ask, "Why do you have to knock Chicago?" He would say it and never mind whether Chicagoans wonder "What's with this Professor? What's he talking? His pilot light is gone out."

Bellow lent Corde aspects and traits of Alexandra so that he could reflect on his domestic life. While drinking plum brandy to generate a little internal heat, Corde leafs through Minna's old books, looks over the furnishings of her old room, and thinks of himself as the inappropriate American married to an astronomer whose business was not of this world, dragged back to her mother's deathbed to watch her mother break her solemn promise to live to ninety. Corde wants to be thought dependable, responsible, practical. He knows he had the reputation of a swinger, a chaser; but has he not long since proved to Valeria and Minna, who had been warned against him, that he can be—is—a good husband, stable, balanced, reliable? Why does he still need to prove to Valeria on her deathbed that he is a gentle soul, not a masked killer, not weak with vice, that she can trust him to protect her daughter? Why, Corde dares to ask himself, should he sacrifice himself for a daughter who knows nothing of the real world and less of him? Why is he fulfilling the life goal of this Macedonian matron? Why has he chosen to become a "crystallized husband"?

I once heard Bellow say, as if to himself, very quietly—this was after *The Dean's December* had been published—he had always thought he could not live alone, that he always had to be married. Now he was not so sure. He could do very well alone. I could not take that up. There was no need. The ambivalence, the tenuous hold husband and wife had on each other is there for any reader of the novel to discern.

While in Vermont, I had copied down a few lines from Alexandra Ionescu Tulcea's article, a reprint from *Probability on Banach Spaces,* and wondered then how her sense of reality could have any significant impact on Bellow.

> The purpose of this note is to give a submartingale characterization of measurable cluster points and to show how a recent result of Baxter, more general than both the "amart convergence theorem" and Chacon's "Generalized Fatou inequality" can be derived directly from the "Doob a.s. convergence theory for submartingales."[2]

Examples of the propositions and theorems, the proofs and consequences, even the remarks in the conclusion, would torment the typesetter, and although I perceived that Alexandra Bellow achieved an understanding of the real character of submartingales, I knew that Saul Bellow's quest for the true nature of reality could have little impact on his wife. I had already read Corde's words:

> Reality is real only when the soul found its underlying truth. . . . In the American moral crisis, the first requirement was to experience what was happening and to see what must be seen.

The generality mind, the habit of mind that governed the world, had no force of coherence—none. Reality does not exist out there. I had read Corde's direct address to Minna:

> . . . he would have told Minna "Imagine, sometimes, that if a film could be made of one's life, every other frame would be death. It goes so fast we're not aware of it. Destruction and resurrection in alternate beats of being, but speed makes it seem continuous. But you see, kid, with ordinary consciousness you can't even begin to know what's happening."

I knew how Bellow could find metaphors to depict reality.

> It was not so much the inner city slum that threatened us as the slum of innermost being, of which the inner city was perhaps a material representation.

The problem for Bellow was not that the vision of probability was basically a subject grounded equally in geometry and measure theory, not that theorems about real or complex numbers seemed to flow from the fact that these are Hibert spaces, but that a man might never discover what is eternal in his spirit, that an Albert Corde might fail to pass the reality of a Dewey Spangler, a sister Elfrida, a wife Minna, a Valeria, a Gigi, a Vlada, a Ridpath, a Varennes, a Petruscu, a Voynich, a Detillion, a Zaehner, an Ebry, a Rick Lester, and yes, an Albert Corde through his soul. That was the project. Without that, the soul was empty, desiccated, a waft of blue smoke that passes in a plume into the ether.

What did Minna know of Corde, the man who never goes to cemeteries because "it was just as easy for your dead to visit you, only by now he would have to hire a hall." She wanted him to join the work of the scientist Beech, an environmentalist who wished to publicize his discovery that it was lead that was destroying the nerve cells of Homo sapiens. Corde tells Vlada, Beech's emissary and Minna's friend:

> "Where Beech sees poison lead I see poison thought or poison theory. The view we hold of the material world may put us into a case as heavy as lead, a sarcophagus which nobody will even have the art to paint becomingly. The end of philosophy and of art, will do to 'advanced' thought what flakes of lead paint or leaded exhaust fumes do to infants. Which of these do you think will bring us to the end of everything?"

What Corde needs is to find the connection between the terror of a young man's widow and the bitterness of an old woman's daughter, between the death of a young man thrown out the window and that of an old woman fed into the fire of the crematorium. He feels close to Valeria, who with a mind "exquisitely vivid" was "studying her death," but he has more in common with that boy Rick Lester, who with a gag in his throat had two or three seconds in which to recognize he was finished. This old woman who believed the Sermon on the Mount knew not one syllable of the truth of the Cabrini-Green housing project. "She didn't have their sort of mind, the modern consciousness, that equivocal queer condition, working with a net of foolish assumptions and so much absurd unwanted stuff lying on your heart." Valeria is dying. "For her this world of death was ending." Rick Lester was dead. However, Corde was alive still with time left to expose the truth, with time left to express his feelings, his rage, his sorrow, his exaltation. Ah, if only he could write one marvelous book before he was closed down! If only he could achieve what he dreams he can do.

At the conclusion of *The Dean's December,* Corde comes as near as he shall ever get to the light; he searches the heavens from his unobstructed observation point on Mount Palomar and acknowledges the sky itself is an unreality:

> And what he saw with his eyes was not even the real heavens. No, only white marks, bright vibrations, clouds of sky roe, tokens of the real thing, only as much as could be taken in through the distortions of the atmosphere. Through these distortions you saw objects, forms, partial realities. The rest was to be felt. And it wasn't only that you felt, but that you were drawn to feel and to penetrate further, as if you were being informed that what was spread over you had to do with your existence, down to the very blood and the crystal forms inside your bones. Rocks, trees, animals, men and women, these also drew you to penetrate further, under the distortions (comparable to the atmospheric ones, shadows within shadows), to find their real being with your own. This was the sense in which you were drawn.

Sky roe! That is a metaphor of the light that knocks out all possibilities of a generative force that is stable. Three decades earlier, Bellow had said in his letter to me, "Writing should derive from the Creation. . . . We should require things to be simpler and simpler, greater and greater." Now Dean Corde is wondering, Suppose simpler and simpler does not mean greater and greater; it may turn out that there is no greater, only shadows within shadows, the light itself a delusion, no difference at all between the real and the ideal, none between appearance and reality, none between the transient world below and the evanescent world above. The man on quest for transcendence desiring to attain a sense of a higher reality is arriving at a suspicion that only tokens and distortions and partials may be found. Above and below.

If a man can find no essence, no real being, what becomes of the universe? If the universe were an appearance only, what becomes of the man?

And where shall a man look? Into what shall he penetrate? The self. Gazing into the freezing heavens, Corde remembers:

> Once, in the Mediterranean, coming topside from a C-class cabin, the uric smells and the breath of the bilges, every hellish little up-to-date convenience there below to mock your insomnia—then seeing the morning sun on the tilted sea. Free! The grip of every sickness within you disengaged by this pouring out. You couldn't tell which was out of plumb, the ship, or yourself, or the sea aslant—but free! It didn't matter, since you were free! It was like that also when you approached the stars as steadily as this.

That the man be free, is all. Owes nothing to appearance or reality. Needs only to be free to try to figure it out. Figure out what? His own real being.

Corde is a professor, yes, a real brain; he has a comprehensive vision, infinite longings, but he has no guarantees, no insurance plans, only freedom to search for a truth that may not even exist, freedom to continue a quest he recognizes will be fruitless, endless, and concludes only with the grave.

Corde is also characterized as an artist, but he fears his art has been weak, "fiddle-faddle."

He has aroused, with his writings and his actions, only horror, indignation, bewilderment, suspicion, puzzlement, and outrage. He was compelled to speak out, however, to rid himself of insulating fictions, driven to seek justice, to denounce the dehumanization of the spirit. The man who gives up the search for truth may just as well climb into his own sarcophagus and give a signal to the grave digger to lower away. "Anger was better. In passivity you only deteriorated."

His art did not float him; his writings seemed very nearly to have taken him out of the human world. Corde thinks of Rilke's lament: "When Rilke had complained about his inability to find an adequate attitude to the things and people about him, Corde had thought, yes, that's very common— that's me, too." Like Rilke, Corde believes he has become a man too impartial, too objective, too given to disinterested judgment. He calls himself "impartiality intoxicated," led away from contact with human beings and with the world. "Lord," Corde thinks as he walks along the corridor of corpse alcoves in the crematorium, "Lord, I am ignorant and strange to my fellow-man. I had thought that I understood things pretty well. Not so."

The witness judges the artist: "If I'm some kind of artist," Corde tells Vlada, "I need to be busy with some kind of art. I wish I knew what it was."

He wonders whether maybe he "wasn't advanced enough to be the artist of this singularly demanding sense of his!" Corde fears his own inadequacy; he confesses this fear came into the world with his freedom and his light and his purpose and now the fear threatens to obscure his light and shake his purpose. He admits he has always tried to set that gnawing truth aside, but it was there all the time, he couldn't get rid of it, and as he grew older it gained strength and he had to give ground.

Albert Corde joins the assembly of Bellow's dolorous narrators, the Joseph and the Asa Leventhal, the Tommy Wilhelm, the Herzog, and Artur Sammler; gone, for *The Dean's December,* is the ebullient Augie March and Eugene Henderson, the yea-saying heroes with their schemes for rehabilitation, Bummidge and Charlie Citrine. The young man with a project and the oh so disheartened and distraught old man will both arrive together in *More Die of Heartbreak,* when Bellow splits his vision of himself into two, the young nephew Ken Trachtenberg and his aging uncle Benn Crader.

20

In Stormy Solitude

Obsessed by his need to justify his new "consciousness level," Bellow said to Melvin Bragg:

> "I don't like to go on producing the same book over and over again. This is a habit of professional writers that I deplore. They learn to write a book and then continue to write that one book from beginning to end. That would bore me and I think it would be an imposition on the reading public."

Bellow is writing the same book over and over again, but each book is a spring forward from the one before. Bellow does not perceive how great a distance he has come. He is the high jumper who raises the bar and lands on his turf with more force, beating his own record each time he plays his game.

In place since *Dangling Man,* his recognizable disjunctive style still served him well for *The Dean's December:* There is the same juxtaposition of events and recollections, the same intentional contrasts of public and private worlds, the same manner of rendering the polarity between the ideal and the real, and the same adversaries, at once cherished and repugnant, besetting the narrator, still cringing, whining, snarling, at bay. However, in *The Dean's December,* the big questions have answers, problems may be dealt with, issues resolved. We cannot defeat death, we may not ever know who we are, the immortal spirit may or may not fulfill its contract with God, but we can improve the prisons, the hospitals, the law courts; we can fight drug addiction, racism, terrorism, child abuse, sexual depravity; we can reclaim the underprivileged, fight poverty, crime, corruption, if we take the first step and that is to fight ignorance, not with great books, not with meditations, but with knowledge of reality. We need only to observe the disorders of the real world in order to begin to reconstruct society. "Who am I?" gives way to "What can I do?" It is Corde who says, "The first act of morality was to disinter the reality, retrieve reality, dig it out from the trash, represent it anew as art would represent it."

Bellow, through the voice of the narrator, instructs himself to turn aside his "poetry" and his "philosophizing" and take upon himself the work of observation.

> He looked out, noticing. What a man he was for noticing! Continually attentive to his surroundings as if he had been sent down to *mind* the outer world, on a mission of observation and notation. The object of which was? To link up? To classify? To penetrate? To follow a sprinting little van-hearse over a gloomy boulevard was the immediate assignment.

Gone, therefore, in *The Dean's December,* are the ebullient catalogues, the extravagant allusions and fanciful metaphors; all the well-known devices of Bellow's diction are compressed into a minimalist mannerism, taking a kind of shortcut to characterization, depending on the reader to get the picture. It's "King Kong delicacy," a "Huckleberry Finn air," a "Lyndon Johnson type of bully," a "William Powell moustache." One-liners do appear from time to time, but the humor is bitter; re Max Detillion: "You swindle a man and then grab even the sense of injury for yourself." Re Elfrida's remarriage: "She saw the handwriting on the nursing home wall."

Corde is after the facts and the truth beneath the facts, and the aura of feeling that such knowledge generates. Corde believes Elfrida's new husband Judge Sorokin is tough; he says, in metonymy, "a rude hand, and all of a piece, as though the fingers were incapable of separate action." The reader perceives that fingers so held together are a fist. An event described in concrete detail stirs the reader's heart with compassion and sorrow although the emotions experienced by those taking part are not named, the meaning not stated. Take, for example, the return home of Tante Gigi, Minna, and Corde after the death of Valeria:

> Gigi served an early dinner. It was eaten listlessly. For Christmas Eve the table had been laid with linens embroidered in red. Corde went to bed early. The twenty-fourth of December had lasted long enough.

The austere rendering continues in the description of Christmas morning:

> On Christmas morning there were presents beside their coffee cups. The old girls saved gift-wrapping paper and ribbons from year to year. There were treasures of all kinds in the cupboards, boxes of pre-Communist ornaments. Gigi brought to the table the Christmas angels Minna remembered from childhood. They were designed to float slowly on wires radiating from a disk set in motion by the heat of a small candle. The toy would not work. "Valeria always could make it go," Gigi said. She wore deep mourning and her neck was strained as she bent to strike more matches. She had combed out the bobbed hair but at the back it still looked like a hayrick. "It may be the candles," she said. She went through the drawers of the buffet, looking for the right kind. She didn't know where Valeria had put them. Corde tinkered with the wires. Americans were supposed to be mechanically gifted, but he could get nowhere with them. He only bent the toy badly. The four angels hung motionless. That was the end of them. Valeria had taken their secret with her.

The little toy is a symbol, but no esoteric knowledge is needed to understand the four angels hanging motionless.

In *The Dean's December,* all the mourners gather around the open coffin to say goodbye to the matriarch. For seven pages, Corde observes the scene in minute detail and as the paragraphs unfold, the event becomes an old-fashioned mural, like a Rivera or an Orozco, with a multiplicity of figures and objects all testifying to human sorrow and human loss, with the ostensible objective observer tottering on the edge of despair. Corde, isolated in the crowd, becomes the impassioned man of good intentions tormented by the spectacle of abject lamentation.

Albert Corde no longer argues in his mind with Freud or Marx or Nietzsche; he leaves behind all his old prosy mentors and talks instead to people, victims and victimizers, asking what has happened to them, and he listens to their answers. He investigates the "pain level" of men and women in the pleasure society and in the society of the iron fist. We remember Artur Sammler's dismay, his disgust and fear, when he was accosted by the black prince of pickpockets waggling his penis before the old man's face. Compare this to Toby Winthrop's telling Albert Corde how he cured himself of heroin addiction and consider the degree to which the remoteness of the dissociated old man Sammler has expired.

> He lifted himself from the tub, and just as he was, in wet clothes, he went down into Sixty-third Street and caught a cab to Billings Hospital, to the detoxification unit. Because of his terrifying looks, the receptionist signaled the police, who grabbed him in the lobby. But they had nothing to hold him on at the station, only vagrancy and loitering. "I bailed myself out. Always a big bankroll in my

pocket. I got another cab back to Billings, but this time I stopped in an empty lot and tore the leg off a table. I went in with it under my coat, and I showed it to the receptionist. I said I'd beat her brains out. That's how I got upstairs. They gave me the first methadone shot. I was in a hospital gown, and I went to the toilet and sat on the floor to wait for the reaction. I put my arms around the commode and held tight to it."

"But you didn't go through with the methadone treatment."

"No, sir. I did not. Something happened. When I came in I had the table leg, I was ready to kill. I would have killed the lady if she called the cops again. But in less than an hour I was called to stop a riot. I had to stop a man breaking up the joint. He was a black man, as big as me, and he had delirium tremens. He smashed the chairs in the patients' sitting room. He broke a coffee table, broke windows. The orderlies and nurses were like kindergarteners around him. He was like a buffalo. I had to take a hand, Professor. There was nothing else to do. I separated from the commode and went out and took control. I put my arms around the man. I got him to the floor and lay on the top of him. I don't say he was listening, but he wasn't so wild with me. They gave him a needle and we laid him on a cart and put him in bed."

"That was Smithers?"

"Smithers," said Winthrop. "I wish I could explain what it was all about. I've told this before. It's as if I kept after it till I could find out what happened that moment I took control of him. Maybe it was because I died twenty-four hours before. Maybe because my buddy left me in the bathtub in the hotel— that was all he knew how to do for me. But when they put Smithers in bed, I sat by him and minded him."

"This was when your own treatment stopped."

"I wouldn't leave him. They had to measure his body fluid. I held the man's Johnson for him. You understand what I'm saying? I held his dick for him to pee in the flask. He had a bad ulcer in his leg. I treated that, too. That was his cure, and it was my cure, at the same time. I was his mother, I was his daddy. And we stayed together since."

Henderson and Dahfu, too, had talked brotherhood after Atti the lion had been returned to its cage; Tommy Wilhelm had sensed his kinship with his fellowman while walking along a subway arcade or standing at the bier of a stranger. In *The Dean's December,* Bellow exemplified the brotherhood in action, not abstract generalization but concrete reality.

For the first time in forty years of writing, Bellow admitted a sister-hood, a woman's network. "This apartment was the center of an extended feminine hierarchy." Corde observes there is humane cooperation among women in Communist society, "the woman connection," he calls it. He goes so far as to trust Dincutza as she beckons him to follow her below to sign for Valeria's body. "He put his faith in her mottled face, brown buck teeth, sparse hair, goodness of heart." He trusted Vlada, "took comfort in her," and she is intelligent! Vlada even has "a reassuring feminine breath."

Happily the nice observations on women reach across to America. "Towards Minna, Miss Porson's female generosity and admiration were boundless." Lydia Lester surprises Corde with her strength and poise in the courtroom and he reflects, "Lots of nice girls are brought up that way, with too faint an image of themselves. The family tells them they aren't strong." Minna, back in Chicago, rises from her sickbed to attend Elfrida's party for Elfrida's sake. "Her motives were wholly feminine."

Oh it's not all hearts and flowers. It was, after all, Bellow writing. Elfrida's party is a birthday party for her dog. Elfrida, with her Vidal Sassoon dye job, her damaged skin, her heavy thighs and hips, "the broad estuary of the lower half, the lower flow of womanliness," is a raunchy woman who wants action. And Fay Porson?

> She had her own sexual fat to fry. She wasn't going to give it to the grave. She was like that lascivious old woman in Aristophanes, claiming equal sexual rights with the other "girls," grabbing at all the handsome young men. And those young men wouldn't know what they were getting into until it was time to do the act.

Minna, to be sure, is a distinguished professor of astronomy with an international reputation; she has a work and that's a switch for Bellow, whose women have been predators, leeches, erotic engines, and what not. Minna is too much the child, however. "When he pleased her, she might jump up and down and clap her hands like a small girl." Her smiles do not signify understanding. "He had learned that these smiles [signified] only confidence that her husband, if she asked him to explain, could give her his grounds, would show why his remarks deserved her smile." She was not really interested in his work, although she wished him well. "Occasionally the gold-star pupil bit did get him down." When she listened in her solemn way, "You never knew what she was hearing or whether her large eyes look at you or through you or past you." Dissociated, Minna lives outside the real world and is too fanatically absorbed in herself.

Corde has nurtured her but he wants above all to join the human race, to unwind his shroud of "mute heart-aching numbness." The good husband is tired of privacy and propriety and civility. He is no scientist absorbed in measurements but an artist whose spiritual loneliness has come of precisely such dissociation. He has lost contact with human beings, with the world. *To be,* one must experience the times, people, issues. His project is to probe "the depth level," here on earth, to find what lies beneath appearances, running the risk that he may find nothing beneath the appearances; a more dangerous project, but perhaps, Corde thinks, he will be like the acrobat in *Huckleberry Finn*, "who falls over his own feet but turns out to be a marvellous equestrian and acrobat." Or perhaps he will be like the Ancient Mariner, who takes the Bridegroom by the sleeve and tells again his story.

It will turn out to be the Ancient Mariner. In the three long stories that followed *The Dean's December*, "Him with His Foot in His Mouth," "What Kind of Day Did You Have?" and "Cousins," and in the novel published soon after, *More Die of Heartbreak*, each narrator remains at once hopeful and hopeless, tormented, agitated, unstable, a victim still of potato love, still out of it, desolate, with all his hysterical symptoms intact.

What had chilled the writer? When Bellow spoke with Michiko Kakutani of *The New York Times* a month before the publication of *The Dean's December*, she asked him why he had turned to political and social issues, and he replied, "After writing *To Jerusalem and Back*, I saw it was as easy to write about great public matters as about private ones—all it required was more confidence and daring."[1]

What became of the confidence and daring? Why return to the life lived, take another, yet another long, long look at the old life plan; why bring all the old characters back, some in not such new clothes, the losers, the louts, the loonies? Why reincarnate the racketeer brother, the swindler brother, the sniping sister, the best friend who is an archdeceiver, the carping journalist, the mistress with spurious intellectual interests, the litigious wife, the bribed judge, the defiled lawyer, the crude, vulgar, manipulating, corrupt, money-loving, ass-grabbing—well, and so on? Bellow goes back to the immigrant days in Chicago, fifty years back to the old old days on the West Side, East Side. Why is Cousin Motty back in the Turkish bath?

Was it the reviews of *The Dean's December*? Bellow knew there would be flak, but he told Michiko Kakutani he had always gone against the stream. He was not afraid of the members of the tired profession, "third rate vaudevillians," "etiolated," "spiritless," who have not had a new thought since they were undergraduates. "They think they know what writers should be and what writers should write," but who are they? "I think these are the reptiles of the literary establishment who are grazing on the last Mesozoic grasses of Romanticism."

Bellow told Eugene Kennedy, who interviewed him for the *Chicago Tribune*, that he knew his novel of "hard knocks" would disappoint readers who expected a "Bellow book," but he was indifferent to outside expectations. "It's the first time that I have based characters and incidents on real persons and events." He named names for Kennedy. "There are two black men in the book. They are based on real persons. I looked far and wide for men of moral imagination and I found only these two." In all Chicago, Bellow had found only an ex–hit man and the former director of Cook County jail as his examples of men of moral imagination.'

Kennedy reported that Bellow sighed as he described the work of some popular novelists, "apparently delivered by truck to the publishers and unedited and uncorrected immediately set into print. I work over my manuscript many times until I feel that there is nothing more that I can change to improve it. I am deeply moved when I write. I get turned on by it. . . . I don't use words loosely. . . . There is a hardness of intention that goes with it. . . . There is no idleness in it." Here, too, Bellow named names. "Most writers cobble out a book on the same last every two or three years. Updike does that."[2]

Updike may or may not have read Bellow's remark; surely he got wind of it. Within the month, John Updike reviewed *The Dean's December* for *The New Yorker*. He began with a comment that ploughed up the ground for his entire review: "The good thing about *The Dean's December* is that it is *by* Saul Bellow. The bad thing about *The Dean's December* is that it is *about* Saul Bellow." Updike said the so-called persona was redescribed every few pages "as if the author were checking to make sure the mask was still in place." He felt the author slipped in little reassuring compliments. It was not egoism but narcissism. *The Dean's December* was "not an integrated novel," he continued. "Let a journalist pass for a dean; but can journalism pass for a novel?" He believed Corde was a "coddled agonist"; "all the characters are stuck fast in the central tarbaby of Corde's ruminations"; "Bellow has it in him, a great poet and fearless mental venturer that he is, to write one of those unclassifiable American masterpieces like *Walden.*" This was not it.[3]

D. M. Thomas, author of *The White Hotel,* writing in the *Washington Post,* was impatient with the novel. He believed it suffered from Corde's decency and detachment—"It's very difficult to make virtue interesting." There is too much flashback, too much secondhand.[4] As expected, Christopher Lehmann-Haupt, writing for *The New York Times,* called the novel "stifling, oppressive, bleak." He expressed his opinion that there was too much lecturing; at the end there was only relief that the book was over. The Mount Palomar section was moving and beautiful, but "I can't honestly swear that I didn't love it because coming to it at last was like not hitting one's head against the wall anymore."[5]

It was Hugh Kenner's review for *Harper's* that outraged Bellow. Never, he said, in all his forty years of writing had he been subjected to so vicious an anti-Semitic attack. Kenner called the "fox-faced creator" of *The Dean's December* a "puppeteer," a "sardonic connoisseur of Old Testament motifs." Kenner went on to say Bellow's stories all reflected "a tribal penchant for arguing." His narrator was a new "impersonation of Job," Bellow's "formula for getting a new book started." On this occasion, the Dean was "not a Jewish Dean from the Bellow Repertory company," but a Jonah fastened to his whale by "a Hebrew safety pin." However, anti-Semitism seemed a minor note. Kenner began with a generalization intended to offend: "A genre has long since defined itself, Nobel-certified; the Saul Bellow Novel. This is the Novel as First-Draft Dissertation." Perhaps Kenner was chosen for his hatchet job by an irate *Harper's* editorial board that was incensed that the two articles Corde wrote were supposed to have appeared in their magazine. Kenner dutifully said, "You have to suspend belief to imagine *Esquire,* let alone *Harper's,* publishing to the extent of two long installments these meanderings of an epigone of Saul Bellow's." Bellow himself, Kenner was sure, would have judged the book dreary. Why had he written it? He had acquired an alter ego named Herzog, who had addled Bellow's head by lecturing his audiences into a generous stupor, who prided himself on the cogency of his moral reflections. It was Herzog who had written those long "swatches" in *Mr. Sammler's Planet* "you may remember skipping"; it was Herzog with his ruminations, his lucubrations, his platitudes from Communications IA who had written *The Dean's December.* "Corde is empathizing with what he feels the Colonel feels about what he feels about the Colonel's nonfeeling." Corde's plight—he had nothing to do but wait, "killing time in limbo"—was like the plight of the author, "who must fill a book with sheer inaction and has consequently piped in what's been all too fluent for him of late years, the Herzogian vitality to be gotten from opinions."[6]

Kenner's review is an example of the "clobbering," as Bellow called it, that *The Dean's December* got at the hands of the critics.[7] It was said: Bellow smug, Bellow at his worst, Bellow in decline. Bellow a thumb-sucker, Bellow cerebrating and boring, Bellow writing in "frustratingly elliptical intellectual shorthand." The critics felt in the race of Bellow's weeping machines—Sammler, Herzog, Wilhelm—Corde won. They wondered: Why had he "decided once again to stand on the bridge of the *Titanic* and peer prophetlike into the mist, shouting 'Iceberg ahead! Iceberg ahead!' " Why was he so touchy? Why was he so belligerent? Who was Bellow to tell us how we live and how we should live? Why should we listen to him rather than to anyone else?

The intellectual community went to town on the writer who had not "kept his fucking mouth shut," but Greater Chicago was silent. Bellow had told the truth and aroused vilification or indifference.

When had he not, however? At the time of his greatest success, in 1965 when he published *Herzog,* Richard Poirier, a professor at Rutgers

University and an old friend of Jack Ludwig, called the reviewers who praised the book "Literary ragpickers!" Poirier said Herzog's letters were uninventive and tiresome, the writing glib and banal, the mental activity of Herzog limp, his thoughts sophomoric tag lines, his sentiments fatuous, and the book, as a whole, claustrophobic, insufferably smug, and a violation of Jewish sensibility. He felt Bellow was writing out of spite, taking vengeance on his friend and his wife, and "The only betrayal in the book is the betrayal of Bellow by Bellow."[8]

Bellow had long ago learned to withstand the lashings he received from his critics and had his own plan for retaliation. In *Humboldt's Gift*, Charlie Citrine recalls his Princeton days:

> At that time I was an apprentice and a bit player and Sewell [R. P. Blackmur] had treated me like one. He had seen, I expect, a soft-fibered young man, handsome enough but slack, with large sleepy-looking eyes, a bit overweight, and with a certain reluctance (it showed in his glance) to become enthusiastic about other people's enterprises. That he failed to appreciate me made me sore. But such vexations always filled me with energy as well. And if I later became such a formidable mass of credentials it was because I put such slights to good use. I avenged myself by making progress.

Bellow's sense of purpose, what Stephen Spender called "the fire at the heart's center," was not something he would extinguish because of those cold winds blowing from the north, the rains and harsh waters of public disapproval.

Bellow burned for connection, but not connection with what Norman Podhoretz called "The Family," those first and second and third generations of tastemakers who edited and reviewed and wrote articles. Podhoretz was so proud of himself when, after daring to write a negative review of *Augie March*, he was admitted to membership, he wrote:

> That I was virtually the only reviewer of the book who was able to see and understand it, even if very imperfectly, in this way settled the issue of my adoption into the family for good. For some it made me an object of bitter personal attack, itself a sign of family membership, and for others it made me a personage to be reckoned with. Warshow, still with his nose firmly to the ground of my career, told me that this was now definitely the case, but even if he had not, I would have known it by the fact that in the midst of the storm my review had kicked up I received a phone call from one of the two Patriarchs, summoning me to what, looking back upon it, I think might fairly be described as a bar mitzvah ceremony which signified, like that ancient Jewish rite itself, that I had finally come of age.[9]

The connection for which Bellow burned was family, and well he knew what family, the family to which he was connected by blood.

In *Dangling Man,* Joseph finds an old photograph of his grandfather.

> Then, studying the picture, it occurred to me that this skull of my grandfather's would in time overtake me, curls, Buster Brown, and all. Still later I came to believe (and this was no longer an impression but a dogma) that the picture was a proof of my mortality. I was upright on my grandfather's bones and the bones of those before him in a temporary loan. But he himself, not the further past, hung over me. Through the years he would reclaim me bit by bit, till my own fists withered and my eyes stared. This was a somber but not a frightening thought. And it had a corrective effect on my vanity.
>
> Only by this time it was not so simple as that, it was not merely vanity. By this time my face was to me the whole embodiment of my meaning. It was a register of my ancestors, a part of the world and, simultaneously, the way I received the world, clutched at it, and the way, moreover, in which I announced myself to it. All of this was private and never spoken of.

Joseph does not speak of it. Bellow does, from this first observation to the present day. In "Seize the Day," Tommy Wilhelm thinks:

> [It] came over you that from one grandfather you inherited such and such a head of hair . . . from another, broad thick shoulders; an oddity of speech from one uncle, and small teeth from another, and the gray eyes with darkness diffused even into the whites, and a wide-lipped mouth like a statue from Peru. Wandering races have such looks, the bones of one tribe, the skin of another. From his mother he had gotten sensitive feelings, a soft heart, a brooding nature, a tendency to be confused under pressure.

All Bellow's narrators know the blood tie, acknowledged, creates the self; human connection is a magnetic force. Kinship generates love, and love, enfeebled or betrayed, is always capable of being invigorated, perhaps not sustained, but always, always sought for. So Charlie Citrine thinks of his brother Julius:

> I loved my stout and now elderly brother. Perhaps he loved me too. In principle he was not in favor of strong family bonds. Possibly he saw brotherly love as an opening for exploitation. My feelings for him were vivid, almost hysterically intense, and I could not blame him for trying to resist them. He wished to be a man entirely of today, and he had forgotten or tried to forget the past. . . . For my part there was nothing that I could forget. . . . My own belief was that without memory existence was metaphysically injured, damaged.

So there is Corde contemplating the sisterhood of family in Bucharest. There is Ijah Brodsky, who recalls his cousin Raphael Metzger, still wearing the expression with which he was born, one of assurance, of cheerful insolence.

> The divine or, as most would prefer to say, the genetic stamp visible even in corruption and ruin. And we belong to the same genetic pool, with a certain difference in scale. My frame is much narrower. Nevertheless, some of the same traits are there, creases in the cheeks, a turn at the end of the nose, and most of all, a tendency to fullness in the underlip—the way the mouth works towards the sense-world. You could identify these characteristics also in family pictures from the old country—the Orthodox, totally different human types. Yet the cheekbones of bearded men, a band of forehead under a large skullcap, the shock of a fixed stare from two esoteric eyes, are recognizable still in their descendants.

Soon there would be Ken, going over it all once again, his beloved Uncle Benn, his father, mother, cousins, and more cousins.

No matter what setting Bellow chooses, whether it be the upper West Side of New York or gold coast Chicago, a village in the Berkshires or estates in Georgia and Texas, condominiums in Florida, a cold room, a cold street in Bucharest, his hero pauses to recall the world out of which Bellow came, to describe again that family and those relatives who afflicted Bellow with pain and aroused in him profound feelings of love. In book after book, in story after story, he dreams of his relatives, living and dead. "Whom did I ever love as I loved them?" asks Moses Herzog. They are all there in the fiction—father, mother, stepmother, sister, brothers, aunts, uncles, cousins— restored to life and meaning, "the elect of my memory." Brodsky's ex-wife says, "You've always been soft about cousins. . . . I used to think you'd open every drawer in the morgue if somebody told you that there was a cousin to be found." And once more she says, "If you had cared about me as you do about all those goofy, half-assed cousins, we never would have divorced." Brodsky thinks that may very well be true. His Cousin Tanky says, "For some reason you keep track of all the cousins, Ijah." Brodsky admits it is so.

The game of solitaire Brodsky plays with himself, taking the cards from the haphazardly shuffled deck in his hands and placing them in a joined series before him on the table, is a game of connection. The cards did not always work out. If they did, it was only a game of cards. The connection with loved ones is the game no Bellow hero can win. Death has taken his loved ones; those who lived betrayed him.

Abraham Bellow scarcely knew what to make of this delicate, book-ish, mother's darling, all nervousness and tears and dreaming, who would not hold on to a decent job and gave no thought to business. Although Bellow quarreled often, sometimes bitterly, with his father, we remember "Seize the Day": "Croak in a flophouse. . . . Go. And don't come to my funeral." We also remember *Henderson* and *Herzog*, "A Silver Dish" and *The Dean's December* and *More Die of Heartbreak*. There was as much love and nostalgia as exasperation and hostility. Once only does Bellow idealize what he longed for his father to be: The aged Artur Sammler does not chastise his crazy daughter, Shula, but pities her, is kind to her, listens to her nonsense and does not judge.

In every conversation I have had with Bellow, he always has made some reference to his family, sometimes briefly, sometimes at length, sometimes in response to my question or by some association in his mind. Always he has paused to speak of them. I was visiting Bellow in February 1985, and although Abraham Bellow had been dead for some thirty years, Bellow talked of him as if he were in the next room.

I reminded Bellow that I had gone with him, years and years ago, to visit his father, probably just to keep him company on the long streetcar ride. We sat in the dim parlor, the old man questioning me closely: Who was my father? My grandfather? Where did they come from? What was the name of the town in Lithuania? What did my father do for a living? What business were my uncles in? When did they come to America? How old were they when they came? Did I know the name of the ship? The stepmother remained in the kitchen, never once coming in to say a word. Bellow did not leave the room. All the way on our ride back, he fumed and groused about his father. He was nosy. He was impolite. He had submitted me to an inquisition. He did not respect his son's friends but grilled them.

I wish today I had paid more attention. I might have recognized the son's hunger for detail, for facts, for names and places in that fiercely inquiring old man. Were it today, I would have gone into the kitchen for a glass of water and met Fannie. However, she is there large as life on the pages of *Herzog*, Taube, withering in the same house I visited in 1940, the house in which Moses finds his father's old gun and his grandfather's rubles. She is also puttering about in a house in Lakewood, New Jersey—Aunt Mildred in *The Bellarosa Connection*.

When Bellow's father died, I, polite and I suppose nicely trained in the ways of family, went to pay a condolence call. Bellow lived then in one of those huge apartment buildings that stand along Riverside Drive. I left the elevator on the seventh floor and walked slowly down the long corridor and stood for a time before the door, listening to the sounds of a record. It was Mozart's *Requiem*. My knock did not interrupt the cheerless music. When

Saul opened the door, he was weeping. He had, he said, been playing Mozart's *Requiem* for two days, which is how I knew what it was.

The immigrant from St. Petersburg, once an importer of Egyptian onions for Russia's borscht, once a bootlegger in Quebec for American rum-runners, once a supplier of firewood for West Side housewives and storekeepers, then a coal dealer, was dead. The son took his share of his father's money and established himself as a squire in rural New York, where no relative had ever lived, and sat down to write of his childhood on St. Dominique Street in Lachine, which he has continued to do until the present day. Rudi Trach-tenberg is a lively old rooster, still challenging his renegade son Ken for "being out of it." Ken agrees with his Uncle Benn, who says: "The earth is a graveyard and the one and only project of humanity is to reclaim it for life. That people dear to us should disappear into eternity is intolerable, and we can't accept it without cowardice. A beginning must be made with the immediate family. Sons and daughters must restore life to those who gave it to them."

In *The Bellarosa Connection,* published in 1989, the father appears briefly, alive and keen, playing chess with his son; the father absorbed in his knights and rooks, glancing sidelong from time to time at his son: "I was at the bar of paternal judgment again, charged with American puerility. When Would I Shape Up, at last!"

Bellow's mother died when he was fifteen. Only twice is her death graphically described. The first occurs in the course of Herzog's reflections on mortality; even while reliving the scene of her death, Herzog shifts his attention away—to his own melancholy self, to his identity as a Jew, to what he was reading at the time, and disagreeing with, to the sounds he hears outside the silent room in which she lay. Not until "Something to Remember Me By" appeared in *Esquire* magazine, in July of 1990, does Louie, the aged narrator, recall the details, the same sorry details of her death from breast cancer, this time shifting his attention away to his foibles as a sexually aroused adolescent.[10]

Usually the "sacred person," as he calls her, remains very much alive, a presence Bellow in every guise longs to retain or at least reach, and although she ages, becoming more and more incapacitated, blind or senile, in her progress through Bellow's fiction, the mother is represented with tenderness. Not until 1982 is the mother finally conceded to be part of the family that left him out. In "Him with His Foot in His Mouth," an elderly Harry Shawmut visits his ninety-four-year-old mother in a nursing home. She does not even know—perhaps never knew—who he is. The conversation between the bald old man and his senile mother is funny and ironic, but underneath we can recognize Bellow, still sore at heart, still reaching out to the one person he believed loved him.

> I preferred to come at mealtimes, for she had to be fed. To feed her was infinitely meaningful for me. . . . I used to feel that I had inherited something of her rich crazy nature and love of life, but it now was useless to think such thoughts. . . . By no means silent, she spoke of her family, but I was not mentioned.

"How many children have you got?" Shawmut asks.

> "Three: two daughters and a son, my son Philip."
> All three were dead. Maybe she was already in communion with them. There was little enough of reality remaining in this life; perhaps they had made connections in another. In the census of the living, I wasn't counted.
> "My son Philip is a clever businessman."
> "Oh, I know."
> She stared, but did not ask how I knew. My nod seemed to tell her I was a fellow with plenty of contacts, and that was enough for her.
> "Philip is very rich," she said.
> "Is he?"
> "A millionaire, and a wonderful son. He always used to give me money. I put it in Postal Savings. Have you got children?"
> "No, I haven't."
> "My daughters come to see me. But best of all is my son. He pays all my bills. . . . I hurt all the time, especially my hips and legs. I have so much misery that there are days when I think I should jump from the window."
> "But you won't do that, will you?"
> "Well, I think: What would Philip and the girls do with a mother a cripple?"

Shawmut sings snatches of the *Stabat Mater,* defined earlier in the story as "the glorious mother who would not stand up for *me,* " and while he sings, he dreams of his childhood.

> Of course I loved my mother, and she had once loved me. I well remember having my hair washed with a bulky bar of castile soap and how pained she was when I cried from the soap in my eyes. When she dressed me in a pongee suit to send me off to a surprise party, she kissed me ecstatically.

And he kisses the old woman, wondering what he had done to earn such oblivion, why fat-assed Philip the evildoer should have been her favorite, the true son. Shawmut explains to himself why this should be so:

My mother, two-thirds of her erased, and my brother—who knew where his wife had buried him?—had both been true to the present American world and its liveliest material interests. Philip therefore spoke to her understanding. I did not.

Perhaps Shawmut believes the generalized abstract reason with which he justifies his mother's not having recognized him, but a social cause of oblivion cannot heal the private wound of separation.

Kenneth Trachtenberg's mother is alive—much good it does him. He goes to visit her in Somalia, where she is working in a relief camp. "She was disappointed in me, even angry. She had wanted me to be a big shot. I should have been the *Times* number one man in Paris, or *chef de Bureau* for *Le Monde* in Washington, or NBC's head for Western Europe with thirty people under me, or *parte-parole* at the Moscow Embassy." Ken's mother's view of her brother, Benn Crader, is just as obtuse. "She didn't have a clue to her brother's real meaning, that he was a citizen of eternity . . . a person of first importance."

This brings us to brothers. Failing connection to father and mother, how is it with brothers? Shawmut is in British Columbia evading extradition, a return to entanglements of lawsuits and lawyers, a predicament caused by his brother. It is Philip Shawmut who has swindled Herschel Shawmut, and once again Bellow's conception of his archetypal brother is back—the high roller, the "main chance" man, the practical, patronizing, caring, contemptuous, yet tender brother, wanting money, wanting power, wanting women, whatever.

We saw him first in *Dangling Man*, and again in *Augie March*, drowned in *Henderson the Rain King*, alive again and loving in *Herzog*, chiseling Citrine in *Humboldt's Gift*, reappearing in *The Dean's December* as the brother-in-law—"He might have started a service called Dial-a-Fraud" —Mason Zaehner, Sr., the Chicago Goering. Dead. In "Him with His Foot in His Mouth," he is the cheat, worse, the criminal, Brother Philip, dead. Convicted of fraud, Philip had jumped bail and escaped to Mexico; there he was kidnapped while jogging in Chapultepec Park, and brought back to Texas. "My poor brother died while doing push-ups in a San Antonio prison yard during the exercise hour." Throughout it all, Abel suffers.

And what of cousins? In "Cousins," the family connections extend across three generations, grandfather, grandmother, aunts, uncles, nephews, nieces, cousins, and more cousins, and their sons and daughters. A family tree based on this single story would enter the names of more than thirty relatives, with Ijah Brodsky remembering each vividly, picturesquely, lovingly. Despite his awareness that love of family is an anachronism in the present world, he believes that "where you come from is who you are" and he restores to memory the extended family, examining them one by one, the immigrants of the first generation, those wondrous men and women of strength and force, and their descendants, corrupted by America, driven, demanding, erotic, manipulating or criminal, and their descendants, too, their children, dropouts or zombies. Except for Scholem Stavis's daughter, who is reserved to take Ijah Brodsky by the arm and lead him off. Ijah is searching for the imprint of himself, not in literature, not in history or tradition, but in his family. The original cousins are dead; those of the present generation are dying: Tanky is "stroke material"; Eunice has had a mastectomy; Scholem has had a malignant tumor removed; and Cousin Motty, ninety, is somatic under his bedclothes.

Benn Crader is Harold Vilitzer's nephew; Kenneth Trachtenberg is Benn Crader's nephew. We have met uncles and nephews before, first in *The Victim*, where poor, lost little Phillip Leventhal clings to his Uncle Asa's hand. Philip grows up to become the dying Elya Gruner, clinging to the memories of the old family that Artur Sammler has in his keeping. Mason Zaehner, Jr., is a thorn in the side of his Uncle Albert Corde. In *More Die of Heartbreak,* uncle and nephew adopt each other. Nephew Ken makes Uncle Benn his project.

One may ask why should a grown man be so concerned with family? A hint of the answer lies embedded in the metaphor with which Bellow concluded *The Dean's December,* and in the image that reappears so significantly expanded in "Cousins." Corde reflected:

> And it wasn't only that you felt, but that you were drawn to feel and to penetrate further, as if you were being informed that what was spread over you had to do with your existence, down to the very blood and the crystal forms inside your bones.

In "Cousins" Aunt Shana had said of Ijah Brodsky, "The boy has an open head," and Brodsky makes sure the reader understands the picturesque metonomy has nothing to do with his being an avid reader. "What she said is best understood as metaphysics." It was not his head that was open, but his soul. "We enter the world without prior notice, we are manifested before we can be aware of manifestation. An original self exists or, if you prefer, an original soul." Brodsky tells the reader—and this is Bellow explaining Bellow—that he has never given up the habit of referring all truly important observations to that original self or soul. Even Corde has been on the wrong track. To observe Chicago and Bucharest does not lead to an understanding of true being. Now Brodsky reflects:

> The seams open, the bonds dissolve and the untenability of existence releases
> you back again to the original self. Then you are free to look for real being under
> the debris of modern ideas, and in a magical trance if you like or with a lucidity
> altogether different from the lucidity of approved types of knowledge.

To Bellow, the essence of real being resides in the single self; the search must uncover the original self. This is a matter of will and cannot be left to mere natural process. Only deliberate introspection, analysis, and observation of private experiences and private feelings, can achieve order, coherence, form, meaning. The soul searches for its imprint in the past, not outside in history or tradition or society or books, but inside, in origin, in family. The second go, then, will be another try at Who am I? Where have I been? What have I done? Out of what have I emerged? To what have I arrived? That is the meaning of the turn in the three stories that followed *The Dean's December* and that is the whole project of *More Die of Heartbreak,* and the center, I would say the radiant center, of *The Bellarosa Connection.*

Thus, in "Him with His Foot in His Mouth," "What Kind of Day Did You Have?" and "Cousins," Bellow turned away from his own command to Forward March! His dangling man, poised to enter the real world, sits down again inside his room, withdrawn "in stormy solitude," to examine his past life, to go over his steps and missteps, in retreat while the parade of the world outside goes by without him. Herschel Shawmut, Victor Wulpy, and Ijah Brodsky, all reenact having been. It is as if each must take up again his quest for identity before he can open his door; or, as in the case of the aged, ailing, querulous Victor Wulpy, before he concedes he must soon close his door.

Shawmut, learning that Miss Rose, a librarian at Ribier College, had been traumatized for life by a remark he had made to her thirty-five years ago, decides to make it up to her by a letter that will describe the tough life he has led in all the years that followed. His letter becomes the occasion for self-examination: What did he do wrong? Why do others persist in inflicting harm on Herschel? Why has he been victimized and swindled? What were his faults, his vices? He remembers the old days on the old West Side of Chicago, the lawsuits and the lawyers, and he reflects on his Jewishness, on eroticism, on authenticity, on America, and cries out at last: "Isn't there anybody, dear God, on my side?"

Wulpy, a world-class, prominent intellectual, contemplates his present sense of displacement and suspects he has become peripheral. Beset with memories of his life on the Lower East Side of New York in 1912, he feels leaden, in a trance, possessed by fear that he is losing ground, falling apart, having "impressions of winter, winters of seven decades superimposed." Lying in a bed waiting for Katrina to come to him, he considers the issue of limits, a question "he had never until lately reckoned with. Now he touched limits on every side." He has a sense of weakness, helplessness. He hears "the underground music which signified (had signified to Marc Antony) that the god Hercules was going away."

Cousin Ijah Brodsky, without contemporaries, isolated, refusing to lend his soul over to actual conditions, is pursuing a life plan that consists mainly of exercises of memory remembering facts about his family in order to absolve them—to penetrate to the "pain level," his. He is the last holdout from real life, sitting in his shadowy rooms, quiescent, staring at his walls of books, at his floors covered by Oriental rugs—he calls his apartment the Holy Sepulchre. "I suspect I create the dark and antipathetic surroundings in order to force myself to revise or rearrange myself at the core."

The engloried soul is in limbo, if not lost; Shawmut, Wulpy, Brodsky are sick souls restoring in their imagination the symptoms and causes of their discomfiture. The world is a pismire beyond dredging. Strivers brood in the dark. Angels tainted by their former existence, having themselves once been human, are fallible and have no strength to prepare bodies for a higher evolution of spirit.

On May 25, 1985, I went to Sheridan Road to pay a condolence call on Bellow, as I had gone so many years ago to Riverside Drive when Bellow's father died. Now it was his brother Maurice.

Bellow was dressed in a beige silk and wool suit, a very dashing well-cut suit with a vest, so sharp, so rich. Before the door was closed, he was saying, "This is my brother's suit." He told me that when he had gone to see Maury, the dying man had insisted on giving him the suit. Maury had put on a lot of weight. He had bought the suit when he went on a diet and lost all that weight, and Bellow had said he did not need it. "Take it. Take it," his brother had told him, and Bellow did, for old times' sake. Maury was always giving Bellow a suit, and so, at the last, they reenacted this ritual between them.

"Yes," I said. "I know." I knew this from reading about the time Amos made a scene when Joseph refused to take some clothes his brother was thrusting on him, and Amos tucked a hundred-dollar bill into Joseph's breast pocket and said, "I wish I knew how it was going to turn out with you. You'll ruin yourself in the end." I knew from the time Simon took Augie March to the barbershop at the Palmer House to get a haircut and a manicure and took him home to dress him in a decent suit of clothes so that he could make a good appearance before the Magnus family. In Paris, Augie thought: "I love my brother very much. I never meet him again without the utmost love filling me up. He has it too, though we both seem to fight it." And Julius—Ulick—

whom Charlie Citrine loved—berates Charlie's appearance: "You were always a slob, Chuckie, and now you spend money on clothes and go to a tailor, but you're still a slob. Who sold you those goddamn shoes? And that horse-blanket overcoat? Hustlers used to sell shoes like that to the greenhorns fifty years ago with a buttonhook for a bonus. Now take this coat." And Julius throws a black vicuna coat with a Chesterfield collar into Citrine's arms.

Bellow told me his brother Maury always wanted some action going, something always had to be happening. Well, Maury did not have much action now. All the senior citizens of Bellow's family were succumbing, and what was he doing? Writing stories. Isolated. When had he ever not been isolated? He thought it would be Sam first, but no, Sam was still alive. It was Maury. Bellow had gone to Georgia to be with him and when he got back, a few days later, he was dead, not of the liver cancer but an aneurysm. Sam, too, had cancer. Their mother had died of cancer. No, he did not feel panicky, he said he was okay. Okay? Well, I would have liked to put my arms around him and say I was sorry, but I cannot do that with Bellow.

We sat talking for hours. Bellow did not even wish to go out on the terrace, let alone go down for a walk. He had no wish more than to sit in his chair and sip aquavit and talk—about his books, for a while, then about himself and his family. He always believed he did not fit, that he was going it alone from his earliest days. He wasn't bitter but nostalgic, sad, talking about his father's bakery, the business of delivering baked goods, the bakery part declining when the supermarkets came, the switch to delivery of wood, then charcoal, then coal, until coal became the business. When his father retired, Sam bought out Maury, and Maury went into building, first in Florida. When Maury was dying and knew he was dying, he told Bellow how all his life was good, was right, how fine a woman his second wife was, and his children, and his home, and all his fine furniture, and Bellow sat there listening, grieving. Maury had shifted to the antiques business and there were two warehouses filled with valuable furniture—he had traveled twice a year to Bristol, England, to buy furniture—and Bellow wondered what they were going to do with all that now. He bought three pieces from Maury while he was there. He showed me a revolving bookcase, a fine old bureau, and a small desk. He didn't need them, but he bought them and they were beautiful.

When Bellow said goodbye to his brother, he knew he would never see him again, but they did not say goodbye. Bellow told him that if Maury needed him, he would come, just to call and he would fly down. Well, one night his brother called him and said if he meant it, if he wanted to come, now was the time. He had better come now. Before Bellow left for the airport to take the plane, a telephone call came to say Maury was dead. So he never saw him alive again. But he had his suit.

I asked about Sam. Sam had sold the coal business and gone into building nursing homes. He built a string of nursing homes and ran them, and out of that, Sam was able to go into real estate. Big, very big in real estate, Sam was rich. Sam was the one who got into trouble with the law. We can read about it in "Cousins." Sam, Bellow said, became Orthodox, the pillar of the observing Jews in Humboldt Park. Sam still lived there, with the same wife; he was the same family man.

"That's Sam who comes to see Herzog?" I asked.

Sam, Bellow said, always tried. Sam always tried but he never knew what to say to his brother Saul. Bellow described the friends who gathered around Sam now, some of them trying to get him to leave a large sum of money to the synagogue, the yeshiva, an old people's home, to this, to that, and he greeted them all. He was too sick now to go to the shul. Sam was the one who had bought a place in Jerusalem. When Sam realized his illness was terminal, he had stopped eating. No one could make him eat until those old Jews had gone to him and said it was a sin to take his own life. He believed them and they had sent him home from the hospital to die.

Bellow stopped talking for a while, then brightened up. Maybe, he said, they were right. As they sat there together, his brother said, "As we began so are we ending. You were there at the beginning. You're here now. It's all on you afterwards." Bellow was taking care of his sister Jane. It was purgatory, he said, to witness the dwindling of his family.

Alexandra came in at five o'clock and looked at Bellow and smiled. "I see you are wearing the suit. It looks very good." He nodded, smoothing the fabric of the sleeve.

21

"Even Adam, who had God Himself to talk to, asked for a human companion"

Like mercury enclosed in a glass tube, Bellow has a quicksilver mind, but quicksilver only takes the measure of the febrile spirit; it cannot allay the fever.

I had a new sense of the nature of that fever on that dreary February afternoon in 1985 when I visited Bellow on Sheridan Road. He spoke to me at length of America as a project-oriented country. It was, he said, going to be the central idea of a new story he was writing and he picked up a few pages and put them down again. He told me it was just a start, a sketch of a Jewish botanist, Professor Chlorophyll and his nephew. He did not know whether it would be a short story or a novella—he likes the form—maybe it would turn into a book. He wanted to show a man with a project impulse. He had once described a relative of his whose project was to be an American.

"It was your brother-in-law, you called him, the one who changed his name to Lake Erie," I said.

"Arkady," Bellow said. Arkady wasn't exactly his brother-in-law, but yes, he did change his name. "Crazy! Lake Erie!" I commented. Bellow laughed, telling me to try the other lakes. It would not work. However, he went on, every American has an idea for a project, not an idea of truth; Something to do—like Rockefeller or Kissinger—an action; a performance. In his mind, he outlines a project that originates in his idea of an action to take. If he leaves out his own nature, however, it comes back to plague him. It was all in Proust.

Bellow got up to find a passage in Proust, which he proceeded to read to me. While he was thumbing through the volume called *Time Regained*, he said the pitiable ones in the world are those who have no project, like Leopold Bloom in *Ulysses*.

"Is it wrong not to have a project?" I asked.

He had, he said, always had a project; he had to engage himself in the pursuit of meaning, not of what is on the surface, not an action, but a search for the essence. As he was glancing through Proust, he was describing what I felt to be his paradox as a writer. His job was to observe, to see, to take note of every detail, but that very act of taking notice prevented him from making a sympathetic connection with the essence. To observe was the task of the writer, and to empathize was the act of the man. At last, he found the passage he wished to read. Proust was on a train on his way back to Paris and he has a thought.

He read the long passage aloud, looking up from time to time to be sure I was following. I was startled by the first sentence:

> The thought of my lack of talent for literature . . . this thought, less painful
> perhaps but more melancholy still if I referred it not to a private infirmity of
> my own but to the non-existence of the ideal in which I had believed, this
> thought . . . struck me afresh and with a force more painful than ever before.

I stopped listening to Proust. I remembered Corde thinking that he wasn't advanced enough to be the artist of this singular demanding sense of his; it was there, he couldn't get rid of it, it gained strength; as he grew older, he had to give ground. I missed the rest of the passage, but I knew where Bellow had been searching and I found the paragraphs a few days later and studied them alone, hearing Bellow's quiet sad voice reading Proust's pensive words.

> The train had stopped, I remember, in open country. The sun shone, flooding
> one half of each of their trunks with light, upon a line of trees which followed
> the course of the railway. "Trees," I thought, "you no longer have anything to

say to me. My heart has grown cold and no longer hears you. I am in the midst of nature. Well, it is with indifference, with boredom that my eyes register the line which separates the luminous from the shadowy side of your trunks. If ever I thought of myself as a poet, I know now that I am not one. Perhaps in the new, the so desiccated part of my life which is about to begin, human beings may yet inspire in me what nature can no longer say. But the years in which I might have been able to sing *her* praise will never return." But in thus consoling myself with the thought that the observation of humanity might possibly come to take the place of an unattainable inspiration, I knew that I was merely seeking to console myself, I knew that I knew myself to be worthless. If I really had the soul of an artist, surely I would be feeling pleasure at the sight of this curtain of trees lit by the setting sun, these little flowers on the bank which lifted themselves almost to the level of the steps of my compartment, flowers whose petals I was able to count but whose colour I would not, like many a worthy man of letters, attempt to describe, for can one hope to transmit to the reader a pleasure that one has not felt?[1]

Bellow had handed me the book, asking if I saw what he meant.

When I read *More Die of Heartbreak*, I saw what he meant to tell me that afternoon when talking about projects and Proust. Ken has a life plan, a general outline of a project that was to create his soul, to make his life a turning point, to alter historical forces. "Inner communion with the great human reality was my true occupation. . . . Unless you made your life a turning point there was no reason for existing." To this end, Kenneth attaches himself to his Uncle Benn. Uncle Benn was his project. The Citizen of Eternity, the man with imaginative powers that let him see things others don't see, the man with the uncommon gift of self-description, possibly rooted in habitual truthfulness, was the only man left with a sense of life derived from love.

With Benn, he could speak of the single community of the dead and the living, of demons and inner spirit, of angels charged with preparing us for a higher evolution of the spirit. With Benn, he could share his "Project Turning Point," his quest for a revelation, a massive reversal, an inspired universal change, a new direction, a desperately needed human turning point.

Alas, it was not to be. Benn has the crying needs and hungers of any man and human attachments have a priority. His blood was charged with longing, and since blood is the medium in which the self lives, blood it must be. "Even Adam, who had God Himself to talk to, asked for a human companion." Uncle Benn, not only an important man in his field, famous for his humorous remarks, his insights, his magics, is also the man who hears the cry of Della Bedell—"What am I supposed to do with my sexuality?"—and in pity copulates with her; the man who sees Caroline Bunge lying in the sun in Puerto Rico and finding his way to her bed is pleased when she switches on the lamp, looks him over, and says, "I'll buy that."

Benn is a sex-abused man who receives too much attention from women and cannot resist their bids. He is a carnal man agitated by his erotic lapses and to escape himself agrees to marry Matilda Layamon.

> In the years before his second marriage he had his hands full, dealing with ladies: flirtations, courtships, longings, obsessions, desertions, insults, lacerations, sexual bondage—the whole bit from bliss to breakdown."

To put an end to his torments, he begins the slide down to a new depth level of suffering. His ideal of classical love endued with beauty and the sublime is annihilated. Love in the real world is a parody of Eros, a matter of limbs, members, and organs.

> "All those mad men and mad women sharing beds. Two psychopaths under one quilt. Do you ever know who is lying beside you, the thoughts behind the screen of 'consideration'? A flick of the thermostat and the warmth of love explodes, a bomb of flame that cremates you. As you float away from your ashes into the etheric world, don't be surprised to hear sobs of grief from your destroyer."

Benn's lust for Matilda is matched by her lust for money, for power, for social position, for action in the big world. She demands that Benn stimulate her with dollars, not foreplay, demands he sue his Uncle Vilitzer for fraud and win back his fortune and lay that at her feet. Benn is trapped. The married man cannot sue family for inheritance, only for violating the covenant of heritage, and there is no litigation for that. Time would take care of it. Benn feels Matilda's cold aggressive shoulders, like bronze, and cannot touch her breasts, too wide apart, and knows he would like not to kiss her throat but strangle it.

> "Is there something I've done? Is there something I'm not doing?" "No, dear, no," she said. This "dear," the dear of contradiction, was laid down like a cement block.

The Citizen of Eternity has made the all but fatal mistake of pursuing human company and he must run as far as he can get outside the real world, to night and ice, to reindeer country on the frozen tundra near Novaya Zembya. "How long will you be gone?" Ken asks. "I can't predict the time. Was it my sister or was it you, who said that I was a phoenix who runs with arsonists? Well, let's see what can be done, when I can rise from these ashes."

And Ken? Recall Proust's words: "The thought of my lack of talent for literature . . . this thought, less painful perhaps but more melancholy still if I referred it not to a private infirmity of my own but to the non-existence of the ideal in which I had believed. . . ." Kenneth has discovered the nonexistence of his ideal: "What had happened to him affected me as well. I could feel the perturbation widening and widening as I lay there and became aware that I had come to depend on his spirit." That spirit has died of heartbreak. Eros vetoed Matilda; Benn ignored Eros and married her. Now he had fallen from grace. The mentor has failed the pupil. Ken's soul cannot create itself; Ken's life would not be a turning point; the colossal purpose would not be achieved.

It is a sad book.

> Mankind was long supported by an unheard music which buoyed it, gave it flow, continuity, coherence. But this humanistic music has ceased, and now there is a different barbarous music welling up, and a different elemental force has begun to manifest itself, without form as yet. Do we consent to go under or do we take advantage of our freedom to search for the original self?

The search is over for now. *More Die of Heartbreak* is a bitter book—at times cruel. It is tender only in its representation of the bond between nephew and uncle. There is compassion for the fate of the uncle and a wistful sympathy for the fate of the nephew. Ken reflects ruefully, "The greater your achievement, the less satisfactory your personal and domestic life will be."

One cold day in January 1986, Bellow came home from a trip he had taken alone to visit old friends. When he walked into his apartment, he saw tags of one color on all his possessions, and tags of another color on all that belonged to Alexandra. The little girl who jumped up and down clapping her hands ordered him to remove all that was tagged Bellow. He did. In the South Side apartment to which he retreated, he sat down to turn his sketch into the novel *More Die of Heartbreak*. Minna the astrophysicist was thrown in with the women who encased their hips in green ribbons; she transmutes into that part of Matilda Layamon, who has shoulders like Tony Perkins in *Psycho*, with breasts that are too far apart, whose "dear of contradiction was laid down like a cement block." The Holocaust survivor who stared at the penis of the Negro pickpocket is now the Russian-looking Jew staring at the satin crannies of Miss Osaka, Miss Tokyo, Miss Nara, Miss Yokohama, Miss Nagasaki, at "the center of desire, the chaste treasure fully opened . . . the thing of things, the small organ red as a satin pincushion."

Bellow's friendly assessment of women began and ended with *The Dean's December*. In the story "Him with His Foot in His Mouth," Shawmut's good wife is dead; Mrs. Pergamon's diamonds on her bosom "lay like the Finger Lakes among their hills"; his brother's wife, Tracy, is a breeder of pit bull dogs; Babette, a relentless talker, is a chatterer with a big underlip. Miss Rose "is a woman whose command of sexual forces made ugliness itself contribute to her erotic power." In "What Kind of Day Did You Have?" the mistress of Victor Wulpy is a flaky suburban housewife in the midst of a divorce; Katrina is a cat's-paw, reckless, restless, awkward, without common sense, without self-respect, seeking sexual excitement and entree into higher cultural circles. Her father thought of her as a "Dumb Dora from north-suburban Chicagoland," and she, too, considers herself a nitwit. Katrina offers her own view of herself: "voluptuous, luxurious beauty, confused sexpot, carnal idiot with piano legs, her looks (mouth half open or half shut) meaning everything or nothing. Just this grace-in-clumsiness was the aphrodisiac of one of the intellectual captains of the modern world." The intellectual captain is retraining Katrina.

In "Cousins," there is Riva who "had come down in the knees like the jack of a car, to a diamond posture. She made an effort to move with speed, as if she were dancing after the Riva she had once been." Riva's mother draws down the veil of her big hat "to keep off the mosquitos and perhaps also to conceal her looks from other players." Hurrying about the hotel on spike heels, Miltie's wife, Libby, is a " 'suicide blonde' (dyed by her own hand)." Eunice Karger is tenacious, determined, limited, primitive, formerly a stammerer, a "layer cake of heartsickness," nosy, "proud of the special vocabulary she had mastered," "vain of her degree in educational psychology," and her daughter Carlotta has the arctic figure of an Eskimo. Her look is febrile. Tanya is a movie fan, who never misses a performance of *Gone With the Wind:* "Oy, Clark Gebble, I love him so!" Isabel Greenspan, Brodsky's former wife, is a woman determined to make an impression of perfect balance; she reflects only unhappy instability.

The women in the course of Bellow's three stories grow worse and worse, preparing for the outbreak of war between Eros and Logos in *More Die of Heartbreak*.

Ken Trachtenberg visualizes the painting by the Douanier Rousseau, "the famous painting of a forest clearing," with a nude at the center "lying on a Recamier sofa with the tigers of desire glaring at her. This is an arcane vision, but more like the real thing. And that's exactly it. That's my subject."

So it is. Uncle Sammler's niece Angela is reactivated by Bellow to dominate the portrayal of women in the novel. Recall that Angela had told old Uncle Sammler, "A Jew brain, a black cock, a Nordic beauty . . . is what a woman wants." Sammler had understood this to be a woman's way, "Putting together the ideal man." In *More Die of Heartbreak,* a cousin, Fishl, tells Ken, "The best husband for most women is a composite. . . . a little Muhammed Ali for straight sex, some of Kissinger for savvy, Cary Grant for looks, Jack Nicholson for entertainment, plus André Malraux or some Jew for brains. Commonest fantasy there is." Ken reflects, "I really liked what Fishl had said about the composite dream husband." Later, Ken approves: "It was a common feminine fantasy to put together an ideal man . . . they assemble parts and elements from here and there—a large cock, a sparkling personality, millions of dollars, a bold spirit like Malraux, the masculine attraction of Clark Gable in *Gone With the Wind,* the manner of a French aristocrat, the brain of a superman in physics." More parts, same concept.

When Ken's quiet friend, Dita Schwartz, who had once been his pupil—"I myself had trained her in Russian literature"—wishes to make a love offering, she submits to a face peeling, hoping that Ken "will fall in love with the angelic face of the real Dita." He understands and accepts her sacrifice. He exclaims, "These torments and martyrdoms to which women submit their bodies, the violent attack they make on their own long-hated faults or imagined deformities! Gladly assaulting themselves. The desperate remedy." Dita is awed by Ken; he is the one with vision. "I think your eyes are placed higher and wider in the head than most people would consider normal." Ken likes that. He agrees with Dita, who says, "You'd be wasting your time with a woman who didn't enjoy hearing you talk—a woman who had no clue as to what you were saying, or what you're all about." Dita does not dismember men, she assaults herself. Ken counsels himself to marry Dita.

Why do women tear men, or themselves, apart to build for themselves a fantasy lover? They "secretly fear that they haven't got what it takes to hold the interest of a man who is powerfully energized by an important task." Women do not follow "a course of life that will enable them to develop their soul." Women "remain in outer darkness where their poor hearts are breaking." I wish these were ironical observations. No, these are Ken's thoughts, his assessment, this version of the young Bellow trying to understand what has happened to his Uncle Benn, the magical mentor, this version of the elder Bellow, fallen into erotic bondage. All the wickedness of the world, all the manifestations of hate, the Armageddon and Apocalypse of the present day, have spiraled down to the abandonment of a good man by a bad woman.

The wound to Herzog's self-esteem has opened once again. Treckie, the child woman, small, small, gives Ken his walking papers, preferring the snowmobile salesman to the widely read, soulful Ken. Matilda Layamon's violet eyes glitter at Benn Crader across the breakfast table in the penthouse. Her greed for money is at the same depth level as Denise on the warpath, suing Citrine for all his worth. True, her hint of her father's secret lust for her—"I've always been the channel for his unclean fantasies"—is Angela's hint to Sammler of her doctor father's interest in her, but there is more in Matilda than erotic allure and female odors emanating from the satin quilt. She is the social climber, once again the cold manipulator, the schemer with a plan to reform her new husband. Benn admits to Ken that Matilda "doesn't like to hear that things strike me as strange." Matilda is contemptuous of the poor-kid slant. Matilda doesn't care "for that far-away-and-long-ago stuff." Matilda does not like Uncle Benn to look back, to cling to the past. It is Madeleine's scoff: "I know your darling mother wore flour sacks." It is Denise's snarl to Citrine: "Ah, here comes the cemetery bit! . . . Why are you hung up on the past and always lamenting some dead party or other?"

Although Bellow believed *More Die of Heartbreak* to be a departure from all his other works, we recognize it as a remodeling, perhaps a correction. Typically, the action is over—the events have taken place last year, last December, last spring. We know Kenneth will live alone in rooms on Chicago's South Side, that Benn will leave his apartment farther north and move on to a penthouse where he will wander about lost, displaced, comforted only by an azalea, reporting to his nephew all that had happened to him this year, last year, and all the way back to his childhood in the old neighborhood. We expect that Ken will tell his uncle all his experiences this year, last year, and all the way back to his youth at the dinner table in his father's house. We are not surprised that these two "valuable oddities" will be the only ones still searching for the right way to live, for the fate good enough, and that they will talk to each other in the dark, in the middle of the night—remembering; both devoted to self-examination, both needing to find order and coherence, neither succeeding; without friends, alone, alone, alone like a stone, as the lament goes. We anticipate that Benn will be characterized as brilliant, observant, a man who has the power of seeing, the power of light, a great reader, but who does not understand women. Of course Benn will go to the cemetery and cry at the graveside of his parents: "Uncle was a man of feeling, especially family feeling." To be sure, plants will convey a message from the dead.

We expect someone somewhere to ask Kenneth why he wants to live in the Midwest: "Such a cultural throwback, unconscious of its philistinism." We know that Kenneth will read books and reject them. Bellow himself had said to me that he had gone through a plethora of books that explain life, and each of them leaves life poorer than it was before. They did not speak the truth. His examination of contemporary life had turned up so many preposterous conditions in the pursuit of life that it had thrust *him* into a preposterous condition. So for a nickel Benn will get from the junkman the book that changed his life. That did not, in the long run, change his life.

We are not surprised to hear that true knowledge comes from experience or from intuitions of the soul, although we are saddened that now souls are contaminated by their link to the body rather than strengthened by their bond to the cosmos, to God. When Ken asks Benn how he pictures death— the same question that awakened Asa Leventhal in the middle of the night— Benn answers not with an explanation from Steiner but with Albert Corde's metaphor of film: "Well, from the very beginning there have been pictures— inside and outside . . . and for me the worst that can happen is that those pictures will stop."

Universities will be in the consciousness-raising business; the art world will be phony: millionaire painters play softball with multimillionaire collectors, and Professor Komatsu reads his delicate verses about his old nanny of seventy-five years ago; music is an art garment that is incomplete: "Obligations to one's fellows perhaps prevent full buttoning by artists."

Again, all humankind is declining. Again Russia and America are compared; now America is worse: In the East, humankind underwent the ordeal of privation; many of the higher human functions were eliminated; in the United States, you have instead a population confined to the lowest level of human interests, and their ordeal is the ordeal of desire.

All the rest of the characters in the book are familiar and predictable. Ken's mother, Hilda, will have gone to Somalia not to help the poor but to escape her womanizing husband; Matilda's mother, Mrs. Layamon, will be happiest with her opal earrings; Treckie's mother, Tanya Sterling, will try to seduce her daughter's lover, Ken; and Caroline Bunge will pursue Benn. Fishl Vilitzer, hastening to his father's deathbed, longing to be cherished at the last by the dying old man, will fail to reach him in time. Judge Chetnik will be "fixed," part of a deal made by lawyers who are corrupt.

An effort is made to update the allusions—Carl Sagan, Qaddafi, Imelda Marcos, Charles Manson, Von Bülow, Pavarotti, Mother Teresa, Margaret Thatcher, Marguerite Duras, Ken Kesey, Schwarzenegger, Pritikin diets—but the tried and true appear—Balzac and Blake and Hegel and D. H. Lawrence, Stendhal, Shakespeare and Kierkegaard, Swedenborg, Freud, Nietzsche—Matthew Arnold is new—and although we have Tony Perkins in *Psycho*, we also have Akim Tamiroff and the "Ed Sullivan Show" and Charlie Chaplin.

The old slang brightens the dialogue: "dumbsock," "not such a big deal," "ditched me," "whatchamacallit," "what's the use of talking," "gave them the business," "old snatch," "schmutzig," "as if I had lost my marbles," "you should have got out and kicked him right in the knackers." The direct address to the reader is updated: "I'm not going to dump ideas on you"; "Now I have to tell you up front."

There are more than the usual parenthetical remarks; indeed, so many dashes and dashes within dashes, it now seems to be a writer's tic, although it may also be intended as a modernizing of the old prose style.

There is renovation of the sicknesses described: Kitty Daimler had the flu, Mimi Villars an abortion, and Henderson's bridgework broke off on a hard bite down; then came Elya Gruner and his aneurysm, Ulick and his open-heart surgery, Valeria and her stroke; then came tumors and cancers— breast, liver, stomach—and a surgically fused knee. Now there is Alzheimer's disease and AIDS, endoscopy of the prostate gland, pruritus ani, with CAT scans and beta blockers, Dalmane and quinidine glutonate, chloral hydrate and pacemakers, and little packets of vitamins from Valhalla.

Perhaps *More Die of Heartbreak* was written in haste or in anger or just to keep going, for there are lapses, repetitions, and dialogue that often seems out of character. It is difficult to credit a man like Uncle Vilitzer, nicknamed by his family "The Big Heat," with going to the university campus to lecture to students on municipal government. Spoof? Maybe. Vilitzer is also the man who sold property to Ecliptic Circle Electronics, which then built the newest Chicago skyscraper, in fact the Illinois State Government Building in the Loop, looked upon by all Chicagoans as a horror and a folly. We can read about the iniquitous Big Heat and the decline of American architecture at the same time; the decline of the Chicago Courts of Justice, too, for Vilitzer is on the parole board so that the televised public hearings of the well-known case of a rape victim who changed her testimony, identifying the rapist, can be used. Danae Cusper's underpants can be exposed to the view of millions and thus the concupiscent media can be reconsidered and recondemned.

The good old one-liners do appear from time to time: Benn is "dredged in floury relationships by ladies who could fry him like a fish if they had a mind to"; "the fallopian tubes like the twin serpents of the caduceus"; "a head as round as that was born to roll"; "His face was very large, with so many tucks and folds under his chin that if he had been a violinist, it would have been hard for him to decide where to put the fiddle"; and so on. However, the pretentious Matilda Layamon, thinking of how she will restore the Roanoke apartment to its former glory, looking around and conceding it's "schmutzig" is not funny, nor is Dr. Layamon laughing at his patients in their beds, calling them "old snatch" or telling his son-in-law, "Listen, son, women have to have suitable activities. If they aren't *engagées* . . . they can get into bad, and I mean really very bad, scheming and double-dealing their menfolk. It's better to let them have these ego satisfactions." Caroline Bunge, stuffing her vagina with bits of Kleenex as a deterrent to sperm, is not so funny. However, that "The balsam fir was the little sister of the bridegroom" *is* funny and profoundly sad at the same time. Why? Because the image of the lonely man at his wedding is also a reminder to those who read Bellow to reflect on the distance between Charlie Citrine's exultation reading Steiner and meditating on a lamp post in lieu of a rose, and Benn Crader's little sister, the balsam fir.

Bellow has told his story again, reinterpreting his old betrayals and treacheries and disappointments, reassigning the blame. Now Kenneth Trachtenberg is betrayed by his Uncle Benn, and if we understand this story to represent a confrontation between the young aspiring Bellow and the older achieved Bellow, between what he conceived himself to be in his thirties and what he knew himself to have become in his, say, sixties, then we see there are nonhistorical, nonphilosophical, nonsocietal, noncultural reasons for betrayal. The young man is telling us where he wished to walk and the older man is telling us why he had to follow where his Gucci shoes led him. Kenneth is engaged in a project to transcend the real world, a project to forge a fate good enough, defying convention and tradition, defying death itself by the power of imagination and the magic of light and the bonding of love; Uncle Benn, inevitably, has fallen prey to his own erotic needs, married to protect himself, married in a fit of absentmindedness, married by mistake, a failure of illumination, a lapse of reason, a submission to the senses, a weakness of heart. *More Die of Heartbreak* represents the failure of the internal man, of the self inside the self.

A poem by Emily Dickinson, written a hundred years earlier, describes the same compulsion, the same need to confront the self:

One need not be a Chamber—to be Haunted—
One need not be a House—
The Brain has Corridors—surpassing
Material Place—

Far safer, of a Midnight Meeting
External Ghost
Than its interior Confronting—
That Cooler Host.

Far safer, through an Abbey gallop,
The Stones a'chase—

Than Unarmed, one's a'self encounter—
In lonesome Place—

Ourself behind ourself, concealed—
Should startle most—
Assassin hid in our Apartment
Be Horror's least.

The Body—borrows a Revolver—
He bolts the Door—
O'erlooking a superior spectre—
Or More—[2]

I think of Bellow when I read this poem. In novel and story and play, he, like Dickinson, chases himself down the corridors of his brain. To the external world, he presents himself as a loyal and good man, charming, could the world but see it, on the right side of truth and justice, faithful, hopeful. However, he, in the guise of his narrator, hero if you like, discovers that to be well-meaning is no protection against treason and betrayal. Augie March, Tommy Wilhelm, Eugene Henderson and Herzog, Citrine and Albert Corde are thwarted and manipulated by the predators who live in the outside world. Worse threatens in the interior world. Ken is betrayed by Benn. In the house of the mind, there has always lurked the more dangerous assassin, the hidden self—the hiding Joseph who requires a special fate, the contentious Asa Leventhal, the contemptuous Sammler, the pretentious and erotic Charlie Citrine, the self-serving Dean Corde—the man of vanity; and each is shadowed by a cooler host who scoffs at the public image the self has generated. A man may aim his revolver at the ghosts of deceivers and frauds but he has no weapon with which to attack his own specter, now become the carnal Uncle Benn and the elite Nephew Ken.

Like Dickinson, Bellow has always known that were he to escape the self, were he to bring his appearance and his essence into harmony by the power of his will, he would still live in danger, for no ego, however firm, can bolt his door against the ubiquitous predator, the inevitable assassin—Death. Neither Dickinson nor Bellow ever overlooked that chilling "More." Until in *More Die of Heartbreak,* Bellow turned away from the specter and faced the final barrier to fulfillment and transcendence—his own self. His cherished freedom to choose is the ultimate assassin because he chooses incorrectly. His adversary is not mortality but sexuality.

Dickinson remained inside her father's house for eighteen years, writing her poems of fanciful confrontations and retreats. Bellow collects experiences like bus fares, traveling by day and by night. The events he reflects upon are real; the people who inhabit his world exist, in part or in whole; his memories, literal or transformed, are authentic. The self behind the self, the subterranean Bellow who lives an isolated life, viewing himself as cut off, bereft, battered, betrayed, defeated, is real, too. He is determined, nevertheless, to talk himself into going another round, pursuing once more his heart's ultimate need, connection—to the cosmos, with God, in the world with a beloved person. Until *More Die of Heartbreak.*

Like Henry Thoreau, who saw the face of Apollo on the face of a woodcutter, Bellow believes the face of the god glows on every man. His hero, be he Augie or Tommy, Herzog or Citrine or Corde, Benn or Ken, gazes into the faces of hoodlums and hypocrites, cheats and pretenders, small-time gangsters, corrupt lawyers, debased judges, dandified journalists, drunk poets, lascivious women, greedy, hard-bitten manipulators old and young. Citrine weeps. He peers into the mirror and his eyes fill with tears at the image of his wrinkles of misery, the sag of his disintegration. What Apollo? Has he, too, bungled it? Was he a bit player? A cheat? A hypocrite? It may be. Yet he, like any man, everyman, has a good face, a good heart. He still feels the old tearing eagerness; and although the women may change, and he knows they will, isn't he still active on his Posturepedic mattress? True, he is a touchy, wisecracking, goofy old chaser with a misunderstood heart, and true, he is still sitting alone in a rented bedroom talking to a patient "Spirit of Alternatives," but he is also still seeking the right way to live, still absorbed in explaining the intellectual comedy of the modern mind, still confident there is a chance to rise straight to the truth despite his fears of the threat of the grave.

> I had waited many thousands of years for God to send my soul to this earth. Here I was supposed to capture a true and clear word before I returned, as my human day ended. I was afraid to go back empty-handed.

The quest for the true and clear word has been the quest since the time of Joseph. The quest for the true and clear word fails with Kenneth Trachtenberg. Uncle Benn goes off and leaves Ken with empty hands.

As in all of Bellow's stories, the hero is a man in distress, living alone, enclosed, inactive as the world judges, and, taking Ken and Benn together, he, too, is passing his soul through his crucible of memory until the glacier of ice at the heart's center reaches the melting point and, like Lazarus, the true self can come forth and the story can end. In *More Die of Heartbreak,* however, the spirit's quest, still moving fitfully, irrationally, in a turbulence of recollections, insights and explanations, reenactments and reinterpretations of old experiences, still moving back, backward and further back, across the years and generations, reaching beyond the known life to counterparts in history, in the natural world, now does not reach out to the supernatural world, to the world beyond life and death, but—as already predicted in *The Dean's December*—to society and politics, to the observed life, to family and friends and associates, to the shared life. Now the soul reaches inward, to childhood and youth, to marriages and divorces, to conflicts of desire, to experiences of the heart. The lamentations are the cries of the man caught in his web of self-scrutiny. Now the soul does not tear the web.

What Bellow believed could happen, ought to happen, to a man is represented by Kenneth Trachtenberg. What did happen, does happen, is represented by Benn Crader. Each discovers a self more lonely and more isolated, not because of what the world thinks, praise or blame, but because of what he knows to be the truth about the precious self: the self is inchoate, disordered in spirit; the heart is consumed with hatred; the spirit itself is an aggressor in good tweeds.

Ken–Benn, fondly thinking of himself as a prototype of everyman, discovers he cherishes his individuality more and will not give up his freedom to join. Ken–Benn, on the higher level of Being, exhorting himself to look forward in optimism and hope and to look back with love and compassion, finds he can only look forward and back in bitterness and despair. There is neither love nor compassion on either side. The dream of the life of reason, of spiritual fulfillment, of the immortality of the soul is a dream fading, weakening, thinning out to threads of a spider's web. Uncle Benn, who seeks comfort in the azalea, discovers he has been in communion with a fake plant, plastic, in sham dirt. Nephew Ken, who seeks a model for Becoming, observes a war between Eros and Logos, and in that real war, Reason and Passion are both defeated. Thanatos is the victor.

A newspaperman calls Uncle Benn for a statement on the dangers of an increasing level of radiation: "It's terribly serious of course but I think more people die of heartbreak than of radiation."

Bellow has always been the participant and the observer, the man who lived the story and the artist who writes about the man who believes that distress understood will be distress alleviated, that once the action of the mind has released the straining soul, the man will emerge to resume his outward transactions.

Remember the dangling man who explained why he dangled, then came out of his furnished room to enlist in the war. Remember the victim of himself, of delusions, of hypocrisies, of contempt, leaving the empty corridor and going back to join his wife and see the show. Recall the larky ingénu who explored the process by which he taught himself, freestyle, to make his record in his own way, and stood finally shuddering on the desolate shores of Dunkerque, then climbed back into his Citroën and drove to Bruges. Recall the abandoned son who tried to conceal his troubles and by the time he came to the end of what Benn Crader will call his "pain schedule," had no more secrets and stood weeping among mourners, united to strangers by the bonding of tears, joined with all the nameless dead and the nameless living. He left the chapel and stepped onto Broadway. The rain king asked, "What made me take this trip to Africa?" Then he explained:

> When I think of my condition at the age of fifty-five when I bought the ticket, all is grief. The facts begin to crowd me and soon I get a pressure in the chest. A disorderly rush begins—my parents, my wives, my girls, my children, my farm, my animals, my habits, my money, my music lessons, my drunkenness, my prejudices, my brutality, my teeth, my face, my soul! I have to cry, "No, no, get back, curse you, let me alone!" But how can they let me alone? They belong to me. They are mine. And they pile into me from all sides. It turns into chaos.

By the time Henderson said goodbye to Romilayu and led his lion cub onto the plane, we have learned all his facts and know why he appointed his soul to lead him out of chaos. He had searched on two continents for how he might signify and had paused before he returned to his world to run around and around in the arctic silence of the Newfoundland airstrip, as if he could outrace his fate by the sheer force of his newfound energy. He boarded the plane that would fly him back to Idlewild.

"If I am out of my mind, it's alright with me," the abandoned husband admitted. "Some people thought he was cracked and for a time he himself had doubted that he was all there." Under a spell, he was writing letters to everyone under the sun. Herzog did not mail the letters; into the valise, he threw his recollections of everything that happened to him in his private world and all his thoughts and feelings about everything that had taken place in the public world, and by the end of his inquiry into himself, he was "confident, cheerful, clairvoyant, and strong." He bought lemons and swordfish steaks, chilled two bottles of wine in the brook, and picked wild flowers. Ramona was coming to dinner.

The old survivor, blind in one eye, searched for a way to explain himself to himself:

> Shortly after dawn, or what would have been dawn in a normal sky, Mr. Artur Sammler with his bushy eye took in the books and papers of his West Side

bedroom and suspected strongly that they were the wrong books, the wrong papers. In a way it did not matter much to a man of seventy-plus, and at leisure. You had to be a crank to insist on being right. Being right was largely a matter of explanations. Intellectual man had become an explaining creature. Fathers to children, wives to husbands, lecturers to listeners, experts to laymen, colleagues to colleagues, doctors to patients, man to his own soul, explained. The roots of this, the causes of the other, the source of events, the history, the structure, the reasons why. For the most part, in one ear out the other. The soul wanted what it wanted. It had its own natural knowledge. It sat unhappily on superstructures of explanation, poor bird, not knowing which way to fly.

By the time the cranky old Artur Sammler finished explaining, he was content that he had assessed rightly the state of contemporary civilization—in America, in Europe and the Middle East—and he had distinguished fairly between the spurious and the true, that he was indisputably right when it came to identifying good fathers and children, good husbands and students and teachers, good wives and mothers, good doctors and patients, and good whites and blacks; good souls, too. Finally, Sammler, ending his prayer over the corpse of his dead nephew, gathered together his flagging energy and took up again the terms of his contract with God.

The poet who survived remembered the poet who died:

I was a student at the University of Wisconsin and thought about nothing but literature day and night. Humboldt revealed to me new ways of doing things. I was ecstatic. I envied him his luck, his talent, and his fame, and I went east in May to have a look at him—perhaps to get next to him.

Humboldt remembered Charlie Citrine:

"Take the case of Charlie Citrine. He arrived from Madison, Wisconsin, and knocked on my door. Now he's got a million bucks. What kind of writer or intellectual makes that kind of dough. . . . who the hell is Citrine to become so rich. . . . there's something perverse with that guy. After making this dough why does he bury himself in the sticks? What's he in Chicago for? He's afraid to be found out."

Charlie Citrine examined all the facts of his case, judged the kind of writer and intellectual he was, confessed what precisely was perverse about himself, and by the time he finally interred Von Humboldt Fleisher, he had unburied himself. There was weight on the coffin lid; there was weight on the grave; but there were crocuses pushing their young green shoots through the soil. Citrine plans to go on to complete what the poet has left undone.

The Dean passed himself through his climacteric alone in an unheated bedroom in Bucharest, reflecting on a much worse Chicago than Augie March had known, observing a worse Europe than Artur Sammler had known. Frozen cold at the grotesque interment of a familiar dead, frozen cold under the dome of the Mount Palomar observatory, the fire to rally himself to have another go must ignite itself from within, from his spirit. He cannot hang suspended between the teeming earth and the glittering night sky. Corde was drawn down, drawn back, drawn to feel, drawn to penetrate further, to have a second try, to complete what he has left undone.

Now, Uncle Benn Crader is an old man in crisis, betrayed, swindled, thwarted in love; now, Nephew Ken is a young man in crisis, betrayed, made a fool of, thwarted in love. Still, both have a weakness for setting things straight, for doing the right thing. Neither knows how. "Professor Chlorophyll" plunges out, away, in fact into the cold, and Ken, who had hoped to "bring to the human world what Uncle brought to plant life," has nothing to complete. Both have all but died of heartbreak.

22

"At times I feel like a socket that remembers its tooth"

Bellow's narrators have carried on a forty-year quarrel with Freud, always satirizing, denouncing, caricaturing his—or anyone else's—psychological insights. Sammler thought:

> What was it to be arrested in the stage of toilet training! What was it to be entrapped by a psychiatric standard (Sammler blamed the Germans and their psychoanalysis for this)? Who had raised the diaper flag? Who had made shit a sacrament? What literary and psychological movement was that?

Corde cannot comfort Minna with spurious psychology. "I'm not the wise psychologist type. Psychology is out of my line. I even dislike it." Ijah Brodsky said, "These psychological terms lying around tempting us to use them are a menace. They should all be shovelled into trucks and taken to the dump." Kenneth Trachtenberg is still denouncing psychoanalytic explanations of behavior:

I trust psychology less and less. I see it as one of the lower by-products of the restlessness or oscillation of modern consciousness, a terrible agitation which we prize as "insight."

I doubt that it can interest Him much to watch the shits at their play. I don't refer now to the Iago type but to people of ordinary stunted imaginative powers. The work of psychology is to explain and excuse these shits.

The not-so-silent vendetta goes on in *A Theft*. Clara Velde visits her psychiatrist, Dr. Gladstone, to talk about her trouble, "mostly to relieve my heart." The narrator comments, "You didn't expect replies from these doctors. You paid them to lend you their ears." Ithiel Regler acknowledges he went through a shrink period himself: "But my doctor had even more frailties than me . . . it occurred to me one day that he couldn't tell me how to be Teddy Regler. And nothing would go well unless I *was* Teddy Regler. Not that I make cosmic claims for precious Teddy, but there never was anybody else for me to be"—these are almost the exact words that restored Herzog to himself twenty-five years earlier—"I have to be that man. There is no one else to do it." Ithiel believes the more we analyze the more injury we do; psychiatry encourages one to build on abuses and keeps one infantile; after the age of forty, a moratorium has to be declared. "You can't afford to be a damaged child forever." Ithiel dismisses psychiatry with a neat one-liner: "If a millipede came into the office, he'd leave with an infinitesimal crutch for each leg."

To put Freud aside as Bellow insists we do does not require that we refuse to recognize a pattern in Bellow's fiction. The formulaic representation of the conflict and its resolution, the recurrence of archetypal personalities, the refashioning of the same old experiences, the reappearance of the narrator who stalks himself and captures himself and lets himself go, in a word, the manner of fashioning his novels and novellas, short stories and plays suggests the art object is itself a metaphor of Bellow's vision of reality.

Had Jung access to Bellow's fiction, he would have been happily affirmed in his theory of the presence of the animus-anima, the male and female coexisting in each individual, and *A Theft* would have served as a fine demonstration of Jung's insight. Clara Velde and Ithiel Regler are so intricately interwoven, loyal and faithful, caring and committed, to each other across decades, their relationship may be interpreted as the anima-animus of Bellow himself.

Teddy Regler has appeared in Bellow's fiction from *Dangling Man* on. Teddy is always thinking significant thoughts (so Clara tells us); he is vain about his looks, irks easily, knows his faults. Like Herzog and Dean

Corde and Uncle Benn, he is a singular person with a singular eye; this
time a wunderkind in nuclear strategy. Teddy has a genius for observing
politics; world figures find Ithiel worth their while; people of great power
put a high value "on his smarts." Like Dean Corde, Teddy "is an expert
witness"—recall what a man Corde was for seeing. Of course it is Ithiel
Regler, the male counterpart of the female, who will one day take hold and
do the wrap-up of wrap-ups, be the Gibbon or Tacitus of the American
Empire, write the book of books. And like Humboldt, Teddy declares, "I
loved my late father. I still love him," and he more than half-expects to see
him in the land of the dead. If it happens, it will be because "we loved each
other and wished for it."

"Tell me. Tell," Clara has begged Teddy for years—not protesta-
tions of love but truths—and like Dita Schwartz in *More Die of Heartbreak,*
like Wulpy's mistress in "What Kind of Day Did You Have?" Clara listens.
Teddy does tell: that the mortal sin is not sex but hatred; that love cannot
be separated from Being; that in the United States the status of the individual
is weakening and probably in an irreversible decline.

So many of Bellow's attitudes are restated as Clara's characteristic
thoughts, it is often difficult to separate her from Bellow's heroes. She has
parents by whom she felt stifled in childhood, and for whom she now feels
a boundless love; like Joseph, she has a wild streak, "a spoonful of something
wild in my mixture"; like Augie, she has her mentor, Ithiel solely and wholly;
like Tommy Wilhelm, Clara dissolves in tears at the end of the story.

> When Clara came out of the revolving door, and as soon as she had the
> pavement under her feet, she started to cry passionately. She hurried, crying
> down Madison Avenue, not like a person who belonged there but like one of
> the homeless, doing grotesque things in public. . . . The main source of tears
> came open. She found a handkerchief and held it to her face in her ringed hand,
> striding in an awkward hurry. She might have been treading water in New York
> harbor—it felt that way, more a sea than a pavement.

Clara does not have Tommy's sense of union with the crowds of people in
the subway passage, no sense of the love rising in his soul; Clara is acerbic
watching the crowds that interrupt her taxi's flow.

> Why are all these people here, idle shoppers or old people with no urgent
> purpose except to break out of confinement or go and scold someone.

Love is not transcendent love but love for Ithiel Regler.

When Clara says to Teddy that if they had become husband and wife, she would not have been so overcharged and confused, she reminds us of the wistful conjecture of Citrine as he gazes at the comfortable dowdy figure of Naomi Lutz. When Clara reflects on Gina, her au pair, it is in the masculine way of an Artur Sammler, an Uncle Benn in Japan: Gina has "the Arabian Night's treasure that nubile girls (innocent up to a point) were sitting on." Like all of Bellow's heroes, Clara has "a death-beat pulse and it tempts me to make out with death. It says, why wait! I'm open to seduction by death."

Familiar as all this may be, still *A Theft* is an odd piece of writing for such a craftsman as we know Bellow to be. He allowed the following to stand unrevised:

> In a sophisticated boardroom Clara could be plain as cornmeal mush, and in such a mood, when she opened her mouth, you couldn't guess whether she would speak or blow bubble gum. Yet anybody who had it in mind to get around her was letting himself in for a lot of bad news.

Bellow uses commonplace phrases such as "this Austrian chick," "blew into town," "overdressed sexpots," "Ithiel was doing very badly now," "she couldn't flap him," "hump another woman," "ball such an awful tramp," "let me check the woman out," "we're going to be bamboozled again," "he'd be totally at sea if I weren't—oops!" "Oops" in a Bellow story—oh well.

Putting this aside as perhaps Bellow's desire to "be with it," to be a swinger in dialogue as well as in fact—Ithiel has his "ground-dragging titzers"; he is a gambler with women—the strange thing about *A Theft* is the narrowness of its concerns, the attenuated conception of what constitutes tormentous problems. Recall the thralldom of a Thea, a Ramona, a Renata, the to-do over the split-up between Herzog and Madeleine, the fuss between Angela and Wharton Horricker, with Sammler counseling, the bondage of Ken and Treckie, the entrapment of Uncle Benn on the silken sheets of Matilda Layamon; Ithiel's wife Francine has left him and all he will say is that "the third Mrs. Regler had hired a moving van and emptied the house one morning as soon as Teddy left for the office." For what reason? "He didn't let her feel that she was sharing his life." And then, "Possibly, too, there was another man in the picture," that "it would have been awkward, after an afternoon with this man, to come home to a husband absorbed in dark thoughts or needing consolation." Nothing more.

Clara has lost a ring taken from her by the Haitian boyfriend of Gina; the ring is restored to her, and Clara goes back to her Park Avenue apartment weeping as she walks. How does such a plot conclude? Gina knows "who she is"; Lucy, a child of ten, has been trusted to replace the ring on her mother's night table, has been given something significant to do, and is equal to it; and Clara, at the last, knows who *she* is—"I do seem to know what it is that's at the middle of me." She is the woman connected to Ithiel Regler.

Bellow names what is at the center of Ithiel Regler in the story that followed *A Theft.*

In a telephone conversation, I think in October of 1988, I casually asked Bellow what he was doing these days. He was writing. "Oh Lord, Saul, I can't keep up with you." Well, he did not know how to do anything else, did he? All he could do was write.

The Bellarosa Connection was published in 1989 and here I had a novella that provided me with a fitting conclusion to my study of the canon of Saul Bellow. It is Bellow's own reprise of his career as a writer. Exquisitely crafted, with familiar characters reflecting on well-known issues, returning to events and situations and relationships borrowed from earlier fiction, the novella jolts us with an insight into the turbulence of spirit of this man who ought not to do anything else but write.

Recall that Dean Corde at the end of *The Dean's December* determines to have a second go; it was not that he had hit too hard in his articles, but that he had hedged, held back, had not recounted the whole of the spoilage of the human spirit, the fullness of the rot and corruption. In *The Bellarosa Connection,* Bellow, in the guise of the Director of the Mnemosyne Institute, the man of memory, has a profoundly moving afterword to communicate to his readers. The narrator has a dream in which he is striving to climb out of a deep hole, not the mass grave into which Sammler fell, but a pit, a trap prepared for him by somebody who knew him well enough to anticipate that he would fall in: "My struggles were watched by the person who planned this for me." Bellow is watching Bellow. What the narrator says of himself will shake the hearts of all who read and admire Bellow, the Ancient Mariner of fiction who takes us once again by the sleeve and tells us, the anxious Clara Veldes of the world:

> Despair was not principally what I felt, nor fear of death. What made the dream terrible was my complete conviction of error, my miscalculation of strength, and the recognition that my forces were drained to the bottom. The whole structure was knocked flat. There wasn't a muscle in me that I hadn't called on, and for the first time I was aware of them all, down to the tiniest, and the best they could do was not enough. I couldn't call on myself, couldn't meet the demand, couldn't put out.

Whence the sorrow? Because of the four wives; the betrayal of friends; the dissociation from family; the deaths of loved ones? Because of the dreadful solitude of the act of writing, and always to be misunderstood, vilified for conservatism, accused of this and of that and of this again? No.

> I was being shown—and I was aware of this in sleep—that I had made a mistake, a lifelong mistake: something wrong, false, now fully manifest.
>
> Revelations in old age can shatter everything you've put in place from the beginning—all the wiliness of a lifetime of expertise and labor, interpreting and reinterpreting. . . .
>
> Your imagination of strength is connected to your apprehensions of brutality, where that brutality is fully manifested or absolute. Mine is a New World version of reality—granting me the presumption that there is anything real about it. . . . It wasn't the dream alone that was so frightful . . . it was the accompanying revelation that was so hard to take. It wasn't death that had scared me, it was disclosure. I wasn't what I thought I was. I really didn't understand merciless brutality.*

When Bellow created Artur Sammler, published in 1970, it was, as he said then, an act of the imagination, a fanciful projection, to see how all his world, and his experiences in his world, would look to a man in his seventies. Almost twenty years later, Bellow has become that man in his seventies and the narrator of this story looks back to see how all that has happened to him, all that he has seen and done, looks to him at the present time.

The characters that collect and hold the memory of this resurrected Sammler are not an Angela with her female generative slime, not a Margo, the sex engine aimed in the right direction, not a crazy Shula, a black pickpocket, the hustlers and losers; there is no manuscript of Govinda Lal with its talk of life on the moon, no sex-obsessed H. G. Wells deserving a memoir, but Eisen, the Israeli with his bag of medals, transformed, and the Jew from the Zamosht forest restored. Now it is the narrator who awaits his death with a soul that flutters—"poor bird not knowing which way to fly"—and it is the narrator who is the timorous bird, caught on the palings of an iron fence, with no strength left to fly.

Unnamed, the narrator characterizes himself as a man of memory:

> I would like to *forget* about remembering. . . . In your twilight years, having hung up your gloves (or sheathed your knife), you don't want to keep doing what you

*Asa Leventhal, decades ago, awakened frightened in the middle of the night, agonized at how little he knew of evil in the real world.

did throughout your life: a change, a change—your kingdom for a change! A lawyer will walk away from his clients, a doctor from his patients, a general will paint china, a diplomatist turn to fly fishing. My case is different in that I owe my worldly success to the innate gift of memory—a tricky word, "innate," referring to the hidden sources of everything that really matters. As I used to say to clients, "Memory is life." . . . but it puts me now in an uncomfortable position because if you have worked in memory, which is life itself, there is no retirement except in death.

As in "Cousins," the narrator is a Jewish-American, this time, from New Jersey, rich, successful, and alone, wifeless, sitting in his fine house, furnished in almost Oriental splendor, with vast rooms, high ceilings, precious old furniture. He is engaged in self-revision, preoccupied with wistful feelings and longings for the past, cautioning himself not to be carried away from the true facts—"whenever I was tempted to fake it, I asked myself, 'and how are things out in New Jersey?' " Deliberately, as once did Mosby and Shawmut, Braun and Charlie Citrine, he brings to mind those who have departed this life: the dead Harry Fonstein and his dead wife, Sorella, his dead father, and dead Billy Rose.

I don't know why Bellow hit upon Broadway Billy Rose for his "legendary personality" to reconstruct, but then I did not know why the caricature of Woody Allen should have been called in to bug Victor Wulpy in "What Kind of a Day Did You Have?" or, for that matter, why Allen Ginsberg was chosen to take part in Shawmut's self-justifying letter to Miss Rose in "Him with His Foot in His Mouth." However, so it is; Billy Rose it is.

The action of the story consists of Harry Fonstein's lifelong effort to find and thank Billy Rose for saving his life. Fonstein had made it halfway through the war but was caught in fascist Rome and imprisoned, waiting his turn to be "trucked to caves outside the city and shot." Billy Rose, Bellarosa, had masterminded the underground operation in Italy to save what Jews he could from annihilation, transporting them out and over to America. Billy Rose will not be met, however, refuses all contact with and responsibility for the Jews he diverted from Treblinka. Rose Productions sends an emissary to tell Harry Fonstein he is on his own; she is Mrs. Hamet, an overripe *drama-tiesten*, once an actress in the defunct Yiddish theater. She gives her journal, a record of the secret life of Billy Rose, a documentation of his bribery, arson, sabotage, sexual impotence, of his "chicken-scratch career," to Harry's wife, Sorella, who confronts Billy Rose with the threat: Meet my husband and let him spend fifteen minutes with you, shake your hand and say thank you, put closure to that part of his life, do this, or I will expose you "for the piece of filth you are." Sorella fails. That is all that happens in Part One.

It is Sorella who interprets the meaning of the relationship between her husband and the showman; she tells the narrator, who has followed the story closely, "If you want my basic view, here it is: The Jews could survive everything that Europe threw at them. I mean the lucky remnant. But now comes the next test—America. Can they hold their ground, or will the USA be too much for them."

When the story resumes, thirty years have passed, a device Bellow has used frequently—the leap back in time in "Cousins" to describe Sholem Stavis, and the leap forward to a meeting with the narrator decades later; the present time of Mosby writing his memoirs, the leap back in time to reconstruct a recollection of Lustgarten, and the leap forward to Mosby in Mexico, in fact standing terrorized in a dark and gloomy tomb, with scarcely the strength to climb the stairway back into the light. It is the technique of "The Old System," "The Silver Dish," "What Kind of Day Did You Have?" and *A Theft,* the device of the man of memory.

The Bellarosa Connection, Part Two, presents the counterpart to Fonstein seeking Rose: The narrator now searches for Fonstein, who is wanted by a rabbi in Israel to succor an old demented Jew, Polish by birth, a beggar with filthy habits, who makes prophetic speeches on the sidewalks of Jerusalem, another survivor of Europe who lives out the dregs of his life in a world of fantasy, not so much the man of *Eisen,* but an ancient Billy Rose. Can Harry save him?

The narrator begins his task of tracking down Harry and Sorella, but they cannot be called. In a surge of disappointment, the narrator cries out:

> I was shocked. Something essential in me caved in, broke down. At my age, a man is well-prepared to hear news of death. What I felt most sharply and immediately was that I had abandoned two extraordinary people whom I had always said I valued and held dear. I found myself making a list of names: Billy is dead; Mrs. Hamet, dead; Sorella dead; Harry dead. All the principals dead.

So are Aunt Mildred and his father, and the narrator's wife, dead? And who lives? Gilbert, Fonstein's son, the little boy who had gone to a mathematics summer camp, now grown up to be a specialist in probability theory, his genius applied to gambling and risk and sex and showmanship, a true American in the Billy Rose style. Gilbert is the present Bellarosa connection. Gilbert's friend who reveals to the narrator the subsequent and final history of the Fonsteins is alive; he has severe narcissistic problems of his own; he is not interested in reckoning with his Jewishness; "the only life he cared to lead was that of an American."

The narrator survives. Brooding on the lost old system, the dead past, he sorrows: "Two more old friends gone, just when I was ready after thirty years of silence to open my arms to them: Let's sit down together and recall the past and speak again of Billy Rose." The narrator reflects that Jews in America are as lost as are the Americans. All he can do is keep the record: "At times I feel like a socket that remembers its tooth."

In the cautionary note preceding the novella, requested by the publisher, Bellow writes, "Although portions of this novel are derived from real events, each character in it is fictional, a composite drawn from several individuals and from imagination. No reference to any living person is intended or should be inferred." Bellow needs no protection from the imagined characters and events taken from his fiction; and borrow he does.

Aunt Mildred, the narrator's stepmother, is still puttering about in a Tante Taube kitchen, preparing her remarkable strudel for her tough old husband, a more placid Dr. Adler from "Seize the Day," still judging his son and finding him on the scale of one to ten a borderline two.

> I was at the bar of paternal judgment again, charged with American puerility. When would I shape up at last! At the age of thirty-two, I still behaved like a twelve-year-old, hanging out in Greenwich Village, immature, drifting, a layabout, shacking up with Bennington girls, a foolish intellectual gossip, nothing in his head but froth.

Thus Bellow views his Augie March, the ingénu, and Charlie Citrine running after Von Humboldt Fleisher. The narrator remembers himself as an "immature unstable Jewish-American, humanly ignorant and loosely kind," a corrected Asa Leventhal. Physically, he is still the lanky Nephew Ken, "a tall old man with a structural curl at the top like a fiddlehead fern or a Bishop's crook." Harry Fonstein wears the orthopedic boot of Gersbach in *Herzog*, dragging along Gersbach's gimpy leg. Like Henderson, Fonstein is "a man acquainted with grief," like Sammler, an immigrant, "a central European Jewish type," saved from the Holocaust.

It is Sorella whom the narrator finds most congenial, Sorella with whom he wishes to spend the remaining years of his life, as Charlie Citrine had fleetingly thought when he visited Naomi Lutz. Sorella is obese, grotesquely so, with a heart beating deep within the folds of her flesh—"a mountain of lipids"—and that is borrowed from Queen Willatale, transported from Africa to the terrace of the King David Hotel in Jerusalem. Sorella is said to have a profound knowledge of Jewish history and that is something wholly new, and not altogether probable unless we are willing to think of her as a vestige of the anima of Bellow himself.

Like Sammler journeying to Israel, so Sorella and Fonstein go too and by chance meet the narrator who is in Jerusalem to open a branch of his memory institutes, as if, he says ironically, Jews in Israel need a memory institute. "They have to keep up with the world and be a complete microcosm," the narrator says, words similar to Bellow's assessment of the Israeli mind-set in *To Jerusalem and Back.* Taking tea, gazing out over the Vale of Hinnom, as once Bellow had done with his friend and guide David Shahar, the narrator accepts Sorella's memory test, as had Citrine when Cantabile challenged him. She asks the name of his second-grade teacher of fifty years ago. "Miss Emma Cox," is his quick reply.

It is true. Bellow is very proud of his memory. When taping a video at Boston University for an archive intended to preserve the record of great American artists, Bellow told Sigmund Koch, the interviewer, he could recall the names of all the schools he had ever attended, and all the names of his teachers. When Bellow returned from a walk around the block during a rest break from filming, he was distraught: "I couldn't remember the names of the flowers planted in clusters around the campus. Imagine. For half an hour I couldn't remember marigolds." So too the narrator has been singing an old song and is devastated by his failure to sing the key word:

> Way down upon the . . .
> Way down upon the . . .
> . . . upon the . . . . . . River . . .
> But what was the river called!

It still suffocates the narrator to think about the Holocaust; so Bellow had said the same to me years ago. When he finished writing *The Dean's December,* a sad mile away from German depredations of the spirit, inside the iron curtain country where violations of body and soul still prevailed, Bellow was ill for many weeks. In *The Bellarosa Connection,* the narrator confesses, "I didn't want to think of the history and psychology of these abominations, death chambers and furnaces. Stars are nuclear furnaces too. Such things are utterly beyond me, a pointless exercise."

The tooth that the narrator worries with his memory is Bellow's past fiction.

Indeed, the conclusion of the novella has its roots in the final lamentation and prayer of Sammler as he stands beside the gurney on which lies the corpse of Elia Gruner. However, this narrator keens a funeral cry for himself, not for his death but his life:

> Whose disappearance will fill you with despair, sir? Whom can you not live
> without? Whom do you painfully long for? Which of your dead hangs over you

daily? Show me where and how death has mutilated you. Where are your wounds? Whom would you pursue beyond the gates of death?

Sammler turned his back on the world and prepared his soul for entry into a new life beyond the grave. This narrator turns his back on the present and gazes back on his past. He sighs: "You can never dismantle all these modern mental structures. There are so many of them that they face you like an interminable vast city." There is worse, however, and this is the point of the story. What kind of a Jew is he? A Billy Rose or a Fonstein? The question was raised and left dangling in *To Jerusalem and Back.* In 1989 Bellow has returned to the issue, answering his own interviewer: Are you a Jewish writer? Or, to borrow the question from Sorella: Can you hold your ground or has the USA been too much for you?

The narrator realizes he is a Jew of an entirely different breed, closer to Billy Rose than to Fonstein. Free and bred in liberty, an equal, strong, there was no way for him to grasp the real facts in the case of the Jew, neither European, nor American. Waking, as he says, in a fifty-fifty bed—half Jewish, half WASP—he realizes "I hadn't understood Fonstein v. Rose."

The case will have to be remanded to another court, delayed for further appeal.

An old man has had a lifetime to learn to control his jitters in the night. Whatever I was (and that, at this late stage, still remained to be seen) I would need strength in the morning to continue my investigations.

And so, there is no answer.

Afterword: "Maybe they believe me because very simply it's true"

No one can presume to hold fast to any theory of Bellow, so complex a man, his mind a constellation of thoughts and feelings and intuitions and sensations, always playing with experiences, some private, some well-known, some fantasy, some obsession, but we have the fiction and we can hold fast to the fiction, tangible pages between covers. He has filled his pages with dreams of the community lost to him; his childhood before the death or corruption of his loved ones; his youth when joy and excitement and ecstasy consumed him, before treason and betrayal and rejection destroyed his love; his manhood, when ambition carried him to knowledge and success, and the life of the spirit seemed immanent, before books defeated him and institutions failed him and the dishonesty and wickedness of men in action debased him. All this is Bellow. It is he who seeks a design, a meaning, a stable self that will enable him to contend with a Chicago, a New York, an America that is variable, corrupt, dangerous, or indifferent, who searches his past to explain his present, believing that if he understands his past he may come better prepared to take charge of his destiny. Nothing is lost. The Chicago Bellow recalls as a child is as alive as the Chicago he observes in the 1980s; father and mother, brothers and sister, wives, children, lovers, relatives remote and nearest of kin, friends, old buddies and new, acquaintances professional and passing by, teachers alive or dead, wrong and right, all appear and reappear as he scrutinizes the stages in his transformation from boy to adolescent to man. He remembers his jobs, the scutwork and the drifting, the misunderstandings and swindles and falsehoods to which he has fallen prey, the betrayals and rejections, the good times and the evil days and the jokes and the Shakespeare and every book he has ever read and the buses and trains and planes and the newspapers. He remembers the money and the money and the money. Whatever the disguise, it is Bellow who has the gift or puts his foot in his mouth or, in the December of his life, observes Rumania and America. He is the nephew whose life project is his uncle; he is the uncle who has been to the dummy school.

It is Bellow who is at once the talented, powerful, successful man, at the same time overcome with a sense of failure, a weak, dependent victim, a loser, a Jew. Yes, he is Joseph and Augie and Wilhelm, Herzog, Bummidge, and all the rest of his narrators; he is also Cantabile and Tamkin and Mintouchian and Basteshaw, Schlossberg and Dahfu, Thaxter and Spangler, Von Humboldt Fleisher and Fishl. All are some part of Bellow.

The names do not matter; all are simulacra of the writer himself, the man who arrives to join the fellowship, the man in retreat. He weeps. His intellect kills. He longs to break through. He longs to keep himself intact. He longs to transcend himself. To join. But what? The human race? He is there already. He is son, brother, nephew, uncle, lover, husband, friend, citizen. Let him change wives and change cities and change hats; he is mortal, taking his vitamin pills, his heart pills, his love pills. It is Bellow who stands at the open door and closes it and stares out the window and keeps the hall light burning.

Can a man like Bellow falter? Does he not know exactly who he is? Haven't the prizes told him? National Book Awards and honorary doctorates and Nobel and Pulitzer and Chevalier and now a Bellow Society have little to do with the quest for identity. Self-discovery is a private matter and to Bellow self-knowledge is the provenance of the soul. His soul is vulnerable as is the soul of all who read him. The soul cannot be protected by a ribbon or fixed on a plaque or inscribed on parchment. Were the soul stable as law, it can take no firm and final hold on anything, be that "anything" outside the self or the light within. Let the soul lead the self out of the quiet space, where memories live and significance glows, into the turbulence of the real world, emerge to take up citizenship in the nation; there will be slippage. Despite Steiner, despite Swedenborg, despite Sinyavsky, despite free will, the soul has no hands for grasping—despite art, despite history, despite family. Let the soul transcend the limitations of the body; let it drift out safe; it drifts away. It leaves the body senseless or sensual, unknowing or uncaring, feeding itself on *nouvelle cuisine* or watering itself with "Cote d'Or, Domaine Roy." Bellow's quest for transcendence remains solely this from first to last, a quest for transcendence. So Bellow instructs us by the form of his canon.

We who read Bellow's fiction are the Spirits of Alternatives who listen to the account of what occurred to him as he sought connection in the ostensible real world. His Spirit, the Self that lies hidden in the heart, explains to our Spirit, and we, the readers of Bellow's inward transactions, are compelled to listen. Why? There is more to it than keeping ourselves posted on Bellow, more to it than the incandescent style, the humor, the intellectual games he plays. We are the Bridegroom—as Bellow tells us—interrupted on the way to the wedding, compelled to hear out the Ancient Mariner—as he calls himself—who tells his tale not to purge himself but for the sake of the Bridegroom. We are plucked by the sleeve by the storyteller who accosts us directly: "Dear friend," "I should tell you, "I can tell you that," "I'm not about to go into it here," "Listen," and as we turn the pages, the bonds of empathy strengthen and we begin to put ourselves in his place.

Often while the Bellow hero laments he is naïve in an unreliable world, trusting in a cynical world, faithfully loyal to scoundrels, uselessly wise among oafs, we pause and begin to think of our own frailties and humiliations, our backslidings and failures of nerve, our disillusions and ambivalence; we fall back into our past and ask ourselves how did we recover our sense of self-worth—or did we?—and we reflect: Have we ever found the way to become responsible for our fate? While we read Bellow, we recognize our energies, too, are wearing thin, our souls, too, feel drained of vitality, and reading, say, *Mr. Sammler's Planet,* we think of our soul, perched unhappily on superstructures of explanation. We ask ourselves how can we continue our quest, or, are we on a quest?

Don't quit. Don't quit, Bellow had said to me in 1979. The one thing all his books are saying to every reader is don't quit. Don't quit! It is true. All of us want not to quit. But how shall we fight?

Charlie Citrine whispered to himself, "Dance!" Citrine is playing racquet ball, a fast and dangerous game; he may collide with other players, or dash himself against the wall, or hit himself in the face with his own paddle, but Citrine is a tough player. He can leap and fling his body full length on the floor to scoop up some dead shot, and even though he knows full well he is not a good player, "too tangled about the heart," too competitive, too flashy, he can still spin around like a Russian dancer and slam the ball hard. "Dance, dance, dance, dance!" Mastery over the game depends on dancing.

Not many of us play racquet ball but we all have the need to dance, we all wish to master the game that Bellow is playing on our behalf. What exactly is that game? Of course it is writing, but there is more to it than that. Bellow's game is as old as the sport of Socrates: how, precisely, to untangle the heart. Citrine says:

> I tell myself that when I achieve mental and spiritual clarity and translate these into play nobody will be able to touch me.

As we read Bellow's stories of men in search of mental and spiritual clarity, we imagine how ascendant we may yet be should we have the courage to confront ourselves, tell ourselves our truths, and so achieve mental and spiritual clarity.

We are heartened to see the flaws in character can be repaired; we root for each Bellow hero who emerges, the soul restored, ready once more to club down the moronic, the fatuous, the illogical, the pompous, to take up the fight against the erudite assassins of the soul. As each book follows the last, we watch the progress of little David gradually evolving to old King David and see that David must once again kill Goliath. Victory lapses between the fictions. Stability disintegrates. Illumination bright and glowing wanes, flickers. New resolves and good intentions have not endured. Finding truths is like finding wives. Finding is not keeping. Love is elusive as truth, truth as short-lived as love.

Bellow knows art is not reality, only sentences, paragraphs, printed pages bound into a book. Fiction itself represents abstractions—character, plot, theme, setting, dialogue, figurative language—all abstractions. It's a queer calling. Bellow, who burns with the single desire to distinguish between appearance and reality in order to transcend both and grasp the essence of spirit and soul, devotes his life to creating the appearance of reality. Writing words, emending, revising, adding to and cutting out, he is creating imitations of his dreams, simulations of his intuitions, artifices of his imagination. Men and women walk steadily to and from their business; Bellow at work goes nowhere. He sits motionless at a table, with only his pen moving back and forth across the page, clothing his hopelessness, his tragic sense of loss in a clown suit, sending his pretended persons out to laugh and weep and rage, to quarrel and love, to be powerless and invincible, to find illumination in tears, relief in clamor and outrage and lamentation, to tap-dance around a floor of allusions and similes and metaphors. We who are his readers transform his words by our acts of imagination into what we believe is reality. Just as mysteriously we believe it is our own discomfitures and disappointments, our neurotic tangles and erotic spoilings that Bellow represents. And all the while there is nothing more tangible between us and Bellow than the printed words on the page of a book.

I once asked Bellow why he does not content himself, calm himself, by thinking of us for whom he always says he writes his books. We are hundreds of thousands of readers all over the world who buy or borrow the hardcovers, the paperbacks. His fiction has appealed to us for more than forty years. It is an oddity, surely, that the more Bellow tells the truth about himself, disclosing his individual and private experiences, the more we recognize ourselves. Describing his singular life, magnifying the drama of his unique self, with all the suffering, that pervasive anxiety, the self-pity and special pleading, the more he evokes in us recognition of some aspect of our experience. We, too, have felt like crying aloud "Havoc! All is havoc!" or "Life—it sucks!" Who has not detested the world, not known self-doubt and castigated the world for its flaws? Usually, we walk along steadily, dressed for wherever it is we are going, resigned or fierce, to do whatever we ought to do, and eventually the trouble passes. Bellow does not permit the trouble to pass. He asks why, why his profound desolation, where has he gone wrong, how can he change? He transforms his consciousness of despair, his dreariness, his anguish; he plays games with his sad self, inventing causes, fabricating experiences, contriving reasons, creating fantasies that so uncannily objectify his forlorn spirit. All this he offers to his imagination and sits down to write us stories.

His private investigations of reality—himself as individual, himself as member, himself as citizen, himself as artist fabricating conflicts between intellect and passion, reason and sexuality, ideals and hoax—are his long letter to us. No matter how much Bellow runs about the world, as if he were a whole team of researchers, he always comes to rest in a place that will enclose him, and within his own four walls he takes up his pen and stares down at his pad of paper with no more rules to guide him than the faint lines on the blank page. "Dear Miss Rose." "My dear Child."

I tried to tell Bellow some of my thoughts one late December afternoon.

"Perhaps you *are* writing to purge yourself of your experiences, to attack your enemies, to justify yourself. I can see that, and if you are, it really doesn't matter why. The question is why do we read you? Here's what I think.

"We sit, your readers, thinking about how to refurnish the den, what kind of rug to buy for the living room, what horse to bet on, which car to buy, which check will bounce, which motel is easier to sneak in and out of on a secret afternoon, should I still contribute to the ACLU, send money to the NAACP or the UJA or both, or neither. We construct conversations with a boss, a child, a lover, a cleaning lady, an old friend, a salesclerk, all the time aware we ought to be thinking about more important things, without the energy or perhaps the courage to do so. Your Citrines and Sammlers and Albert Cordes are reflecting on significant questions, tough ideas, seeking purpose and meaning, talking about God and the soul and death and time and history and nature and I am glad to have them speculate for me. It's like 'Let Ken do it.' I have thoughts about death but I have a way to put them aside. Should I have thoughts about my soul? Yes. Usually I don't. You figure it all out for me. As long as your soul says 'I want, I want,' my soul can lie low and leave me free to decide what to wear to the wedding."

To all this Bellow said only that his soul went into this work he does; he wished it were so, what I was saying, he wished it were so.

I got carried away. I see that now. However, when Bellow sits there, listening, that happens. Usually he talks, but when he falls silent and seems to be attuned to what the other is saying, one goes on in a rush, taking a chance, trying to get it all in. There I was, explaining Bellow to Bellow.

"I'll put it this way, Saul. You know, I have been where you have been, seen what you have seen; thousands of us know what you know but we cannot say it, cannot tell. We all have relatives. I read the books and say Yes, Yes, I've seen it, felt it, suffered and cried, exulted and laughed, cheated, swiped, pretended, run away, begged, prayed. Even if I do not go past a desk clerk at the Plaza, I did at the Biltmore; if I did not kill a German soldier, I might have; my arteries are clean now but I may some day be trapped on a hospital bed. I would like to win at a big poker game in some café in Mexico. My father is in the cemetery and I wish he could hear me sing. What I am trying to say is that you are telling it for me. Evidently my secrets are not so secret. You have heard what I have said in silence to myself when I look in the mirror. You are my proxy. You take notice. You make my record while I, also driven, harassed, tormented, striving, failing, go about my day."

He got up to pour some more tea, or maybe it was Jack Daniel's, or whatever it was that got me started. He wished, he said, I didn't have to smoke my cigarettes; the smoke irritated his eyes.

I continued to talk. "And when I get creepy at how I waste my days, I can always brew a fresh cup of coffee and light a cigarette, yes, smoke a cigarette, and pick up Herzog or "Seize the Day" and become Tommy who asks, or Herzog who asks, and maybe feel a little relieved that they have no answers, either. And if they do, they don't keep them very long, and even if their wisdom should prove durable, it makes no difference to the world. We get it. We lose it. We get it. We lose it. That's good news to me. Remember all that illumination Charlie Citrine has and then he looks down at the massive coffin and thinks how does the soul get out? It did not, did not. You stayed, you stayed. And you end up with 'What's the name of this flower, Papa?' 'How should I know? Am I in the millinery business?' Citrine sees the light and you tell us he has to go to the Goetheanuum for instruction."

I remember Bellow smiling as he reminded me that Citrine lived in Chicago. Smiling at me? At what I was saying? At some thought that welled up from his memory of another time, another person? Who knows? Then he said there was something I was forgetting. Yes, he found what I was saying interesting and maybe this idea of mine, of his being a spokesman—a proxy, I called it—was right, but wasn't I overlooking something?

"What?" I asked.

Bellow sat quietly and then suggested, softly, that maybe people believe what he says because very simply it's true.

I do not know whether that meant he agreed with me or whether he was just uncomfortable with all this talk about Bellow. Well, but he does like to talk about Bellow. Bellow had said, "I don't like to be pigeonholed, figured out, analyzed." Maybe he doesn't like others to say.

Anyhow, I have talked. I know that for Bellow there is only one box to which he will consign himself, into which he will helplessly fit. He has no way to evade that measured space. Until then, he will go on. When last I spoke to him, he was writing a new story. It's as my father always said: "Six inches above the ground you can always move; six feet under you stay still."

Appendix A:

The Writings

of Saul Bellow

MAJOR WORKS

Dangling Man (New York: Vanguard Press, 1944)
The Victim (New York: Vanguard Press, 1947)
The Adventures of Augie March (New York: Viking Press, 1953)
Seize the Day and Other Stories (New York: Viking Press, 1956)
Henderson the Rain King (New York: Viking Press, 1959)
Herzog (New York: Viking Press, 1964)
The Last Analysis (New York: Viking Press, 1965)
Mosby's Memoirs and Other Stories (New York: Viking Press, 1968)
Mr. Sammler's Planet (New York: Viking Press, 1970)
Humboldt's Gift (New York: Viking Press, 1976)
To Jerusalem and Back (New York: Viking Press, 1976)
The Dean's December (New York: Harper & Row, 1982)
Him with His Foot in His Mouth and Other Stories (New York: Harper & Row, 1984)
More Die of Heartbreak (New York: William Morrow and Company, 1987)
A Theft (New York: Viking Penguin, 1989)
The Bellarosa Connection (New York: Viking Penguin, 1989)

SHORT FICTION AND PLAYS

"Two Morning Monologues," *Partisan Review* (May–June 1941)

"The Mexican General," *Partisan Review* (May–June 1942)

"Dora," *Harper's Bazaar* (November 1949)

"A Sermon by Dr. Pep," *Partisan Review* (May–June 1949)

"The Trip to Galena," *Partisan Review* (November–December 1950)

"Looking for Mr. Green," *Commentary* (March 1951)

"Address by Gooley MacDowell to the Hasbeens Club of Chicago," *Hudson Review* (Summer 1951)

"The Wrecker," *New World Writing* (one-act play) (New York: New American Library, 1954)

"A Father-to-be," *The New Yorker,* February 5, 1955

"The Gonzaga Manuscripts," *Discovery,* No. 4, ed. Vance Bourjaily (New York: Pocket Books, 1956)

"Seize the Day," *Partisan Review* (Summer 1956). Reprinted, in *Seize the Day and Other Stories* (New York: Viking, 1956). *Seize the Day,* Viking Compass Edition, 1961

"Leaving the Yellow House," *Esquire,* January 1958

"Scenes from *Humanitis*—A Farce," *Partisan Review* (Summer 1962)

"Out From Under" (one-act play), unpublished.

"Orange Soufflé" (one-act play), *Esquire,* October 1965

"A Wen," *Esquire* (one-act play), January 1965

"The Old System," *Playboy* (January 1968)

"Mosby's Memoirs," *The New Yorker* (July 20, 1968). Reprinted, in *Mosby's Memoirs and Other Stories* (New York: Viking, 1968)

"Zetland: By a Character Witness," *Modern Occasions,* ed. Philip Rahv (New York: Port Washington, 1974)

"A Silver Dish," *The New Yorker* (September 25, 1978)

"Him with His Foot in His Mouth," *Atlantic Monthly* (November 1982)

"What Kind of Day Did You Have?" *Vanity Fair* (February 1984)

"Cousins," *Him with His Foot in His Mouth and Other Stories* (New York: Harper & Row, 1984)

"Something to Remember Me By," *Esquire* (July 1990)

OCCASIONAL PIECES

ESSAYS, SPEECHES, TRIBUTES

"Spanish Letter," *Partisan Review* (February 1948)

"The Jewish Writer," *Commentary* (October 1949)

"How I Wrote Augie March's Story," *The New York Times Book Review,* January 31, 1954

"The Creative Artist and His Audience," a symposium, *Perspectives USA* (Autumn 1954)

"Isaac Rosenfeld," *Partisan Review* (Fall 1956)

"The University as Villain," *The Nation*, November 16, 1957

"Distractions of a Fiction Writer," *The Living Novel: A Symposium*, ed. Granville Hicks (New York: Macmillan, 1957)

"Deep Readers of the World, Beware!" *The New York Times Book Review*, February 15, 1959

"Illinois Journey," *Holiday*, September 22, 1959

"The Sealed Treasure," *The Times Literary Supplement*, July 1, 1960

"Literary Notes on Khrushchev," *Esquire*, March 1961

"Facts That Put Fancy to Flight," *The New York Times Book Review*, February 11, 1962

"The White House and Artists," *The Noble Savage*, volume 5 (October 1962)

"Where Do We Go From Here: The Future of Fiction," *Michigan Quarterly Review* (Winter 1962). The Hopwood Lecture for 1961. Copyright, The Regents of the University of Michigan

"Recent American Fiction," The Gertrude Clark Whittal Poetry and Literary Fund Lecture, the Library of Congress, January 1963. Reprinted, "Some Notes on Recent American Fiction" (*Encounter*, November 1963)

"Literature," *The Great Ideas Today*, eds. Mortimer Adler and Robert Maynard Hutchins (Chicago: Encyclopedia Brittanica, 1963)

"The Writer as Moralist," *Atlantic Monthly*, March 1963

"My Man Bummidge," *The New York Times*, September 27, 1964

"A Comment on Form and Despair," *Location* (Summer 1964)

"Mind Over Chatter," *The New York Times*, April 4, 1965

"Cloister Culture," Keynote address to International PEN Congress, New York, June 13, 1966. *Page Two*, ed. by E. F. Brown, New World Writing, pp. 592–3

"Report on Israel," *Newsday*, June 12, June 13, June 16, 1967

"Skepticism and the Depth of Life," *The Arts and the Public*, eds. J. E. Miller and P. D. Herring (Chicago: 1967)

"Culture Now, Some Animadversions, Some Laughs," *Modern Occasions*. (Winter 1971). Address to the Annual Literary Awards Banquet at Purdue University, April 30, 1970

"World-Famous Impossibility," *The New York Times Book Review*, December 6, 1970

"John Berryman, Friend," *The New York Times Book Review*, May 27, 1973

"Literature in the Age of Technology," *Technology and the Frontiers of Knowledge*, ed. Frank K. Nelson (New York: Doubleday Lecture Series, 1973)

"Starting Out in Chicago," *American Scholar* (Winter 1974–1975)

"An Interview With Myself," *New Review*, Vol. 2, No. 18 (1975), pp. 53–56

"A World Too Much With Us," *Critical Inquiry* (Autumn 1975). Address to the International PEN Congress, Jerusalem, 1974

"Why Not?" *Bulletin: The American Academy of Arts and Sciences*, Vol. 30, No. 4 (January 1978). Address to the Emerson-Thoreau Society

"The Day They Signed the Treaty," *Newsday*, April 1, 1979

"On John Cheever," *The New York Review of Books*, February 17, 1983

"The Civilized Barbarian Reader, *The New York Times Book Review*, March 8, 1987

REVIEWS

"Italian Fiction: Without Hope," *New Leader,* December 11, 1950. (On *The New Italian Writers, An Anthology,* ed. Marguerite Caetani, New York: New Directions, 1950.)

"Dreiser and the Triumph of Art," *Commentary* (May 1951). (On *Theodore Dreiser* by F. O. Matthiessen.)

"Gide as Writer and Autobiographer," *The New Leader,* June 4, 1951. (On *The Counterfeiters, with Journal of the Counterfeiters* by Andre Gide.)

"Laughter in the Ghetto," *Saturday Review of Literature,* May 30, 1953. (On *Mottel the Cantor's Son* by Sholom Aleichem, trans. Tamara Kahana.)

"Hemingway and the Image of Man," *Partisan Review* (May–June 1953). (On *Ernest Hemingway* by Philip Young.)

"A Personal Record," *New Republic,* February 22, 1954. (On *Except the Lord* by Joyce Cary.)

"Pleasures and Pains of Playgoing," *Partisan Review* (May–June 1954). (On the 1954 season on Broadway.)

"The French as Dostoevsky Saw Them," *New Republic,* May 23, 1955. Published in an extended form as "Introduction" to reprint of *Winter Notes on Summer Impressions* by Dostoevsky, 1957

"Rabbi's Boy in Edinburgh," *Saturday Review of Literature,* March 24, 1956. (On *Two Worlds* by David Daiches.)

"Two Faces for a Hostile World," *The New York Times Book Review,* August 26, 1956. (On *Five A.M.* by Jean Dutourd.)

"Man Underground," *Commentary* (June 1959). (On *Invisible Man* by Ralph Ellison.)

"The Swamp of Prosperity," *Commentary* (July 1959). (On *Goodbye, Columbus* by Philip Roth.)

"The Uses of Adversity," *The Reporter,* October 1, 1959. (On *Five Families* by Oscar Lewis.)

"The Riddle of Shakespeare's Sonnets," *The Griffin* (for The Readers' Subscription) (June 1962). (On *The Riddle of Shakespeare's Sonnets,* ed. Edward Hubler.)

"The Art of Going It Alone," *Horizon,* September 5, 1962. (On the films of Morris Engel.)

"Buñuel's Unsparing Vision," *Horizon,* November 5, 1962. (On *Viridiana,* a film by Luis Buñuel.)

"The Mass-Produced Insight," *Horizon,* January 5, 1963. (On film in general.)

"Adrift on a Sea of Gore," *Horizon,* March 5, 1963. (On *Barabbas,* a film by Dino De Laurentiis.)

"Beatrice Webb's America," *The Nation,* September 7, 1963. (On *Beatrice Webb's American Diary,* ed. David A. Shannon.)

"Barefoot Boy," *The New York Review of Books,* September 26, 1963. (On *A Precocious Autobiography* by Yevgeny Yevtushenko, trans. by Andrew R. MacAndrew.)

"On Jewish Storytelling," *Jewish Heritage* (Winter 1964–1965). Published as "Introduction" to *Great Jewish Short Stories* (New York: Dell, 1963)

"Writing About Presidents," *New York Herald Tribune Book Week,* January 1966. (On *A Thousand Days: JFK in the White House* by Arthur Schlesinger, Jr.; *The Making of a President* by Theodore H. White; *Kennedy* by Theodore Sorensen.)

"Solzhenitsyn's Truth," *The New York Times Book Review,* January 15, 1974. (Letter to the Editor.)

UNPUBLISHED LECTURES

(The manuscripts are in the Saul Bellow Papers in the archives of the Regenstein Library, University of Chicago.)

"On Flaubert" (c. 1955)

"The Modern Religious Novel" (c. 1966)

"The Next Necessary Thing" (c. 1967)

"Joyce's *Ulysses:* A Personal View" (c. 1970). Perhaps the lecture at Northwestern University in 1970, or, at Franklin and Marshall College in 1973

The Jefferson lectures, I and II. The first lecture was delivered in Washington, March 30, 1977; the second lecture in Chicago on April 1, 1977

"On Culture and Creativity: With a Brief Conducted Tour of Division Street," presented at the Library of Congress, Conference on Creativity, 1980

Appendix B:

Interviews with

Saul Bellow

"Talk with Saul Bellow," with Harvey Breit, *The New York Times Book Review,* September 20, 1953.

"On an Author," unsigned, *New York Herald Tribune,* October 4, 1953.

"Saul Bellow: A Mood of Protest," with Bruce Cook, *Perspective Chicago,* February 1963.

" 'Successor' to Faulkner?" with Nina A. Steers, *Show,* September 4, 1964.

"Talk with Saul Bellow," with Robert Gutwillig, The *New York Times Book Review,* September 20, 1964.

"Saul Bellow Tells (Among Other Things) the Thinking Behind *Herzog,* " with Robert Cromie, *Chicago Tribune Books Today,* January 24, 1965.

"Saul Bellow: An Interview," with Gordon Lloyd Harper, *Paris Review,* Winter 1965.

"Gloria Steinem Spends a Day in Chicago with Saul Bellow," with Gloria Steinem, *Glamour,* July 1965.

"Saul Bellow: An Interview," with John Enck, *Wisconsin Studies in Contemporary Literature* (summer 1965).

"Saul Bellow Revisited," with Alice Albright Hoge, *Chicago Daily News,* February 18, 1967.

"Mystic Trade—the American Novelist Saul Bellow," with Jim Douglas Henry, *The Listener,* May 22, 1969.

"Mr. Bellow Considers His Planet," with Jane Howard, *Life,* April 3, 1970.

"A Conversation with Saul Bellow," with Chirantan Kulshresthta, 1971, *Chicago Review,* Winter 1973.

"Saul Bellow of Chicago," with Joseph Epstein, *The New York Times Book Review,* May 9, 1971.

"Saul Bellow in the Classroom," with Sanford Pinsker, *College English* (April 1973).

"Literature and Culture: An Interview with Saul Bellow," with Robert Boyer, Robert Orrill, Ralph Ciancio, Edwin Mosely, *Salmagundi,* Summer 1975. The public interview took place in 1973.

"An Interview with Saul Bellow," with Joyce Illig, *Publishers Weekly,* October 22, 1973.

"Saul Bellow at 60," with Robert Robinson, *The Listener,* February 13, 1975.

"An Interview with Saul Bellow," with Karyl Roosevelt, *People,* September 8, 1975.

"Off the Couch by Christmas, Saul Bellow on His New Novel," with Melvyn Bragg, *The Listener,* November 20, 1975.

"Saul Bellow Taking Laureateship Lightly," with Herbert Mitgang, *The New York Times,* November 14, 1976.

"Bellow's Gift," with Richard Stern, *The New York Times Magazine,* November 21, 1976.

"A Talk with Saul Bellow," with Joseph Epstein, *The New York Times Book Review,* December 5, 1976.

"Common Needs, Common Preoccupations: An Interview with Saul Bellow," with Jo Brans, *Southwest Review,* Winter 1977.

"Free to Feel," with Maggie Simmons, *Quest,* February 1979.

"The Quintessential Chicago Writer," with Steve Neal, *Chicago Tribune Magazine,* September 16, 1979.

"With Bellow in Chicago," with Herbert Mitgang, *The New York Times Book Review,* July 6, 1980.

"The Graying of Saul Bellow," with Helen Dudar, *Saturday Review,* January 1982.

"If Saul Bellow Doesn't Have a True Word to Say, He Keeps His Mouth Shut," with William Kennedy, *Esquire,* February 1982.

"A Cry of Strength: The Unfashionably Uncynical Saul Bellow," with Cathleen Medwick, *Vogue,* March 1982.

"Saul Bellow Picks Another Fight," with Al Ellenberg, *Rolling Stone,* March 4, 1982.

"A Conversation with Saul Bellow," with Alvin P. Sanoff, *U.S. News & World Report,* June 28, 1982.

"Bellow Visits NY for Rare Public Reading," with Edwin McDowell, *The New York Times,* January 19, 1985.

Appendix C:

Table of Contents of

Each Issue of

The Noble Savage

VOLUME I, FEBRUARY 1960

EDITORS: Saul Bellow, Keith Botsford, Jack Ludwig
CONTRIBUTING EDITORS: John Berryman, Ralph Ellison, Herbert Gold, Arthur Miller, Wright Morris, Harvey Swados

VOLUME II, SEPTEMBER 1960

VOLUME III, MAY 1961

VOLUME IV, OCTOBER 1961

VOLUME V, OCTOBER 1962

EDITORS: *Saul Bellow, Keith Botsford, Aaron Asher*
CONTRIBUTING EDITORS: *John Berryman, Ralph Ellison, Herbert Gold, Arthur Miller, Wright Morris, Harvey Swados*

Sources

CHAPTER 1

1. *The Adventures of Augie March* bears the solemn dedication "To My Father." Abraham Bellow's letter is on deposit in the Saul Bellow Papers, archives of the Regenstein Library at the University of Chicago. All unpublished lectures, essays, and speeches by Bellow, as well as personal correspondence, referred to in my study are in the archives.

2. Saul Bellow, "Isaac Rosenfeld," *Partisan Review* (Fall 1956), pp. 565–567.

3. Saul Bellow, "Zetland: By a Character Witness," *Modern Occasions,* edited by Philip Rahv (Port Washington, N.Y.: 1974), pp. 9–30.

4. Saul Bellow, "Starting Out in Chicago," *American Scholar* (Winter 1974–75): pp. 71–77.

5. Melvin Bragg, "Off the Couch by Christmas," *The Listener,* November 20, 1975, pp. 218–219.

6. Alfred Kazin, *New York Jew* (New York: Random House, 1978), pp. 60–61.

CHAPTER 2

1. Saul Bellow: "Two Morning Monologues," *Partisan Review* (May–June 1941), pp. 230–236; "The Mexican General," *Partisan Review* (May–June 1942), pp. 178–194; "Notes of a Dangling Man," *Partisan Review* (September–October 1943), pp. 402–438.

CHAPTER 3

1. William Targ, *Indecent Pleasures* (New York: Macmillan, 1975).

2. The Nobel lecture was delivered on December 12, 1976; the limited edition was published by Targ Editions, New York, 1979.

3. Richard Stern, "Bellow's Gift," *The New York Times Magazine,* November 22, 1976, pp. 42–44.

4. When *Dangling Man* was issued in England at the turn of the year, 1946–1947, it was reviewed in *The New Statesman and Nation, The Spectator, The Sunday Times, The Observer,* and *The Times Literary Supplement,* altogether a notable reception for an American first novel.

5. Edmund Wilson, "Doubts and Dreams: 'Dangling Man' and 'Under a Glass Bell,'" *The New Yorker,* April 1, 1944, pp. 78, 81. Wilson wrote a review of Henry James's *Notebooks* for *The New Yorker,* December 13, 1947. Just below, in the "Briefly Noted" section on fiction, an unsigned paragraph praised *The Victim,* but it is doubtful Wilson wrote it.

6. William Barrett, *The Truants: Adventures Among the Intellectuals* (New York: Anchor Press/Doubleday, 1982), p. 49.

7. Bellow has said many times that he could not face the realities of the Holocaust; indeed it was not to become part of his subject until 1970, in *Mr. Sammler's Planet,* and even then it emerges as the recollection of an old man who survived and came to America. Nor does Bellow probe the realities of the criminal state until 1982, when Albert Corde observes the oppressive society of Rumania and links the evils of tyranny in Rumania with the moral torpor of political and social leaders in America.

CHAPTER 4

1. Richard Match, "Anti-Semitism Hits a Jew," *New York Herald Tribune,* November 23, 1947. "Unsigned," "Suffering for Nothing," *Time,* December 1, 1947. Hugh Kenner, "From Lower Bellowvia," *Harper's,* February 1982. Diane Johnson, "Point of Departure," *The New York Review of Books,* March 4, 1982.

2. Martin Greenberg, "Modern Man as Jew," *Commentary* (January 1948). Leslie Fiedler, "The Fate of the Novel," *Kenyon Review* (Summer 1948). Professor Trilling of Columbia University wrote only a handful of short stories; *The Middle of the Journey* was his first and last novel.

3. Alan S. Downer, "In Chungking and Manhattan," *New York Times Book Review,* November 30, 1947, p. 29.

4. Saul Bellow, "Starting Out in Chicago," *American Scholar* (Winter 1974–1975), pp. 71–77.

5. Nina A. Steers, " 'Successor' to Faulkner," *Show,* September 4, 1964, pp. 36–38.

6. Gordon Lloyd Harper, "Saul Bellow: An Interview," *Paris Review* (Winter 1965), pp. 48–73.

7. Jim Douglas Henry, "Mystic Trade—The American Novelist Saul Bellow Talks to Jim Douglas Henry," *The Listener,* May 22, 1969, pp. 705–707.

8. Chirantan Kulshrestha, "A Conversation With Saul Bellow," *Chicago Review* (Winter 1973), pp. 7–15. The interview took place on January 12, 1971.

9. The United States Cultural Center in Tel Aviv sponsored the panel discussion on June 28, 1970. The quotation is from a transcript of the proceedings.

10. Joseph Epstein, "Saul Bellow of Chicago," *The New York Times Book Review*, May 9, 1971) pp. 4, 12, 14, and 16.

11. Sanford Pinsker, "Saul Bellow in the Classroom," *College English* (1973), pp. 975–982.

12. Only Joseph F. McCadden wrote extensively on the subject of Bellow's women, in his monograph titled *The Flight From Women in the Fiction of Saul Bellow* (Lanham, Md.: University Press of America, 1980).

13. Saul Bellow, "Dora." *Harper's Bazaar*, November 1949, pp. 118, 188–191 and 198–199.

14. Saul Bellow, "A Sermon by Dr. Pep," *Partisan Review*, May–June 1949, pp. 455–462.

15. In his biography of Robert Lowell, Ian Hamilton tells us the most vigorous champion of Ezra Pound was Allen Tate. John Berryman helped Allen Tate gather seventy-three signatures on a letter of defense of the committee. *Robert Lowell, A Biography* (New York: Random House, 1982), pp. 142–143.

16. Saul Bellow, "The French as Dostoevsky Saw Them," *New Republic*, May 23, 1955, pp. 17–30. It was later published in extended form as "Introduction" to a reprint of Dostoevsky's *Winter Notes on Summer Impressions*, first published in 1863.

17. The stories were: "A Trip to Galena," 1950, *Partisan Review;* "Address by Gooley MacDowell to the Hasbeens Club of Chicago," 1951, *Hudson Review;* "Looking for Mr. Green," 1951, *Commentary.* The reviews were: "The Jewish Writer," *Commentary,* 1949; "Italian Fiction: Without Hope," on *The New Italian Writers, An Anthology*, ed. Marguerite Caetani, *New Leader,* 1950; "Dreiser and the Triumph of Art," on *Theodore Dreiser* by F.O. Matthiessen, *Commentary,* 1951; "Gide as Writer and Autobiographer," on *The Counterfeiters,* with *Journal of The Counterfeiters* by André Gide, *New Leader,* 1951; "Laughter in the Ghetto," on *Mottel, the Cantor's Son* by Sholom Aleichem, *Saturday Review of Literature,* 1953; "Hemingway and the Image of Man," on *Ernest Hemingway* by Philip Young, *Partisan Review,* 1953.

18. 1949, Chapter 1, "From the Life of Augie March," *Partisan Review;* 1951, Chapter 2, "The Coblins," *Sewanee Review;* Chapter 5, "The Einhorns," *Partisan Review;* 1952, Chapter 25, "Interval in a Lifeboat," *The New Yorker;* 1953, Chapters 15–16, "The Eagle," *Harper's Bazaar;* Chapter 24, "Mintouchian," *Hudson Review.*

CHAPTER 6

1. Gordon Lloyd Harper, "Saul Bellow: An Interview," *Paris Review* (Winter 1965), pp. 48–73.

2. See the following reviews: Robert Gorham Davis, *The New York Times Book Review,* September 20, 1953; Norman Podhoretz, *Commentary* (October 1953); Ray B. West, Jr., *Shenandoah* (Winter 1953); Anthony West, *The New Yorker,* September 26, 1953; T. E. Cassidy, *The Commonweal,* October 2, 1953; Henry Curtis Webster, *Saturday Review,* September 19, 1953; Robert Penn Warren, *New Republic,* November 2, 1953; Delmore Schwartz, *Partisan Review* (January–February 1954); Henry Popkin, *Kenyon Review* (Spring 1954); Maxwell Geismar, *The Nation,* November 14, 1953.

3. Harvey Breit, "Talk With Saul Bellow," *The New York Times Book Review*, September 20, 1953.

4. See Bellow archives.

5. Dupee wrote his letter December 9, 1953; Malamud on November 28, 1953; and Fiedler on October 9, 1953.

6. See Bellow Archives. Bellow is quoting from Ralph Waldo Emerson, "The Transcendentalist," *Essays and Lectures* The Library of America, N.Y., 1983, p. 204.

7. Norman Podhoretz, *Making It* (New York: Random House, 1967).

8. *Time*, September 21, 1953; Orville Prescott, *The New York Times*, September 18, 1953; Milton Crane, Chicago *Tribune*, September 20, 1953; Arthur Mizener, *New York Herald Tribune*, September 20, 1953; Granville Hicks, *New Leader*, September 21, 1953; V. S. Pritchett, *The New Statesman and Nation*, June 19, 1954; Charles Rolo, *Atlantic Monthly*, October 1953.

9. Saul Bellow, "Laughter in the Ghetto," *Saturday Review of Literature*, May 30, 1953, p. 15.

10. Ira Berkow, *Maxwell Street* (Garden City, N.Y.: Doubleday, 1977), pp. 182–189.

11. Sanford Pinsker, "Saul Bellow in the Classroom," *College English* (April 1973), pp. 975–982.

CHAPTER 7

1. Saul Bellow, *The Wrecker, New World Writing*, 1954, pp. 271–287.

2. Saul Bellow, "A Father-to-be," *The New Yorker*, February 5, 1955, pp. 26–30.

3. Saul Bellow, "Seize the Day," *Partisan Review* (Summer 1956), pp. 295–319, 376–432.

4. All this is ably explored by Eusebio L. Rodrigues in his article "Reichianism in *Henderson the Rain King*," *Criticism* (1973), pp. 212–233.

5. "Seize the Day" appeared as the title story in a collection of short stories published in 1956 by Viking Press. Included were "A Father-to-be," "Looking for Mr. Green," "The Gonzaga Manuscripts," and *The Wrecker*. Weidenfeld & Nicolson, London, brought the book out the following year.

CHAPTER 8

1. Ray B. West, Jr., "Six Authors in Search of a Hero," *Sewanee Review* (Summer 1957): pp. 498–508.

2. Herbert Gold, "The Discovered Self," *The Nation*, November 17, 1956, pp. 435–436; Alfred Kazin, "In Search of Light," *The New York Times*, November 18, 1956, pp. 5 and 36.

3. Walter Allen, "New Novels," *The New Statesman and Nation*, April 27, 1957; pp. 547–548. John Bayley, "New Novels," *Spectator*, June 7, 1957, p. 758; Francis Wyndham [n.t.], *The London Magazine*, August 1957, p. 66; "Bad Company," *Times Literary Supplement*, unsigned, May 10, 1957, p. 285.

4. Saul Bellow, "Distractions of a Fiction Writer," in the *The Living Novel: A Symposium*, ed. Granville Hicks (New York, Macmillan, 1957), pp. 1–20.

5. Saul Bellow, "The University as Villain," *The Nation*, November 16, 1957, pp. 361–363.

CHAPTER 10

1. Saul Bellow, "Deep Readers of the World, Beware!" *The New York Times Book Review*, February 15, 1959, pp. 1 and 34.

2. Carlos Baker, "To the Dark Continent in Quest of Light," *The New York Times Book Review*, February 22, 1959, pp. 4–5.

3. Orville Prescott [n.t.], *The New York Times*, February 23, 1959, p. 21.

4. Richard Chase, "The Adventures of Saul Bellow," *Commentary* (April 1959), pp. 323–330.

5. Charles Rolo, "Reader's Choice," *Atlantic Monthly*, March 1959, p. 88.

6. Elizabeth Hardwick, "A Fantastic Voyage," *Partisan Review* (Spring 1959), pp. 299–303. Dwight Macdonald's "Letter to the Editors" appeared in the same issue.

7. Reed Whittemore, "Safari Among the Wariri," *New Republic*, March 16, 1959, pp. 17–18.

8. Theodore J. Ross, "Notes on Saul Bellow," *Chicago Jewish Forum* (1959), pp. 21–27.

9. *The Noble Savage* appeared five times: Volume I, February 1960; Volume 2, September 1960; Volume 3, May 1961; Volume 4, October 1961; Volume 5, October 1962. See Appendix C on page 349 for the "Table of Contents" of the five journals. At the front of each TNS there was an "Arias" section consisting of unsigned editorial reflections on the general scene, literary and political. Some are recognizably by Bellow.

10. Rosette C. Lamont, "Bellow Observed: A Serial Portrait," *Mosaic* (1970), pp. 247–57.

11. Saul Bellow, "The Sealed Treasure," *The Times Literary Supplement*, July 1, 1960; "The Writer as Moralist," *Atlantic Monthly*, March 1963; "Some Notes on Recent American Fiction," *Encounter*, November 21, 1963.

CHAPTER 11

1. Jack Ludwig, "The Wayward Reader," *Holiday*, February 1965, pp. 16 and 18–19.

CHAPTER 12

1. Saul Bellow, "My Man Bummidge," *The New York Times*, September 27, 1964, pp. 1 and 4.

2. Barry Hyams, "Play Out the Truth," *The Reconstructionist*, October 13, 1964, pp. 13–15.

3. Harold Clurman [n.t.], *The Nation*, October 19, 1964, pp. 523–524.

4. "From Womb to Gloom," *Time*, October 9, 1964, p. 92.

5. Robert Brustein, "Saul Bellow on the Dragstrip," *New Republic,* October 24, 1964, pp. 25–26.

6. "The Last Analysis, 'inspired . . . lunacy' " [anon.], *Vogue,* November 15, 1964, p. 64.

C H A P T E R   1 3

1. Tom Prideaux, "Don't Let Bellow Get Scared Off," *Life,* October 30, 1964, p. 17.

2. Robert Lasson, "Will Mr. Bellow's counsel approach the bench?" *Chicago Tribune,* October 20, 1968, p. 6.

3. Charles Thomas Samuels, "Action and Idea in Saul Bellow," *Atlantic Monthly,* November 1968, p. 126.

4. Tony Tanner, "Profile: Tony Tanner writes about the American novelist, Saul Bellow," *The Listener,* January 23, 1969, pp. 113–114.

5. The address, delivered to the PEN Congress on June 13, 1966, was titled "Cloister Culture."

6. Saul Bellow, "Skepticism and the Depth of Life," published in *The Arts and the Public Life,* edited by J. E. Miller and P. D. Herring (Chicago: University of Chicago Press, 1967).

7. Mark Harris, "Saul Bellow at Purdue," *The Georgia Review* (Winter 1978), pp. 715–754.

8. Saul Bellow, "Culture Now: Some Animadversions, Some Laughs," April 30, 1970, reprinted in *Modern Occasions,* edited by Philip Rahv, 1970–1971.

9. Saul Bellow, *Newsday,* June 12, June 13, June 16, 1967.

10. Jack Ludwig, *Above Ground* (New Canadian Library, McClelland and Stewart, 1968).

C H A P T E R   1 4

1. Christopher Lehmann-Haupt, "The Monotonous Music of the Spheres," *The New York Times,* January 26, 1970; Anatole Broyard, "What a complicated machine an Old School European is," *The New York Times Book Review,* February 1, 1970, p. 45.

2. Robert Kiely, "In an unbalanced world . . . Saul Bellow's balanced man," *Christian Science Monitor,* February 5, 1970, p. A11. John Bayley, "More Familiar than Novel," *The Listener,* July 9, 1970, pp. 51–52.

3. Irwin Stock, "Man in Culture," *Commentary* (May 1970), pp. 89–94.

4. Beverly Gross, "Dark Side of the Moon," *The Nation,* February 9, 1970, pp. 153–155.

5. L. E. Sissman, "Uptight," *The New Yorker,* January 31, 1970, pp. 84–87.

6. Alison Lurie, "The View from the Moon," *New Statesman,* July 10, 1970, p. 19.

7. Raymond Sokolov, "West Side Lear," *Newsweek,* February 2, 1970, p. 77.

8. Charles Thomas Samuels, "Bellow on Modernism," *New Republic,* February 7, 1970, pp. 27–30.

9. Alfred Kazin, "Though He Slay Me . . . ," *The New York Review of Books,* December 3, 1970, pp. 3–4.

10. Edward Grossman, "The Bitterness of Saul Bellow," *Midstream* (August–September 1970): pp. 3–15.

11. Joseph Epstein, interview, *The New York Times Book Review*, May 9, 1971, pp. 4 and 12–14.

CHAPTER 1 5

1. Marjorie Farber, "Journey into Life," *New Republic* (June 3, 1946), p. 809: "But in the second portion of the book, which carries an exhaustive analysis of motives to the point of tediousness . . . novelistic problems are attempted, and partially solved, of such formidable difficulty that I shall call this a 'failure' only tentatively, in quotes." Elizabeth Hardwick, "Fiction Chronicle," *Partisan Review* (Vol. 13, 1946), p. 392: "*Passage from Home* is creditably written but it lacks vigor and fictional inspiration and seems more the act of an intelligent will than of a compelling imagination. Unfortunately the subject matter [a youth as the central character] makes it impossible for us to have more than a hint here and there of Isaac Rosenfeld's intellectual gifts. They are of the sort that may, if he finds the right theme to utilize them, make him an exciting writer." Diana Trilling, "Fiction in Review," *The Nation* (May 18, 1946, p. 606): "But whatever the shortcomings of Mr. Rosenfeld's book, they are of only minor consequence compared to its major accomplishment—the taking of life at such a high moral pitch." Richard Sullivan, "Growing Up," *The New York Times* (May 12, 1946), p. 5: "The prose is warm, neat and eminently readable. At times its simple direct clarity is brilliant; at other times, particularly in passages of analysis, its subtlety becomes a trifle burdensome. More explanatory than evocative, more reflective than dramatic, it is always completely controlled writing that never sprawls or spills; and although it is often slow, it is always full of a quiet, almost deliberate energy. But despite the sound craftsmanship of the writing, and despite the potential importance of the matters treated—there remains a peculiar insufficiency in this novel. It is as if a dimension were missing, or a part suppressed." Richard Match, *Herald Tribune*, May 12, 1946, p. 8: "Like a medieval scholar splitting hairs, Mr. Rosenfeld dissects emotions and responses, postulates motives and counter-motives and counter-counter-motives to the third or fourth degree." In the *Chicago Sun*, the *San Francisco Chronicle*, *The New Yorker* and the *Saturday Review of Literature*, brief notices appeared.

2. Irving Howe, "Of Fathers and Sons," *Commentary*, Vol. 2. (1946): pp. 190–192.

3. Isaac Rosenfeld, "Life in Chicago," *Commentary* (June 1957): Collected in the posthumous volume *An Age of Enormity* (Cleveland and New York: The World Publishing Co., 1962), pp. 323–347.

4. Eileen Simpson, *Poets in Their Youth: A Memoir* (New York: Random House, 1982), pp. 218 and 222–223.

5. The incident was described by Bellow in a tribute, "John Berryman, Friend," printed in *The New York Times Book Review*, May 27, 1973, and was used as a foreword to Berryman's novel, *Recovery*, published posthumously by Farrar, Straus & Giroux in 1973.

6. Irving Howe, *A Margin of Hope: An Intellectual Autobiography* (New York: Harcourt Brace Jovanovich, 1982), pp. 133 and 164.

7. William Barrett, *The Truants* (Garden City: Anchor Press Doubleday, 1982), p. 112.

CHAPTER 17

1. Norman Mailer, "Modes and Mutations: Quick Comments on the American Novel," *Commentary* (March 1966), pp. 37–40. Mailer read the essay at the Christmas convention of the Modern Language Association in Chicago; *Commentary* printed the essay.

2. Christopher Lehmann-Haupt, "The Monotonous Music of the Spheres," *The New York Times,* January 26, 1970.

3. Alfred Kazin, "Though He Slay Me . . . ," *The New York Review of Books,* December 3, 1970.

4. Richard Gilman [n.t.], *The New York Times Book Review,* August 17, 1975, pp. 1–3.

5. Daniel Aaron, "Marginal Notes on a New Novel," *New Republic,* September 20, 1975, pp. 28–30.

6. John Updike, "Draping Radiance with a Worn Veil," *The New Yorker,* September 15, 1975, pp. 122–130.

7. Roger Shattuck, "A Higher Selfishness," *The New York Review of Books,* September 18, 1975, pp. 21–23.

8. Maria St. Goar [n.t.], *Newsletter,* Anthroposophical Society in America (Autumn 1975), pp. 11–12.

9. Alan Howard [n.t.], *Anthroposophical Quarterly* (Spring 1976), p. 22.

10. Nick Lyons, *Journal for Anthroposophy* (Autumn 1975), pp. 77–79.

11. Paul Margulies, "A Letter to Saul Bellow," *Newsletter,* Anthroposophical Society in America (Spring 1976), p. 15.

12. Owen Barfield, *Saving the Appearances: A Study in Idolatry* (New York: Harcourt Brace & World, [no date]).

13. Owen Barfield, *Unancestral Voice* (Middletown, Conn.: Wesleyan University Press, 1965).

14. Jo Brans, "Common Needs, Common Preoccupations," *Southwest Review*, Winter 1977, p. 2.

15. William Kennedy, " If Saul Bellow Doesn't Have a True Word to Say, He Keeps His Mouth Shut," *Esquire*, February 1982, pp. 48–50.

16. Walter Clemons and Jack Kroll, "America's Master Novelist," *Newsweek,* September 1, 1975, pp. 32–34 and 39–40.

17. Barfield, *Saving the Appearances,* pp. 67–68. See also pp. 149, 154–155, 157–166, 168, 171–173, 176, and 181.

18. Seymour Epstein, "Bellow's Gift," *University of Denver Quarterly* (1976), pp. 35–50.

19. Owen Barfield, *Worlds Apart* (Middletown, Conn.: Wesleyan University Press, 1963).

20. Owen Barfield, *Orpheus: A Poetic Drama* (West Stockbridge, Mass.: The Lindisfarne Press, 1983).

21. Louis Simpson, "The Ghost of Delmore Schwartz," *The New York Times Magazine,* December 7, 1975, pp. 38–43, 48, 52, and 56.

CHAPTER 18

1. Christopher Lehmann-Haupt, "Ill at Ease in Zion," *The New York Times,* October 18, 1976, p. 27.

2. Anthony Burgess, "A Resonant Bellow," *Spectator,* November 27, 1976, p. 26. The

original version of *To Jerusalem and Back: A Personal Account* appeared first in *The New Yorker.* Burgess's article, "The Jew as American," appeared in *Spectator,* October 7, 1966, pp. 455–456.

3. Irving Howe [n.t.], *The New York Times Book Review,* October 17, 1976, pp. 1–2.

4. Irving Saposnik, "Bellow's Jerusalem: The Road Not Taken," *Judaism* (Winter 1979), p. 43.

5. Sarah Blacher Cohen, "Saul Bellow's Jerusalem," *The Modern Jewish Studies Annual* (1979), pp. 16–23.

6. Louis Ehrenkrantz, "Bellow in Jerusalem," *Midstream* (November 1977), pp. 87–90.

7. Peter Prescott, "Passage to Zion," *Newsweek,* October 25, 1976, pp. 108 and 110.

8. Stefan Kanfer, *Time,* "Tour de Force," November 8, 1976, p. 108.

9. Paul Johnson, "The Issue of Israel," *The Times Literary Supplement,* December 3, 1976, p. 1509a.

10. Amanda Heller, "Short Reviews: *To Jerusalem and Back,*" *Atlantic Monthly,* December 1976, pp. 113–114.

11. John Hollander, "Return to the Source," *Harper's Magazine,* December 1976, pp. 82–85.

12. Roderick Nordell, "Saul Bellow's *To Jerusalem and Back,*" *Christian Science Monitor,* November 3, 1976, p. 29.

13. Carlos Baker, "Bellow in the Holy Land," *Theology Today* (January 1977), pp. 407–408.

14. Henry Fairlie, "Epistle of a Gentile to Saul Bellow," *New Republic,* February 5, 1977, pp. 18–20 and 22–23.

15. See, for example, Ralph Berets, "Repudiation and Reality Instruction in Saul Bellow's Fiction," *Centennial Review* (1976, pp. 75–101); Robert Boyers, "Nature and Social Reality," Ben Belitt, "Saul Bellow: The Depth Factor," Harold Kaplan, "The Second Fall of Man," all in *Salmagundi* (1975), an issue devoted entirely to articles on Bellow. Also *Modern Jewish Studies Annual* (1978), *Modern Fiction Studies* (1979), and *Studies in the Literary Imagination* (1984) consisted wholly of essays on Bellow. See, too, Brigitte Scheer-Schazler, *Saul Bellow* (New York: Frederick Ungar Publishing Co., 1972); Sarah Blacher Cohen, *Saul Bellow's Enigmatic Laughter* (Urbana, Ill.: University of Illinois Press, 1974); M.Gilbert Porter, *Whence the Power? The Artistry and Humanity of Saul Bellow* (Columbia, Mo.: University of Missouri Press, 1974); Joseph F. McCadden, *The Flight From Women in the Fiction of Saul Bellow* (Lanham, Md.: University Press of America, 1980); Daniel Fuchs, *Saul Bellow: Vision and Revision* (Durham, N.C.: Duke University Press, 1984). Jeanne Braham, *A Sort of Columbus, The American Voyages of Saul Bellow's Fiction,* (Athens, Ga.: University of Georgia Press, 1984); Judie Newman, *Saul Bellow and History* (New York: St. Martin's Press, 1984); Jonathan Wilson, *On Bellow's Planet, Readings from the Dark Side* (Washington, D.C.: Associated University Presses, 1985). Three books on Bellow were brought out in well-known series: Twentieth Century Views, Twayne's United States Authors Series, and the London Contemporary Writers.

16. Mary McCarthy's remarks were printed in full in *The New York Times* Sunday edition, May 6, 1979, pp. 12 and 30.

17. Saul Bellow, "Why Not?" *Bulletin,* American Academy of Arts and Sciences (January 1978). The Jefferson lectures have not been published; they are in the Bellow archives. "On Culture and Creativity, with a Brief Conducted Tour of Division Street" was the title given the keynote address, unpublished; it can be found in the archives.

CHAPTER 19

1. The essay was eventually published: Ruth Miller, "Invisible Man: A Parable for Our Times," *Scripta Hierosolymitana*, Vol. XXV, Publications of the Hebrew University (Jerusalem: The Magnes Press, 1973), pp. 261–282.

2. Alexandra Ionescu Tulcea Bellow, "Submartingale Characterization of Measurable Cluster Points," *Probability on Banach Space*, ed. James Kuelbs (New York and Basel: Marcel Dekker, 1978), pp. 69–80.

CHAPTER 20

1. Michiko Kakutani, "A Talk with Saul Bellow on His Work and Himself," *The New York Times Book Review*, December 13, 1981, pp. 1, 28 and 30–31.

2. Eugene Kennedy, "Bellow Awaits Heat from Novel of Hard Knocks," "Bookworld," *Chicago Tribune*, January 10, 1982, pp. 1–2.

3. John Updike, "Toppling Towers Seen by a Whirling Soul," *The New Yorker*, February 22, 1982, pp. 120–128.

4. D. M. Thomas, *"The Dean's December,"* *Washington Post*, January 10, 1982, pp. 1–2.

5. Christopher Lehmann-Haupt, "Books of the Times," *The New York Times*, January 11, 1982, Section 3, p. 17.

6. Hugh Kenner, "From Lower Bellowvia," *Harper's*, February 1982, pp. 62–65.

7. See: James Atlas, "Interpreting the World," *Atlantic Monthly*, February 1982; Jack Beatty, "A Novel of East and West," *New Republic*, February 3, 1982; Walter Clemons, "A Tale of Two Cities," *Newsweek*, January 18, 1982; David Evanier, "Bare Bones," *National Review*, April 2, 1982; Diane Johnson, "Point of Departure," *The New York Review of Books*, March 4, 1982; Gabriel Josipovici, "A foot in the stockyard and an eye on the stars," *The Times Literary Supplement*, April 2, 1982; George Stade, "I, Me, Mine," *The Nation*, January 30, 1982; Ruth R. Wisse, "Saul Bellow's Winter of Discontent," *Commentary* (April 1982); James Wolcott, "Dissecting Dean," *Esquire*, March 1982.

8. Richard Poirier, "Bellows to Herzog," *Partisan Review* (Spring 1965), pp. 264–71. Poirier eventually became editor of *Partisan Review*. Bellow never published there again, nor did *Partisan* ever review anything further by Bellow.

9. Norman Podhoretz, *Making It* (New York: Random House, 1967), p. 124.

10. Saul Bellow, "Something to Remember Me By," *Esquire*, July 1990, pp. 64–79.

CHAPTER 21

1. Marcel Proust, *Remembrance of Things Past*, volume 3, *Time Regained*, trans. by C. K. Moncrieff, Terence Kilmartin, and Andreas Mayor (New York: Random House, 1981), pp. 886–887 (the New French Pléiade Edition). The influence of Marcel Proust on Bellow would be a fruitful topic for study. Bellow lectured on Joyce and Flaubert but never wrote on Proust, whose ideas on romanticism and realism, on the search for essence not facts, on boredom, on the concept of simultaneity and conventional time in the novel,

on the aura of the soul that surrounds human beings and objects in nature, and whose technical device of interweaving memory and incident all surely were absorbed by Bellow and contributed to his formulation of his purpose and style in art.

2. Poem #670, *The Poems of Emily Dickinson,* ed. Thomas H. Johnson (Cambridge, Mass.: Harvard University Press, 1963).

Index